Writing through Jane Crow

D1496475

810.9896
H264

Writing through Jane Crow

Race and Gender Politics
in African American Literature

AYESHA K. HARDISON

University of Virginia Press

CHARLOTTESVILLE AND LONDON

University of Virginia Press
© 2014 by the Rector and Visitors of the University of Virginia
All rights reserved
Printed in the United States of America on acid-free paper
First published 2014

9 8 7 6 5 4 3 2 1

LIBRARY OF CONGRESS CATALOGING-IN-PUBLICATION DATA

Hardison, Ayesha K., 1978–
  Writing through Jane Crow : race and gender politics in African American literature /
Ayesha K. Hardison.
    pages   cm
  Includes bibliographical references and index.
  ISBN 978-0-8139-3592-8 (cloth : alk. paper)
  ISBN 978-0-8139-3593-5 (pbk. : alk. paper)
  ISBN 978-0-8139-3594-2 (e-book)
  1. American literature—African American authors—History and criticism.
2. American literature—Women authors—History and criticism. 3. American
literature—20th century—History and criticism. 4. African American women in
literature. 5. Racism in literature. 6. Sex discrimination in literature. I. Title.
PS153.N5H2235 2014
810.9'896073—dc23

                                                              2013039219

Portions of chapter 3 were previously published in *African American Review*. Quotes
from Gwendolyn Brooks's letters are reprinted by consent of Brooks Permissions.
Photographs of Joe and Marva Louis are used with the permission of the *Chicago
Defender*; images of *Candy* and *Patty-Jo 'n' Ginger* are courtesy of Tim Jackson; and
images of *Torchy in Heartbeats* are courtesy of Nancy Goldstein.

A book in the American Literatures Initiative (ALI), a collaborative
publishing project of NYU Press, Fordham University Press, Rutgers
University Press, Temple University Press, and the University of Virginia
Press. The Initiative is supported by The Andrew W. Mellon Foundation.
For more information, please visit www.americanliteratures.org.

For Shirley, Marie, Leola, and Willie Mae

Contents

Acknowledgments

In an effort to remember those who helped me develop a question into a monograph, I begin my acknowledgments with this project's genesis. My doctoral exam committee sagely encouraged me to "go back earlier" when I discussed only post-1970s literary representations in my exploration of black women's sexual empowerment and social resistance. I thank Arlene R. Keizer, Ifeoma K. Nwankwo, and Patricia Yaeger for advising, supporting, and challenging me throughout the writing process and afterward. I now recognize that Claudia Tate latently inspirited my study of 1940s and 1950s African American life and culture, as she introduced me to microfilm and mid-twentieth-century popular icons during the undergraduate Princeton Summer Research Experience. I am grateful for the opportunity to have developed intellectually, professionally, and personally under these scholars' guidance, just as I am compelled to acknowledge Lawrence P. Jackson, Ann duCille, Stacy I. Morgan, Farah Jasmine Griffin, Gene A. Jarrett, and Alex Lubin, whose critical works on mid-twentieth-century African American literature have inspired my own.

Willing readers as well as expert readers are a crucial part of the writing and revision process, and I am beholden to my colleagues and friends who have given me constructive feedback on my monograph and its early iterations. I tried to address all of their helpful comments, but of course, any shortcomings in the book are my own. To my oldest cherished interlocutors Lydia Middleton, Shawn A. Christian, and Clare Counihan: infinite thanks for never saying no to my requests for one more reading and for always affirming the validity of my ideas. No call was too trivial or too late for Clare, who has been a wellspring of patience and encouragement. I am appreciative too of my colleagues in the English Department at Ohio University. Thank you to Amritjit Singh for his genuine camaraderie, esteemed mentorship, and conviction in all matters and to Paul C. Jones for offering pragmatic strategies for my "tenure book" while also advocating for the intellectual ardor I maintained for my monograph. I want to share a special thank you with Mara Holt for her unwavering integrity, Marilyn Atlas for her special mix of idealism and candid acumen, Ghirmai Negash for his calming wisdom, Nicole Reynolds for shoring my writing efforts, and all those in the department who attended my faculty colloquiums. Additionally I am fortunate to have had colleagues near and far act as valuable resources, generative sounding boards, and positive motivators at various stages of this project: Jacqueline Goldsby, Rebecca Wanzo, Thadious M. Davis, Stefanie Dunning, Ruth Iyob, Irma Carmichael, Joyce A. Joyce, Michele Elam, Christina Sharpe, Sharon Lynette Jones, SallyAnn H. Ferguson, Joycelyn Moody, David Ikard, Mark Halliday, Simone Drake, Ronald J. Stephens, Venetria K. Patton, Cherene Sherrard-Johnson, Koritha Mitchell, P. Gabrielle Foreman, Ayana Haaruun, Michael B. Gillespie, Lisa Harrison, Tehama Lopez Bunyasi, Michael Gerardo, and Adom Getachew. Christina Bucher, Brittney Cooper, and Maryemma Graham generously—and serendipitously—shared materials and resources with me that undoubtedly made *Writing through Jane Crow* a better book. Maryemma deserves additional acknowledgment, but her unconditional collegiality and consummate mentorship are, in fact, beyond words.

The research and writing of this monograph also benefited from the institutional and financial support made available at Ohio University by Joseph McLaughlin as chair of the English Department and Benjamin M. Ogles as dean of the College of Arts and Sciences. My gratitude goes to the Black Metropolis Research Consortium (BMRC) for awarding me a 2009 Short-Term Fellowship in African American Studies. My monograph was shaped in wonderfully unexpected ways by the brilliant scholars and artists I met through the BMRC, including Vera Davis, Adam Green, Michael Flug, Cynthia Hawkins, Barbara E. Allen, Monica Hairston O'Connell, Christopher R. Reed, Marcus Shelby, and Bonnie Harrison. I would also like to extend a special thanks to Beverly Cook, an archivist at the Vivian G. Harsh Research Collection of Afro-American History and Literature, who took me down an exciting archival rabbit hole that summer with Era Bell Thompson. I am indebted to the National Research Council and the Ford Foundation for awarding me the 2005–6 Dissertation Fellowship that supported me on this intellectual journey at its inception and the 2010–11 Postdoctoral Fellowship that enabled me to complete this project. Over the years the Ford Fellows community has nurtured me intellectually, emotionally, and spiritually, and I credit it for continuously sustaining me in the academy. I want to express my heartfelt gratitude to Madhu Dubey for graciously mentoring and engaging me during my postdoctoral fellowship as well as securing the institutional support of the Department of African American Studies at the University of Illinois at Chicago, where Michelle R. Boyd kindly shared her office space, scrap paper, and comfy chair. Marisha Humphries, Lorena Garcia, and P. Zitlali Morales invited me into their academic writing group, and I appreciate the accountability and fellowship I found in their circle. I am happy that in my monograph's later stages I was able to benefit from the critical insights of Trudier Harris, Evie Shockley, and Dana Williams about the African American literary tradition during the 2012 National Endowment for the Humanities Summer Institute, directed by Lovalerie King at Pennsylvania State University. The provocative discussions among the Summer Institute's dynamic cohort rejuvenated my research, writing, and teaching. I especially want to acknowledge the intellectual rigor and savvy of Aisha D. Lockridge, Therí A. Pickens, Kameelah L. Martin, Thabiti Lewis, Beauty Bragg, Cherise A. Pollard, Nicole L. Sparling, Lanisa Kitchiner, Shaila Mehra, Brandon Manning, Earl Brooks, and David B. Green.

The following libraries, institutions, and individuals also deserve my sincere thanks: the Beinecke Rare Book and Manuscript Library, Yale University; Black Women Oral History Project, Schlesinger Library, Radcliffe Institute, Harvard University; Manuscripts Division, Department of Rare Books and Special Collections, Princeton University Library; and Special Collections and University Archives, Rutgers University Libraries. Nancy Goldstein was extremely charitable in opening up her home and taking the time to talk about her passion.

Last but certainly not least, *Writing through Jane Crow* came to fruition with the commitment of my editor, Cathie Brettschneider, and the assistance of two anonymous readers, whose thoughtful, detailed feedback greatly enriched the book. I believe this is also the appropriate place to thank my dear friends Cherri Hendricks, Travis Gatling, Colette McLemore, Alicia Boards, Reneé Matthews, and Robert

Johnson for grounding me and giving me balance in my life as I undertook this research. I must express my profound gratitude to Andreá N. Williams for going first and rallying behind me and to Chavella T. Pittman for being an intuitive listener and a pillar of strength and courage. This book also owes its existence to my mother, Jean Brooks Hardison, who would have loved me anyway but always maintained faith that I would finish it.

Writing through Jane Crow

Introduction: Defining Jane Crow

*In my preoccupation with the brutalities of racism, I had failed until now
to recognize the subtler, more ambiguous expressions of sexism.*
—PAULI MURRAY, SONG IN A WEARY THROAT: AN AMERICAN PILGRIMAGE

The shadow of Jim Crow loomed over African Americans' bodies and
imaginations throughout the first half of the twentieth century. As
the personification of racial discrimination, Jim Crow was a mocking
nineteenth-century stereotype performed by blackface minstrels and a
system of laws and customs practiced by whites to oppress black subjects
after Reconstruction.[1] The withdrawal of federal troops from the South
in 1877 and the *Plessy v. Ferguson* U.S. Supreme Court decision in 1896
imposed racial segregation on housing, work, leisure, public transportation, and civil rights protest. The southern white policeman in James
Baldwin's short story "Going to Meet the Man" (1965) swaggers, "Well,
Big Jim C. and some of the boys really had to whip that nigger's ass
today."[2] Jim Crow embodied the federal legislation that touted "separate
but equal" as well as the local common-law vigilante violence governing
the interactions between blacks and whites. This institutional inequality
continued roughshod until what C. Vann Woodward terms the "Second Reconstruction," initiated by the desegregation of schools with the
Brown v. Board of Education U.S. Supreme Court decision in 1954.[3]

Yet even at its nadir, the moniker Jim Crow did not address the patriarchal conventions also subjugating African American women politically, economically, and socially. In the *Negro Digest* article "Why Negro
Girls Stay Single" (1947), black civil rights lawyer and feminist activist
Pauli Murray contends, "The rationalizations upon which this sex prejudice rests are often different from those supporting racial discrimination in label only."[4] Murray employs the term *Jane Crow* to identify

the gender oppression preventing black women's full participation in society because "it is so strikingly similar to 'Jim Crow.'" By exposing black women's harassment under the union of Jim and Jane Crow, she rejected the prevailing assumption that black women should privilege race matters over gender issues despite what Gloria Wade-Gayles would later describe as the "double jeopardy" of racism and sexism.[5] Instead Murray equates the black male chauvinism hindering black women's economic mobility with the white supremacy restricting African Americans' collective political enfranchisement. "The successful outcome of the struggle against racism," she wagers later in "The Liberation of Black Women" (1970), "will depend in large part upon the simultaneous elimination of all discrimination based upon sex."[6] "Why Negro Girls Stay Single," then, was not a question but a declaration.

Writing through Jane Crow: Race and Gender Politics in African American Literature argues that black writers explored both racial and sexual discrimination during the heyday of social realism through their representations of black women. Rather than focus singly on black women's racial oppression under Jim Crow, I recast the term *Jane Crow* to consider the intersections of race, gender, class, and sexual politics in a literary moment defined by its pragmatic portraits of subjection and protest. The cultural production of texts between the Harlem Renaissance and the Black Arts Movement, amid World War II and the *Brown* decision, is a turning point in the African American literary tradition. In this epoch female-centered texts challenge the privileging of race over gender. They confront tensions between the expectations of middle-class respectability and the desire to express black female sexuality. These works grapple with the Jane Crow practices prescribing black women in the public sphere of work, citizenship, and an emergent popular and consumer culture. In turn they interrogate the Jane Crow proprieties delimiting black women in the private sphere, which included the politics of domesticity performed in the kitchen and the bedroom. The latter is particularly important, as Karla F. C. Holloway argues, because black and female bodies have "a compromised relationship to privacy" due to the fact that white patriarchal culture—always and already—depicts them as Other in the public sphere.[7] What I identify as a Jane Crow discourse, however, is historically contingent. It surfaced in the wake of Richard Wright's critically acclaimed, commercially successful, and masculinist novel *Native Son* (1940). Moreover it anticipated the Black Women Writers' Renaissance, introducing Alice Walker, Toni Morrison, Gloria Naylor, and Gayl Jones. Shaped by blacks' disillusionment after the war, this Jane Crow discourse preceded the modern civil rights movement of the 1950s and 1960s and the women's movement of the 1970s.

The specter of Jane Crow marks a rupture in twentieth-century African American literature. The moniker describes the burdening of black female subjectivity under a specific set of social conditions: mass migration, changing gender relations, class anxiety, and racial strife. As a result, the Jane Crow text is a work that contemplates these social conditions. Each chapter in *Writing through Jane Crow* traces the nuances of this discourse by examining the work of black female and male writers who share an investment in redressing black women's oppression. This selection of Jane Crow texts attempts to redefine black female agency within the public and private spheres, and these works try to imagine social change for the black collective within black women's purview. The Jane Crow text is unheralded perhaps, but it decisively imagines new identity formations for black female subjectivity within literary and social contexts.

Writing through Jane Crow also traces mid-twentieth-century black writers' efforts to gain literary agency under the strictures enforced by publishers and critics.[8] My map of Jane Crow outlines the politics of representation shaping the black text as well as those dictating the black writer's critical reception during the period. Wright, for example, rejected Zora Neale Hurston's folkloristic novel *Their Eyes Were Watching God* (1937) as "serious fiction" because the black female writer "*voluntarily*" participated in the minstrel tradition.[9] Hurston then chided Wright for his "elemental and brutish" characters in *Uncle Tom's Children* (1938) and dismissed the short story collection as a book of "hatreds."[10] Such politics of representation continue to inform mid-twentieth-century literary history's celebration of black male writers like Wright, who wrote naturalistic fiction, to the detriment of their female contemporaries like Hurston, who deviated from that writing formula.[11] *Writing through Jane Crow* examines how the intersections of race and gender affected black female and male writers as well as how both genders endeavored to publish beyond such proscriptions. I deconstruct the politics-versus-arts debate that framed Wright and Hurston's aesthetic binary by analyzing the understudied texts of both canonical writers. I also seek a broader understanding of quasi-canonical fiction by Gwendolyn Brooks and Ann Petry. Finally, *Writing through Jane Crow* surveys the fiction and nonfiction work of four commonly neglected writers: Dorothy West, Curtis Lucas, Era Bell Thompson, and Pauli Murray. Whether looking at texts written by black female or male authors, I place representations of black women at the center of my study in order to reconsider the parameters of social realism, mid-twentieth-century American arts and letters, and black women's cultural history.

Although I primarily use the term *Jane Crow* to name the social oppression black women endured in the World War II and postwar eras, the personification also addresses the cultural and intellectual practices negating the specific contributions black women made to the postwar civil rights moment. Historian Maureen Honey, for example, calls attention to mainstream media's exclusion of black women's labor and domestic efforts from popular narratives about the war in favor of white images like Rosie the Riveter and the brave mother. However, black women themselves recognized American society's active denial of their contributions as industrial workers and preservers of the home front. In the essay "What My Job Means to Me" (1943), published in *Opportunity* magazine, Hortense Johnson declares, "America can't win this war without all of us, and we know it. We must prove it to white Americans as well—that our country can't get along without the labor and sacrifice of her brown daughters."[12] Still, contemporary narratives of World War II often overlook, as Megan Taylor Shockley argues, "the gendered roots of the modern civil rights movement."[13] Black female factory workers and clubwomen fought to claim citizenship through the Double V campaign, in which the mantra "Victory at home, Victory abroad" linked the struggle against American racism to the war against European fascism. They also fought for the right to enter industry and meet war labor demands by appealing to the Fair Employment Practices Committee, which enforced the 1941 executive order preventing racial and religious discrimination. The presence of black women in the war factory defied traditional strategies for racial uplift by shifting their energies from the domestic to the public sphere.

Black women's lived experience with Jane Crow oppression was also inscribed on their bodies. Hypersexual stereotypes of black women were established in slavery to justify white men's systematic rape of them, and the gross sexual exploitation of black female bodies continued during and beyond Jim Crow. However, the terrorism white men carried out against black men by way of lynching figures prominently in the Jim Crow narrative of racial violence, and often the civil rights movement is portrayed singly as a struggle between black and white men. Danielle L. McGuire's historical study helps to address this oversight by focusing on blacks' organized efforts to challenge the racial superiority and economic power whites exercised through the ritualistic sexual assault of black women in white employers' homes, in public places, and on modes of public transportation. In fact Rosa Parks, known for her civic disobedience during the 1955 Montgomery bus boycott, began her career as an investigator and antirape activist for the National Association for the Advancement of Colored People (NAACP). As McGuire documents, Parks mobilized unions, leftist publications, and black civic organizations in defense of Recy Taylor, a black woman who was kidnapped and gang-raped by seven white men in Abbeville, Alabama, in 1944. Taylor, a working wife and mother, was framed initially as a diseased prostitute during the investigation of her rape. National media scrutiny forced authorities to charge Taylor's rapists, but the all-white jury failed to indict the men despite a confession, witnesses to the abduction, and whites' character statements about Taylor. The judicial farce maintained that black women had no authority over their bodies, and there was no legal recourse for white men's targeted sexual violence against them until Betty Jean Owens's rape trial in 1959.[14] Darlene Clark Hine reveals that black women developed a culture of dissemblance, a "self-imposed invisibility," in response to this targeted sexual violence in order to protect their inner selves or private lives.[15] Black women's dissemblance resulted in their silence on domestic violence in addition to the omission of interracial rape from historical narratives of their lives.

While the de facto sanctioning of black women's sexual abuse is arguably the apex of their gender oppression during the segregation era, black women's activism during the Montgomery bus boycott evidenced their agency. Black domestic workers' refusal to ride city buses mitigated the social, political, and economic conditions undergirding Jane Crow. Most Americans remember that Rosa Parks's unwillingness to sit in the back of the bus launched a social movement led by a dynamic Martin Luther King Jr. Few remember that Jo Ann Gibson Robinson, president of the Women's Political Council, threatened a boycott a year before Parks's arrest. In a letter to the mayor, Robinson requested that bus drivers permit black passengers to pay and enter at the front of the bus. She also suggested that drivers end reserved seating for whites and allow black passengers to fill the vehicle from the back to the front. "Please consider this plea, and if possible, act favorably upon it," Robinson writes, "for even now plans are being made to ride less, or not at all, on our busses. We do not want this."[16] The ensuing boycott projected black humanity in the public space and on the national stage by protesting the verbal and physical abuse blacks suffered at the whim of white bus drivers. It also changed black women's relationships with their white employers by reminding the latter of the value of domestic work. Black women were the Montgomery boycott's "trailblazers," to borrow Mary Fair Burks's word, while King was a "torchbearer" who utilized and brought their "truth" to fruition.[17] Still, many historical accounts foreground King, or singularly Parks, over the many black domestic workers who sacrificed their livelihood or walked when they could not ride. Erica R. Edwards's recent work disrupts this privileging of "charismatic leadership," which she defines as a singular narrative of normative masculinity, in the fictions of African American history and literary studies.[18]

Writing through Jane Crow moves black women writers and female-centered texts from the periphery to the focal point of mid-twentieth-century literary history. I shift the conversation from a dialogue among black male writers to a tête-à-tête between black female and male writers about black women. This move makes possible a new understanding of writers on the margins of literary studies like Dorothy West. She faced Jane Crow politics in her conflict with the white editors of the *Ladies' Home Journal*, who feared the loss of advertising if they serialized her novel *The Living Is Easy* (1948). Additionally West clashed with Wright over the journal *New Challenge*, which produced only one issue, in 1937. His political aesthetic and her financial backing exacerbated their conflict regarding the publication's editorship. In the end West agreed to sign the journal over to Wright because of his affiliations with the Communist Party.[19] "Maybe you don't realize it," she explains in an interview with Deborah McDowell, "but it was very hard for one little woman back then. . . . I guess you could say I was passive. Plus, I was small and my voice soft."[20] Cultural expectations, West suggested, stunted the voice of the black woman writer. Notwithstanding this silencing, mid-twentieth-century black female and male writers were in conversation. Lawrence P. Jackson's tome *The Indignant Generation* (2010) attests that literary critics, institutional support, and cultural brokers created a social milieu for black writers from the height of 1940s protest fiction to the American liberalism and high modernism of the 1950s. During the period's Black Chicago Renaissance, for example, Wright recommended Gwendolyn Brooks's poems to publisher Harper & Brothers and the Julius Rosenwald Fund, an endowment that supported academic and creative projects.[21] *Negro Digest* printed Ann Petry's and Era Bell Thompson's opposing views on black men's romantic and social relations with black women. Whereas these black writers were in literal conversation, Wright's and Petry's best-selling novels along with Brooks's prize-winning poetry meant that their writing contemporaries were also in metaphorical conversation with them.

Although black writers articulated critiques of Jane Crow oppression, many literary histories of the mid-twentieth century continue to focus entirely on race. Evie Shockley sees the tenets of the Black Arts Movement retroactively shaping the reception of literary texts produced prior to 1960—even when the "Black Aesthetic" is rebuffed and "caricatured" by literary critics as prescriptive.[22] Kenneth W. Warren's critique *What Was African American Literature?* (2011) takes its cue from the 1950 special issue of *Phylon*, the flagship journal for black intellectuals during the segregation era. The special issue contains a who's who of critics and creative writers, including Langston Hughes, Margaret Walker, Robert Hayden, William Gardner Smith, Nick Aaron Ford, and J. Saunders Redding. Contributors provided a "sober appraisal" of the past and forecast the future of African American letters.[23] Hugh M. Gloster argues that the preponderance of racial themes "helped certain critics and publishers to lure [the black writer] into the deadly trap of cultural segregation by advising him that the black ghetto is his proper milieu."[24] Gloster uses the imagery of spatial segregation to criticize the thematic tyranny thrust upon black writers by white publishers. Comparably Charles I. Glicksberg looks forward to the figurative integration of African American literature. "Whites hold a mortgage even on this segregated sector and dictate the terms of the lease," he writes. "They decide what is unique in Negro genius."[25] The economic power of white publishers dictated the aesthetic limitations placed on postwar black writers.[26] Their narratives about blacks' oppression assuaged white readers' angst regarding cold war alienation.[27] Alain Locke, dean of the Harlem Renaissance, closed the special issue of *Phylon* with his conclusions on the literature produced during the first half of the twentieth century. Although he once professed the birth of the "New Negro," Locke elucidates that black gatekeepers also hold black writers in bondage. He argues that the black middle class, characters of mixed-raced heritage, and intraracial prejudices are forced into "closed closets like family skeletons."[28] White publishers imposed Jim Crow on black writers and their subject matter; black writers chafed against conventional boundaries.

Instead of a complex history of mid-twentieth-century African American literature, critics reduce the period into an Oedipal dynamic between Wright (the father), James Baldwin (the prodigal son), and Ralph Ellison (the literary heir). Wright's essay "Blueprint for Negro Writing," published in the single issue of *New Challenge*, differentiates his script for interwar black texts by disparaging the Harlem Renaissance artists, "who went a-begging to white America" and entered the public stage "in the knee-pants of servility, curtsying."[29] In turn Baldwin deconstructs dangerous stereotypes of blacks by likening *Native Son* to Harriet Beecher Stowe's well-intentioned though damaging novel *Uncle Tom's Cabin* (1852). Wright's protagonist Bigger Thomas, Baldwin lambastes, "admits the possibility of his being sub-human and feels constrained, therefore, to battle for his humanity according to those brutal criteria bequeathed him at his birth."[30] Though most literary scholars interpret Ellison's high modernism in *Invisible Man* (1952) as the end of the Wright school of protest, William J. Maxwell registers Oedipal anxieties in Ellison's work.[31] Black male writers who attempted to model, refine, or critique the literary blueprint for protest Wright executed in *Native Son*, such as Carl Offord, Willard Motley, and Chester Himes, swells this "boys' club" of Jim Crow arts and letters.

The schema for social protest in the mid-twentieth-century novel is often costly for the black male dissident and his black female counterpart. In *Native Son* white society convicts Bigger for the rape and murder of white Mary Dalton, while the court simply uses the violated black body of Bessie Mears, whom Bigger does rape and premeditatedly murder, as evidence. Proving the pervasive influence of Wright's novel, Chester Himes references the text in his novel *If He Hollers Let Him Go* (1945) with a brief yet provocative book club discussion, in which participants debate Wright's aesthetic and social politics. This intertextual moment illustrates the masculinist focus of both black male writers' novels. In *If He Hollers Let Him Go* the failure of shipyard crew leader Bob Jones as a patriarch is the lens through which he understands Bigger's social, economic, and political oppression.[32] "I'm scared to ask a white woman to do a job," Bob explains to fellow discussants. "All she's got to do is say I insulted her and I'm fired." In contrast, three black female social workers vehemently criticize Bigger and ultimately Bob, who is sentenced climactically to the army because of a false rape accusation. One female reader complains, "*Native Son* turned my stomach. . . . It just proved what the white Southerner has always said about us; that our men are rapists and murderers."[33] A second suggests that Wright is naïve about the implications of his text. *If He Hollers Let Him Go* delivers these criticisms through black female voices even as it signifies on *Native Son*'s male-centered social critique. Himes's reiteration of the protest novel explores black male subjugation in relation to white women, but Bob Jones is not conscious of his own corruption, culpability, or misogyny.

By examining mid-twentieth-century female-centered texts, *Writing through Jane Crow* explores proto-feminist protest. In *The Street* (1946)

Petry's black female protagonist literally strikes back at the black man who tries to rape her as well as symbolically fights the segregation that prevents her physical and economic mobility. The novel's representation of violent resistance significantly acknowledges black women's protest of Jim and Jane Crow. Yet Petry strategically depreciates the cultural significance of the protest novel later in her essay "The Novel as Social Criticism" (1950): "After I had written a novel of social criticism (it was my first book, written for the most part without realizing that it belonged in a special category) I slowly became aware that such novels were regarded as a special and quite deplorable creation of American writers of the twentieth century." Petry's best-selling novel was deemed in vogue because it easily fit into the profitable formula *Native Son* created. Her feigned ignorance of the genre, however, alludes to critics' reductive reading that all social criticism originated with Marxist protest fiction, which was censured later by 1950s liberalism and cold war containment. "There were fashions in literary criticism," Petry explains, "and . . . they shifted and changed much like the fashions in women's hats."[34]

Writing through Jane Crow charts black female protest, but it also reconsiders the centrality of the protest genre to the period. Mid-twentieth-century authors of female-centered texts utilized aesthetics, techniques, and tropes beyond the conventions of the social protest novel to portray black female subjectivity. Dorothy West refines the domestic novel, Curtis Lucas capitalizes on pulp fiction, and Gwendolyn Brooks composes a novella. Zora Neale Hurston creates a "white-plot" novel with only minor black characters, whereas Era Bell Thompson constructs an autobiography that projects promise for interracial relations. Even Wright, the author of the black masculine archetype Bigger Thomas, aimed to refine the social protest novel with the black female protagonist in his unpublished manuscript "Black Hope," drafted shortly after *Native Son*. I engage these diverse works to stress the elasticity of the period shaped by its representations of black women.

My study is in conversation with Stacy I. Morgan's book *Rethinking Social Realism* (2004) and Gene A. Jarrett's work *Deans and Truants* (2006), which reimagine this literary period in regard to the politics of texts and the dynamics between writing contemporaries. Morgan contends that social realism extends beyond its zenith in the 1930s to include not only the protest novel of the 1940s, with which most black writers of the period make their debut, but also the integrationist writing of the 1950s. Comparably Jarrett reconceptualizes social realism by discerning the relationship between canonical "deans" like Wright, who established literary conventions, and less critically engaged "truants" like Frank Yerby, whose historical romances resisted dominant aesthetic forms. Both Morgan and Jarrett remark upon the gender question in their work, but neither distinguishes the influence of sexual difference beyond a cursory glance.[35] My work is in debt to their scholarship, but *Writing through Jane Crow* departs from these projects in its gendered lens to create an even more textured narrative of the period.

Drawing on black feminist approaches, I trouble the masculinist mid-twentieth-century narrative of black literary production that has remained the primary focus of contemporary scholarship. Womanist and feminist literary scholars have recovered several black female writers from critical obscurity. Alice Walker not only provided the "lost" Hurston with a headstone for her grave, but she also relocated Hurston's body of work within the tradition of African American literature. Walker claimed Hurston as a literary foremother and what Michael Awkward terms an "inspiriting influence" for her own work.[36] Similarly Thadious Davis, Ann duCille, Mae G. Henderson, Deborah McDowell, and Cheryl A. Wall have reinstated the works of Nella Larsen and Jessie Fauset to the critical conversation. The unprecedented production of texts during the Harlem Renaissance, however, tends to overshadow the critical recognition of works published during the heyday of social realism. Likewise the racial politics of the Black Arts Movement often preempt the significance of mid-century texts for contemplating black women's intersecting race, class, and gender oppressions. Barbara Christian, Maryemma Graham, Trudier Harris, Hortense J. Spillers, and Mary Helen Washington have returned to the work of black female authors writing during the Jane Crow period. Yet to a great extent, current gender surveys focus on the intertextual dialogues between women writers of the Harlem Renaissance and those publishing after the emergence of black feminist criticism. Conversely critical surveys of mid-twentieth-century fiction are typically single-author studies. In the following discussion, I make a case for the significance of the period and the concerns of the Jane Crow text by examining a medley of works.

Writing through Jane Crow recovers the lost work of obscure writers and restores the lesser-known works of canonical writers. I look at visual texts as well as written works; examine the protest novel as well as texts whose conventions critique that genre; and consider the contributions of men as well as women to this gender discourse. A compilation of disparate texts in conversation, *Writing through Jane Crow* resists a superficial coherence of the period by exposing the political squabbles, aesthetic fissures, thematic overlaps, editorial compromises, and literary dead-ends found across texts produced by and about black women. Placing these episodic works in context, I identify a triptych of objectives for the Jane Crow text. First, it attempts to create art outside the confines of the protest tradition, which overdetermines the tragic end of its protagonist. Second, it tries to conceive ways for black women to resist racism, sexism, and the expectations of middle-class respectability, which proscribe a reductive model of black femininity. Third, it indicts those complicit in black women's oppression, including white women and black men who benefit from racism and patriarchy. Each chapter of *Writing through Jane Crow* explores the manner in which selected texts address these aims— albeit each work accomplishes these goals with varying degrees of political and commercial success. These Jane Crow texts do not necessarily resolve the issues they take up, but they lay the groundwork for the more liberating narratives published later.

Naming Jane Crow: A Model Reading

The title of my book invokes Pauli Murray's term for black women's gender oppression. Her posthumously published autobiography, *Song in a Weary Throat: An American Pilgrimage* (1987), yields a template for understanding the Jane Crow text.[37] Murray was one of the leading minds of her generation, and she dedicated her extraordinary career as a black activist, feminist, lawyer, priest, and poet to fighting racism and sexism from the Depression era to the women's movement. She also faced the multiple oppressions black women endured during this period. *Song in a Weary Throat* illustrates her confrontation with Jane Crow in her life and written text.

As her autobiography's original title suggests, Murray's efforts to contribute to an emerging modern civil rights movement were exhaustive. For example, in 1938 the U.S. Supreme Court ruled in *Missouri ex rel. Gaines v. Canada* that the University of Missouri Law School was required to admit black applicants because a "separate but equal" law school did not exist in the state. That same year Murray applied to graduate school at the University of North Carolina, but the school rejected her due to her race. (It did not accept its first black student until 1951.) Murray notes in *Song in a Weary Throat* that NAACP lawyer Thurgood Marshall declined to take her case because the North Carolinian lived in New York when she applied. Historian Glenda Elizabeth Gilmore supposes that other reasons also likely informed Marshall's decision:

Murray's letter-writing campaign in the press regarding her rejection, her communist affiliations, and the fact that she "did not conform to feminine standards."[38] Murray often dressed as a man, lived with women, and sought psychiatric help for her same-sex desire.[39] Although in her autobiography she critiques the sexism obstructing her efforts to fight Jim Crow, she treads carefully in regard to the politics of sexuality contributing to the injustices she experienced during the segregation era. The NAACP did not pursue her desegregation case, but she went on to attend Howard University Law School, where she was one of the first to propose a frontal assault on the constitutionality of segregation rather than challenge individual states' application of the "separate but equal" statute. As a civil rights attorney, Murray published *States' Laws on Race and Color* (1950) to support legal challenges to segregation statutes, and her 1944 law school essay theorizing that "separate" is inherently unequal was one of the briefs in the *Brown* case argued by Marshall.

Song in a Weary Throat also discusses Murray's "spirited corre-spondence" with First Lady Eleanor Roosevelt, in which she criticized President Roosevelt's moderate position on segregation, discrimination, and lynching.[40] While she admits that her fervent words often stirred Mrs. Roosevelt "to use strong language" in defense of the White House, Murray concedes, "At least I had her ear."[41] Finding prolific synergy between her activism and creative passions, Murray expressed in prose her frustrations with the federal government's ambivalent stance toward racial inequity. In the poem "Mr. Roosevelt Regrets," she censures the president's inadequate response to the 1943 Detroit riots. The narrator demands:

> What'd you get when you cried out to the Top Man?
> When you called on the man next to God, so you thought,
> And you asked him to speak out to save you?
> What'd the Top Man say, black boy?[42]

The poem answers: "Mr. Roosevelt regrets . . . ." Murray achieved artistic integration in her writings as a poet and activist, both of which worked in concert with her legal contestations to Jim Crow.

At the same time that Murray's autobiography chronicles her regular stands against racism, *Song in a Weary Throat* documents her evolving feminism, incited by her recurring encounters with gender oppression during the long civil rights movement. Toward the end of her narrative, she explicitly articulates the two-pronged social intervention she desired to make with an account of her developing political consciousness. "What I really wanted to do," she clarifies, "was to write an autobiographical book upon Jim Crow and Jane Crow—racism and sexism as they had impinged on my life."[43] *Song in a Weary Throat* details her experiences with racism and sexism in the interest of exhibiting her triumph over them: she was the first African American to receive a doctor of juridical science degree from Yale Law School, in 1965; she was one of the twenty-eight founders of the National Organization of Women (NOW) in 1966; and she was the first African American woman ordained as an Episcopal priest, in 1977.[44] Despite her achievement as a civil rights attorney and feminist activist, Murray confesses in her autobiography, "[In the 1940s] breaking the code of respectability . . . was as formidable a psychological barrier to [social] action as the prospect of police brutality."[45]

African Americans' efforts to obtain the rights of citizenship rested, in part, on black women's performance of bourgeois respectability, which represented sexual restraint and domestic propriety in private and public.[46] This racial-uplift strategy policed black female bodies in order to dispel myths of their licentiousness rooted in slavery, to protect black women from sexual assault, and to give evidence of African Americans' collective worthiness for citizenship. Even as Murray acknowledges the politics of middle-class respectability in her narrative, *Song in a Weary Throat* manifests the psychological repercussions that race, gender, and class oppressions imposed on her figurative body. That is to say, the union of Jim and Jane Crow disenfranchised Murray within her historical context, and it compromised her narrative voice, though her autobiography was written decades later. The mandates of middle-class respectability demanded Murray's silence on her sexuality in her memoir, as the politics of Jane Crow circumscribed not only black women's literal bodies but also their textual representation.

Murray first explores her subjection to Jane Crow oppression in her autobiography by exposing the sexism perpetrated by black men who were committed to abolishing racial injustice. Sharing these men's aims, Murray explains that she attends Howard University Law School "with the single-minded intention of destroying Jim Crow." The 1942 execution of black sharecropper Odell Waller motivates her to apply to law school, as Waller's legal lynching teaches her the importance of legal expertise to civil rights advocacy. An all-white jury sentenced Waller to death for murdering his white landlord—though allegedly in self-defense—in a dispute over their jointly owned crop. On behalf of the Workers Defense League, Murray travels to raise funds for the case and bring attention to the plight of black sharecroppers. "I might as well become a lawyer," she half-jokingly tells a Howard law professor, "if I kept bumping into the law as I had been doing." Her tenure at the all-black institution, however, allows her to perceive the oppression she experienced specifically due to her sex. Prior to attending Howard, Murray completed her undergraduate education at Hunter College in 1933, which she recognizes in retrospect as "a natural training ground for feminism." She explains that observing women in the faculty and student body take leadership roles "reinforced our egalitarian values, inspired our confidence in the competence of women generally, and encouraged our resistance to subordinate roles." In contrast, she reflects, "if Howard Law School equipped me for effective struggle against Jim Crow, it was also the place where I first became conscious of the twin evil of discriminatory sex bias, which I quickly labeled Jane Crow. In my preoccupation with the brutalities of racism, I had failed until now to recognize the subtler, more ambiguous expressions of sexism." The nuances of sexism virtually "condemned" Murray to silence as the only woman in her class at Howard. She recalls that her male classmates' voices "obliterate[d]" her softer voice, and the school's legal fraternity excluded her from its membership. The fact that male faculty members discriminated against Murray, men whom she "deeply admired because of their dedication to civil rights, men who themselves had suffered racial indignities," fostered her "incipient feminism."[47]

Murray not only exposes black men's patriarchal privilege, but she also reveals that Jane Crow oppression included the politics of respectability, limiting how she confronted Jim Crow segregation. For example, Murray and a female friend were arrested for creating a public disturbance on a bus trip from Washington, D.C., to Virginia when they refused to sit on a broken seat in the back of the bus. The court initially convicted Murray and her companion for breaking segregation laws practiced by the bus company, although the state legally required only that blacks not sit in seats adjacent to whites. As a result, a misinformed first lady concluded in a letter that Murray's means did not justify her ends. "As long as these laws exist," Eleanor Roosevelt writes, "it does no one much good to violate them." Murray admits in her narrative that she was bothered by the first lady's response, but she explains, "It was hardly surprising that she seemed to disapprove of our resistance to discrimination in the climate of 1940. Unlike the 1950s and the 1960s, when the Supreme Court had outlawed segregation, and going to jail in the civil rights struggle was commonplace, in 1940 it was somehow horrifying to 'respectable' people." Murray acknowledges the social consequences, in addition to the psychological barriers, the politics of middle-class respectability posed for interracial alliances and partisanship within the black community. "For all my bravado, deeply engrained notions of respectability filled me with distress," she writes.⁴⁸

Traditionally, racial violence manifested itself in particular ways: black men were more often the targets of lynching and black women were more vulnerable to rape. Nineteenth-century codes for black female propriety had been the primary defense against sexual violence, and Murray confirms in *Song in a Weary Throat* that violating the codes of respectability remained particularly appalling for black women. "Many parents of Howard University students, particularly the parents of teenage girls, adhered to middle-class standards of respectability," she relays, "and would be horrified at the thought of their daughters tangling with the police, being arrested and thrown into jail." She explains that black female students at Howard University during World War II felt "an extra responsibility to carry on the integration battle" because "an accident of gender exempted [them] from military service."⁴⁹ Yet few mid-twentieth-century histories credit these black female students for initiating the sit-in tactics that became nationally recognized when students integrated southern lunch counters in 1960.⁵⁰ Black female activists defied the classed expectations imposed on their gender performance, but the significance of their work was relatively minimized in later civil rights campaigns. Anne Standley observes that "the widespread use of the metaphor of reaching manhood to describe the self-confidence that blacks gained from the movement" failed "to consider the impact of the movement on black women's consciousness, and to recognize the contributions of women in making this racial pride possible."⁵¹ Masculinist discourses occluded black women's specific gender oppression as well as their activist efforts during the 1930s, 1940s, and 1950s. In *Song in a Weary Throat* Murray critiques such chauvinism as well as the borders of respectability it regulated. Both, she intimates, undermined radical social change.

Despite her pioneering stand, Murray was hampered by the conventions she opposed. The literary inscriptions of Jane Crow inhibited her representation of black female subjectivity. Her same-sex desire and questions regarding her biological sex remain suppressed in *Song in a Weary Throat* because the autobiography, as Joanne M. Braxton contends, "is a vision not of an individual, but a collective wholeness."⁵² Murray's self-conscious construction of self does not jeopardize the black community's social progress with any controversy her sexuality might have elicited.

Her autobiography instead negotiates her public and private selves with omissions. In this way her twentieth-century narrative exhibits the conventions of nineteenth-century black women's autobiography.

The politics of respectability repeatedly represses Murray's narrative voice. For example, in the chapter "Among the Unemployed" she describes her antagonistic relationship with the director of Camp Tera (Temporary Emergency Relief Administration), a women's recreational program she attended in 1934, established under Roosevelt's New Deal. Murray attributes the conflict to the director's dislike of her "cockiness" as well as her friendship with camp counselor Peg Holmes. She complains that the director "discouraged any social contact between campers and counselors outside of scheduled activities, despite the fact that we were all adult women."[53] Though she affirms a bond with Holmes founded on mutual intellectual interests, Murray is unable to write about the intimate relationship between herself and Holmes documented in her archived diary, photos, and personal correspondence.[54] Rather Murray suggests that her expulsion from Camp Tera is based on two misunderstandings: she claims she did not stand with other campers when the first lady toured the camp because the women were not being officially introduced, and she brought an unread copy of Marx's *Das Kapital* with her to the program. The camp director finds the first act disrespectful, but the second infraction evidences Murray's social and political threat, though she does not become a communist until after the accusation. Notwithstanding Murray's progressive politics throughout her life, the reference to Marxism in *Song in a Weary Throat* effectively replaces a potentially more radical critique of heterosexuality with a class critique.

Most strikingly Murray omits from her autobiography her series of hospitalizations in the late 1930s and 1940s, which were attributed to her struggle with her sexuality and gender identity. Arguably her psychological turmoil is displaced onto recollections of her father's mental illness earlier in the text. Murray shares that her father, whose "most marked characteristic" was to improve his education and excel in his profession as a teacher, was prone to "unpredictable attacks of depression and violent moods" due to the chronic effects of typhoid fever.[55] After her mother's death when Murray is four, different relatives raise her and her siblings while her father is placed in a mental hospital. Her characterization of her father as being frustrated intellectually by racism and stigmatized socially due to the ignorance of mental illness queers or "quares" him as a black subject, to use E. Patrick Johnson's term for blacks' lived experience as the racial and sexual Other.[56] Murray's telling of her father's murder in 1923 when she is thirteen stands in for the psychological violence she suffers under Jane Crow oppression. A contentious exchange between her father and a bigoted white hospital attendant, which purportedly escalates to the latter's threat to "get that nigger later," culminates in the attendant beating Murray's father to death with a baseball bat.[57]

Her father's institutionalization and murder inspire Murray to question her own mental health in her autobiography. She confides, "My father's death had left the question of hereditary insanity unanswered." She recognizes her father's death as a casualty of racially motivated violence, but she normalizes this brutality by questioning her own threatened response to this trauma. She admits, "I developed an irrational fear of being hemmed in or struck from behind, as my father had been. I always tried to get an aisle seat when going to the theater and to sit in the last row in the movies, at church, or other public places."[58] Her supposedly illogical fear is a response to the violence that racism and segregation constantly posed for blacks. Meanwhile *Song in a Weary Throat* denies her fears about her own "quare" identity. Her aporia and ellipses in the narrative signal her added anxiety regarding her sexuality and enact their own psychological violence. Murray's self-denial in the autobiography implicitly expresses what Candice M. Jenkins terms the "salvific wish": a middle-class desire to protect black subjects from sexual pathology through the promotion of conventional bourgeois propriety.[59] In the chapter titled "Saved by the WPA," Murray's account of the Great Depression does not address her month-long stay in a mental hospital in 1937 after her relationship with Holmes. When she discusses student activism at Howard University, she does not disclose that she was hospitalized a third time during law school after allegations that she had a relationship with a female undergraduate.[60]

Song in a Weary Throat resounds with silence on Murray's same-sex desire and questions regarding her biological sex, but her private letters and notes kept during her hospital stays fill in the gaps required in her published writing. Murray discusses the possibility that she was a homosexual as well as developments in hormone therapy with her doctors. Complicating her struggle with her sexual identity is the fact that she was aware, according to Anne Firor Scott, that she was attracted to what she was not: white and feminine.[61] Murray suspected that her attraction to women indicated that she was biologically male, and in 1947 she underwent abdominal surgery to reveal the internal male sex organs she believed she possessed.[62] Her emotional conflict reflects the disapproval activists in the civil rights and women's movements had for homosexuality;[63] thus she only gestures toward her masculine identification in *Song in a Weary Throat* when she occasionally discusses her resistance to conventional femininity. "I was much more at home with a pencil than a needle," she writes.[64] She abruptly mentions her marriage only when she informs readers of its dissolution. More than once she expresses her reluctance to return home, as a single woman, to care for elderly family.

Murray rewrites the narrative of Jim Crow segregation by unmasking Jane Crow oppression in *Song in a Weary Throat*, but her life story remains constrained by Jane Crow's intersecting race, class, gender, and sex politics. One could argue, as Barbara Smith does about Toni Morrison's novel *Sula* (1973), that Murray's memoir is innately lesbian because it "refuses to do what it is supposed to do, . . . there are strong images of women and . . . there is a refusal to be linear."[65] One could also conclude, as James Olney suggests, that because autobiography "takes on a life of its own . . . the self [represented in the text] . . . is a fiction and so is the life."[66] Perhaps a more productive approach is acknowledging the text's covert Jane Crow inscriptions. *Song in a Weary Throat* explores the effect of racism and sexism on Murray's public life, but the absences in the narrative point to the psychic and textual consequences of Jane Crow. There is no space in the text for Murray, as a "respectable daughter" of the civil rights movement, to discuss her sexuality given that her black female writing contemporaries also glossed heterosexual desire in their fiction. The fact that Murray's 1987 autobiography adheres to these sexual codes illustrates the outgrowth of such censure. In effect *Song in a Weary Throat* displays the self-control required of a black woman living and writing through the Jane Crow period.

Nonetheless these silences do not negate what Murray set out to do in *Song in a Weary Throat*: to tease out the intersections of racial and gender oppression. Like her epic poem "Dark Testament" (1943), her memoir bears witness to blacks' perseverance despite disenfranchisement. "Hope is a crushed stalk / Between clenched fingers," the poem laments. "A word whispered with the wind, / A dream of forty acres and a mule, / . . . Hope is a song in a weary throat."[67] Murray's autobiography shares the poem's desire to sustain hope, and to this end the narrative documents her accomplishments overcoming racism for the benefit of the black collective.[68] Murray outlines her contributions to the civil rights movement in her autobiography too, to challenge sexism, and she demonstrates what she achieved in spite of her race and sex.

Song in a Weary Throat also makes a significant contribution to a literary history of black female sexuality. It is only within her poetry that Murray claims public discursive space to explore her desire. For example, in the poem "Without Name" (1948) the thing that goes unspoken is love. "Let this seed growing in us / Granite-strong with persistent root / Be without name," the poem encourages, "or call it the first / Warm wind that caressed your cheek / And traded unshared kisses between us."[69] Although in the poem feelings remain unnamed and kisses unshared, the something between the lovers is persistently growing. In *Song in a Weary Throat* such silence illustrates the ways the politics of Jane Crow affected the configuration and legibility of black women's social and textual bodies.

Writing through Jane Crow

In codifying the race, gender, class, and sex politics of mid-twentieth-century African American literature, I do not argue that any of the texts included in my project preempt history, offer solutions to racism and sexism, or usurp the politics of respectability. On the contrary, I read the Jane Crow text as a product of a particular cultural juncture. In *What Was African American Literature*, Kenneth W. Warren contends that the tradition "is not a transhistorical entity ... but ... constitutes a representational and rhetorical strategy within the domain of a literary practice responsive to conditions that, by and large, no longer obtain."[70] As Jim Crow discrimination and protest writing defined African American literature, Warren claims that the fiction emerging after the long civil rights movement is no longer limited by the political demands of the segregation era and therefore is no longer African American literature. Instead I am interested in reading the discontinuities between the representations of black women assembled in this book: the stops in addition to the starts of mid-twentieth-century African American literature, the plateaus, twists, and rebounds of this cultural moment.

The following chapters are concurrent yet distinct portraits of black female agency and subjection. I embed each work within its specific social and literary context, uncovering its theoretical, aesthetic, and historical layers. Arguing episodically, I advance interlocking claims about black women's lived experiences, the politics of representation in black female-centered texts, and the intertextual dialogues between black female and male writers. As a final point, I do not discuss playwright Alice Childress's work in depth because her major drama, *Wedding Band: A Love/*

Hate Story in Black and White (1966), is outside the chronological scope of my project. However, I briefly explore how two of Childress's earlier works resonate with a few of the Jane Crow texts examined in my study. Her column "Conversations from Life," which features a black domestic worker's verbal exchange with her friend, was published first in Paul Robeson's newspaper *Freedom* from 1951 to 1955, then the *Baltimore Afro-American*, and later as a book in 1956 under the title *Like One of the Family . . . Conversations from a Domestic's Life*. Childress's play *Florence* (1949), which deliberates women's alliances across divides of race and class, also exposes black women's multiple oppressions.[71] *Writing through Jane Crow*, of course, is by no means a comprehensive study of mid-twentieth-century black women's writing, but it does represent a critical intervention in how one perceives the significance of this cultural work in terms of the period and tradition.

Chapter 1, "At the Point of No Return: A Native Son and His Gorgon Muse," traces Richard Wright's efforts to adjust the "blueprint" he establishes in *Native Son*. Wright historically occupied an antithetical position in relation to many of his black female writing contemporaries, and I do not desire to reify his work, celebrated, in part, by African American literary critics because of those masculinist politics. Rather this chapter contemplates the complex gender and sex politics Wright wrestles with in his unpublished manuscript "Black Hope"—his only work propelled by black women's specific political needs. Among the first readings to engage with this text substantively, the chapter looks at "Black Hope" as a not yet fully realized turning point in Wright's oeuvre. I compare the canonized Wright of *Native Son*, whose black male protagonist scorns his mother and sister as well as rapes and murders his girlfriend, with a little-known Wright who struggles to empower black women in "Black Hope." Wright has difficulties overcoming the politics of Jane Crow in his creative process. However, he materializes "black hope" in the narrative's conclusion with a domestic workers' union organized to confront the economic and sexual exploitation of Jane Crow. As the manuscript languishes unfinished, this accomplishment remains latent and undervalued.

Turning to the fiction of black women writers, chapter 2, "Gender Conscriptions, Class Conciliations, and the Bourgeois Blues Aesthetic," examines Ann Petry's and Dorothy West's critiques of black women's social immobility, a fixed economic state founded on racial segregation. This immobility is furthered by patriarchy's relegation of black women to domestic labor or the domestic space. I juxtapose Petry's working-class protagonist in *The Street* and West's middle-class protagonist in *The Living Is Easy* in order to tease out the complexities of black women's bourgeois blues, which I define as an irreconcilable conflict between the black female protagonist's displaced desire for white middle-class respectability and the text's critique of those politics. The blues are complexly a site of personal trauma and empowerment for black women artistically, economically, and sexually. The bourgeois blues aesthetic in Petry's and West's novels negotiates black women's command of vernacular culture, class aspirations, and sexual vulnerability. In contrast to the masculine working-class protagonist privileged in the protest novel, Petry and West construct middle-class conscious narratives to depict black women's disenfranchisement within white society and working-class black enclaves. The chapter explores the bourgeois blues as a metaphor for the performance of black femininity, and it analyzes the bourgeois blues as a trope for discussing black women's unsanctioned class ambitions.

Moving from the Jane Crow blues of working-class and middle-class black women, chapter 3, "'Nobody Could Tell Who This Be': Black and White Doubles and the Challenge to Pedestal Femininity," looks at concentric representations of black and white women in Zora Neale Hurston's white-plot novel *Seraph on the Suwanee* (1948) and Petry's racially provocative text *The Narrows* (1953). Petry's career as a novelist began during the height of social realism, and together chapters 2 and 3 show the development of her gender discourse by examining her first and last adult novels, respectively. *The Narrows* follows the course of an interracial romance, and *Seraph on the Suwanee* focuses on the cross-class romance of a white couple. My analysis of these two less critically engaged texts highlights their subversive narratives regarding the potentials and limits to social bonds between women of different race and class backgrounds. Each novel acknowledges black and white women's comparable disenfranchisement under patriarchy. Yet each work also critiques the complicity of elite white and middle-class black women in the subjection of working-class black women because of their respective race and class privilege. In Hurston's and Petry's novels, white and black women function as mirrors or doubles for one another. Both are disadvantaged during the Jane Crow period by the pedestal figure of femininity, which is narrowly conceived of as white, middle-class, chaste, respectable, domesticated, and self-sacrificing.

Chapter 4, "'I'll See How Crazy *They* Think I Am': Pulping Sexual Violence, Racial Melancholia, and Healthy Citizenship," explores Curtis Lucas's depiction of black women's psychological response to sexual assault in *Third*

Ward Newark. A forgotten mid-twentieth-century text, *Third Ward Newark* is one of few black male-written and female-centered novels during the social realist era. This chapter establishes a cultural context for Lucas's work by examining the novel's evolving cover art: the 1946 Ziff-Davis hardcover introduces its black female protagonist as perfectly coiffed on its dust jacket, whereas the 1952 Lion Books pulp reprint presents her with shirt askew and a torn skirt on the verge of her rape by two white men. These contrasting covers reflect the Jane Crow politics of a white-male-dominated publishing industry. Comparably the novel's melodramatic plot straddles the genre boundaries between protest, which is invested in sobering social critiques, and pulp fiction, which is marketed for entertainment. Lucas's use of popular psychoanalysis in the novel manifests this friction. His protagonist's psychic trauma critiques black women's exclusion from pedestal femininity just as her emotional distress sensationalizes black women's supposed sexual pathology. In reading Lucas's pulp rendition of black women's protest, the chapter mines the political value of popular texts for expanding one's understanding of social realism.

Shifting from a black male writer's pulp production of black female subjectivity to a black female writer's critique of popular black discourses, chapter 5, "Rereading the Construction of Womanhood in Popular Narratives of Domesticity," assesses Gwendolyn Brooks's novella *Maud Martha* (1953) as a metafiction responding to representations of black femininity promoted in contemporaneous African American publications. *Maud Martha*'s nontraditional form and self-reflexive moments of reading challenge the fictions of middle-class domesticity perpetuated in print media. Brooks presents critical reading as an act of social and private protest in the collected sketches of the novella. *Maud Martha* constructs its titular protagonist as a savvy reader of literary and social texts even though she is relegated to the doldrums of the domestic space. The text also draws attention to the masculinist discourses of an emerging black popular culture depicting black women as textual bodies to be read—that is, commodified and consumed. Thus the chapter positions *Maud Martha* in relation to black-owned publications circulating around Brooks's protagonist: the *Chicago Defender,* a newspaper mentioned in the novella, as well as the magazines *Negro Digest, Ebony,* and *Tan Confessions* produced by John H. Johnson during the Black Chicago Renaissance. This discussion juxtaposes Maud Martha's private reading with her public performance of black female subjectivity. The chapter additionally compares Brooks's portrait of black womanhood to the visual images published in the black press in order to pinpoint how selling sex and, conversely, marketing middle-class respectability perpetuate Jane Crow.

Chapter 6, "The Audacity of Hope: An American Daughter and Her Dream of Cultural Hybridity," brings my book full circle by analyzing Era Bell Thompson's autobiography *American Daughter* (1946), whose title signifies on *Native Son* while its narrative content revises Wright's autobiography *Black Boy* (1945). Typically left out of Black Chicago Renaissance surveys, Thompson's cold war classic rejects Wright's "blueprint" and attempts to write black women into the national narrative of migration, upward mobility, and interracial relations.[72] *American Daughter* promotes her nontraditional childhood as a motherless black girl growing up winningly in a family of men and a predominantly white community on the prairies. Moreover Thompson writes herself into subjectivity via an idyllic representation of a united America that nurtures its native daughters. The chapter charts the race and gender themes inspiring Thompson's life story as well as the cultural production of her memoir. An extraordinary example of the white male publishing industry's calculated promotion and control of African American literature during the postwar era, Thompson's memoir about her racial isolation in North Dakota and racial frustration on the South Side of Chicago is her first publication. The narrative's success led to her editorship at *Ebony* magazine. The chapter explores *American Daughter* as an important work for contemplating racial reconciliation and progress during the segregation era, but it also traces the material and immaterial obstacles to black women's writing under the politics of Jane Crow.

Writing through Jane Crow examines the different approaches midtwentieth-century black writers employed to construct black female subjectivity. This cultural history embraces the political fissures between Wright and Thompson; thematic overlaps between Hurston, West, Petry, and Brooks; and the curious, uneven trajectory of the obscure though prolific Lucas. In doing so *Writing through Jane Crow* notes the past and present stratagems involved in the canonization, publication, and censure of African American literature. The epilogue to this discussion looks at the visual texts of the first black female cartoonist, Jackie Ormes, whose contemporaneous comics published in the *Chicago Defender* and *Pittsburgh Courier* refashion black female subjectivity. Ormes's stylish illustrations assert black women's sexuality in ways the novels could not. Together the written and visual work in *Writing through Jane Crow* is as telling of the heyday of African American social realism as that which is critically celebrated—perhaps even more so.

1 / At the Point of No Return: A Native Son and His Gorgon Muse

"This is not a novel with a 'feminist' theme!" he insisted.
—HAZEL ROWLEY, *RICHARD WRIGHT: THE LIFE AND TIMES*

To "see" nouns in quotation marks is to question their straightforward, direct meaning—to highlight through a specific ironic staging a queer multiplicity or polymorphous perversity.
—JENNIFER DEVERE BRODY, *PUNCTUATION: ART, POLITICS, AND PLAY*

In the essay "How Bigger Was Born" (1940), Richard Wright first discusses the impetus behind his best-selling first novel, *Native Son* (1940), then divulges his intentions to complete a new, unnamed work theorizing the distinct grievances of black women. Wright credits his northern migration and participation in the labor movement for engendering *Native Son*'s black male protagonist as a universal signifier for the politically disenfranchised and disinherited. Throughout his southern maturation, the writer knew personally several "Bigger Thomases" whose bullying swagger, intraracial violence, defiance of Jim Crow laws, social restlessness, and recurring melancholy fated their broken spirits, imprisonment, and death. The southern migrant also came to understand that there were numerous white "Biggers" around the world who shared black men's economic oppression as well as their potential for fascism or communism. Despite these revelations, Wright admits in his exegesis that he felt fear and shame while writing *Native Son*. He questioned what white people would think and how middle-class blacks would respond to his work. These doubts made *Native Son*'s social commentary necessary as much as they made it possible. Although he grapples with the various influences shaping his work in "How Bigger Was Born," Wright acknowledges that "reluctantly, [the writer] comes to the conclusion that to account for his book is to account for his life, and he knows that is impossible."[1] Wright, however, concedes *Native Son*'s flaws, including his privileging of morality over the plausibility of certain plot points and his overall investment in character destiny. "With what I've learned in the writing of this book, with all of its blemishes, imperfections, with all of its unrealized potentialities," he discloses, "I am launching out upon another novel, this time about the status of women in modern American society."[2] Just as the new text is informed by his experience writing *Native Son*, Wright reveals that this female-centered work "goes back to my childhood just as Bigger went, for, while I was storing away impressions of Bigger, I was storing away impressions of many other things that made me think and wonder." The fascination—and amity—with which Wright briefly gestures toward the double jeopardy of racism and sexism in "How Bigger Was Born" is in stark contrast to *Native Son*'s dismal representations of black women, who emasculate Bigger or are violated by his machismo exertions. "I don't know if *Native Son* is a good book or a bad book. And I don't know if the book I'm working on now will be a good book or a bad book," Wright confesses. "And I really don't care. The mere writing of it will be more fun and a deeper satisfaction than any praise or blame from anybody." After delineating *Native Son*'s preoccupations, the black male writer intimates his plans to retire the novel's critically and commercially successful blueprint in his next revisionary work.

The resulting manuscript, "Black Hope," is Wright's first novelistic attempt to conceptualize a complex black female protagonist, yet the work is neither actualized nor recognized fully as a turning point in the writer's oeuvre and critical legacy.[3] Critiques of Wright's failure to address black women's multiple oppressions and his understood oppositional stance in relation to contemporaneous black female writers who effectively take up this project are due, in part, to the anonymity and neglect of the unfinished manuscript. While "Black Hope" remains unpublished, its explicit consideration of Jane Crow politics is not prioritized or resolved in his previous or subsequent fiction. *Native Son* exposes the systematic segregation and Jim Crow practices that sentence the benighted Bigger to death, and the novel initiates a series of disenfranchised black male protagonists defining Wright's later work. In contrast, "Black Hope" presents a socially aware, articulate, and yet flawed agent in Maud Hampton, who shuns true love and stunts her political consciousness by passing for white. Maud's willingness to ingest arsenic to escape racism, poverty, and the circumscriptions of domesticity illustrates the hierarchical power dynamics of black women's interracial, intraracial, and heterosexual relationships.

Moreover the manuscript's unexpected portrayal of middle-class black, working-class black, and elite white women's comparable subjugation in white patriarchal society exposes the interconnectedness of whites' racism, black men's chauvinism, and the class dissidence between women. With a triptych relationship between the educated and passing Maud, her southern migrant black maid, Ollie Knight, and her wealthy white stepdaughter, Lily Spencer, Wright tries to imagine "black hope." The manuscript's working title is a sardonic comment on Maud, who dies at the end of the narrative, like Wright's other defeated black protagonists. This catalogue includes but is not limited to Bigger, Mann and Silas of *Uncle Tom's Children* (1938), and Cross Damon in *The Outsider* (1953). Yet the manuscript's working title is also an earnest compliment to Ollie, as Wright materializes "black hope" in the conclusion via her participation in a domestic workers' union organized to confront black women's economic and sexual exploitation. Wright attempts to refine the palimpsest *Native Son* with a black female protagonist and a more productive strategy for social protest in "Black Hope." Granted, the unpublished work's obscurity means that the manuscript is not a definitive statement on Wright's body of work. Nonetheless the text's exploration of Jane Crow oppression attests to the complex gender politics shaping the black male writer's career. Wright's unrealized efforts to address sexism in "Black Hope" undoubtedly also informed his published, more critically engaged fiction.

In spite of Wright's apparent enthusiasm for the manuscript and its political objectives, a succession of productive waves and slack wanes delayed the publication of "Black Hope" and its exploration of black female subjectivity. In May 1939 Wright received a Guggenheim Fellowship to finish *Native Son* and begin his new work, which was then titled "Little Sister." The manuscript's initial title potentially nods to, Sondra Guttman suggests, Bigger's little sister, Vera, in *Native Son*. Whereas Bigger makes Vera feel like "a dog" within his denigrating gaze, Wright's impending text promised to foreground a black woman's perspective.[4] By December 1939 Wright had a five-hundred-page draft of "Little Sister," and as early as March 1940, the date of *Native Son*'s publication, the *New York Sun* publicized Wright's "960-page first draft of a new novel dealing with the plight of Negro women, especially domestics in Manhattan and Brooklyn."[5] In the summer of the following year Wright continued to promote the work in the *New York Herald Tribune* as "a sort of feminine counterpart of *Native Son*."[6] He settled on the title "Black Hope" in 1942 after deliberating numerous alternatives that signified on *Native Son* but spotlighted the status of women, alluded to the passing plot, or centralized the exploitation of domestic workers. During the fall of that same year Wright's publishers Harper & Brothers scheduled "Black Hope" for production, while Warner Brothers studio considered translating the work into film.[7] Wright produced more than one draft of the lengthy manuscript as well as a distinct, shorter version of the narrative with a revamped black female protagonist, but he ceased all efforts to finish "Black Hope" in 1948. That year the prolific writer directed his focus toward drafting *The Outsider*—only his second novel published thirteen years after *Native Son*.

Wright's sundry revisions to "Black Hope" stall at a defining cultural and historical moment that would later dictate the race and gender politics of his oeuvre. The fiction of Ann Petry, Dorothy West, and Zora Neale Hurston demonstrates that mid-twentieth-century black female writers managed to devise and contest Jane Crow oppression in ways Wright did not in his work published during the heyday of social realism and lauded long afterward. Yet the materiality of "Black Hope" problematizes the critical nature of Wright's canonicity even as the text's unpublished status recapitulates it. The writer's most noted contribution to the tradition, as Paul Gilroy contends, is an articulation of blackness as "a distinct mode of lived masculinity."[8] Consequently black feminist critics often conflate *Native Son*'s misogyny with Wright's own chauvinism. The enmity Bigger directs at his sister, mother, and girlfriend in his gaze as well as by his hands is at the behest of Wright's pen. The writer's failure to complete "Black Hope" affirms such critiques, and his multiple drafts of the manuscript suggest the impasse black female subjectivity posed for him.

Still, "Black Hope" warrants critical study. As Wright's only female-centered text, the manuscript's publication might have changed the classification of the writer and his oeuvre in literary history. In the biography *Richard Wright: The Life and Times*, Hazel Rowley suggests that living with his first wife and her mother inspired him to privilege the social and psychological aspects of female subjectivity. Rowley contends that the race and gender politics motivating "Black Hope" coalesce around one primary question: "If blacks were placed in positions that made them dependent, and black women even more so, how far would a highly intelligent, restless black woman be prepared to go to acquire freedom, money, and power?"[9] Maud goes so far as to sever her connections with the black community and pass for white in order to nullify the handicap of race and obtain agency. In the *Unfinished Quest of Richard Wright*, Michel Fabre qualifies, "Although Maud finds herself caught between the two races, her principal concern is her role as a woman, and the racial aspect of her dilemma merely supplies the pivot for the plot. Wright did not set out to describe the place of women in modern society as a piece of 'feminist' propaganda, but he cannot help concluding that they are victims more often than not."[10] Fabre identifies Maud's "role as a woman" as the manuscript's main subject, but he notes Wright's discomfort actualizing her in the context of a mass woman's movement.

"Black Hope" endorses political alliances between black and white women as well as between working-class and middle-class women, but one would be remiss to read the manuscript simply as feminist agitprop—or not. As if retreating to a familiar masculinist agenda, Wright stresses in a letter that his work in progress "is *not* a novel with a 'feminist' theme!"[11] He offsets his aversion to a feminist reading of the manuscript with scare quotes and creates symbolic distance between his intentions and their perceived misinterpretation. The use of quotation marks, as Jennifer DeVere Brody infers, "questions the status of that which passes for the naturalized and the normal."[12] By interrogating the validity of a feminist reading, Wright's use of scare quotes calls into question the female-centered focus of "Black Hope" and problematizes a more generous reading of his gender politics. At the same time, the scare quotes indicate feminism's cultural currency regardless of his oeuvre's masculinist focal point.

Wright's reticence to name his new writing trajectory "feminist" reflects the tensions surrounding the term during the postsuffrage and interwar period. Early twentieth-century feminists struggled for economic independence, called for the end of the sexual double standard, and desired equal opportunity in civic and professional arenas. However, other women and chauvinists characterized feminists as anti-male, women who wanted to force femininity onto men, and lesbians.[13] In "Black Hope" Maud passionately expresses her condemnation of men's desires to relegate her to the labors and obligations of the domestic space, but the third-person narrator makes it clear that she neither detests men nor desires to be a "man." The manuscript maintains women's conventional gender roles, while its black female protagonist attempts to circumvent the institutional oppressions of race, class, and gender. As the Communist Party was a cultural broker for Wright's early work, its censure of feminists as bourgeois separatists—potential workers who privileged their gender over class oppression—underwrote his rejection of "feminist" ideology.[14] Modern feminism ostensibly had an inherent paradox: it asserted "woman" as an individual while promoting the need for women's collective awareness. In "Black Hope" women's social and political desire, which Wright characterizes as class-conscious and collective, and not their performance of gender, which he essentializes as heterosexual and feminine, seems to be his primary concern.

Thus "Black Hope" invokes a female-centered discourse that documents Wright's efforts to usurp Jane Crow social oppression, but it also demonstrates his concession to Jane Crow's literary politics. In the biography *Richard Wright: Daemonic Genius*, Margaret Walker posits that the writer's frustrated relationship to racism, classism, and sexism is emblematic of the Greek mythological figure Medusa. Walker claims Medusa "was part of his *ambivalent* self—sexually, politically, and racially. She was a teasing presence all his life, sometimes appearing beautiful and benevolent and at other times reversing her face and revealing the twisted, malevolent, serpent-ridden monster. Medusa is a woman!"[15] The enigmatic trope is useful for thinking about Wright's circuitous gendered discourse in "Black Hope." The binary or two-faced conceptualization of "woman" reflects his aesthetic struggle both to theorize black women's subjugation and realize their subjectivity in the manuscript. Maud transcends her social immobility by marrying white and rich and then murdering her aged husband. Yet as a privileged white widow, she economically exploits her black female domestic worker, Ollie; she literally perpetuates intraracial class conflicts and symbolically reenacts the interracial oppression she escapes by passing. Like Medusa, Maud is a double-dealing agent within a matrix of intraracial, interracial, and gender violence; she is both black and white, victim and perpetrator. The stony gaze of Wright's gorgon muse attested to black women's multiple oppressions, but Medusa's duplicity also signaled the limitations of his Jane Crow text. Though Maud is Wright's protagonist, she is complicit as an antagonist in "Black Hope."

In lieu of advancing an explicit feminist or womanist project, "Black Hope" unsettles neat literary histories of mid-twentieth-century social realism dominated by not only a masculinist Wright but also a naturalist Wright. Gene A. Jarrett suggests Wright's oeuvre is more complicated than typically recognized. In identifying Frank Yerby as a lesser-known truant writer in the context of Wright's predominance as dean, Jarrett also asks, "How do we reconcile Wright's persona in the late 1930s and the 1940s and his persona in the 1950s, when he wrote *Savage Holiday* (1954)?"[16] Jarrett points to the obvious differences between Wright's work when he was a Depression-era, Communist Party loyalist and when he published the white-plot novel as an American expatriate. The writer's nuances during World War II, however, are far subtler. Although *Native*

Son is the quintessential novel of mid-twentieth-century African American protest fiction, Wright experimented with naturalist conventions in the text. This is exemplified in the novel's conclusion, when Bigger faces his impending execution, by his struggle to articulate his personhood and the reason he commits murder. *Native Son*'s indeterminacy in this moment is what James Baldwin criticized as the novel's racist sentimentality and overdetermination of Bigger as a cipher and not a subject.[17] If Wright's preeminent fiction is more an exploration than a testament to naturalism, how might critics rethink the novel's testament to masculinity? More specifically, how might the unpublished "Black Hope" complicate critics' understanding of the black male writer's generic and gendered conventions? "Black Hope" is what Claudia Tate terms a "latent narrative" in Wright's oeuvre; it reflects the conflict between the conventional, commercial demand for the black male protagonists repeatedly featured in his published work and the writer's unknown efforts to represent black female subjectivity.[18] The manuscript points to an underlying narrative of potential black female social protest, in spite of its perpetual deferment, throughout Wright's divergent oeuvre. Ironically in "Black Hope," Maud's suicide negates her subjectivity but precipitates the emergence of her maid Ollie's proletarian consciousness.

The aim of the following discussion is neither to recover Wright as a covert feminist nor to undermine the contribution his conceptualization of black masculinity makes to the African American literary tradition. Instead this analysis reconsiders his rough proto-feminist gestures in relation to the entrenched masculinist political agenda impinging upon the work of mid-twentieth-century black writers—men and women, emergent and accomplished alike. In contrast to his contemporaries, Wright was a highly praised and widely read black male writer when he attempted to fix a publishing formula that, for all intents and purposes, was not broken. Nonetheless the hundreds of pages he devoted to constructing black female subjectivity denote "Black Hope" as another episode in the series of starts and stops, missteps, and mitigated successes during the epoch of the Jane Crow text.

The Black Female Continuum in Wright's Masculinist Oeuvre

In order to discern the significance of "Black Hope" for its cultural moment as well as for contemporary literary scholarship, it is important to contextualize Wright's female-centered effort with his fictional, expository, and autobiographical publications. While the manuscript shares his oeuvre's primary objective to actualize a realist politics for black subjectivity, "Black Hope" directly addresses the intricacies of Jane Crow oppression not reconciled elsewhere in his work. Hence "Black Hope" intimates Wright's interest in the full spectrum of gender politics during the height of a celebrity career established on outlining the complexities of black masculinity. Fabre perceives the intertextual dialogue between Wright's texts not in print and his more well-known writings as revelatory of his entire writing corpus: "In Wright's case, the number of unpublished manuscripts makes it imperative to take them into consideration, . . . to consider everything that Wright was working on at the various stages of his artistic evolution, to show how an essay perhaps foreshadows or contradicts a successful piece of work, or how a recurring theme or metaphor betrays its importance in the subconscious of the writer."[19] Wright's oeuvre self-consciously focuses on the construction of black masculinity—exhibited by a series of short stories foregrounding the plight of black men with titles such as "The Man Who Was Almost a Man" (1939) and "The Man Who Lived Underground" (1944)—but "Black Hope" proposes that a more complicated gender discourse runs throughout the fiction and nonfiction produced before and after his manuscript on black women's social condition.[20] This subtle discourse on black womanhood, appearing as early as the autobiographical sketch "The Ethics of Living Jim Crow" (1937) and as late as the collection *Eight Men* (1961), exemplifies Wright's efforts to theorize the intersectionality of race, class, and gender oppression. Admittedly he differentiates the lived experience of subjugated black femininity from disenfranchised black masculinity with varying degrees of success, as his short stories in *Uncle Tom's Children* (1938) and photo-essay *12 Million Black Voices* (1941) present African American women only in the gestating stages of social consciousness.

In his self-reflective essay "The Ethics of Living Jim Crow," Wright recalls his experiences with bigotry as a black man in the South while offering glimpses of black women's distinct subjugation under racism and patriarchy. He mainly focuses on elucidating his "Jim Crow education" in various predominantly white workplaces, but he also tacitly acknowledges three unsettling incidents of Jane Crow oppression by differentiating his emasculation from black women's always and already sexual violation.[21] In fact he employs his inability to respond to black women's double jeopardy to heighten his masculinist experience of social disenfranchisement and psychological subjection in the essay. First while working as a porter in a clothing store, Wright listens to two white men beat a black woman because she has not paid her bills. Subsequently the police arrest the woman for alleged public intoxication even though it is obvious she has been assaulted. In turn Wright's employers give him a cigarette as a "gesture of kindness," which signals his exemption from such violence as well as a symbolic contract for his silence.[22] When Wright shares the story with fellow African American porters, one points out that the abused woman is "a lucky bitch" because she is only beaten and not raped. This first portrait of victimized black womanhood is followed by a story that more explicitly exhibits white men's sexual exploitation of black women and, resultantly, black men. In the second sketch Wright recalls the police forcing a black bellhop to marry a pregnant black maid even though the courting couple never had intimate relations. White men at the hotel explain the light complexion of the couple's baby by joking that a white cow must have frightened the woman during her pregnancy. The jest denies the sexual impropriety of the white man who actually fathered the maid's child. More important, the white men emasculate the bellhop by negating the respectability of the maid. Wright didactically discloses in the conclusion of the sketch that, in the presence of the white men's repartee about blacks' social and sexual violation, he also is expected to laugh.

A third sketch in "The Ethics of Living Jim Crow" nods toward the union of Jim and Jane Crow and personally escalates the complexity of white men's emasculation of black men by way of black women's economic and sexual exploitation. In this portrait of racial subjection, Wright witnesses a white night watchman assault a black maid with a slap to her buttocks. The writer must then verbally acquiesce to the maid's molestation as an additional affront to black masculinity. "Nigger, don't yuh like it?" the white man threatens. Wright is too ashamed to face his female coworker after his capitulation, but she chides, "Don't be a fool! Yuh couldn't help it!"[23] Their interlocking subjugation triggers his psychological unmanning, which virtually supersedes the man's physical violation of the woman. Given that the night watchman is rumored already to have murdered two African Americans, he presumably presents a greater bodily threat to Wright than the woman, even though she too is always in danger of interracial violence. Like the previous two portraits, this last recollection in "The Ethics of Living Jim Crow" centralizes the delicate balance black men must maintain to survive in a racist society, but it also illustrates the interdependent economic and sexual exploitation of their black female counterparts. Since black women are polemically a means to an end in "The Ethics of Living Jim Crow," Wright embeds his commentary on white men's sexual abuse of black women within his critique of white men's emasculation of black men. He portrays his "uneducated" self in the processes of southern racialization. Yet he depicts the black woman in the last sketch as a more learned subject who recognizes the hierarchical racial and sexual dynamics structuring the politics of Jim and Jane Crow oppression.

Black women's peripheral role in Wright's mapping of black male subjugation is reiterated in the collection *Uncle Tom's Children*. Even in the short stories that feature black women as pivotal characters, namely Sarah in "Long Black Song" and Aunt Sue in "Bright and Morning Star," Wright ultimately privileges the literal and symbolic struggles between black and white men. For instance, in "Long Black Song" Wright ambivalently characterizes Sarah as both empathetic and traitorous to her husband, Silas. She is both a collaborator and a victim to the white male that disenfranchises him. Although she is unfulfilled in her roles as wife and mother, Sarah knows that "Silas was as good to her as any black man could be to a black woman. Most of the black women worked in the fields as croppers. But Silas had given her her own home."[24] The domestic security Silas provides his family presumably proves that "he was as good as any white man," but a white salesman easily violates the couple's home by leaving a clock-gramophone as proof of his economic and sexual exploitation of Sarah in Silas's absence. Sarah is an ingénue to the white salesman's arrogant rapaciousness, as he presses her to buy his wares just as he enters her bedroom without invitation. However, she is also complicit in the white man's seduction of her and emasculation of her husband. Silas sees the clock-gramophone as evidence of Sarah's infidelity but not rape, and he kills the salesman upon the latter's return for payment. Engaging the intricacies of Jane Crow oppression, "Long Black Song" renders the various abuses black women suffer: the white salesman's sexual exploitation of Sarah; Silas's physical abuse in response to her infidelity; and the narrative's climactic censure with the lynch mob's murder of Silas. Despite the intricacies of her subjugation, Sarah pragmatically surmises the spectacle between black and white as "men killing and being killed" when she observes the racial drama of retributive violence.

Sarah's agency in the story is ambiguous, but it is difficult to reduce her subject position to simply a victim of Silas's or Wright's misogyny given her importance to the narrative. In her reading of "Long Black Song," Joyce Ann Joyce contends that Sarah is the text's center of consciousness and concludes that "the position that Wright was not empathetic, that he was totally warped in his characterization of black women is in itself biased and extreme."[25] Indeed Sarah furthers the writer's exploration of the compounded race, class, and gender dynamics dictating the triangular exchange between black men, black women, and white men. Sarah additionally occupies a privileged perspective in the short story when she watches from above the violence between the salesman and Silas, who appear to her "like two dolls, a white doll and a black doll." Black women's multivalent oppression, however, does not motivate the central conflict in "Long Black Song"; their collusion in black men's physical and psychic injury elicits the text's denouement. A soon-dead Silas confides to the reposed salesman, "When mah eyes is on the white folks to keep em from killin me, mah own blood trips me up!"[26] His words reflect a historically exclusive conversation between black and white men (in which, to refer to another Wright work, white men do not listen) and configure Sarah as an audience to the drama enacted by and about them. "Long Black Song" acknowledges Jane Crow oppression, but the short story is preoccupied with black male and not black female subjectivity.

"Bright and Morning Star," the final short story in *Uncle Tom's Children*, similarly maintains the primacy of masculinist strife even though Aunt Sue is the heroine of the narrative. Sherley Anne Williams identifies the character as the strongest woman in the short story collection, but the literary critic deduces from the black male writer's corpus that "Wright seldom loved his black female characters and never liked them, nor could he imagine a constructive role for them in the black man's struggle for freedom."[27] In "Bright and Morning Star" the communist activism of Aunt Sue's sons inspires the black matriarch's developing social consciousness framed by her religiosity: "The wrongs and sufferings of black men had taken the place of Him nailed to the Cross; the meager beginnings of the party had become another Resurrection."[28] Aunt Sue's attempts to reconcile her faith in spiritual deliverance with her tentative trust in the Party's interracial coalition illustrate her growing social consciousness, but she unknowingly betrays blacks' political salvation by naming her sons' comrades to a white Judas-like traitor. She becomes critical to the contest between southern white supremacists and the black proletariat in "Bright and Morning Star" when she performs the violence and martyrdom typically coded as masculine in Wright's literary imagination. Aunt Sue, whom whites dismiss as an exploited washerwoman, assassinates the treacherous informant before he can brief the town's segregationists. In the wake of one son's imprisonment and the other's death, she concludes that the cause for which she surrenders her own life is a "black mans fight [that] takes *everthin!*"[29]

Published before Wright began drafting "Black Hope," *Uncle Tom's Children* employs representations of alternately disloyal and self-sacrificing black women to examine the disenfranchisement of southern black men. Comparably the photo-essay *12 Million Black Voices*, which was compiled during his early efforts to portray black women's economic and sexual exploitation in "Black Hope," documents the evolution of black workers from slavery to wage labor. Wright's folk history of African Americans' migration from south to north spotlights the sharecropper, waiter, stevedore, and industrial worker as working identities fostering black male subjectivity. As Houston A. Baker explicates, within this masculinist gaze "black men are industrial workers of the world; they are 'in the making' because they have become making men. . . . Rather than workers in the public world of Western progress, [black women] are 'domestics.'"[30] Wright depicts black women's subject positions as fundamentally stagnant in comparison to self-making men, as the women's belabored domesticity delimits their personal and political efficacy. By critiquing black women's roles as plantation mammies who emasculate black men in *12 Million Black Voices*, Wright returns to the representation of the blind matriarch and disaffected domestic worker he derides in *Native Son*. He uses first-person narration to convey a collective black voice that accuses black women of barring black men from their patriarchal roles until "we men were freed and had moved to cities where cash-paying jobs enabled us to become the heads of our own families."[31] Whereas northern migration enables black men to evolve into empowered actors in both public and private spaces, black women's labor remains unchanged in the domestic space: the antebellum mammy is now the automaton maid.

Though *12 Million Black Voices* impugns black women's agency, it does not ignore the fact that both race and gender structure the social institutions specifically subjugating them. The photo-essay reveals the domestic worker's distinct economic and spatial oppression by juxtaposing images of her in two rigidly constructed domestic spaces. "In the Black Belts of the northern cities," Wright expounds, "our women are the most circumscribed and tragic objects to be found in our lives . . . because their orbit of life is narrow—from their kitchenette to the white folk's kitchen and back home again."[32] He exemplifies this point with the picture of a black woman and child standing at either side of a worn stove, which is positioned as the focus of the photograph (Figure 1). Ironically

FIGURE 1. Woman and child in rented apartment kitchen in Chicago, Illinois, 1941. (Photograph by Russell Lee; Library of Congress, FSA/OWI, LC-USF34-038777-D)

the dilapidated kitchenette's emptiness dominates most of the image. As Farah Jasmine Griffin observes of Wright's autobiography *American Hunger* (1977), the kitchenette "serves as a synecdoche for all the forces that act in the construction of a black urban dweller. . . . Its effect is that of genocide."[33] Wright's black female peers share this image of the kitchenette in their fiction. In Gwendolyn Brooks's poem "kitchenette building," the urban space is "grayed in, and gray," which conveys the decay of blacks' hope to achieve the American Dream.[34] Similarly in *The Street* (1946), Ann Petry intimates that black women's particular disillusionment with the kitchenette is due to their inability to model in their homes the "miracle of a kitchen" in which they work.[35]

Correspondingly in *12 Million Black Voices* the photograph accompanying the image of a tenement kitchenette features a uniformed black maid feeding a white baby in a suburban-looking kitchen. In contrast to the former image, the composition of this second photograph is filled with spotless modern conveniences that sanitize the black woman's domestic labor (Figure 2). Together the contiguous photographs demythologize

FIGURE 2. Domestic worker and child in modern kitchen in Atlanta, Georgia, 1939. (Photograph by Marion Post Wolcott; Library of Congress, FSA/OWI, LC-USF34-T01-051738-D)

the American Dream in the context of black women's social and spatial realities. "Surrounding our black women are many almost insuperable barriers: they are black, they are women, they are workers," Wright theorizes, "they are triply anchored and restricted in their movements within and without the Black Belts."[36] Wright privileges black male enterprise, but he briefly speaks to Jane Crow oppression in his compilation of poignant colloquy and photographs. The portrait of the domestic worker in *12 Million Black Voices* is reminiscent of the disquieting sketches of working black women in "The Ethics of Living Jim Crow," and it complements the portrayal of domestic labor in "Black Hope." In Wright's continuum of black female representation, his critiques of labor exploitation more progressively depict black women than his profiles of the romantic or familial relationships between black men and black women.

This reading of Wright's Jane Crow discourse logically relies on his work published during the 1930s and 1940s, but an analysis of the short story "Man of All Work," published posthumously in *Eight Men*, is also critical to charting the trajectory of the writer's gender politics. The sketch explores the economic and sexual exploitation of black female domestic workers through the firsthand experience of a black male protagonist disguised in women's clothing. Interestingly, in "How Bigger Was Born" Wright uses the metaphor of dressing-up to explain his writing process: "Emotions are subjective and [the author] can communicate them only when he clothes them in objective guise; and how can he ever be so arrogant as to know when he is dressing up the right emotion in the right Sunday suit?"[37] Wright professes the arbitrariness of signs to account for his authorial intent in *Native Son*, but he later authorizes his critique of black women's double jeopardy by way of his protagonist's masquerading observation in "Man of All Work." Literally stepping into a black woman's shoes, Carl encounters racial and gender oppression while working for the humorously unknowing Fairchild family. Wright's creative representation of racial, gender, and class subjection via drag performance complicates his misogynist branding. "Man of All Work" contemplates black women's lived experiences in addition to the social construction of black masculinity. Carl's temporary transvestism does not deconstruct gender performance like the African American dandy, for example, who Monica L. Miller conceives of in her work *Slaves to Fashion* as a simultaneously hypermasculine and feminine subject that challenges the conventions of heterosexuality and race. Rather Wright's work registers sexual anxiety regarding a black man's gender-bending. Yet cross-dressing is indisputably an additive to the story's consciousness raising. The fiction presents black women as equal partners in the struggle for racial equality, while it enlightens black men to the intersectionality of racial and gender oppression.

Written as a radio play, "Man of All Work" depends on the witty innuendo of the characters' direct dialogue to show Carl's "passing" as a black female domestic worker. The story invokes the specter of racial passing despite the absence of visual irony. Confident in his performative skill, Carl justifies, "I've got on a dress and I look just like a million black women cooks. Who looks that close at us colored people anyhow? We all look alike to white people."[38] He takes up domestic work in order to pay his mortgage after he is laid off and his wife, Lucy, is incapacitated following childbirth, but Lucy is fearful that his performance will unsettle their domestic roles. "Can she be thinking of the implications of emasculation that there are in a black man's doing a black 'woman's work'?" Trudier Harris questions, "Is the emasculation involved in black women's being able to find jobs when their men cannot relevant to her overreaction here?"[39] In addition to her concern about her husband's unmanning, Lucy's apprehension reflects her angst about her own displacement. Carl figuratively replaces his wife by using her clothes as well as her name in his transvestism, and he plays her role so well that his white employers violate "Lucy's" sexual boundaries. Though he planned to maintain his subterfuge for two months, Carl admits, "I was a woman for almost six hours and it almost killed me. Two hours after I put that dress on I thought I was going crazy."[40]

This sartorial realization regarding the psychic burdens of African American womanhood speaks to the limited roles ascribed to black women during and after the Jane Crow era. Carl is unprepared for his employers' relegation of "Lucy" to the mammy and jezebel stereotypes. Mrs. Fairchild requests that her employee play the role of the asexual nursemaid in an intimate bathing scene, which effectively signifies on myths of the black male rapist. Meanwhile Mr. Fairchild attempts to codify his aggressive sexual advances toward "Lucy" as playful wrestling in front of his precocious daughter, who is the only person to recognize Carl's mannish appearance. In this eroticized homosocial exchange, Wright physically exorcises both black women and white women from the confrontation between black and white men, though, in this case, black women and not white women maintain a symbolic presence in this historical exchange. Mr. Fairchild's racist presumption that "Lucy" is a wanton black woman motivates his rapacious assault, but the altercation manifests white men's desire to subjugate black men's assumed sexual prowess. Historically white men enforced their supremacy through the lynching and castration of black men. As a result the multiple significations of black, white, man, and woman in "Man of All Work" code Carl's performance of black female subjectivity as queer or "quare." E. Patrick Johnson explains that the latter term "connote[s] something excessive—something that might philosophically translate into an excess of discursive and epistemological meanings grounded in African American cultural rituals of lived experience."[41] Carl amusingly bests his supposedly white male superior, but "Lucy" becomes a "nigger bitch" to Mr. Fairchild.[42] Moreover Mrs. Fairchild shoots the maid upon catching her husband in another compromising position, almost castrating Carl with an injury to his thigh. The shooting ultimately reveals his biological sex to his beguiled employers and restores his masculinity in short order. He receives enough hush money to pay off his mortgage in addition to a change of clothes from Mr. Fairchild as reparations.

Carl's hesitation to articulate this series of events to his wife, who could empathize with and substantiate his experience, cogently differentiates between Jim and Jane Crow oppression and raises questions about the authenticity of his performance. All Carl can confirm is that he "worked" for the money, and he qualifies for his skeptical wife that "it was all kinds of work"—alluding to his sexual abuse. The Fairchilds' sexualized violence illuminates the gendered experience of black men and black women for the short story's readers, but it is Carl's new insight into the double jeopardy of black womanhood that leaves him traumatized and speechless. "But, Carl, I warned you," his wife admonishes, "It's not easy for a man to act like a woman." Lucy explicitly comments on the credibility of Carl's performance, yet she intimates, See, it's not easy to *be* a black woman. She must negotiate her sexual vulnerability daily in order to survive in a racist and patriarchal society, while playing a black woman for several hours nearly castrates Carl. Admitting his prior ignorance of black women's specific sexual oppression, Carl proclaims, "I wouldn't be caught dead again in a dress."[43] His avowal winks at his recuperated masculinity while expressing a new level of respect for black women. The homage to the domestic worker is prefigured saliently in "Black Hope."

Notwithstanding the intertextual dialogue between "Man of All Work" and "Black Hope," *Native Son* most concretely correlates with the manuscript given the texts' chronology and appositional themes. Maria K. Mootry contends that in *Native Son* "all of Wright's women . . . are Mothers or Whores" because Bigger's limited purview dominates the novel: his mother is "at once demanding, critical, bitchy," and Bessie is the "embodiment of need, of suffering, of willessness, of mindless whoredom."[44] The latter's social condition as a domestic worker is a portrait Wright returns to and refines in *12 Million Black Voices*, "Black Hope," and "Man of All Work." "I just worked hard every day as long as I can remember, till I was tired enough to drop," Bessie explains, "then I had to get drunk to forget it. I had to get drunk to sleep. That's all I ever did."[45] For many critics, Bessie's abject life and brutal death sum up the significance of black female subjectivity in Wright's work. In contrast, Gilroy argues that scholars have been too preoccupied with Wright's theme of violence to complicate the writer's gender politics productively. Gilroy posits that critics "should also be able to connect [Wright's] uneven misogyny to his path-breaking inauguration of a critical discourse on the construction of black masculinity as well as to the few tantalising feminist and proto-feminist statements sprinkled around his work."[46] Themes of racial violence evidence the masculinist hegemony of Wright's oeuvre, but his discursive gestures toward proto-feminist frameworks become apparent when one contextualizes his published texts with "Black Hope." Wright's representations of black men after *Native Son* arguably become more contrived and conventional when one contends with the manuscript.

Wright's reimaging of *Native Son* through a series of black male protagonists hindered his attempts to represent black female subjectivity in "Black Hope." According to Rowley, Wright was "too distracted" by the negative criticism and leveling sales of *Native Son* to finish the manuscript.[47] Then his subsequent efforts to rewrite his first novel into various generic reproductions diverted his attention from the manuscript. In 1941 Paul Green staged a dramatic adaptation of *Native Son*, with Orson Welles as the director and Canada Lee as the star. The same year Wright discussed a filmic interpretation of the novel, but he did not make the movie until 1950. Directed by Pierre Chenal and scripted by Wright, the Argentine production of *Native Son* restyles Bessie as a blues singer and stars Wright as Bigger Thomas. Bigger—and seemingly Wright—laments his mistreatment of Bessie in this filmic version.[48] Soon one black man after another took precedence over actualizing Wright's black female protagonist in "Black Hope."[49] Wright began and completed the novella "The Man That Lived Underground." Shortly thereafter he traveled with Horace Cayton to Fisk University, where the response to his speech about his southern migrant experience motivated him to compose his autobiography. Then the commercial success of *Black Boy* (1945) apparently compelled him to return to the masculinist writing formula, shaping short stories such as "The Man Who Killed a Shadow" (1946), in which a black man murders a white woman who falsely accuses him of rape. Finally, Wright put aside "Black Hope" in order to write *The Outsider*. This succession suggests a compulsory engagement with black masculinity that permanently stymied the progression of his female-centered text.

Once, Twice, Three Times the Woman in "Black Hope"

Although Wright perpetually postponed the manuscript, publishing "Black Hope" was important to his livelihood. The manuscript would have secured his career as a novelist given that he published a photo-essay, an autobiography, and several expository writings prior to returning to the fiction for which he became famous. Before the publication of *Native Son*, Wright's literary agent Paul R. Reynolds fastidiously laid out the publishing terrain by explaining that novels had more profit and prestige attached to them and that it would be difficult to find venues for the writer's short stories because of his provocative subject matter. The agent also cautioned Wright about publishing "Black Hope" too soon after *Native Son* because one's latest work typically affects the demand for the preceding text. However, in 1942 Reynolds writes that the success of "Black Hope" would decide Wright's "fair chance of being somewhat a fixed star in the publishing firmament," but the manuscript's commercial failure would make it difficult for the writer to have another successful novel and be known for anything other than as the author of *Native Son*. With the hope of staying the latter, Reynolds sent Wright four pages of recommended revisions. "Anyone reading all this criticism would think I didn't like the novel at all and I can only say with all the emphasis possible that the reverse is true," he writes.[50] His suggestions include encouraging Wright to reduce scenes in which it appeared that the novelist and not his characters were speaking and to increase the plausibility of certain plot points. In 1940 Wright had submitted a nine-hundred-page draft of "Black Hope" with the disclaimer, "I am aware that this manuscript is in a crude condition."[51] His letter assured his agent that *Native Son* was in the same condition when first submitted to Harper, and he enclosed a detailed outline, as Fabre documents, for clarifying the manuscript's "study of the feminine personality in general, as it developed from feudalism to fascism."[52] Furthering his critique of despotic social systems, Wright's representation of racial passing and domestic work in "Black Hope" underscores black women's gender oppression, especially their sexual vulnerability. Yet the narrative also conspicuously traces the political and psychological parallels between middle-class black women, working-class black women, and elite white women.

The first woman in Wright's female triptych is the light-skinned African American protagonist Maud Hampton, who myopically endeavors to transcend race, gender, and class oppression by passing for white. A classic trope in African American literature, racial passing has both a symbolic and a structural function in the manuscript.[53] The thematic device moves the setting from the bleak reality of the segregated black world, which ruins Maud's health in her daily struggle as a social worker, to the mansion of the white elite, which she barely enjoys as a rich widow before she is blackmailed by her corrupt male collaborators. Maud's racial passing invokes what Abdul R. JanMohamed terms the archaeology of the death-bound-subject present throughout Wright's oeuvre. Inherently socially alienating and dangerous, Maud's consumption of arsenic to lighten her skin illustrates that her new life as well as her previous one are symbolic social deaths due to her multivalent oppression and its repercussions for her health and livelihood.[54] Furthermore

"Black Hope" stresses Maud's sexual vulnerability, as she is reminded constantly that she cannot prevent her victimization at white or black men's hands. Her lover Freddie Rogers's summation that black women's existence consists of physical abuse, excessive work, familial obligation, and ultimately abandonment drives Maud to risk her life to escape discrimination, poverty, and domesticity. Wright claims that his novel is not "feminist," but Maud's racial passing challenges the Jane Crow politics circumscribing black women's lives. Analogous to the inefficacy of the writer's ill-fated black male characters, Maud subverts Jim Crow's racial and class inequities only to be subjugated by sexism as a supposedly privileged white woman.

While Wright devises political agency for black female subjectivity, "Black Hope" explores sexuality as a site of subjection and a recourse for self-determination. Like the working women in "The Ethics of Living Jim Crow," Maud is always and already a potential victim of rape. Thus she tries to reappropriate her sexuality as ammunition in the battle between the sexes. As a white woman Maud negotiates her sexuality when she marries her wealthy, elderly employer, Cleveland Spencer, who acquires his assets by exploiting others; he profits from unethical bank loans, steals oil from Mexican farm workers, and sexually harasses Maud on her job as his housekeeper.[55] In comparison to Maud's emblematic social death under Jim Crow segregation, Wright configures Spencer and his exploits as the decrepit and diseased body of white masculinity, American capitalism, and colonial power within the global labor caste system. Maud's manipulation of the invalid white patriarch is vindicated, then, but her commodification of her sexuality does not empower her as an oppressed black woman. Her marriage actually precipitates her sexual violation. Spencer anxiously consummates their union because Maud coincidentally looks like his late first wife, and she acquiesces in order to orchestrate his death with a postcoital overdose of sleeping pills. This sequence of events implies that Maud murders so that she can inherit her husband's wealth without any legal objections and to redress her sexual capitulation.

To further illustrate this point, Wright juxtaposes black women's potential sexual violation in the context of racism and patriarchy with their possible sexual agency in relation to black men. "Black Hope" implies that Maud's inability to differentiate between interracial violence and her domestic obligations foretells her literal death: she is willing to forgo her love affair with Freddie and suffer Spencer's sexual subjugation for money. While Maud's and Freddie's conflicting politics epitomize the battle between the sexes, their romantic discord also manifests Wright's difficulty depicting black female subjectivity, as the writer gives weight to Freddie's negative opinion of Maud's priorities. Rowley too recognizes that Freddie "is obviously an idealized Richard Wright figure." Freddie gives up his job at the post office to pursue a writing career, which will portray "the lives of men and women who had been sucked under in the whirlpool of steel and stone." Hence Freddie's criticism of Maud's supposed ignorance of her disenfranchised social status recalls Wright's early communist philosophy and lays bare the text's ambivalent gender politics. Likely typifying what Reynolds gauged as Wright's conspicuous bearings in the text, Freddie complains about the criticism black men elicit when they attempt to educate black women about their oppressed class condition instead of indulging their weakness for superficial luxuries like cosmetics and fashion. A cipher for Wright's ventriloquism, Freddie seemingly exhibits the writer's anxiety about the potential anti-male interpretation of the manuscript's political objectives. His objection to accusations of chauvinism is also a rejoinder to feminist pundits, as Freddie reiterates Wright's masculinist discourse by reducing Maud to girly goods. From Freddie's perspective, misguided Maud does not understand that he can help her develop a collective social consciousness, which has more value than the pleasure she gains as an individual from material objects. From her perspective, well-meaning Freddie would chain her to a life of economic immobility if she were to marry the starving artist devoted to "puny words."[56] The couple's disjuncture echoes the marital disconnect in "Long Black Song," inasmuch as black women's inchoate class consciousness disenfranchises them economically and emotionally in the domestic space.

Wright editorializes Maud's bourgeois and separatist objectives, and yet he depicts her sexual desires without censure. The manuscript criticizes her materialist desire, but the sex scene between her and Freddie is relayed in erotic detail with approbation. Maud injects spermicide into her diaphragm in anticipation of Freddie's return from the grocery store. Her act suggests Wright's investment in women's sexual and economic liberation by disregarding society's sexual double standard as well as the reproductive expectations of religious conservatism. After Maud and Freddie's coital moment, the two remain intimately intertwined as they kiss and feed each other ice cream in the extreme heat. In the context of the bitch-and-whore binary depicted in *Native Son* and Wright's puritanical childhood described in *Black Boy*, the equitable sensuality of this moment is unmatched in the writer's other work. For example, in his autobiography Wright recalls a beating he received for naïvely using obscene language when he directed his deeply religious grandmother to "kiss back there" while she bathed his backside.[57] With his reference to female genitalia in "Black Hope," Wright does not pathologize black female sexuality but makes Maud an agent in the intimate moment. Nonetheless Wright's portrayal of female subjectivity in the early draft of the manuscript would probably have been cut from the published text due to editorial constraints imposed on his representations of sexuality. Reynolds advises him, "One or two of the sex scenes should be toned down as a matter of taste."[58] Accordingly, this erotic moment is not included in a later draft of the manuscript.

The most surprising turn in Wright's opus on the social status of women, however, is the parallel he draws between middle-class black, working-class black, and elite white women. Wright explores the shared oppression of black and white women by presenting Spencer's young adult daughter, Lily, as the second figure in his female triptych. In the letter to his agent laying out his intended revisions, Wright identifies Lily as Maud's psychic foil. He makes the similarities between his passing black female protagonist and seemingly privileged white female character overt in a late draft of the manuscript. He characterizes Lily as the madwoman in the attic, who experiences a different kind of social death in white male hegemonic culture. For Sandra Gilbert and Susan Gubar, the madwoman is an avatar for the nineteenth-century woman writer as well as the antithesis of the angel of the house who "arises like a bad dream, bloody, envious, enraged, as if the very process of writing had itself liberated a madwoman, a crazy and angry woman, from a silence in which neither she nor her author can continue to acquiesce."[59] Gayatri Spivak and other literary scholars have criticized Gilbert and Gubar's universalizing of women's experience irrespective of racial difference due to the fact that the quintessential madwoman is a displaced Creole in *Jane Eyre* (1847).[60] However, the madwoman is a productive trope for thinking about Lily's social confinement and struggle for articulation in "Black Hope," as she is emblematic of patriarchal oppression in the text. Quite literally the emotionally unbalanced white woman hidden upstairs, Lily frequently appears in the manuscript screaming in her room and walking around the house nude.

Lily embodies not only suffering due to patriarchy but also black and white women's suppressed desire for retribution as Maud's psychological mirror. Wright is transparent in revealing the affinities between the two women since Maud physically resembles Lily's mother and recognizes

Lily as her repressed self. In particular Lily fulfills Maud's unspoken wish to free herself from her white male antagonist, Henry Beach. If Freddie is Maud's black political consciousness, Beach is her white male id that plans her husband's murder. As Spencer's lawyer, Beach is complicit in white, patriarchal, and capitalist exploitation. He and his delinquent son, Junior, are white Bigger Thomases who embrace fascism instead of emancipating themselves through communism. Whereas Junior is sentenced to death for a fatal robbery, Beach blackmails Maud for Spencer's murder in order to fund the xenophobic National American Union Rehabilitation. The organization targets African Americans, Jews, and Catholics as the source of white men's burdens, and it castigates women for disabling men in the public and private spheres. A sycophant who capitalizes on the frustrations of the dispossessed, Beach scapegoats racial, ethnic, and gendered Others in order to enfranchise himself. He is another example of crippled white male subjectivity in "Black Hope." Consequently Lily mistakes Beach for her abusive father and restages the latter's murder by mercilessly decapitating the lawyer. Although race and class differentiate Maud's and Lily's lives, their vengeful murderous acts imply that both black women and white women are vulnerable to the oppressive violence of white patriarchal society.

Commensurate in this brutal gender oppression, the domestic worker Ollie is the pivotal third woman in Wright's triptych of black women's political and psychological subjugation. The manuscript's two disparate portraits of black womanhood cogently critique intraracial classism. Maud is college-educated, and Ollie is unlearned; Maud transgresses social boundaries, and Ollie is socially inert. Wright presents the domestic worker as the most disenfranchised in "Black Hope" because she is utterly nescient, although Maud and Lily are disadvantaged in varying ways due to their gender. Yet Maud feels superior to Ollie in her identity as a middle-class black woman, and she participates in Ollie's economic exploitation in her role as the white lady in relation to the black maid. Also Maud conspires with Mr. Downey from the Afro-American Employment Bureau to cheat the live-in domestic worker out of her wages: Mr. Downey claims part of Ollie's income as reimbursement for fronting the southern migrant's travel expenses, and Maud siphons a part of Ollie's earnings for herself. As Wright's two-faced, double-dealing archetype, Maud only briefly considers the hypocrisy of her malfeasance. She knowingly colludes in the exploitation of the working-class black woman in spite of her own efforts to circumvent racial and economic oppression.

Wright's research on black domestic workers' social condition informs his depiction of Ollie's economic exploitation, which institutional racism and black middle-class avarice structures. Working as Wright's research assistant during the drafting of "Black Hope," Ralph Ellison collected materials on New York's "slave market." The term highlighted the similarities between African Americans' nineteenth-century bondage and black women's domestic servitude during World War II. Louise Mitchell notes that on the modern "slave market" black women stood on "street corner auction blocks" to gain temporary employment and "were exploited beyond human endurance."[61] The domestic workers were paid less than what they negotiated, and they worked longer than they initially agreed to. Maud's participation in this contemporary slave economy demonstrates her flawed individualist and capitalist character, but she justifies her mistreatment of Ollie by displacing the domestic worker as a primitive anachronism of her past. Reminiscent of Wright's colloquy in 12 Million Black Voices distinguishing self-making men from black female automatons, Ollie is not an actor but a working drudge who is acted upon in Maud's esteem. Ollie's social condition ensures her ignorance and economic exploitation as a domestic worker and temporarily assuages Maud's conscience. However, once Freddie tells her that she does not receive a competitive wage for her labor, Ollie requests a raise from Maud and begins to exhibit an emergent political consciousness.

The denial of a decent living wage, social security, workman's compensation, and retirement plan for black domestic workers exploited their labor during the postwar and early modern civil rights eras. Along with their economic oppression, black women's historical sexual exploitation in domestic work prefigures Ollie's psychological subjection. When Mr. Downey forces Ollie to collect her pay from his home instead of his office, he not only physically violates the maid but also denies her humanity in his sexual assault of her with a dog. Ollie's violation under gunpoint is so traumatic that it seems almost implausible, but Wright's qualitative research on domestic workers inspired the details of her abuse. In addition to conducting interviews with judges, welfare employees, and city workers, the writer conversed directly with the Domestic Workers' Union in Brooklyn and Harlem about black women's experiences being physically and economically vulnerable while laboring in white employers' homes. The domestic workers were more forthcoming when Wright spoke with them as a group rather than as individuals, but most did not fully disclose their sexual exploitation.[62] Wright's interview notes include a domestic worker's secondhand account of forced bestiality similar to the sexual degradation Ollie describes. Ollie's nearly incomprehensible retelling of this sexual assault testifies to the literal and figurative debasement of domestic workers. Wright first introduces the concept of black women as the "dogs" of society with Vera and Bessie in *Native Son*.[63] In "Black Hope" the metaphor is not a misogynist reference to black women as emasculating bitches but as the "dogged" victims of racist, classist, and patriarchal culture. Wright strengthens this affecting imagery in a later draft of the narrative by depicting Ollie in a state of despair physically abusing herself after her assault. This portrait confirms the black domestic worker as the definitive subjugated human being.

Whereas middle-class black women and elite white women historically betray working-class black women, the former's social responsibility to the domestic worker is the literal and figurative foundation of "Black Hope." Wright signifies on the bonds of sisterhood affirmed in Zora Neale Hurston's novel *Their Eyes Were Watching God* (1937) when Janie Crawford feels free to tell her story to Pheoby because, as she says, "mah tongue is in mah friend's mouf."[64] In his review of Hurston's novel, Wright faults the black female writer for "*voluntarily*" participating in the minstrel tradition previously "*forced*" onto black expressive culture for white entertainment.[65] However, "Black Hope" conjures Hurston when Freddie appeals to Maud's conscience and effectively asks her to be Ollie's voice. Maud rejects the idea of testifying for the abused Ollie, just as she reneges on indicting Ollie's rapist because of her culpability in the domestic worker's economic and sexual exploitation. She believes her redemption will come from settling into domesticity with Freddie and her unborn child, whose uncertain paternity conveys the futility of her passing and renders her gender politics suspect. The conclusion of "Black Hope" insists that the cause of Maud's psychological suffering and political failure is twofold: she does not build a coalition with disenfranchised workers, and she does not realize the value of the domestic space (and black men) until too late. As Wright's work uniformly promotes his protagonists' developing social awareness, Maud's arrested political consciousness fixes her in the bedlam of society and drives her to suicide. Because she tries to best a white world dominated by men, Freddie repudiates her, her child, and her gender politics. Maud exacerbates her social death when she passes for white, but she hastens her literal death when she impedes black workers' struggle for political subjectivity. She protects herself rather than champion the disinherited, and her guilt over this duplicity pressures her to self-destruct. She falls far short of her individualist pursuits in the end, when her blackness is exposed posthumously and the funeral home buries her in a segregated plot. Yet in order to atone for her transgressions, she wills her house to the domestic workers' union for its headquarters and thus facilitates collective "black hope."[66]

The manuscript complicates notions of social success and textual failure for Wright in addition to his black female protagonist. As Jan-Mohamed posits about the writer's published works, Wright's death motif in "Black Hope" endorses symbolic death as a means to achieve political consciousness, counter to the social death whites inflicted upon oppressed black subjects. The domestic workers' union sustained by Maud's suicide—an autonomous symbolic death—begets her moral salvation while challenging racist and sexist institutional structures subjugating working-class black women. The finale of "Black Hope" harkens back to the utopian conclusion in Wright's short story "Fire and Cloud," in which poor whites and blacks march together on city hall to demand relief during the Depression. Reverend Dan Taylor realizes in "Fire and Cloud" that political power lies in collective action and not in his prior accommodations to white elites. Comparably "Black Hope" anticipates a promising future for black and white female laborers. However, the union's interracial and working-class coalition invalidates Maud's critique of her economic and domestic confinement. In Freddie, Wright recognizes the intersection of race and gender oppression in terms of domestic labor, but he does not take stock in middle-class black women's repression within heteronormative domestic spaces. In terms of the manuscript's narrative development, Maud's speciously desperate turn to build a family with Freddie in the conclusion delegitimizes the vehemence of her previous stand against patriarchal domestication. The text focuses on its female characters, but it never stabilizes its inconsistencies in regard to its gender politics.

"Black Hope" fails in the sense that Wright never overcomes the obstacles problematizing the manuscript, so much so that he rewrote the narrative's premise in a distinct second manuscript. In "Slave Market," Wright abandons his less developed white characters and combines the competing passing and domestic worker plotlines into one black female protagonist. Kidnapped and raped, the reenvisioned Maud is forced to migrate north and whiten her skin as part of a black crime boss's trafficking of southern black women into domestic work and prostitution. In contrast to the hundreds of pages he devoted to refining "Black Hope," Wright completed only roughly a hundred pages of this second attempt to address the plight of black women. The shelving of both manuscripts evinces the black male writer's difficulty representing black women's complex textuality.

A Radical Vision for Black Female Politics

Although Wright's bourgeois protagonist brings to fruition black women's emancipation from economic exploitation, the domestic worker is the heroine of "Black Hope" because of her figurative resurrection in the wake of her overdetermined social death. Wright affirms as much in his introductory comments at a public reading of the manuscript for the League of American Writers in 1941, during which he foregrounds Ollie as a woman coming into subjecthood. While highlighting Maud's self-destruction, the domestic worker's birth into political consciousness delivers the manuscript's optimistic denouement regarding black women's emergent political movement. Maud's self-abnegating passing, subjugating marriage to Spencer, and extortionate partnership with Beach perpetuate her racial and gender oppression. She dies tragically because she cannot create a productive domestic or political space under such social conditions.

Inspiringly the domestic workers' union is born out of this nexus of white male patriarchy and middle-class black elitism, and it effectively substitutes the class-based partnership for the failed romantic coupling in the text. Ollie's inheritance of the estate's possessions inverts conventional racial, gender, and class hierarchies by reconfiguring the historically disenfranchised as the newly endowed. At the close of "Black Hope" she helps the union take inventory of the mansion and serendipitously relays that the house is full of art, which includes several oil paintings by Matisse. More than what the increased worth of the property means for the union, Wright privileges the value of the domestic worker's proclaimed voice. The manuscript succinctly concludes with Ollie taking center stage in the narrative's political struggle, and "Black Hope" becomes her story. It is noteworthy, however, that Ollie does not understand fully the importance of the paintings or her knowledge of the house. The domestic worker embodies "black hope," but Wright is unable to author or authorize the consciousness of an organic Jane Crow intellectual.

In order to evaluate Wright's political agenda for working-class black women, it is helpful to consider "Black Hope" briefly in the context of a contemporaneous popular narrative that also addresses the intersection of race, gender, and class oppressions. Based on the novel *Quality*

(1946) by Cid Ricketts Sumner, the film *Pinky* (1949) is a fitting text for comparison not only because of its passing plot but also because of the public discourse debating the progressiveness of the narrative's politics. Directed by Elia Kazan, *Pinky* stars Ethel Waters as Aunt Dicey and Ethel Barrymore as Miss Em. The film centers on the return of Patricia "Pinky" Johnson, portrayed by white actress Jeanne Crain, to the South after years passing while attending nursing school in the North. Whereas the trope of racial passing is traceable to the beginnings of the African American literary tradition, Judith Smith argues that "the portrayal on film of even qualified racial indeterminacy at a time when segregation was being challenged was in itself provocative."[67] Contemporaneous critics praised *Pinky*'s depiction of black women's subjection under police brutality and sexual predation. In one scene, two white policemen detain and degrade Pinky's black female rival by searching under her skirt; Pinky suffers the same sexual violation when they eventually realize that she too is African American. In another scene, two white men warn Pinky about the dangers of walking alone at night. They try to rape her once they become aware of her racial identity, and they prove that they and not the black residents pose the threat to her.

These provocative scenes expose white men's racial and gendered violence toward black women, but *Pinky* also upholds white paternalism and stereotypes of black complacency. Aunt Dicey faithfully urges her granddaughter Pinky to care for her dying white employer, which allows Pinky to open a segregated clinic and nursery school when she inherits Miss Em's house after a contentious legal battle. Leaving behind her northern white life, Pinky affirms, "You can't live without pride." Walter White, then head of the NAACP and a consultant on the film, publicly expressed his disappointment with *Pinky*'s lack of militancy because the film "accepts without visible objection the philosophy that the Negro has his 'place,' that he accepts that place, that all white people are united in agreement that colored people must forever stay in a position of inferiority."[68] The film essentially celebrates Pinky's return to the plantation and the economic and sexual condition from which she attempted to escape by passing. Academy Award nominations for Waters, Barrymore, and Crain in addition to the success of the film in southern theaters is also telling of the film's recapitulation of entrenched hierarchies enabling racial and sexual subjugation.

In light of Jane Crow's critical and commercial acclamation in *Pinky*, Wright more radically challenges racial and gender hierarchies in "Black Hope." However, the manuscript's unpublished status exemplifies the effect of Jane Crow politics on mid-twentieth-century black cultural production. *Pinky* is a Hollywood concession to the racial climate of the film's historical moment, with its depiction of Aunt Dicey as the faithful washerwoman and Pinky as the tragic mulatto. The film limits the possibilities for black women's transgressive action in domestic spaces. In comparison, "Black Hope" emphasizes the socially conscious potential of the maid, who traditionally was perpetuated in film and other popular cultural texts as the ignorant and loyal servant. Wright's shift toward representing black female subjectivity was a logical progression in his creative and political processes given his investment in black workers. Yet nowhere else in his fiction do black women achieve maturation as subjects, as "Black Hope" is an artifact of his distinct 1940s persona. How might critics' framing of Wright's adversarial association with his black female writing contemporaries change if "Black Hope" were a part of the conversation? How might "Black Hope" complicate our understanding of his masculinist discourse? Equally important to mapping the gender politics of Wright's works published during the social realist era is considering "Black Hope" in comparison to his later twentieth-century work, including *The Long Dream* (1958) and the posthumously published *Lawd Today* (1963). The obscurity of "Black Hope" implies that the text is a casualty of past Jane Crow politics as well as the gender politics defining the writer's oeuvre now.

As the most celebrated writer of his moment, Wright bears the burden of gender politics, albeit differently than the mid-twentieth-century black woman writer. On one hand, he succumbs to his gorgon muse. The two-faced enigma prevents him from completing his opus on black women's intersecting racial, gender, and class oppressions. On the other hand, he invests enough time and energy to write hundreds of pages about the plight of black women. In its absence, "Black Hope" relates the gender politics of the Jane Crow text and the mid-twentieth-century black male writer maybe more persuasively than the lack of strong black female characters in Wright's published work.

2 / Gender Conscriptions, Class Conciliations, and the Bourgeois Blues Aesthetic

The young girl who wishes to make the wheels of life run smoothly for herself and those with whom she comes in contact remembers that:
A lady,
1. Is polite when entering or leaving a room.
2. Passes behind people....
8. Awaits her turn; never bruskly pushes ahead....
12. Plays fair and works fair....
15. Listens to and follows simple directions....
17. Is always well-groomed, appropriately dressed, scrupulously clean in body and attire with hair carefully arranged....
19. Does not make advances for acquaintance of young men or go out of her way to attract their attention....
24. Accepts courtesy of young men graciously.
   —CHARLOTTE HAWKINS BROWN, "THE EARMARKS OF A LADY,"
   IN *THE CORRECT THING TO DO—TO SAY—TO WEAR*

You never get nothing by being an angel child
You'd better change your ways and get real wild...
'Cause wild women don't worry, wild women don't have the blues.
   —IDA COX, "WILD WOMEN DON'T HAVE THE BLUES"

In *The Correct Thing to Do—to Say—to Wear* (1940), educator Charlotte Hawkins Brown offers the etiquette advice in the first epigraph as an early twentieth-century script for African American women's performance of middle-class respectability. The list of twenty-four do's and implied don'ts constitutes the chapter titled "The Earmarks of a Lady." Deemed by contemporary scholars Charles W. Wadelington and Richard F. Knapp as the "first lady of social graces," Brown encourages decorum and admonishes uncouthness for the junior and senior high school students attending her Palmer Memorial Institute in North Carolina in addition to the adult readers of her text.[1] Brown addresses both the private and public constructions of black femininity by counseling African American women on how "to make the wheels of life run smoothly" for home and travel, church and school, dances and theaters, as well as afternoon teas and formal dinners.[2] Exhorting that genuine ladies stay "well-groomed, appropriately dressed, [and] scrupulously clean in body and attire," she suggests that only a disreputable woman would forget how others might perceive her appearance and deportment. Brown's rubrics for bourgeois black respectability are, as Carol C. Denard denotes, "self-conscious attempts to achieve practical and political aims."[3] Pragmatically drawing on the ideals of elite white femininity, Brown contends that an African American woman of refinement "is polite when entering or leaving a room," "passes behind people," and "listens to and follows simple directions." These maxims, which were devised in a patriarchal culture in response to racism, enforced prescriptions for black women's prudent conduct. Brown instructs that a proper lady "does not make advances . . . or go out of her way to attract [male] attention" yet welcomes the "courtesy of young men graciously." Such rules of social engagement corrected stereotypes of black women's sexual salaciousness established during slavery; they also evidenced black women's legitimacy to enter the cult of true white womanhood during the segregation era. Thus "The Earmarks of a Lady" defines a canon for black womanhood and promotes class codes for the black collective's social mobility. The recommendations strategically stress congeniality in this social and political race work.

Brown's earmarks are a definitive program for mid-twentieth-century woman-making and a modality for performing class and racial identity. Hence the directives set the terms and the tenor of black women's resistance to their multivalent oppression. Given that a lady "awaits her turn" and "plays fair" in spite of the ignobility of Jane Crow oppression, *The Correct Thing* intimates that black women's efforts to obtain the full rights of citizenship must similarly "go slow," "be nice," "accommodate" others, and work within the boundaries of "respectability."[4] For example, in her autobiography, *Song in a Weary Throat* (1987), Pauli Murray, who coined the term *Jane Crow* to name the gender discrimination she experienced during her 1940s civil rights activism, confesses, "Breaking the code of respectability . . . was as formidable a psychological barrier to action as the prospect of police brutality."[5] As Victoria W. Wolcott observes of other interwar racial-uplift stratagems, the code of respectability underlying Brown's compendium reflects "more than simply bourgeois Victorian ideology; it was a foundation of African American women's survival strategies and self-definition irrespective of class."[6]

Affirming late nineteenth- and early twentieth-century Victorian morality, *The Correct Thing* attempts to safeguard black female bodies from economic and sexual exploitation by refashioning them within the cloak of propriety. The extent to which black women were respectable presumably determined the degree of whites' acceptance, as blacks' bourgeois conformity demonstrated their proclivity for normative gender roles, sexual behavior, and cultural civility. "Let us take time, therefore, to be gracious, to be thoughtful, to be kind," Brown rallies, "using the social graces as one means of turning the wheels of progress with greater velocity on the upward road to equal opportunity and justice for all."[7] *The Correct Thing* was published the same year as Richard Wright's protest novel *Native Son*, which criticizes society's racism through protagonist Bigger Thomas's anger, bullying, and gendered violence. Meanwhile Brown's code of etiquette encourages black women to pit ladylike affectation against the unmannered and inequitable.

Revising Wright's masculinist blueprint for racial protest, Ann Petry's novel *The Street* (1946) and Dorothy West's novel *The Living Is Easy* (1948) evidence some of Brown's earmarks for respectability. Together the black women writers demonstrate the importance of the lady archetype for blacks' racial pride, economic progress, and ultimate integrationist aims. However, *The Street* and *The Living Is Easy* also articulate the inevitable contradictions in ceding to the conscriptions of pedestal white womanhood; the texts stress the bourgeois blues intonations in black women's performance of subjectivity under Jane Crow oppression. Even as they admire the touted figure of femininity defined as chaste, obedient, and self-sacrificing, Petry's and West's black female protagonists entertain the recalcitrant blues lyrics in the chapter's second epigraph. "You never get nothing by being an angel child," blues woman Ida Cox sings. "Wild women are the only kind that really get by."[8] It is hard to imagine Brown's proper lady having an interview with Cox's wild woman, but Petry and West position Lutie Johnson in *The Street* and Cleo Jericho Judson in *The Living Is Easy* at the crossroads of such an exchange. Each novel's bourgeois blues aesthetic is signified in the texts' literal and figurative representations of the vernacular. This bourgeois blues aesthetic also manifests in each text's irreconcilable conflict between the protagonist's desire for social mobility and the narrative's representation of black women's historically fixed social condition. Black women's bourgeois blues maintain the ironic balance between tragic and comic responses to racial trauma—"laughing to keep from crying," as Langston Hughes so keenly phrased it. They further address the conciliations black women make between the sexually repressed lady construct as a recuperative strategy and the classic blues woman figure as an erotic emancipatory improvisation. Despite black women's efforts to be angels of middle-class domesticity, Petry's and West's novels consider whether it might be more effective to "get real wild" and transgress the social practices enforcing Jane Crow oppression.

The blues matrix in *The Street* and *The Living Is Easy* illustrates black women's social, economic, and political disenfranchisement during the Jane Crow era by exposing their inherent exclusion from the racist and patriarchal cult of true white womanhood. Barbara Christian and Hazel V. Carby theorize that ideologies of white womanhood are constructed in opposition to—and are thus dependent upon—stereotypes of black femininity. Because race bars black women from this feminine ideal, You-me Park and Gayle Wald argue that black women are "complicit with as well as victimized by the myth of bourgeois respectability and domesticity that prohibits them from reaching out to alternative communities and public spheres."[9] In *The Street* working-class Lutie literally sings the blues at her Harlem neighborhood bar while she aspires to the middle-class domesticity of her white suburban employers. Recognizing the consequences of racial segregation as well as the class codes of bourgeois respectability, Lutie deduces, "No one could live on a street like this and stay decent."[10] In contrast, in *The Living Is Easy* Cleo is a member of the middle-class black Bostonian elite who financially compromises her husband by moving her sisters and their children out of the Jim Crow South and under her more privileged purview. Although she prides herself on publicly exhibiting that a "proper Bostonian never showed any emotion but hauteur," Cleo criticizes the pretensions of auspicious ladyhood by privately admitting that she "had no desire to resemble a fish."[11] She does not literally sing the blues but attempts to negotiate her folk past and bourgeois present through creative storytelling and a revisionist oral history. Cleo and Lutie are on different rungs of the economic ladder, but neither woman is able to secure access to the pedestal figure of white femininity or embrace fully the symbolic bodies of "low" culture black folk. The bourgeois blues, then, are a metaphor for the performance of black femininity regardless of class. Both Petry's working-class protagonist and West's middle-class protagonist struggle to reconcile the concessions intrinsic in their deference to the social strictures undergirding their Jane Crow oppression. Hence *The Street* and *The Living Is Easy* contemplate black women's relationship to vernacular culture, class desire, and the domestic sphere through bourgeois blues tropes.

Classic blues music was a source of empowerment for black women given its unconventional image of femininity and penchant for proto-feminist critique. In addition to the cultural capital and financial sovereignty the blues provided black women singers as the first to record race records in the 1920s, Angela Y. Davis contends that the blues offer "fascinating possibilities of sustaining emergent feminist consciousness" because "they often construct seemingly antagonistic relationships as noncontradictory oppositions."[12] When Cox sings, "You'd better change your ways and get real wild . . . / 'Cause wild women don't worry, wild women don't have the blues," she advises her female listeners to manage their blues condition under racism and patriarchy by breaking with the restrictive covenants domesticating black womanhood. The alternative wild woman is the archetype of a nonconforming, self-determining woman synonymous with the eroticized image of the female blues singer. Carby explains that blues women of the 1920s and early 1930s employed the musical genre as "a discourse that articulates a cultural and political struggle over sexual relations: a struggle that is directed against the objectification of female sexuality within a patriarchal order but which also tries to reclaim women's bodies as the sexual and sensuous subjects of women's song."[13] Since classic blues women did not hesitate to articulate their desires, sexual innuendo saturates their lyrics, including euphemisms of male prowess as well as homoeroticism. References to marriage, motherhood, and domesticity, which are markers of middle-class respectability, are noticeably limited. In effect this sexual commentary expresses proto-feminist values and anticipates queer theory's critique of heteronormativity, which Cathy Cohen elucidates is aligned with white supremacist ideologies invested in regulating the sexuality of various marginal and oppressed subjects.[14] Classic blues women's rejection of heteronormative domestic identities contested the elitist politics of racial uplift as well as the racism and patriarchy subjugating black women. Though this early twentieth-century image of the erotically empowered blues woman did not survive the Depression (Hollywood films subsequently subordinate blues singers like Hattie McDaniel and Ethel Waters in roles as nurturing domestics), "the blues muse" influenced the evolution of jazz and gospel music, according to Guthrie P. Ramsey Jr., well into the 1940s.[15]

Black women writers who published during the interwar period were often precluded from the classic blues modality, but the "blues-ing" nuances of African American women's novels, to use Ramsey's term, can be traced throughout the fiction of the Harlem Renaissance and the social realist texts of the post–World War II era.[16] The representation of the lady was critical to "New Negro" racial uplift and the refutation of blacks' exotic primitivism perpetuated in the period's racial and sexual discourses. As a result black women writers of the 1920s and 1930s made the explicit sexuality expressed by contemporaneous blues women latent in their work. In *The Coupling Convention* (1993) Ann duCille demythologizes the classic blues' explicit sexuality by questioning to what degree blues women singers created and exploited this cultural moment and to what extent the recording industry created and exploited the artists. DuCille in turn delineates bourgeois blues "inscriptions" or "subtle, frequently subversive responses to the oppressive, materialist rhythms" in the fiction of Jessie Fauset, Nella Larsen, and Zora Neale Hurston.[17] She argues that the fiction of Fauset and Larsen, who wrote about northern middle-class communities, and Hurston, who is most obviously linked to the southern folk, shares the classic blues' concerns with black female desire and erotic relationships. The bourgeois blues in these Harlem Renaissance women writers' work, duCille contends, are a cultural critique symbolized in the marriage trope, which explores social conventions and gender relations in economic and geographical transition.

Petry's and West's novels similarly speak to domesticity's constraints for defining black female subjectivity. Additionally *The Street* and *The Living Is Easy* were produced in a comparable moment of historical transition. The second phase of the Great Migration signals this shift, along with a corresponding change in literary conventions due to an evolving racial and gender consciousness. Drawing on and extending duCille's concept, the bourgeois blues inscriptions in post–World War II black women's fiction do not promote the explicit sexuality of the classic blues. Yet unlike the novels of Harlem Renaissance women writers, the mid-twentieth-century articulation of the bourgeois blues directly addresses black women's sexual exploitation as well as their efforts to expand the definition of the erotic beyond sex. These bourgeois blues concretize the conflict between the ideals of bourgeois white womanhood and the intersection of race, class, and gender oppression in the 1940s. Differentiating between singing the blues (as a conscripted lady) and improvising the performance of black female subjectivity (as a wild woman), Petry's and West's Jane Crow texts reconsider the potentialities and limitations of the vernacular for reconfiguring African American womanhood.

The Street and *The Living Is Easy* elide social realism's race-writing formulas and explore black subjectivity from the self-consciously gendered and classed perspective of the bourgeois blues. With their social commentary on Jane Crow oppression, Petry and West rewrite the traditionally male-dominated protest novel and migration narrative genres. On one hand, *The Street* is a protest novel in the tradition of the Wright school, as Lutie's alienating environment pushes her to murder her would-be rapist in order to claim subjectivity. On the other hand, Petry departs from the conventions of the protest novel and focuses on black women's experiences with sexual as well as labor exploitation. She further moves beyond the naturalist tradition by emphasizing Lutie's choices. While Lutie's environment determines her inability to access true womanhood, her decisions contribute to her perpetual exclusion from it. Extrinsic to the protest novel genre, *The Living Is Easy* rejects the mandates of the Wright school and depicts the domestic conflicts of middle-class blacks. As Sharon L. Jones observes, West's work demonstrates "an appreciation of the folk, the proletarian sense of communality between humans, and a necessity for the socioeconomic progress of bourgeois values but not at the expense of the community."[18] The writer deviates from the strict urban and working-class ambits circumscribing black subjectivity during the mid-twentieth-century social realist literary period. In West's gendered revision of the migration novel, Cleo's sexual and economic exploitation in the South drive her to migrate, while her discontent with middle-class domesticity delimits her life in the North.

Recasting these two black male writing traditions, Petry and West provide a cross-class, intergenerational critique by accenting black women's bourgeois blues in two distinct yet related historical settings. When read jointly, the novels become "before" and "after" narratives of black woman-making: *The Living Is Easy* details Cleo's migration from the South just before World War I in order to obtain economic and sexual agency, whereas *The Street* intimates the loss of folk culture and community owing to blacks' northern migration during the World War II era. The women's gains and losses as a result of migration at the interstice of the wars substantiate their specifically gendered experiences. If the blues are a "metaphor for what happens to the migrants when they arrive in the city," as Farah Jasmine Griffin states, then Huddie "Leadbelly" Ledbetter's song "Bourgeois Blues" conveys, only in part, Cleo's and Lutie's experiences with racism and classism.[19] "I heard a white man say: I don't want no niggers up there," Leadbelly's narrator reflects. "Me and my wife we went all over town / Everywhere we go the colored people would turn us down."[20] The blues man's song describes black migrants' confrontations with interracial prejudice and intraracial elitism. Petry's and West's novels articulate a similar critique, but the writers' appropriation of the bourgeois blues aesthetic also impugns the union of Jim and Jane Crow denying black women's public expression of sexual desire and negating their authority over their private domestic space.

The Living Is Easy and *The Street* depict black women's struggle to define subjectivity under the oppressions of racism and sexism, within the circumscriptions of respectability, and outside the conventional representations of black women. In this way the novels' bourgeois blues aesthetic marks black women's "disidentification" with the protocols of respectability associated with elite white femininity. José Esteban Muñoz theorizes that "disidentification is the third mode of dealing with dominant ideology, one that neither opts to assimilate within such a structure nor strictly opposes it; rather, disidentification is a strategy that works on and against dominant ideology."[21] Cleo and Lutie cannot attain the pedestal figure of white womanhood or escape its oppressive paradigm; instead they ambivalently construct subjectivity through their performance of the bourgeois blues. As Muñoz argues more broadly about the performance of identity politics by queer people of color, Cleo and Lutie "desire [the white ideal] but desire it with a difference."[22] In *The Living Is Easy* Cleo's duality as policing agent and rebel against prohibitive class codes manifests her bourgeois blues. She impersonates the earmarks of bourgeois respectability to obtain social mobility, but she adroitly manipulates its principles to maintain authority over her domestic space. Comparatively in *The Street* Lutie's bourgeois blues ensue from the disparities between the harsh realities of the urban neighborhood in which she must live and the idealized space of white domesticity she is relegated to as a domestic worker in suburban Connecticut. Her white employers disavow her identity as wife and mother and assume that she is promiscuous because she is black. Concurrently her black neighbors deduce that she is primed for prostitution because she is poor. Both Cleo and Lutie disidentify with elite white womanhood by embodying the bourgeois blues, which compels them to covet and reject the pedestal figure in their efforts to define black womanhood for themselves.

Lamenting the compromises made in the pursuit of true womanhood, the bourgeois blues in *The Street* and *The Living Is Easy* suggest two strategies for black female agency. First, maintaining authorial control over the fictions of ladyhood relies upon black women's command of vernacular cultural forms. Second, demystifying the myths of pedestal white femininity depends upon black women's intimacy with other black women. Not only do the blues provide a model of improvisation to contest white society's overdetermination of black subjugation, but they also offer a gender-conscious discourse with which to confront Jane Crow's subjection of self-empowering black women. A literal and symbolic trope for reimagining black female desire, the bourgeois blues encourage womanist communions to counter the stipulations imposed upon the race and the sex. When blues woman Cox conspiratorially discloses, "I want to tell you something, I wouldn't tell you no lie . . . wild women don't have the blues," she builds and models a womanist cooperative with her advisory lyrics. Cox's address to "you" in the song speaks to an implied female community for whom her "I" performs and to whom she counsels on the extemporizations of black womanhood. While the blues create intimacy between the singer and her audience, the bourgeois blues aesthetics in Petry's and West's novels impart the consequences of this cultural loss and community absence.

Champagne Tastes and Beer Money in *The Living Is Easy*

In *The Living Is Easy* Cleo Jericho Judson's bourgeois blues consist of disidentifying with the demands of feminine propriety that proscribe her domestic roles as daughter, sister, wife, and mother. While the official earmarks of a lady decree that true women are polite, obedient, and fair, Cleo is a shrewd critic of the fictions of womanhood and rejects being an angel of the house. In the South her gender performance challenges the union of Jim and Jane Crow that relegates black women to domestic work and represses their sexual agency. In the North she resists the physical obligations of marriage as well as self-sacrificial modes of motherhood. As her most ambitious act, Cleo creates a woman-centric domestic space that she alone dominates by manipulating her three married sisters to move north without their husbands. Her deviation from traditional scripts for middle-class domesticity rejects patriarchy while embracing her gendered role as matriarch. Yet her self-indulgent tactics also contribute to the social forces disabling her sisters' self-actualization and culminating in her husband's financial demise. Hence the tragic conclusion of *The Living Is Easy* leads one contemporaneous reviewer to dismiss West's protagonist as a "predatory female."[23]

Cleo's efforts to remodel the domestic structures of bourgeois respectability, however, are attempts to confront the historical racism and patriarchy that render her female-centered domestic sphere unthinkable. West's novel is set on the cusp of World War I, but her publishing moment is the post–World War II era. "As a strong, determined, controlling, beautiful woman of some means with an adoring husband," Adelaide Cromwell explains in the afterword to *The Living Is Easy*, "Cleo is new to black literature."[24] West's representation of black womanhood is unique because it is neither romanticized nor idealized. Whereas Cleo seeks the privileges of bourgeois respectability, she transgresses the morality and social edicts of ladyhood to achieve contradictory objectives: the annuities of middle-class materialism and a sisterhood of black folk. Cleo's figurative bourgeois blues convey her difficulty reconciling these individualist and collective aims socially and psychically. As E. Patrick Johnson posits about the politics of blackness and authenticity, "It is in the performance site . . . where the cognitive dissonance between life as lived and life as imagined is less conflictual."[25] For Cleo, modeling the bourgeois lady and reifying the folk are competing objectives, but she negotiates them in her makeshift performance of femininity within her discomfited family, disjointed northern black community, and declining middle-class way of life.

The Living Is Easy explores the politics of middle-class respectability conscribing black femininity just as the novel's production exemplifies black women writers' distinct contributions to mid-twentieth-century social realist literature. At one end of the publishing spectrum, Richard Wright criticizes black writers' disregard of the proletariat and outlines a formula for the racially authentic, politically conscious, and ultimately commercially successful black text in his essay "Blueprint for Negro Writing" (1937). At the other end of the spectrum, Zora Neale Hurston bares the consequences of Wright's mandates in her essay "What White Publishers Won't Print" (1950), which was inspired by publishers' rejection of her proposed novel on middle-class African Americans. Hurston acknowledges that white publishers "are not in business to educate, but to make money. Sympathetic as they might be, they cannot afford to be crusaders."[26] Still, she cautions that neglecting to diversify the black literary landscape will create a museum of "UNNATURAL HISTORY," where black subjects become racialized objects. Hurston wrote her white character–driven novel *Seraph on the Suwanee* (1948) in response to the apartheid-like restrictions white publishers placed on black writers and their racial subject matter. Coincidentally her understudied final novel was published the same year as West's neglected first novel, *The Living Is Easy*.

A contemporary of both Hurston and Wright, West encounters several obstacles to publishing her work, which spans from the Harlem Renaissance to her final novel, *The Wedding* (1995). When West submitted short stories to magazines early in her career, white editors rejected her fictions about middle-class blacks, discouraged her narratives about characters they erroneously assumed to be white, and advised her to write about what they presumed she knew well: working-class blacks.

She confronted similar challenges with *The Living Is Easy*, as the novel was scheduled initially for publication in the *Ladies' Home Journal* and then shelved. "I have always felt," West intimates in an interview with Deborah McDowell, "that they feared the loss of advertising revenues by serializing a novel by a Black woman about Black people."[27] The forty-seven-year publication gap between West's first and last novels, Jones contends, reflects the recurring debates in the African American literary tradition about which aesthetics will take precedence. The radical politics of the Black Power movement delayed the publication of *The Wedding*. Prior to that, the protest novel's predominance reflected the colliding race, gender, and class politics at play in *The Living Is Easy*'s publication and reception. There was a limited literary context in the 1940s for a black female protagonist's unconventional performance of middle-class respectability.

While West's novel invokes blues women's critiques of pedestal femininity's idiosyncrasies, Cleo's bourgeois blues are inspired by the writer's familial history. Like Cleo, West's mother migrated north because of the sexual danger southern white men posed due to her attractiveness and lighter complexion. Like Cleo's husband, Bart Judson, West's father was known as the "Black Banana King" because of his entrepreneurial success, which established the family's middle-class standing among Boston's elite black enclaves. Although the title of West's novel is a line from the George and Ira Gershwin song "Summertime," featured in DuBose Heyward's opera *Porgy and Bess* (1935), *The Living Is Easy* is not an affirmation of the southern pastoral but an ironic reference to blacks' precarious northern privilege. In other words, the living is not easy for Cleo, and the novel's title refers to her elitist aspirations, not her economic security. The text's bourgeois blues aesthetic manifests in the temporal and spatial interchanges West employs to disrupt structures of female desire. *The Living Is Easy* juxtaposes storylines about the elite Binney family, whose deceits maintain their waning old-money reputation, with details about the rural Jerichoes, who naïvely migrate because of Cleo's chicanery. The narrative's temporality transitions between the northern present and southern past. Because Cleo enjoys the class advantages of the former (the Binneys, North, and present) and remains nostalgic for the familial intimacies of the latter (the Jerichoes, South, and past), she believes that money will guarantee her some middle ground between both pulls.

The dualities in *The Living Is Easy* mirror the ambivalence of the blues. Bessie Smith's song "Money Blues," which relays a recurring conversation between a couple about their indigent financial situation, exemplifies Cleo's irreconcilable bourgeois blues. With two tiers of narration, "Money Blues" relates a husband's telling of his wife's material consumption as sung by a blues woman. "Fast as I can lend it, how you like to spend it / It disappears somehow / I've got beer money, you like champagne / If you don't stop spendin'...," the man cautions.[28] The woman later insistently bemoans in the song's chorus, "Daddy, I need money... Daddy, I need money now." Provoking similar censure in *The Living Is Easy*, Cleo subverts male dominance over domestic economies and bucks the conventions of wifedom and motherhood by swindling money from her husband and stealing coins from her daughter's piggy bank. More than cash, Cleo's "money blues" concomitantly express her urgent need for distance from rural poverty, refuge in new-money airs, and her sisters' presence even though she cannot afford them.

In this blues matrix, Cleo's double consciousness as middle-class policing agent and dissident from such gender restrictions transforms her uneven performance of bourgeois respectability into a discursive critique of her gendered possibilities. She adheres (at least publicly) to the codes of pedestal womanhood in order to differentiate herself from recent migrants and working-class blacks, while she finds power, ironically, in breaking the rules of decorum. For example, when her daughter Judy expresses excitement at seeing a puppy, Cleo instructs, "Don't show your gums when you smile, and stop squirming. You've seen dogs before. Sit like a little Boston lady. Straighten your spine." Cleo perpetuates the gendered strictures in which she feels trapped by teaching Judy to straighten her spine, to showcase her refinement, as well as pinch her broad nose to lessen her racial distinction. Despite her valuation of ladylike civility, Cleo quickly deserts its principles with those she deems her social inferiors. In the presence of a black maid she chides her daughter, "Always remember... that good manners put you in the parlor and poor manners keep you in the kitchen." With this recitation she offers a lesson on the economics of deportment for black women: etiquette determines who is a lady and who is a domestic. However, Judy, who has a Boston governess responsible for teaching her manners, knows that "a lady must keep her voice low, and never boast, and never, never say anything that might hurt somebody's feelings." When Judy informs Cleo that the maid overheard her mother's comments, Cleo responds, "Well, I expected her to hear. Who did you think I was talking to? I certainly wasn't talking to you."[29] Cleo simultaneously performs and negates bourgeois respectability. She elevates herself as a lady over the domestic and then insults the maid in an unladylike manner.

Cleo feigns born and bred class superiority, but her migration narrative highlights white women's exploitation of black women's domestic work and policing of black female sexuality. Before "the wildness in the child might turn to wantonness in the girl," Cleo's white schoolteacher urges the Jerichoes to send their eldest daughter north.[30] Presumably there is cause for concern when Cleo's childish impropriety earns her a whipping for brazenly turning cartwheels and showing off her underwear. Like the dress-clad black female child in *Seraph on the Suwanee* who performs a headstand without any drawers, mischievous Cleo is budding with dangerous artistic desire. She dreams of the masculine freedom life as a stage actress offers in the face of the realities home tenders, which include working as a cook in her white childhood friend's kitchen. Her migration promises opportunity, yet the move curbs her literal performative ambitions when she becomes the charge of a white spinster. Instead of a formal education, Cleo receives cultural disciplining in the symbolic performance of gender, as Pamela Peden Sanders suggests, by learning "how to construct her outside—her 'female' social mask, her feminine manners."[31] She also gains social practice in creating what historian Darlene Clark Hine terms a "culture of dissemblance" with which black female migrants shielded their private selves from public subjugations.[32] Cleo's "conscientious custodian" initially keeps her from being corrupted or courted by the "temptations along the way in the guise of coachmen and butlers and porters."[33] Cleo goes on to emulate the spinster's class chauvinism and condescends to more recent migrants, working-class laborers, and her own unsophisticated relatives.

Despite patronizing her supposed social inferiors, Cleo practices elitist snobbery to usurp strategically Jane Crow's interlocking racism and patriarchy. Resolute in the belief that "men were nothing but stomach and the other thing. It would be a happy day for women if both could be cut out," she marries out of self-preservation and not in pursuit of domestic fantasies or sexual desire. Her compulsory marriage to Mr. Judson, who is twenty-three years her senior, helps her escape the lustful advances of her white guardian's nephew, and her husband's class standing enables her social mobility. To avoid the increasing population of southern black migrants, the Judsons move to a predominantly white neighborhood where there are "no stoop-sitters anywhere, nor women idling at windows, nor loose-lipped loiterers passing remarks." The bigger house is a gender and class performance site for Cleo to reinvent herself, though she makes Mr. Judson believe that the new home is for the son he dreams will inherit his business. "What was there to being a boy? What was there to being a man?" Cleo pridefully asks. "It was women who did the lying awake, the planning, the sorrowing, the scheming to stretch a dollar. That was the hard part, the head part. . . . A woman had to be smart."[34] Toward this end she lies to her husband that their new rent is forty-five dollars instead of twenty-five dollars so that she can pocket the extra money without his scrutinizing her activities. She also fails to tell him that their new addition to the house is not a baby or a boarder but her nonpaying sisters and their children. Cleo, whom duCille describes as "a kind of robber baron/grande dame," siphons Mr. Judson's dollars to ensure that she is the boss of her own house.[35]

More valuable than her financial shenanigans, Cleo revises traditional feminine scripts and rewrites the official history of slavery that dehumanizes black women. Slavery contrived an image of black women as chattel, but Cleo portrays her female ancestors as always and already actors despite their bondage. She believes their suicides prove the respectability of black womanhood because "when they couldn't live proud, they preferred to die."[36] She refuses to teach her daughter about the horrors of slavery. Instead she wants her to know about her great-aunt who hanged herself after her master whipped her and her great-grandmother who walked into the river after her missus scolded her for burning biscuits. Preserving the agency of the Jericho women, Cleo inscribes her version of history with a blues-voiced narration that, as Houston A. Baker contends about the vernacular, "negotiate[s] an obdurate 'economies of slavery' and achieve[s] a resonant, improvisational, expressive dignity."[37] Cleo's oral history effectively highlights her ancestors' acts of self-worth within an institution that values black female bodies in terms of production and profit. Her reenvisioning of African American women's history gives her authorial control over her own narrative and gendered performance. Thus oral history is a performance event for Cleo, defined by her temporal setting, intended audience, and staged presentation of self.[38] Her revisionist account is constructive for her as well as Judy's self-definition. Nonetheless Cleo's esteem for those who committed suicide rather than those who survived also advances a kind of reductive performance of empowered womanhood.

Marriage is also a performance event that allows black women to access the privileges of white middle-class respectability while also potentially subjecting them to patriarchal oppression. The bourgeois blues in *The Living Is Easy* do not reiterate classic blues women's copulating discourse but critique the double jeopardy of race and gender via the collateral damage childbirth engenders. Cleo views her mother as a cautionary tale for heterosexual desire's fatal consumption of black women, and she criticizes her mother's privileging of romantic love over mother-daughter bonds: "Mama loved Pa better than anyone. And what was left over from loving him was divided among her daughters. Divided even." Her mother's death while delivering a stillborn child suggests that love and sex destroy black female subjectivity, as "Pa had just as good as killed her." Cleo subsequently invokes her bourgeois blues when she decides "she wasn't going to sing an old love-song with any greasy-haired coon." Whereas she watches her "sisters turn into wives," she dominates her marriage to Mr. Judson by withholding sex and engaging in verbal play to achieve domestic despotism. Cleo informs Mr. Judson "that she had no intention of renouncing her maidenhood for one man if she had married to preserve it from another," even though there is "no real abhorrence of sex in her." One night her sexual desire weakens her resolve, and they conceive Judy. Yet she repeatedly rejects marital intimacy and embraces frigidity—an extreme distortion of white women's idealized sexuality—in her battle of the sexes with Mr. Judson. Cleo's marriage legitimates her ascension to the role of respectable lady; in turn she disparagingly calls her husband "Mister Nigger" to fix him in his rural southern roots.[39] With this epithet she does not belittle the primitivism of the folk in favor of black middle-class pretensions; she critiques the trivialities of both.

Mimicry of middle-class white femininity would typically place a black woman outside the classic blues woman tradition, but Cleo's improvised gender performances indicate her character's bourgeois blues inscriptions. With her ambivalent stance toward lies of omission and outright lies, she adroitly runs verbal circles around Mr. Judson and convinces him that she is pregnant despite their lack of intimacy. When he realizes she has misled him in order to bilk money from him, he accuses, "You never talk straight."[40] Cleo's double-talk and circumvention of fixed truths demonstrate that the vernacular's power lies in the ambiguity of its meaning. Her storytelling is synonymous with telling stories—that is, lies—and lying is as benign as black cultural signifying when it comes to her attaining economic security or the undivided attention of her sisters. Her command of language initiates what Lisa Krissoff Boehm terms a female migration route, on which black female migrants traveled north as much for better economic opportunity as to keep company with female relatives who were war brides and childless elders.[41] Cleo spins tales to her siblings to persuade them to visit without their spouses, and she turns their trips into permanent stays by exploiting their husbands' weaknesses, including one's wandering eye and another's insecurities in regard to colorism. The sisters' migration creates a female-centric space that allows Cleo to embrace the folkisms she cannot express among Boston's black elites. Though she views recent southern migrants as "little knotty-head niggers" whose "accents prickled her scalp," she admits, "Sometimes you felt like cutting the fool for the hell of it. Sometimes you hankered to pick a bone and talk with your mouth full." She solicits an audience that enjoys her "great Negro laughter, rich, belly-deep, body-shaking, with little gasps for breath"; applauds her "fool stories"; and appreciates the art of her "lies."[42]

The exclusive female community Cleo structures briefly works and then stalls on three levels. First, her complicated ties with her mother and siblings ground her bourgeois blues. Drawing on Claudia Tate's psychoanalytic reading of the racial politics imposed on black novels, Cleo's chicanery in response to society's racial and gender expectations "negotiates the tension between the public, collective protocols of race and private, individual desire."[43] Cleo publicly imitates pedestal womanhood, but she privately desires to recuperate her deceased mother, whom she did not appreciate as an example of empowered womanhood during her girlhood. Her attempts to reconcile folk nostalgia (in spite of the racial oppression in the South) and urban alienation (despite the economic opportunities in the North) reflect her longing for her lost mother. This contradictory relationship with her mother is emblematic of her problematized relationship to domesticity and what Griffin describes as Cleo's "odd combination of disdain, identification, and need" with the South.[44] Cleo performs middle-class Bostonian hauteur, but she has yet to achieve selfhood beyond the concept of her mother or the South. With her sisters' presence, she attains "mirrors in which she would see Mama."[45] Moreover she reconfigures the maternal South in the North in order to get the unconditional acceptance she craves for her unconventional gender performance.

By privileging being a sister over being a wife, Cleo restructures the heterosexist foundations of domesticity in her female-centered household. She believes she can provide better for her sisters in the North than their husbands can in the South. Recounting the Jane Crow oppressions of the South, she reminds her sisters, "But all you know, all any of us know, is how to cook and clean for white folks."[46] In addition to the personal benefit the sisters' migration has for her subjectivity, Cleo encourages them to define their lives outside the roles racist, patriarchal society prescribes for black women: wife, Jezebel, mother, and Mammy.

She would rather her sisters be single mothers in her household than "slaves" to whites as domestics or black men as spouses. Whereas economic exploitation and heteronormativity maintain white supremacy, Cleo's sisterhood has the potential to be a transformative space for gender equity in her grasp at power.[47] Sisterhood is fundamentally egalitarian in feminist terms, but it is also one of few relationships in which Cleo can assert hierarchical rank and authority.

Finally, Cleo's relationship with Judy complicates Cleo's own identity as a daughter because their bond recapitulates Cleo's conflicts with the conscriptions of middle-class femininity and the "low" culture of southern folk. Cleo reconstructs her mother and the South in her female-centered space, but she also deconstructs herself and the South in her mothering of Judy. She views her child as a contradictory projection of herself: "I want [Judy] to be a Bostonian, but I want her to be me deep down.... Be me as my sisters are Mama."[48] As she pushes her daughter to aspire to bourgeois respectability in order to cement her own standing within the cult of true womanhood, Cleo admits that Judy will not be self-willed like her female Jericho ancestors. Judy is neither prepared for the interracial and intraracial politics she experiences at school nor desiring of anything beyond marriage and children.

Cleo accomplishes her dream of having all the Jericho women under her roof and her control; however, this feat does not resolve the class or sexual conflicts of her bourgeois blues. As rural migrants, Cleo's sisters are too afraid to socialize with her cultured friends. As black women, they are still restricted to jobs as cooks and live-in domestics. After months of "easy living" with the extended family's financial burdens, one of Cleo's sisters gains a significant amount of weight to satiate the lack of passion in her life. Another sister concludes that she would rather be "back down home working steady in the white folks kitchen, knowing at night [she] was coming home to [her] husband." This ironic turn infers that neither migration nor bourgeois respectability overcomes black women's racial and sexual oppression during the Jane Crow era. Further, the sisters' bluesy lament suggests that romantic love is not woman's destruction but the black collective's survival. The sisters' physical and psychological deterioration inspires Cleo to reconsider the constitution of her marriage just as World War I forces Mr. Judson to abandon the family to find work. With the collapse of his business, he relinquishes his money and concedes to his wife that she now runs their household. His concession only serves to confirm that she is "the boss of nothing but the young, the weak, the frightened."[49] Amid limited social power, strained financial resources, and overwhelming debt, Cleo is the queen of "a pygmy kingdom."

Therefore Cleo closes *The Living Is Easy* still metaphorically singing the "money blues." Admittedly her ambitions strain Mr. Judson's budget, but ultimately she is not the source of his economic decline or her sisters' narrow lives. It is exactly because Cleo is not "the boss" that the war, traditionally enacted and meted out by men, overthrows her domestic despotism. The politics of middle-class respectability promise social mobility to the southern migrant, racial equality to black elites, and esteem to black womanhood. However, the Jerichoes' debilitation and the Judsons' decline show that the bourgeoisie's allowances are transitory. The social razing of the poor and the privileged proves that black women are most vulnerable. This is the point of *The Living Is Easy*: the limitations of bourgeois respectability mean that ladyhood must be usable and negotiable.

The Lost Domestic Fantasy in *The Street*

Ann Petry's black female protagonist in *The Street* is a historical daughter to Cleo's culture of dissemblance in *The Living Is Easy*. A single mother estranged from her husband, Lutie Johnson does not reap the benefits of social mobility promised to the children of southern migrants or acquire the privileges of respectability assured black women during the interwar period. Housing discrimination and a lack of economic opportunity prevent Lutie from moving to middle-class white suburbia, and her block is just one of countless streets in working-class Harlem functioning as "the North's lynch mobs, . . . the method the big cities used to keep Negroes in their place."[50] Wright uses similar imagery in *12 Million Black Voices* to describe the migrants' encounter with segregated urban neighborhoods. "And how were we to know," he asks, "that, the moment we landless millions of the land—we men who were struggling to be born—set our awkward feet upon the pavements of the city, life would begin to exact of us a heavy toll in death?"[51] Petry invokes naturalist critiques in *The Street* by concretizing the city's oppressive environment in the kitchenette and indicting its culpability in the social death of urban black female subjects. In addition to representing the effects of racism on black communities, Petry explores the challenge Jane Crow oppression poses for working-class black women's claims to pedestal femininity. While white society debases black maids as sexual threats to domesticity, the street repeatedly propositions single black women as prostitutes. Unlike Cleo, who publicly exhibits venerable womanhood while privately enervating the rules of respectability, Lutie maintains a persistent belief in ladyhood and her ability to master the fictions of middle-class white domesticity. Nonetheless her social condition historically dictates the inevitability of her subjugation, and her fidelity to the politics of respectability produces her bourgeois blues.

Just as classic blues music represents seeming contradictions as concordant, the bourgeois blues aesthetic in *The Street* affirms black female agency, even as it castigates society for disabling black subjects. In a 1946 interview with James W. Ivey published in *The Crisis*, Petry explains that her "aim [in the novel] is to show how simply and easily the environment can change the course of a person's life."[52] *The Street*'s representation of black women's economic vulnerability overdetermines their inability to model the edicts of true white womanhood: "[Black] women had to work to support the families because the men couldn't get jobs and the men got bored and pulled out and the kids were left without proper homes because there was nobody around to put a heart into it."[53] Petry exposes this cycle of poverty and disaffection, ensuring Lutie's fate as an abandoned wife and absent mother in the vein of the protest novel. Interestingly in her essay "The Novel as Social Criticism" (1950), Petry speciously alleges that *The Street*, her first work, is "written for the most part without realizing that it belonged in a special category."[54] Her claim cannot be taken at face value, as Alex Lubin's collection *Revising the Blueprint* shows that she was immersed in the Left enough to be more than well-acquainted with the conventions of social realism. Rather Petry's pretense in "The Novel as Social Criticism" suggests her efforts to avoid having the success of her first novel define the rest of her career and to preempt Baldwin's and others' later critiques that the protest novel was sociology with no literary craft.

The Street, however, does not adhere strictly to the naturalist blueprint of social realism, and thus the novel challenges its generic conventions. Petry's text significantly weighs the repercussions of Lutie's decisions against her oppressive surroundings. For example, before the encroaching predation of the street sentences her son to reform school and forces her to commit murder to avert her rape, Lutie acknowledges that she has "a choice a yard wide and ten miles long."[55] She has limited options, but the repercussions of her decisions are far-reaching. Lutie prefers to live under the menacing gaze of the predatory super of her rented apartment rather than with her inept father and his tacky girlfriend. Notions of decorum dictate her unwitting decisions and their

reverberating consequences for her safety. As a result Ivey characterizes her as "a somewhat naive, often bewildered, and occasionally smug
mother" in his contemporaneous review of *The Street*.[56] Petry highlights
hegemonic society's subjection of Lutie and calls attention to her mea-
sured choices. In doing so she employs the conventions of naturalism
but moves beyond them by depicting her black female protagonist, to use
Nellie McKay's words, as more than "a mere victim" of circumstance.[57]

Lutie's commitment to performing middle-class respectability, in spite
of racist white society and the disenfranchised black community's collusion, incites the bourgeois blues matrix in *The Street*. As in *The Living Is
Easy*, the blues in Petry's text function as a metaphor for the conciliations
black women make in an attempt to model elite white femininity. Lutie's
relegation to domestic work conflicts with her traditional domestic roles
as wife and mother. More specifically she struggles to reconcile her disin-
tegrating marriage with the illusions of middle-class white domesticity,
her need to work with the glorified image of sacrificial motherhood, and
her sexual exploitation with the stratagems of racial uplift. As Candice
M. Jenkins contends, Lutie's desire for pedestal womanhood reflects a
"salvific wish" not only to protect herself with the inviolability of ladyhood but also "to rescue the black community from racist accusations of
sexual and domestic pathology through the embrace of bourgeois propriety."[58] The restrictive covenants of middle-class respectability, however,
actualize Lutie's subjugation under racial and patriarchal oppression.
The salvific wish is characteristically a middle-class black's response to
white society's pathologizing, and Lutie cannot claim the privileges of
middle-class social mobility as a fixed working-class subject.

Without membership in the cult of true white womanhood or a circle of
black elites, Lutie typifies blues women's critiques of sexual objectification
as well as the constraints of bourgeois respectability. *The Street*'s bourgeois
blues aesthetic reveals the incongruities between Lutie's middle-class aspirations and her working-class realities. Petry uses the blues as an analogy
for the performance of everyday life and literally manifests the vernacular in Lutie's brief employment as a blues singer. If she chose to negotiate
the politics of middle-class respectability, Lutie could perform femininity
as a "blues lady" similar to the way jazz singer Billie Holiday embraces
propriety and profanity as noncontradictory oppositions in her autobiography, *Lady Sings the Blues* (1956). If Lutie chose to reject completely the
precepts of true womanhood, she could stage herself as a blues woman
in the mien of classic blues singer Ida Cox, who proselytizes, "You never
get nothing by being an angel child" in the song "Wild Women Don't

Have the Blues." Because Lutie pursues the tenets of middle-class white domesticity as a survival strategy, she lives the blues and does not extemporize them. Ma Rainey's song "Misery Blues," which laments a husband's deception, is emblematic of the bourgeois respectability that first seduces and then disillusions Lutie. "He told me that he loved me, loved me so / If I would marry him, I needn't to work no mo'," Rainey rues. "Now I'm grievin', almost dyin' / Just because I didn't know that he was lyin'."[59] Just as Rainey's narrator regrets her beguilement and mourns the lost domestic fantasy, Lutie's "misery blues" demystify reveries of domestic leisure and domestic labor. Her desire for middle-class respectability rooted in white supremacy inhibits her from joining the classic blues women's tradition of sexual reclamation. Lutie's bourgeois blues, then, problematize her relationship to folk culture and prevent her kinship with black women who transgress the traditional conventions of gender performance.

Lutie's white employers are not paragons of middle-class respectability, but the Chandlers are the primary source for her idealized image of domesticity. Whereas she encounters commercial advertising that romantically constructs bourgeois domesticity as a white couple with white appliances in a "miracle" kitchen, the Chandlers' suburban house includes maid's quarters. Lutie's domestic work underlies the image of effortless white femininity perpetuated in the media insofar as it is the underpinning of the Chandlers' "miracle" home. The family's source of income makes transparent the fragility of their bourgeois respectability. Mr. Chandler manufactures paper towels, napkins, and handkerchiefs and boasts, "Even when times are hard, thank God, people have to blow their noses and wipe their hands and faces and wipe their mouths." The Chandlers profit from decorous accessories that are both purposeful and disposable, and the family can afford to throw away social conventions without censure: the stable husband drinks too much; the devoted wife flirts with married men; their financially privileged child is neglected emotionally; and a relative's suicide is ruled officially an accident, though witnessed by Lutie. Disregarding her intimate knowledge of the myths of middle-class white domesticity, Lutie aspires to be similarly beyond reproach. Yet her construction of subjectivity is even more tenuous than the family's tissue-thin propriety. Lutie is devoted to wifedom and motherhood as revered duties of pedestal womanhood, but Mrs. Chandler suspects that she is a "wench with no morals who would be easy to come by" and a threat to the virtue of the Chandlers' domestic space.[60]

In actuality, working for the Chandlers and internalizing their capitalist spirit devastates Lutie's aspirations for middle-class respectability and proves that she has little social power despite her unlimited ambition. Signifying on her bourgeois blues, Lutie's marriage "bust[s] up, cracking wide open like a cheap record," while she creates her employers' idyllic domestic space as their live-in maid. She chooses to save her earnings rather than spend them on visits home, which further escalates her unemployed husband's insecurity about his role as provider and ends in the couple's permanent estrangement. Lamenting the dissolution of the domestic fantasy, Lutie questions, "Yet what else could she have done?"[61] In what Hazel Arnett Ervin calls bivocal utterance, Petry conflates the omniscient third-person narrator and the protagonist's limited perspective.[62] Lutie's rhetorical question intimates doubts about her responsibility in the marriage's failure while also demonstrating her increasing awareness of the institutional structures working against her.

Similarly Lutie's relationship with her son, Bub, reveals the futility of working-class black women's efforts to enter the cult of true white womanhood founded on the union of Jim and Jane Crow oppression. At the same time that Lutie models sacrificial motherhood, her efforts to protect Bub from the exploitations of the street force her to perform mothering, as Marjorie Pryse argues, in "its ultimate grotesqueness."[63] Lutie slaps Bub because she believes his shining shoes—as she puts it, "like the rest of these little niggers" on the street—portends a life of manual labor, though her efforts to work, save, and move inspire his endeavor. Lutie's industriousness also makes Bub susceptible to the super, who convinces him to steal mail to earn money. At the conclusion of the novel, Lutie decides to leave Bub in reform school because "a kid whose mother was a murderer didn't stand any chance at all."[64] However, her selfless act guarantees his fate just as her abandonment of him exemplifies her exclusion from true womanhood. The difference between the "money blues" in *The Living Is Easy* and the "misery blues" in *The Street* is that Cleo deliberately transgresses the traditional boundaries of the wife and mother constructs with the hope of reconfiguring middle-class domesticity to her advantage. In contrast, Lutie's devotion to the canon of middle-class respectability, despite her lack of success with the directive that a lady "plays fair and works fair," attests to her powerlessness to achieve financial security while triply disadvantaged in society's race, gender, and class hierarchies.

Whereas Cleo attempts to reconcile the bourgeois and the folk in *The Living Is Easy*, Lutie's adoption of white materialism results in her familial and cultural alienation in *The Street*. She moves out of her father's home because he and his girlfriend, Lil, exemplify disparate moral values: "There seemed to be no part of it that wasn't full of Lil. She was always . . . trailing through all seven rooms in housecoats that didn't quite meet across her lush, loose bosom."[65] Lil's boundless lasciviousness offends Lutie's policing gaze, as Lutie characterizes Lil as all bodily excess and reveals herself to be all bourgeois asceticism.[66] Lutie tries to differentiate herself from the raw sensuality Lil embodies, but she moves from a bad situation to a worse one. Her apartment on 116th Street is where "respectable tenants . . . included anyone who could pay the rent. . . . The good people, the bad people . . . would all be wrapped up together in one big package—the package that was called respectable tenants."[67] Housing discrimination and economic exploitation erase the spatial and social boundaries between neighbors, and Lutie's new home places her in close quarters with additional women from whom she desires to distinguish herself, namely Mrs. Hedges and Min.

The black women on Lutie's street are like the "hustling women" pathologized in St. Clair Drake and Horace R. Cayton's study *Black Metropolis* (1945) who were more concerned with financial security than bourgeois morality during the interwar period.[68] Min and Mrs. Hedges are similarly "fallen" women in the race's pursuit of pedestal femininity. However, within the context of the street, Mrs. Hedges, who has never been married and commodifies black female sexuality, and Min, who has had a series of pseudo-husbands to help bear her economic burdens, function as alternative models for performing black female subjectivity. Mrs. Hedges is a monstrosity too big for her small southern town, and her northern migration scars her disfigured body physically and psychically. Initially believing that "if she had enough money she could pick out a man for herself," Mrs. Hedges eventually snubs the patriarchal politics of respectability and predatorily capitalizes on the single women who relieve their economic despair with prostitution. Lutie refuses Mrs. Hedges's propositions, but she soon realizes that the domestic ideal to which she aspires is "a fantastic structure made from the soft, nebulous, cloudy stuff of dreams. There hadn't been a solid, practical brick in it." She cannot afford a divorce and thus will never remarry. In contrast, Min constructs domestic spaces outside of middle-class frameworks and meets her monetary and emotional needs by cohabiting with men. Lutie derides Min as a "drudge so spineless and so limp she was like a soggy dishrag," but Min demonstrates blues woman grit, as Kimberly Drake contends, when she calls upon a conjurer to gain power over the abusive super.[69] Min utilizes a cross as well as a protection powder to stay in the super's apartment, and then she abandons him in anticipation of a better helpmate. As if singing the refrain of a blues song, she affirms, "A body's got the right to live." Her Africanisms are comparable to the mother-wit Lutie inherits from her grandmother. Yet Min's "low" culture improvisation of black female subjectivity is unacceptable to Lutie's middle-class ambitions, as Lutie categorizes her grandmother's acumen as "a lot of nonsense" antithetical to her dream for class advancement and racial assimilation.[70] Unbeknownst to her, Lutie's mother-wit helps her instinctively recognize the super as a sexual threat while the intervening acts of Min and Mrs. Hedges—though not enforcers of true womanhood—prevent him from raping her.

Ancestral wisdom and the street's vernacular culture would strengthen Lutie's communal ties, but she imagines prospering through solitary discipline and single-minded hard work. Petry suggests Lutie's vital need for black folk by juxtaposing the character's daydream about eighteenth-century white Philadelphian Benjamin Franklin with African American girls jumping double-dutch rope in modern Harlem. Lutie desires to join the girls and put down her burdens in the form of scant groceries she must stretch to satisfy several meals, but she chastises, "You'd better get dinner started, Ben Franklin." Her mental return to the white founding father demonstrates her subscription to myths of meritocracy rather than recuperative African American cultural traditions. However, the American Dream Franklin represents is less tangible than Lutie's inundation with dominant white discourses designed to capitalize on the black community's disenfranchisement. It is also less accessible than the abundance of black counterdiscourses conceived to salve the psychological effects of that exploitation. The street's "misery blues" are a composite of contradictory exhortations: radio commercials that encourage, "If you wanta be beautiful use Shirley Soap"; swing records bolstering, "Rock, Raleigh, Rock"; and church revivals promising, "This is the way, sisters and brothers. This is the answer. Come all of you now before it's too late."[71] This cacophony of materialist culture, which includes the secular and the sacred, conveys the exigency of blacks' self-determination. Petry gestures that it is difficult for consumers to differentiate which escapist discourse is invested in satiating, profiting, or commodifying the street.

Blues music in the novel is more than a metaphor for black women's oppressed social condition; it is an economic and psychological way for Lutie to flee the predations of the street. In an attempt to break away from her abject poverty, she indulges in the temporary escape consumerism provides by going to the neighborhood bar for a beer. What she experiences is a connection with the working-class black community when she absently sings along with a blues record playing. "There's no sun Darlin',"

Lutie laments, "There's no fun, Darlin'." The lyrics express her personal bourgeois blues of wanting and lacking, but her singing articulates the collective blues of the street. The record is "a story that all of them knew by heart and had always known because they had learned it soon after they were born and would go on adding to it until the day they died."[72] While the blues song narrates African Americans' experiential trauma, blues singing gives voice to black subjectivity in a white-dominated society that silences its speech-acts and denies its cultural value. In singing the blues, as in her dreams, Lutie leaves the oppressions of the street, and she bonds with the black community, which she undervalues. A less costly and transient form of escapism than consumerism, the blues, as Lindon Barrett argues, are "fully capable . . . of exposing, entering, and altering the dominant economy."[73] Lutie's singing mourns the lost domestic fantasy and critiques the racism and sexism that subjugate her. She briefly alters her reality as a budding blues artist instead of simply enduring her blues condition.

In *Lady Sings the Blues* Billie Holiday proffers the vernacular's recuperative possibilities for black women by narrating her journey from prostitute to "Lady Day." She recalls that she is sentenced to reform school when a man rapes her at age ten and that she first hears jazz while running errands in a brothel. Yet as Gerald Early explicates, the main gendered conflict in Holiday's memoir remains "her own persistent belief in ladyhood."[74] *Lady Sings the Blues* is saturated with coarse language that would traditionally exclude Holiday from true womanhood (she calls various women she dislikes "bitches"), but she also explains that she earned her professional moniker because she refused to bend over as she took customers' tips in the club where she danced. "The other girls used to try and mock me by calling me 'Lady,'" she reveals, "because they thought I thought I was just too damn grand." There is restorative dignity in the title "lady," but Holiday is conscious that the term is socially constructed. "Uptown a whore was a whore," she writes. "Downtown it was different—more complicated. A whore was sometimes a socialite."[75] Holiday cogently navigates the urban geographies of race, class, and sexuality despite her seeming contradictions, an assertion that Sherrie Tucker maintains "made the term *lady* cross the color line and transformed it to include a range of women traditionally excluded from the pedestal: women of color, women from poor families, women who cussed people out, women who were jazz singers."[76] The memoir presents Holiday as neither *either* nor *or* but *both*: she is a lady and a blues woman.

The narrative's juxtaposition of Holiday's jail time and drug abuse with her "Lady Day" persona is a lesson in improvising black womanhood. Serendipitously Holiday realizes the cultural and economic value of her singing voice when she vows to no longer perform sex or domestic work: "I was through turning tricks as a call girl. But I had also decided I wasn't going to be anybody's damn maid."[77] Refusing to commodify her body or, more important, relinquish control over its signification, she employs her voice and makes a lady out of jazz. She transforms it from "whorehouse" music into a genre with cultural and monetary worth. Holiday's singing also refines her as a lady. Her staging and performance of black womanhood with formal gowns, perfectly coiffed hair, and a flower accessory earn her the esteem of her audience and peers. She unsettles the typical gender division of labor in jazz music by collaborating with male musicians; she listened to the instrumentalists and vice versa as equally respected soloists in the band.[78] Holiday's self-representation as "Lady Day" on stage as well as in her memoir balances the scripts of middle-class respectability with the improvisations of jazz music.

Comparably in *The Street* Lutie glimpses new prospects for bourgeois respectability when she performs on stage and embodies the figure of a "blues lady." Blues musician Boots Smith and his male band mates initially dismiss Lutie as a singer because she is attractive. However, once Boots and the band share the stage with her, their musical collaboration dispels any presumption that she is simply a sexual conquest for Boots or an object of erotic consumption for the audience. The male instrumentalists demonstrate their respect for Lutie's talent as another soloist in the band by ceremoniously deferring to her. "It was an exaggerated gesture," the narrator describes, "for they bowed so far from the waist that for a moment all she could see were their backs—rounded and curved as they bent over."[79] A brief scene in the novel, this equitable gender exchange is an important one given the daily subjection Lutie experiences. It is one of the few times she collaborates with others, and it is also the first time that she is acknowledged for her merit. The men's public showing of reverence and the attention they direct toward her as a "blues lady" do not come at the cost of her objectification.

Lutie momentarily feels triumphant with the respect she receives as a blues singer, but her performance of black female subjectivity does not rival the erotic power classic blues women exhibit. Her investment in middle-class respectability prevents her from challenging society's signification of black female bodies as objects of desire, and it inhibits her from reclaiming her body as a desirous subject. As a result Lutie enter-tains Boots's romantic attention only to ensure a job with his band. She stops far short of sex or promises of it, but her efforts to secure permanent employment are notably strategic. Unaware that white gangster Junto's sexual interest dictates her singing career, Lutie is confident that she can manipulate Boots in a game of cat and mouse to her advantage with the principles of proper etiquette. She describes her interactions with men as progressing predictably like a multicourse meal during which only the quality of the silverware, napkins, and glasses differ. And as a single woman of propriety, she belabors how to effectively host such occasions. Because Boots appears to be "one of the thin glass, thick napkin, thin china, polished silver affairs," Lutie does not inform him of her estranged husband, celibacy, or son. Because she desires financial security and not the man, she carefully monitors the development of their symbolic repast: "The soup plate would be removed and the main course brought on. She always ducked before the main course was served, but this time she had to figure out how to dawdle with the main course, appear to welcome it, and yet not actually partake of it."[80] A euphemism for sex as well as a testament to her respectability, the dinner analogy lays out Lutie's intentions to orchestrate the exchange like a lady without being consumed like a promiscuous woman.

This tête-à-tête demonstrates Lutie's denial of the erotic and her polic-ing of her sexuality. When she realizes the disjuncture between how she conceives her intentions and how Boots perceives her actions, she criticizes the way she covets the singing job. She blames her economic need for propelling her to go carelessly "leaping and running into his car, emitting little cries of joy as she went. It hadn't occurred to her until this moment that from his viewpoint she was a pick-up girl."[81] Lutie's discon-nect reflects the historical shift from courting with the intention of mar-riage to the new sexual values and practices associated with social dating during the World War II era. Although Lutie has no intention of directly exchanging sex for money, indulging Boots engages in what Elizabeth Alice Clement calls "treating," a sexual bartering system that operates as a middle ground between prostitution and courtship.[82] Lutie's attempt to best Boots is different from Mrs. Hedges's exploitation of Mary, a deserted wife who learns from Mrs. Hedges not to give "free loving" and to demand money for sex.[83] Since Lutie is disadvantaged similarly in the street's sexual economy, she negotiates Boots's desire for her with the hope that she can dodge his advances and secure the job without offending him. In doing so she asserts a degree of sexual agency in spite of the street's targeted exploitation of single African American women. Still, Lutie is unable to express her sexuality outside the conscriptions of bourgeois respectability; social dating is not an option for her. Her intersecting race and gender oppressions firmly position her as an object of desire, one that Boots can manipulate and abuse.

Ultimately Lutie has no dominion over her singing career or the objectification of her body. Between the exploitative efforts of Mrs. Hedges, Junto, and Boots, Lutie is trapped in what Bill V. Mullen calls a "triangular sexual plantation."[84] Boots is the middleman in this affective blues economy. He defers payment for Lutie's singing and reneges on a loan so that she will succumb to Junto for the money she needs to get her son out of reform school. Consequently Boots is the final disavowal of Lutie's domestic fantasy. The disillusioned wife in Rainey's song "Misery Blues" laments, "Now I'm grievin', almost dyin' / Just because I didn't know that he was lyin'."[85] In *The Street* Lutie's "misery blues" are constantly present just below the surface of her consciousness, and they fully emerge once she realizes that Junto controls her fate. She finds herself "wanting to hum a tune and at the same time thinking about killing that man," but she kills Boots in self-defense when he physically tries to silence her voice—her "no"—with an attempted rape.[86] Boots's murder climactically thwarts Lutie's efforts to maintain bourgeois respectability; his blood stains her white gloves, which are her last anchor to ladyhood. In this moment she embodies the "blues lady."

By the novel's end Lutie has failed to resolve her bourgeois blues because she plays by the rules of middle-class respectability and works hard to meet the expectations of ladyhood. That is not to say that if she had acquiesced to Boots, slept with Junto, or prostituted herself for Mrs. Hedges, she and Bub would have obtained enough money to actualize her domestic fantasy in middle-class white suburbia. That is a highly doubtful alternate conclusion to Petry's novel given the text's naturalist elements. What Lutie's ill-fated ending affirms, then, is that abiding by the earmarks of respectability is a legitimate claim to agency in a historical moment when black women's sexuality is proscribed, their labor exploited, and their blues singing inevitably corrupted. If Lutie had no bourgeois desire, she would have fallen prey to the street long before. However, her commitment to the edicts of middle-class respectability too is a failed effort. The final image of Lutie on a bus to Chicago demonstrates her renewed resolve to resume her pursuit of pedestal femininity, though Chicago's social circumscriptions will not differ from those in New York. This final image intimates the ubiquitous quality of the blues for black identity and vernacular culture, which Amiri Baraka terms "the changing same."[87] Excluded from true white womanhood by systematic racism, sexism, and classism, Lutie is not naïve but remains convinced about the integrity of her performance as a respectable lady.

A Conversation among Black Women

Petry's and West's novels examine the disidentifying strategies mid-twentieth-century black women employed to define their liminal subjectivity between society's objectification of black female bodies and the pedestal figure of white femininity that negated them. Whereas Lutie is devoted to modeling middle-class respectability despite the various obstacles impeding her social mobility, Cleo exploits the rules of middle-class respectability in order to maintain her economic independence. Regardless, both women fail to actualize a domestic space in which they are empowered personally and can contribute to the black community's social uplift. Their utter alienation from the community—especially from other African American women—heightens their resultant bourgeois blues. Cleo strives to create a domestic space for black woman-making outside the racist gaze of whites and the patriarchal purview of black men, but her despotism makes her siblings long to return to the oppressive South and their impoverished lives with their husbands. In contrast, Lutie does not recognize the value of befriending black women even though her narrative is just another "note of resignation" in the street's collective blues compiled by abandoned wives and single mothers.[88] Lutie's alienation is a contributing factor and not the primary cause of her fate. However, she would have benefited from the counsel of other women at critical moments in the novel given her sexual and economic exploitation: a conversation with Min, who suspects the super's predatory intentions; a parlay with Mrs. Hedges, who is a co-conspirator with Junto; or a sit-down with another estranged wife, who might have told Lutie that freeing Bub did not require borrowing money to pay for a lawyer.

Lutie and Cleo sing the bourgeois blues, but neither shares classic blues women's commitment to offering the benefit of their experience or taking direction from the know-how of other women. The dialectic between the singing subject and the imagined community of listeners connects black women along the continuum of womanhood—from respectable lady to wild woman—by way of the blues' intimate confession and self-reflective instruction. As Davis explains, this "aesthetic community" emerges when blues women exchange stories and advice with their "sisters" about their relations with men.[89] In her song "Lady Sings the Blues," Billie Holiday expresses the catharsis found in articulating women's blues troubles for both the singing subject and the avid listener: "Lady sings the Blues / I'm tellin' you / She's got 'em bad." The lyrics create a figurative confidence between Holiday's "I" and the listening "you," as the singer conveys that the blues condition is no longer a burden to the song's heartbroken lady or Holiday's audience of kindred women. "But now the world will know / She's never gonna sing them no more."[90] The song narrates the story of its female constituents and gives them a talking cure. If Lutie were able to continue singing the blues, she would have benefited from voicing her troubles and gained insight from the counsel of other black women. Cleo gives an abundance of unsolicited advice, but she is a one-note record when it comes to black heterosexual relationships. Although her savoir-faire helps her master the vernacular's ambiguities, she lacks the understanding to recognize the noncontradictory oppositions of sexual desire. Cleo and Lutie live the blues, and yet they cannot realize the full potential of the blues aesthetic as storytellers, singers, or bearers of oral histories. *The Street* and *The Living Is Easy* bear witness to the importance of aesthetic communions rooted in the vernacular.

Petry and West engage an intertextual, intergenerational, and cross-class dialogue as their works consider the gendered discourse of mid-twentieth-century African American social realist literature. Both writers explore the bourgeois blues as a metaphor for the evolving construction of black female subjectivity during the interwar period, and their novels demonstrate black women writers' distinct contribution to the aesthetic shifts in this literary landscape. Petry refines the conventions of the protest novel in order to envision black women's agency in the context of their disenfranchisement, and West reconceptualizes social protest by setting black women's remonstrations within middle-class domesticity. Each writer uses her respective genre to propose a bourgeois and feminine alternative to the working-class black male protagonist traditionally found in the protest novel and the migration narrative. Petry and West are in conversation with each other as well as with their contemporary Wright, with whom literary critics liken mid-twentieth-century African American writers in an attempt to situate their work (as in Petry's case) or to tease out their differing politics (as in West's case). Both Petry and West, however, depict more nuanced representations of black women in regard to the blues trope than does the more celebrated black male writer.

Wright defines his figurative blues woman by her stagnant social condition, not her fluid performance of subjectivity. In his depictions of black women's relationship to the vernacular, the blues woman is as socially immobilized in the North as she is culturally fixed in the South. For example, Maria K. Mootry characterizes Bessie's Chicago blues love for Bigger in *Native Son* as "undemanding, with no expectations, laced with pain and an acute sense of *temporariness*."[91] In Wright's autobiography *Black Boy* (1945), he encounters a woman named Bess who is eager to marry him presumably because he has manners. On his way to Chicago by way of Memphis, Wright is disenchanted with Bess's lack of critical consciousness: she "had no tensions, unappeasable longings, no desire to do something to redeem [herself]."[92] Bessie and Bess essentially share the same name and malaise due to their blues condition. Neither inhabits the dynamism of Cleo's gendered performance or the self-possession of Lutie's "blues lady." In fact Wright's blues aesthetic emphasizes his masculinist individualism. His "black boy," as Ellison argues in his review "Richard Wright's Blues" (1945), must transition from a collective to an individual consciousness in order to become the emergent writer. Wright's blues expose the black collective's complicity, especially black women, in white society's emasculation of black men.[93]

In contrast, the bourgeois blues in *The Street* and *The Living Is Easy* acknowledge the conflict between black women's desire for middle-class white respectability and their inevitable exclusion from it in a culture bound by Jane Crow politics. Black women's multivalent oppression creates a disabling culture in which black men are complicit. The bourgeois blues aesthetic criticizes black women's privileging of individualism over communal ties and the cultural connections between African American women. Hence Petry's and West's novels are not bookends to the gendered blues discourse initiated by black women writers of the Harlem Renaissance. Black women writers publishing after the Black Arts Movement like Toni Morrison and Gayl Jones return to the blues aesthetic when exploring black female subjectivity and sexual trauma. Jones literally and figuratively employs the blues to structure her nonlinear narrative *Corregidora* (1975), while Morrison's titular protagonist in *Sula* (1973) is characterized as dangerous because she has no art form with which to express the erotic. Repositioning mid-twentieth-century African American literary production within a genealogy of women writers is pivotal for recognizing interwar contributions to the tradition. The period manifests the tensions between black female sexuality and middle-class respectability, and its Jane Crow texts explore the mythology of pedestal femininity for both middle-class and working-class black women.

3 / "Nobody Could Tell Who This Be": Black and White Doubles and the Challenge to Pedestal Femininity

The female body in the West is not a unitary sign. Rather, like a coin, it has an obverse and a reverse: on the one side, it is white; on the other, not-white or, prototypically, black. The two bodies cannot be separated, nor can one body be understood in isolation from the other in the West's metaphoric construction of "woman." White is what woman is; not-white (and the stereotypes not-white gathers in) is what she had better not be.

—LORRAINE O'GRADY, "OLYMPIA'S MAID: RECLAIMING
BLACK FEMALE SUBJECTIVITY"

Despite the historically entrenched social and political divisions between black and white women, Zora Neale Hurston's and Ann Petry's works wrestle with Jane Crow oppression by signifying on the ironic congruity between the seemingly privileged and the institutionally disenfranchised. For example, in Petry's short story "The Bones of Louella Brown" (1947), the exhumed bodies of the titular black laundress and a white countess are so indistinguishable that they are reburied together. Initially Louella is laid to rest in the outskirts of the all-white Yew Tree Cemetery at the behest of her white female employer, whose charge intimates a gender alliance between the two women regardless of their race and class differences.[1] Louella's plot eventually claims a prime location as the cemetery's grounds expand, and the current owners plan to move her corpse back to the periphery while also transferring the Countess of Castro to an exclusive mausoleum. When the staff confuses the two bodies, the owners realize there is no visible distinction between the women. Both the laundress and the countess have "a very neat set of bones," "thick glossy black hair," and their own teeth. They never had children, and they are buried within two weeks of each other in 1902.[2] Every white male with the power to classify the racial and gendered Other (from scientist to state governor) expresses his consternation with the women's similitude: "Nobody could tell who this be."[3] No one can differentiate the two bodies in order to return them to their segregated final resting places, and the cemetery is forced to bury the women together in the countess's vault. "Here lies Elizabeth, Countess of Castro or Louella

Brown, Gentlewoman," the burial plaque reads. "They both wore the breastplate of faith and love; And for a helmet, the hope of salvation."[4] The story's closing words affirm that the women's undying partnership is modern society's deliverance.

The resolute statement regarding the nobility of black femininity in "The Bones of Louella Brown" vividly exemplifies the deconstruction of racial hierarchies and gender binaries in Hurston's novel *Seraph on the Suwanee* (1948) and Petry's novel *The Narrows* (1953). While the final words of Petry's short story imply that the redemption of racist society lies in acknowledging the eternal unity of black and white women, Hurston and Petry also recognize the significance of racial and class difference in their respective bodies of work. Specifically *Seraph on the Suwanee* and *The Narrows* represent the interchangeability of racialized, classed, and gendered bodies in an attempt to demystify the pedestal figure of femininity as white. Hence the novels debunk the stereotypical image of black women as wanton and intractable. Petry and Hurston problematize constructions of white female subjectivity as a "unitary sign," to draw on Lorraine O'Grady's theory of black female subjectivity, and thus refute the fictions of true womanhood singly casting white women as chaste, refined, and estimable.[5]

For their mid-twentieth-century publishing moment, *Seraph* and *The Narrows* are provocative in terms of their content and genre. Hurston crosses the Jim Crow color line in her last work by writing a "white-plot" novel that concentrates on the trials and tribulations of her white female protagonist. Arvay Henson Meserve's insecurity about her impoverished rural background troubles her relationship with her entrepreneurial husband, Jim, and their socially mobile children. However, her fears regarding her inferiority also surface in her exchanges with those race, class, and ethnic Others she deems her social inferiors. After losing her children to their adult lives and alienating her spouse with disaffection, Arvay submits to Jim's authority and commits to maternal love in service to her husband at the end of the novel. *Seraph* primarily focuses on their marital union, but Hurston also invokes the artist-and-patron relationship characteristic of the Harlem Renaissance, which clearly demarcates racial and class hierarchies. At the same time the commensurability of black and white female bodies as targets of patriarchal subjection in *Seraph* intimates that "nobody could tell who this [woman] be." Hurston connects *Seraph*'s secondary black and ethnic female characters to Arvay by their lack of underwear at critical moments in the text, which symbolizes the vulnerability of all women's sexual difference.

In a complementary project aimed at dismantling racial boundaries, Petry extends the themes in "The Bones of Louella Brown" and juxtaposes elite white, middle-class black, and working-class black women in her final adult novel, *The Narrows*. Petry's black male protagonist Lincoln "Link" Williams has an undergraduate degree in history, but he falls victim to its legacy when he has an affair with the married, rich, and white Camilla Treadway Sheffield, who goes under the assumed name Camilo Williams. Link attempts to escape the limitations placed upon him by his adopted mother Abbie Crunch's bourgeois expectations. Yet he cannot avoid the repercussions of Camilo's false rape accusation spurred by her mistaken belief that he is carrying on with married, working-class, and black Mamie Powther. Petry criticizes racial taboos in *The Narrows* when Camilo's family murders Link, essentially for loving her. The writer further unsettles class and racial hierarchies with the condemnation Link's female constituents express about each other's gender performance. Meanwhile these distinctly raced, differently classed women are virtually undifferentiated in his masculinist gaze. Link deems Camilo, Abbie, and Mamie as guilty too in his demise.

The central conflict propelling *The Narrows* is an interracial romance, whereas the main storyline of *Seraph* is a cross-class romance. However, a secondary motif regarding the exigency of interracial and cross-class bonds between women undergirds both novels. Neither the white-plot focus of *Seraph* nor the integrated cast of *The Narrows* features a fully realized black female protagonist or materializes feminist alliances. Nonetheless both novels explore black and white women's subjugation under Jane Crow racism and sexism as well as women's collusion with such oppressive politics. *Seraph* tacitly addresses Jane Crow's proscriptions by exploring white women's investment in whiteness, which makes them complicit in black women's multivalent oppression. Analogously, by depicting middle-class black women's investment in modeling respectable white womanhood, *The Narrows* highlights their shared complicity in working-class black women's class and sexual oppression. In complicating the boundaries between black and white, middle-class and working-class women, Hurston and Petry expose the socially constructed power and privilege of white femininity. Together they map the homosocial complexities of Jane Crow politics.

The excogitation of whiteness in the African American literary tradition provokes critical debates regarding black writers' obligation to confront "the Negro problem," especially during the heyday of social realism, when an emergent modern civil rights movement heightened

Jim Crow tensions. In *The Negro Novelist* (1953) Carl Milton Hughes recognizes the series of white-plot novels published after World War II by both rising and celebrated black writers as a welcome return to the study of whiteness began as early as Charles W. Chesnutt's novel *The Colonel's Dream* (1905). The critic viewed the recovery of white character–driven novels as a much-needed quieting of the black writer's sociopolitical rallying. For example, one of the most prolific yet understudied African American writers of the mid-twentieth century, Frank Yerby, set his first novel, *The Foxes of Harrow* (1946), among the white aristocracy of the antebellum South. Yerby wrote eleven novels over the next ten years and published at least twenty more until the 1980s. Similarly Willard Motley's first novel, *Knock on Any Door* (1947), explores the urban struggles of ethnic whites; two years later Hollywood translated Motley's novel into a film of the same title starring Humphrey Bogart. In addition to the writers who initiated their careers with the white-plot novel, several of the period's established writers shifted from images of blackness to portraits of whiteness. Hurston, renowned for her folk contributions to the Harlem Renaissance, wrote *Seraph*. After his semi-autobiographical novel *Go Tell It on the Mountain* (1953), James Baldwin subsumed racial difference in his depiction of a Parisian homosexual affair between a white American and his Italian lover in *Giovanni's Room* (1956). Finally, Petry and Wright, who are distinguished by their employment of naturalist conventions, wrote texts centered on white male protagonists: *Country Place* (1947) and *Savage Holiday* (1954), respectively.

For contemporaneous literary critics like Hughes, a thematic focus on whiteness broadened the black writer's racial perspective and universalized his or her subject matter. "Writing a white life novel was thought to have a liberating effect," Robert Fikes Jr. clarifies, "releasing [the black writer] on parole from a literary ghetto and permitting him to focus on 'art' relieved of distracting ethnic concerns."[6] Exclusive treatments of whiteness offered black writers creative sovereignty (freeing Yerby, for example, from contemplating slavery in depth in his historical novels). Moreover white-plot novels gave black writers access to mainstream audiences, including white moviegoers who promised commercial success. For the African American writer, regardless of generic forte, foregrounding white protagonists was a type of creative emancipation as well as a kind of literary assimilation. When one also considers the gender politics of black writing and white publishing, one notices that white characters enabled black women writers to ignore the tacit mandates of the black literary tradition and to privilege female identity in their use of white characters.[7] *Seraph* reflects Hurston's desire to broker a movie deal and her "revisionary ambition" to rewrite *Their Eyes Were Watching God* (1937), as Claudia Tate argues, with a gender critique of romantic love, which Hurston could not address within the latter novel's black context.[8]

In novels that foreground black characters, the inclusion of secondary white characters allows African American writers to define black subjectivity while deconstructing whiteness. Toni Morrison demonstrates in *Playing in the Dark* (1992) that minor black characters function as an imagined Africanism to shape (and equate) ideals of rightness and whiteness in American literature. Conversely, minor white characters in mid-twentieth-century African American texts signal black disenfranchisement and critique whites' moral, spiritual, and cultural bankruptcy. Representations of white women are particularly crucial to this social commentary, as their bodies typically serve as signifiers of black male subjugation or harbingers of black men's death. Like Mary Dalton, whose murder incites the police and the press to pathologize black men as beasts in Wright's novel *Native Son* (1940), Madge in Chester Himes's novel *If He Hollers Let Him Go* (1945) triggers the myth of the black male rapist. First, Madge asks Himes's protagonist Bob Jones to "rape" her in their consensual sex act as part of her sexual fantasy; then she falsely accuses him of rape as retaliation for his rejection. *Native Son* ends with Bigger Thomas's execution, while Himes's novel concludes with Bob's sentencing to the army and quite possibly his death. Similarly Ralph Ellison parodies white women's duplicity as white men's victim and black men's victimizer in his novel *Invisible Man* (1952). When an intoxicated Sybil discloses her rape fantasy to Ellison's black male protagonist, he leaves her unconscious after writing on her stomach that she has been raped by Santa Claus. The joke is on Sybil, as Santa Claus is as much a myth as the invisible man is a rapist. In *The Narrows* Link and Camilo's romance precipitates rather than averts his murder when he ends their affair. However, for Petry's black female characters in the novel, Camilo apes black women's racial subjection and underscores the novel's intersecting race and gender politics.

Highlighting the racism and patriarchy constructing idealized portraits of white femininity, Hurston and Petry dispute black women's exclusion from the cult of true womanhood and question white women's exclusive membership. The writers demonstrate in their respective novels that there is little distance between the white pedestal figure and that on which it is built: black women. The "woman" construct, as O'Grady writes, is "like a coin, it has an obverse and a reverse: on one side, it is white; on the other, not white or, prototypically, black."[9] In *Seraph* black, white, and ethnic women are linked in a chain of signification, tied together by their sexual oppression in a culture that privileges white masculinity. Hurston explores white women's gender oppression in patriarchal society, but she also queries white women's dependence on a racialized artist-patron dynamic. This hierarchical exchange reinforces black women's occlusion from respectable womanhood despite claims that such artistic and economic associations defied Jim Crow segregation during the Harlem Renaissance. Likewise in *The Narrows* elite white, middle-class black, and working-class black women are sometimes doubles, sometimes mirrors for each other. Petry's comparison of middle-class black and elite white women boldly calls attention to their shared misguided attachment to the racist and patriarchal ideals of middle-class white femininity. *The Narrows* criticizes both black and white women's maintenance of racial and class hierarchies, as their devaluing of gender allegiances contributes to Link's death and subjugates working-class black women like Mamie.

In effect both black women writers discard the conventions of the protest novel, which focuses on race, and they subvert fixed conceptualizations of black and white women, which perpetuate reductive gender and racial binaries. Elizabeth Schultz observes that American novels depicting black and white women typically rely upon the "paradigm of mistress and servant, victimizer and victim, with only an occasional reversal which converts the historical victim to victimizer, the historical victimizer to victim."[10] Hurston and Petry engage neither dialectic in *Seraph* or *The Narrows*. Instead they rewrite such tropes by looking at the parity between black and white, middle-class and working-class women in addition to the historical divides between them. It is perhaps no surprise, then, that *Seraph* and *The Narrows* are among Hurston's and Petry's less critically engaged texts, as the novels do not abide by the characteristics of early twentieth-century black literary production that established both women's writing careers. That is to say, the writers diverge from representing the black folk reveled in during the Harlem Renaissance and the working-class masses exalted after the Depression.

To appreciate the politics in Hurston's white-plot novel and Petry's integrationist text is also to understand the politics influencing the critical reception of the black woman writer during the social realist era. *Seraph*'s obscurity in African American literary histories reflects the deliberate crafting of this tradition; the novel's slight reveals the genre conventions shaping the nature of its author's canonicity. Hurston's

"New Negro" treatments of black folk are unquestioned as significant contributions to African American literature. However, the Hurston who writes about whiteness after World War II still remains, to some extent, unrecovered. Comparably the success of Petry's first novel, *The Street*, is unrivaled by the critical engagement of her later work. Despite publishing three adult novels during the heyday of social realism (she produced two texts of young adult fiction and a collection of short stories afterward), the relative neglect of Petry in comparison to Hurston evidences the invisibility of the black woman writer after the Harlem Renaissance and prior to the Black Arts Movement. The demotion of *Seraph* and *The Narrows* in Hurston's and Petry's oeuvres suggests that the Jane Crow politics of mid-twentieth-century black literary production obscure both writers' commitment to confronting racism and sexism throughout their careers. Hurston is fixed as a Harlem Renaissance writer, and Petry's withdrawal from personal celebrity after *The Street* is uncontested by the limited literary criticism on her subsequent work. Granted, neither writer resolves the racial and gender tensions in her fiction. Arvay Meserve refuses to step out of her position of power as a white woman in *Seraph*, and Abbie Crunch models middle-class white femininity to her detriment in *The Narrows*. However, both novels infer the potential of interracial, cross-class feminist bonds under Jane Crow; they also exemplify black women writers' challenge to the tenets of social realism.

Patronage and Subjection in *Seraph on the Suwanee*

From her first published short story, "Drenched in Light" (1924), to her final novel, *Seraph on the Suwanee*, Hurston's work depicts how bodies of black art are esteemed and devalued alternately in American culture. In the afterword to her autobiography, *Dust Tracks on a Road* (1942), Henry Louis Gates Jr. contends, "Hurston *wrote* herself, and sought in her works to rewrite the 'self' of 'the race,' in its several private and public guises."[11] Hurston ponders her subject position as a black female artist and the problematic of the performing black body in "Drenched in Light," in which the young black female protagonist Isie dances in her grandmother's tablecloth for white tourists. Hurston culminates this problematic in *Seraph*, in which eight-year-old Belinda Kelsey performs for money without underwear. As in these works of fiction, Hurston differentiates between a private folk art and the public's commodification of it in her nonfiction texts: her personal essay "How It Feels to Be Colored

Me" (1928), collection of folktales *Mules and Men* (1935), and autobiography *Dust Tracks*. These works fix the writer, Barbara Johnson contends, as a "threshold figure," a black female artist straddling segregated black and white audiences.[12] Hurston's goal as a writer and anthropologist is to document the contributions of black folk art to American culture, but her body of work also contemplates the censure, misappropriation, and subjugation of the threshold figure. She distinguishes between the black artist's product and creative process in *Mules and Men* when she writes that the white spectator "can read my writing but he sho' can't read my mind."[13] In addition to the discursive gulf between subject and interlocutor, racial and gender politics affect the exchanges between black artist and white patron in Hurston's fictional and autobiographical depictions of herself.

Despite the Harlem Renaissance's agenda to attain racial equality and to exhibit African Americans' humanity in the literary and visual arts, Hurston's collaboration with her white patron, Charlotte Osgood Mason, maintained the traditional social hierarchies engendering racism and patriarchy.[14] White patrons wanted to control the artist and his or her art to ensure that they—with all the economic and erotic connotations Ralph D. Story's choice words conjure—"got what they paid for."[15] Marlon B. Ross explains in *Manning the Race* that relationships between black male artists and white female patrons were fraught with racial tensions that were compounded by conventional gender roles and an artistic ardor patterning heterosexual libidos. In comparison Hurston's portrayal of the homosocial intricacies between black and white women manifests the patron's more ambivalent desires: to imbibe the black artist's talent and yet to differentiate herself from black women. Hurston magnifies the power differential in the black-white, artist-patron binary with representations of the black female artist as a child. Whereas the innocent child-artist retains creative integrity in her art, the motivations of the adult patron oscillate between engaging in philanthropy, affirming her whiteness, and subjugating the racial and classed Other.

Hurston initiates this discussion of the racial and gender tensions between artist and patron in "Drenched in Light," in which Isie finds a sponsor to support her craft despite her grandmother's censoring efforts. Markedly Hurston valorizes the white female patron in the short story published during the Harlem Renaissance. However, she amends her position in *Seraph*, which is set during the Depression and was published after World War II. The novel projects the social politics dividing black and white women onto the artist-patron collaboration and reconsiders white women's ability to "appreciate" their racial and class Others. *Seraph* primarily explores the marital conflicts between Arvay and Jim Meserve, but Hurston uses the couple's whiteness to examine gender oppression in the context of Arvay's parity with black, ethnic, and working-class women. The writer represents the interaction between artist and patron as mutually beneficial to both the black child and the white woman in "Drenched in Light." Be that as it may, Arvay's investment in whiteness makes her a poor patron for the black child-artist in *Seraph* as well as a reluctant ally to ethnic and working-class women.

In "Drenched in Light" Hurston contrasts a white woman's maternal patronage of a black child with the familial censure of black art. As the story's threshold figure, Isie sits at the gatepost watching white travelers on the road to Orlando while her grandmother criticizes, "You'se too 'oomanish jumpin' up in everybody's face dat pass." The grandmother fears that the child's curiosity may be read as not so innocent. Isie's dancing at a local carnival brings these concerns to fruition when her grandmother finds her standing in the middle of a "gaping" audience, costumed in a new red tablecloth, "reeking" of lemon extract, and danc-ing like a gypsy. Isie's first transgression is shirking her domestic duties to attend the carnival, and then her dancing body is clothed in exotic sexuality. Before her grandmother can punish her for the spectacle, a traveling white female spectator offers to pay for the soiled tablecloth. The new patron also requests an encore: "The little thing loves laughter. I want her to go on to the hotel and dance in that table-cloth for me. I can stand a little light today."[16]

The white female spectator reimburses Isie's grandmother for the ruined tablecloth, but, more important, she purchases a body of black folk culture. The monetary exchange between the grandmother and the woman implies that Isie is commodified and culturally appropriated at the same time that she is esteemed and valued. The patron explains, "I want brightness and this Isis is joy itself, why she's drenched in light!" Her emphasis on light denies Isie's association with darkness or being a "darky." Furthermore the story suggests the equability of the cultural exchange between the child-artist and her patron. Isie obtains finan-cial support for her art, but the woman's male companion jokes that Isie has adopted *her*. "Ah'm gointer stay wid you all," Isie tells her new benefactress. Pleased by the thought of being tied permanently to black culture, the white woman ends "Drenched in Light" affirming that she has discovered a source from which to absorb black folk: "I want a little of [Isie's] sunshine to soak into my soul. I need it."[17] While the woman's needy desire for light signals her latent desire *for* Isie and to *be* Isie, the grandmother's desire to make Isie presentable for the public performance indicates the potential for the girl's misappropriation. Thus the story celebrates the role of the white patron, but it also gestures toward the consequences of whites' adoption of black folk. Given the woman's racial desire and cultural lack, Isie's folk art is subjected potentially to whites' love and theft.[18]

Hurston retells the story of a curious girl at the gatepost in her personal essay "How It Feels to Be Colored Me" and autobiography *Dust Tracks*. In the essay Hurston recalls that as a child-artist she offered to "speak pieces" and "dance the parse-me-la" for white tourists and received unsolicited coins in exchange. She also remembers that "the colored people gave no dimes" because they "deplored any joyful tendencies in [her]."[19] Her performance unsettles the protection an all-black community provides from economic, cultural, and sexual exploitation, and its refusal to patronize the writer is an unwillingness to participate in her commodification. In *Dust Tracks* Hurston explains that she volunteered to "go a piece of the way" with white travelers who passed her gatepost, admitting that it "must have caused a great deal of amusement among them."[20] In this version of the gatepost story, Hurston's deliberate assertion that she initiated these interactions confirms her agency, for she adds, "My self-assurance must have carried the point, for I was always invited to come along."[21] As E. Patrick Johnson warns about the racial politics of performance, Hurston's repetition of the gatepost in her short story, essay, and autobiography bids the black community "to be cognizant of the arbitrariness of authenticity, the ways in which it carries with it the dangers of foreclosing the possibilities of cultural exchange and understanding."[22] Yet a black child journeying with white travelers, to use Carole Boyce Davies's graphic imagery, possibly "means taking a route cluttered with skeletons, enslavements, new dominations, unresolved tensions and contradictions."[23] Hurston's parents punish her for such precarious encounters, and her grandmother cautions, "Setting up dere looking dem white folks right in de face! . . . Youse too brazen to live long."[24] Scared that the child will enact a powerful black subjectivity in the presence of whites, Hurston's grandmother voices the black community's concern for safeguarding the child's racial and gender identity.

Hurston presents whites' patronage of the joyful and talented child-artist positively in both her fiction and autobiographical writing despite blacks' critique. However, in *Dust Tracks* the writer's brief depiction of her patron casts doubt on Mason's genuine admiration of black culture.

While Hurston's notorious lies about her age imply that her threshold figure's innocence cannot be taken literally, her self-representation in her memoir also mitigates the authenticity of her adult folk performances. Her characterization of her relationship with Mason accordingly wavers between proclaiming the psychic bond the writer shared with her "God-mother" and detailing the critical subjection she endured under her scrutiny. *Dust Tracks'* characterization of Mason is aligned with depictions of white female patrons "mothering" black artists with cultural, spiritual, and social guidance in order to offset the "gender-bending irregularities," as Ross contends, associated with women patrons.[25] Mason's paternalistic letters to Hurston intuitively accuse "You have broken the law!" when the writer supposedly disobeys her rules, and the women's direct encounters make the writer "feel like a rabbit at a dog convention." Moreover Mason's desire for authentic primitivism demands that Hurston "tell the tales, sing the songs, do the dances, and repeat the raucous sayings and doings of the Negro farthest down" upon her return from research trips.[26] Nathan Huggins argues that it is difficult to discern "who was being fooled" in *Dust Tracks*, as the writer who had been known for "putting on an act . . . had become the act."[27] Yet Mason's financial support and contractual ownership of Hurston's findings undoubtedly determined the various layers of Hurston's "act" as well as her rendering of the artist-patron exchange throughout her oeuvre.

With its subtle critique of this dynamic, *Seraph* pivots Hurston's discourse regarding the interplay of black and white women's performances of race and gender. Contemporary critics label *Seraph* Hurston's most unsuccessful and disappointing work, but the novel's racial politics makes it an important text with which to consider her gender discourse.[28] In turn the novel's gender politics makes it a critical text with which to think about Hurston's racial commentary. Still, *Seraph*'s move away from Hurston's traditional black focus and its less than empowering female protagonist has determined its anomalous position in the African American literary tradition.[29] "Apparently, Zora wrote this strange book to prove that she was capable of writing about white people," Mary Helen Washington opines.[30] It is particularly difficult for critics to reconcile the ambiguities of the white-plot novel with Hurston's long-standing efforts to document black folk culture. Susan Edwards Meisenhelder points out that *Seraph*'s protagonist Arvay is essentially "the white woman 'settin' on the porch' Nanny romanticized and naively wanted Janie to be" in *Their Eyes Were Watching God*.[31] Although Janie cannot sit high like Arvay, Arvay is also no Janie. Arvay concludes her narrative on the ocean's horizon, embracing traditional wifely duties and universal motherhood. She does not reach the proto-feminist conclusion Janie attains when the latter returns to Eatonville alone—after having shot a rabid Tea Cake—and pulls in the horizon as though in a big fish net.

This intertextual dialogue between Hurston's black feminist text and her white-plot novel highlights the writer's intersection of race and gender politics in *Seraph*. Ann duCille notes that black men as well as white men exhibit patriarchal ideologies in both novels, but she contends that Hurston's emulation of white women's romantic fiction in *Seraph* allows her to complicate the text's representation of sexuality.[32] Whereas Tea Cake beats Janie to prove his masculinity to a color-struck Mrs. Turner in *Their Eyes Were Watching God*, Jim labels marital sex "rape" in *Seraph* to maintain dominance in his marriage. Tea Cake's domestic abuse unnerves readers' starry-eyed idolization of him, but his actions do not irreparably tarnish his luster as Janie's ideal romantic interest in the novel.[33] On the contrary, the sexual violence discussed in *Seraph* rarely appears in African American literature prior to the Black Women Writers' Renaissance of the 1970s and 1980s due to black women's sexual vulnerability during and after slavery.[34] Both black and white women's rape accusations were systematically discredited until the women's movement. However, masculinist white social structures frequently legitimized white women's allegations of rape against black men, effectively reinforcing white supremacy, ideals of racial purity, and patriarchy, while such structures disavowed interracial sexual violence targeting black women, essentially denying blacks' subjectivity. Black women's discriminate historical experience of rape nonetheless informs *Seraph*'s discourse on configured white femininity, as Arvay struggles with her husband's race, class, and gender privilege.

More specifically *Seraph*'s construction of white femininity forwards the text's heterosexual romance while undermining interracial and cross-class homosocial bonds. Arvay's bigoted investment in middle-class whiteness encourages her to deny her own gender oppression. Hurston signals Arvay's subjection with the character's missing underwear and rape, and she links Arvay to a series of racialized secondary female characters: Belinda, the black female child-artist who bares her naked behind; Lucy Ann Corregio, the daughter of a Portuguese laborer who is physically assaulted; and Fast Mary, the derided town prostitute who flashes her private parts. Because her poor and rural background threatens her whiteness, Arvay rejects her kinship with these raced and classed women in order to embody the pedestal figure of femininity and manage her cross-class marriage. "We ain't nothing but piney-woods Crackers and poor white trash. Even niggers," she complains to Jim, whose ancestors owned a plantation, "is better than we is, according to your kind."[35] In a letter to Burroughs Mitchell, Hurston reassures the Scribner editor that her portrait of aspiring white femininity is authentic. Though Arvay's racial epithet likely offended black readers, the writer explains, "I know, as they know honestly, that the heroine would have certainly used that word."[36]

In Arvay's understanding of race, blackness is the antithesis of a privileged subjectivity, and subjects with "legitimate" claims to whiteness exclude "unsuitable" groups such as poor whites, ethnic immigrants, and immoral bodies. However, in *Seraph*'s Depression-era context, whiteness is perceived increasingly as a racial monolith including various ethnicities. The term *race*, as Matthew Frye Jacobson explicates, was defined as a white-black racial dichotomy, in which "race itself was recast as color."[37] Arvay cleaves to the antiquated idea of stratified white races while affirming her own racial privilege—in spite of her class background—through her distinction from African Americans and racialized whites. Because she believes her whiteness is probationary, her prejudices betray what Chuck Jackson identifies as a "cultural paranoia" about the purity and morality of intraracial difference.[38] In another letter to Mitchell, Hurston admits, "I get sick of her at times myself. Have you ever been tied in close contact with a person who had a strong sense of inferiority? I have, and it is hell."[39] Arvay's insecurities strain her marriage as well as inhibit her interracial homosocial relationships.

Many of Arvay's conflicts with her husband emerge from her lack of racial confidence, which is crippled by Jim's disregard of rigid interracial and intraracial boundaries as a white male subject. Described as "black Irish," Jim enjoys social privilege despite his close association with black laborers.[40] In fact his interracial relationships are the basis for his white male subjectivity as the patron to Joe Kelsey, his "pet Negro." Joe is critical to Jim's identity as a capitalist entrepreneur and patriarchal husband. He encourages Jim to make Arvay "knuckle under" her husband's dominance, and he manages the black workers who build Jim's homestead, distillery, and citrus grove. Arvay, as a result, views Joe as her rival for her husband's affections. "You give him more credit for sense then you do me," she moans. "All I'm good for is to lay up in the bed with you and satisfy your feelings and do around here for you." She fears that Jim and Joe's interracial homosocial bond threatens her wifely influence;

however, Joe's subjection as a "pet Negro" mocks Arvay's degradation as her husband's "pet angel."[41]

Similarly the Meserves' sons embody *Seraph*'s racial politics and confirm Arvay's gender oppression. Arvay's youngest child, Kenny, is "the spitting image of Jim. Couldn't have been anymore like Jim if Jim had spit him out of his mouth," but her oldest son, Earl, resembles her "queer" Uncle Chester and, for her, evidences her questionable whiteness. Jim and Arvay's first premarital sexual encounter, which is referred to as a rape in the novel, appears responsible for Earl's physical defects and bestial behaviors. With her torn underwear hanging from a tree, Arvay feels defiled by the act, whereas Jim claims her as his bride after the exploit. "You're going to keep on getting raped," he promises. When their first-born assaults the Portuguese Lucy Ann Corregio, the attack signifies upon Earl's conception. Emphasizing that white men commit sexual violence too, the two assaults displace the racialized myth of the black male rapist. Additionally the assaults underline the commonalities between white and black women as victims of sexual violence. Arvay prejudicially refers to the Corregios as "those Gees," but Lucy Ann epitomizes white femininity in her violation, while Earl assumes the role of the rapacious white male. His bites to her neck, hands, and thighs incite a posse to protect her, "a clean-living, pretty white girl," and other vulnerable white women. Earl symbolizes, then, the patriarchal violence directed at all women—including Arvay, who is "attacked ferociously" when nursing him. Yet the posse shoots Earl when he targets Jim with his aggression. Earl's death confirms Arvay's expulsion from privileged white subjectivity, as she constantly feels she and her son are "shut off in loneliness, by themselves."[42]

Arvay is afraid that her "cracker" background will manifest itself in Kenny because of Earl's depravity. Just as Jim's economic exploitation of black bodies characterizes his subjectivity, Kenny's appropriation of black folk culture defines his whiteness.[43] The similarities between father and son materialize when an eight-year-old Kenny encourages Belinda Kelsey to perform a handstand for white travelers. To the audience's shock the trick not only displays Belinda's skill but also her naked bottom: "Belinda was innocent of underwear. She was there on her head, . . . with her shining little black behind glinting in the sun." This staging of subjection exhibits not black culture but the black female body itself: its vulnerability and, to some, its vulgarity. Kenny figures if they will pay a quarter to see Belinda perform, they will pay more to stop witnessing the transgression. Bartering to "turn her down," he collects over nine dollars in Belinda's skirt. The children's ingenious spectacle shames Arvay, but the act affirms both father's and son's mastery and privileged white male subjectivity. "That Kenny Meserve! He took after his Pappy all right," the community declares. "Nobody but a Meserve would have thought up such a thing."[44]

Belinda's display—especially the implied exposure of her vagina—offends Arvay's moral sensibilities. The black girl's nakedness, however, metaphorically buttresses Arvay's pedestal femininity. Belinda is only eight years old, but Arvay blames her for the public spectacle and Kenny's moral corruption. "I try to raise my children clean and right," she protests. "I don't intend to have nobody around here toling a young'un of mine off and leading him astray." On the contrary, Kenny's objectification of Belinda as his "pet Negro" empowers him as a white male subject, and eventually Arvay realizes that Belinda's subjection allows her to claim another configured white identity: patron. Arvay "so far forgave Belinda's little bare body" that she gives the child all of her daughter's old clothes, and she swaddles Belinda in Christian morality by making the girl a new white church dress. With these acts of missionary aegis, Arvay enjoys "her first glimmering of really being Jim Meserve's wife," and she superimposes the figure of privileged white femininity onto the image of the benevolent white patron with her newfound racial confidence. Belinda parlays Arvay's policing into pride with her new clothes and avows, "Yes I is Miss Arvay's little girl too. . . . Yes I is her little girl so!"[45] Echoing Isie's adoption of her patron in "Drenched in Light," Belinda performs the primitive stereotype for Arvay's benefaction. Subsequently Arvay becomes Belinda's patronizing godmother and the angel of the house, or the titular seraph on the Suwanee. Unlike "Drenched in Light," *Seraph* upholds the hierarchical artist-patron dynamic with Arvay's self-serving altruism and Belinda's naked primitivism.

Hurston's novel challenges the historical divisions between white women and their racial and classed Others by demystifying the white woman construct. By giving Belinda a white dress rather than underwear, Arvay projects her class passing and sexual repression onto Belinda. The child appears virginal, but her bottom (like Arvay's "cracker" roots) might still show. Felicia Corregio (Lucy Ann's sister) analogously performs white womanhood through clothing. Arvay insists that the Corregios are "not to be treated white," but Jim facilitates Felicia's racial assimilation by buying her an outfit to attend a college football game as Kenny's date. Exotic-looking Felicia is "dressed in a *white* sweater suit, topped by a perky *white* tam over one eye, *white* buckskin oxfords, and a loose-fitting light-weight *white* coat," while Kenny performs ragtime so authentically with his band at the postgame party that "you could almost think those were colored folks playing." It is Kenny's right, as a privileged white male subject, to Americanize "darky music," and Felicia and Kenny are coupled together because of their racial performances.[46] Yet Arvay polices the tenuous boundaries of white femininity in an effort to access privilege and power, though she is subjugated under the auspices of racist and patriarchal culture.

Hurston deconstructs white femininity by drawing thematic parallels between Arvay and those she deems her racial and class inferiors: Belinda, Lucy Ann, and a prostitute named Fast Mary. Belinda shows she has no underwear when she stands on her head, and a twelve-year-old Kenny peeks under Fast Mary's skirt when she sits on her porch stairs without any underwear. Arvay clings to the pedestal of middle-class white femininity, but her own torn underwear proves, as Meisenhelder states, "that, no matter how comfortable her life . . . , her relation to white men often betrays surprising parallels to those of black women she distrusts and resents."[47] The concord between black and white women is also true of ethnic and classed female bodies in *Seraph*. Arvay and Lucy Ann are victims of sexual assault, while Arvay and Fast Mary, respectively, represent the sexually repressed and exploited. Hurston makes Arvay's relation to the eroticized Other concrete when Kenny calls Fast Mary's vagina a mulberry pie, which is the very fruit tree under which Arvay is raped. Arvay dismisses the insult because Fast Mary is "too good-looking and too available" for respectable women and "not pretty enough for any man to excuse her generosity and want to protect her."[48] A case study for the accusation "The lady doth protest too much," no one protected Arvay from Jim. *Seraph* suggests, then, that "woman" is "Other." Arvay perpetuates white male supremacy when she affirms her commitment to her marriage in the conclusion of *Seraph* instead of building female coalitions across race and class divisions.[49] She submits to the traditional role of wife as mother praised in the patriarchal cult of true womanhood.

In her essay "What White Publishers Won't Print" (1950), Hurston intimates that she wrote *Seraph on the Suwanee* because publishers rejected her manuscript on the black middle class. The proliferation of black stereotypes in the white male–dominated publishing industry, she criticizes, makes "the average, struggling, non-morbid Negro . . . the best-kept secret in America."[50] Hurston's white-plot novel correspondingly reveals the second best-kept national secret: white women's racial privilege and social mobility are dependent upon structures of racism and sexism. The commodification of Belinda, the assimilation of the Corregio girls, and the stigmatization of Fast Mary signal the fragility of middle-class white femininity. In other words, Arvay participates in and benefits from Jane Crow oppression despite her own hardships as a desperate housewife. For the creative collaborations between black and white women, this means that the white female patron capitalizes on her hierarchical position in relation to the black female artist, and she takes pleasure in the privileges white femininity affords her. Hurston contends that the artist-patron relationship during the Harlem Renaissance can overcome Jim Crow segregation through interracial cultural exchange, but her post–World War II writing reconsiders such associations. She critiques the perpetuation of Jane Crow politics in white publishers' implicit mandates for African American literature produced in the advent of the protest novel. As a result she amends her recurring representation of her alter ego as an autonomous artist.

Desire and Doppelgangers in *The Narrows*

Similar to that of her contemporary Hurston, Petry's oeuvre includes a critical discourse regarding the interdependency of black and white womanhood. Each of Petry's novels bears distinct plotlines, but all of her texts consider the complexities of race and gender. *The Street* is a novel in the naturalist tradition; *Country Place* is a white-plot text; and *The Narrows* is an interracial drama. Yet all three novels are invested in demythologizing American culture, whether in the urban black center or the small, predominantly white New England town.[51] Petry's works problematize the American Dream for both black and white aspirants by deconstructing racial stereotypes of African Americans. Moreover her work debunks what Martin Japtok calls the "Gospel of Whiteness" with a warning to readers about becoming engrossed in the fallacies and abstractions of "whiteness."[52] For example, Petry challenges stereotypes of black women's hypersexuality in *The Street*. Lutie Johnson's white employers assume that she is sexually available and wanton despite her marital status, and her black neighbors attempt to bait her into prostitution once she becomes a single mother. Petry also interrogates the cult of true womanhood in *Country Place* with her characterization of a working-class white mother and daughter duo; Lillian Gramby and Glory Roane strategically negotiate their sexuality for their social mobility and economic gain. Finally, Petry dismantles the pedestal figure of white femininity along with the myth of the black male rapist in *The*

Narrows, in which Camilo accuses Link of rape after their consensual affair.

This fictive web of black and white, male and female protagonists evidences Petry's intertextual commentary on the intersections of race and gender. While hegemonic society stereotypically typecasts Link and Lutie in the complementary roles of rapist and whore, Petry demonstrates the significance of gender as well as race in overdetermining black men's supposed sexual threat and black women's sexual subjection. Hurston displaces the racialized myth of the black male rapist with white male sexual violence in *Seraph on the Suwanee*, but Petry exposes the myth with Camilo's vengeful rape accusation precipitating Link's murder in *The Narrows*. Conversely in *The Street* Lutie's physical and economic vulnerability to rape provokes her to commit murder at the novel's conclusion. Petry's representations of black and white women across her novels illustrate black women's double jeopardy under racism and patriarchy. Both *The Street* and *Country Place* critique the cult of true womanhood that excludes black women from respectability (in spite of Lutie's efforts to model middle-class white femininity) and privileges white women with permanent access (even though Lillian's profligate sexuality violates the rules of respectability). *The Narrows* further outlines the junctures between the politics of race and gender in the novel's construction of middle-class black femininity. There is neither a fully realized black female subject nor any outright feminist treatise in *The Narrows* given that the novel foregrounds Link's masculinist gaze. Nevertheless the text's interlaced character framework creates an implicit dialogue between elite white, middle-class black, and working-class black women. Camilo Treadway, Abbie Crunch, and Mamie Powther function as distorted mirrors for each other and thus intimate the importance of interracial, cross-class homosocial bonds. In recognizing middle-class black women's complicity in and subjugation under the myths of white femininity, Petry examines the contracts and conflicts between black and white, middle-class and working-class women.

Petry first suggests the potential of proto-feminist alliances in *The Street* with her portrayal of the scripted hierarchical relationship between Lutie and her employer, Mrs. Chandler. Lutie admires the appurtenances of Mrs. Chandler's middle-class life, but her race and class prevent her from having Mrs. Chandler's coveted "miracle of a kitchen." The media negates Lutie's maintenance of this idealized domestic space by only advertising white porcelain fixtures and not acknowledging black women's domestic work. Moreover Lutie's employment as the Chandlers' live-in maid estranges her from her own husband, child, and domestic space. Mrs. Chandler assumes that Lutie will be open to Mr. Chandler's sexual advances, which occludes the domestic worker from respectable womanhood. Mrs. Chandler also believes herself to be an exemplary model of femininity, though she pays more attention to other women's husbands than her own and neglects her son. Hence racial and class hierarchies entitle Mrs. Chandler, and she works to maintain them. During a shared train ride to New York, Lutie notices that "the wall between them wasn't quite so high." However, upon arrival Mrs. Chandler affirms her superior position and dismisses Lutie in a "voice [that] unmistakably established the relation between the blond young woman and the brown young woman."[53] The fictions of middle-class white domesticity underwritten by racism and patriarchy beguile both women. Mrs. Chandler's seemingly idyllic though dysfunctional domestic fantasy tyrannizes over Lutie as much as the segregated, impoverished street on which Lutie lives.

Petry advances her vision for women's interracial and cross-class alliances by briefly returning to the black domestic worker and white female employer dynamic in *Country Place*. In contrast to *The Street*, Neola and Mrs. Gramby challenge blanket attributions of respectability to all white women and create a united front against the latter's daughter-in-law, Lillian, whose déclassé deportment offends elite whites as well as venerable blacks. More confident than Arvay, whose belabored performance of white femininity reveals her racial insecurities, Lillian takes it for granted that her whiteness elevates her to the rank of "lady of the manor" despite her working-class origins and promiscuous reputation. Arvay's use of racial epithets illustrates her anxiety about her "cracker" background, and Lillian similarly employs racial epithets to cement her presumed superior racial and class identity. "Who ever heard of a nigger divorce?" Lillian asks, referring to Neola's estrangement from her husband. Lillian tries to claim true white womanhood by questioning the maid's propriety. "How can a black woman be a divorcée if she is not respectable enough to be a wife?" she implicitly demands. She also extends her bigotry to ethnic whites and frequently abuses Mrs. Gramby's Portuguese gardener and Irish cook. Upon learning that the late Mrs. Gramby has willed her house to her diverse staff, Lillian frantically attempts to co-opt her mother-in-law's empowered subjectivity and claim the property: "I won't have niggers living here—this is my house— . . . everybody in the will but me—I am the one."[54] Lillian's frenzied rant reveals her social degradation just as her bigotry, according to

Emily Bernard, "is the ultimate sign of [her] actual moral inferiority."[55] Lillian marries into wealth and attempts to murder her mother-in-law in order to keep it, but she is neither white nor right enough to be among the privileged elite.

In contrast, Neola, the Portuguese gardener, and the Irish cook deftly assert their agency and effectively differentiate whiteness in *Country Place*. They refuse to defer to Lillian as "ma'am" or as "Mrs. Gramby" and instead treat her like "an undesirable paying guest." The staff is Mrs. Gramby's "loyal army" in the domestic warfare over the politics of respectability, and her daughter-in-law is "the enemy" embodying the sexual corruption and moral decadence of the white elite.[56] Like the mansion in Wright's manuscript "Black Hope" that becomes the site of the domestic workers' union, the Gramby estate in *Country Place* houses an interracial, interethnic alliance between the elite and the working class. Petry also signifies upon the promise of integrated "unions" with Neola and the gardener's impending nuptials. As Laura Dubek points out, the couple's "sincere affection for one another underscores the pettiness and disrespect for marriage vows displayed by the primary white couples. Their 'otherness' thus gives meaning to and simultaneously mocks postwar ideologies of whiteness."[57] Petry juxtaposes Lillian's exploitative marriage with Neola's collectively affirming merger and contests the racism and patriarchy that subjugates black women as white women's inferiors. Also *Country Place* refrains from reiterating white women's traditional role as an abettor in black women's multiple oppressions, as Mrs. Gramby and Neola are allies in the defense of merited and respectable womanhood.

Petry furthers this discourse on the historical conflicts and potential bonds between black and white women by delineating the liminality of middle-class black female subjectivity in *The Narrows*. In *The Street* and *Country Place* Petry critiques white women's complicity in black domestic workers' Jane Crow oppression. Race and class differences create the symbolic distance between Lutie and Mrs. Chandler and instigate the domestic struggle between Neola and Lillian. In *The Narrows* Petry tacitly heightens these conflicts. She unveils white women's collusion in the lynching of black men and invokes a history in which black women are not recognized as victims of rape. What is more, *The Narrows* highlights middle-class black women's collusion in policing the boundaries of respectability established intrinsically to proscribe blackness and regulate women. African Americans' intraracial classism, then, particularly subjugates working-class black women, while whites' racism perpetuates all black women's exclusion from the cult of true womanhood.

Thus a subversive endorsement of interracial, cross-class homosocial bonds underlies *The Narrows*'s ill-fated interracial, heterosexual
romance. Lincoln is the "link" between the novel's elite white, middle-
class black, and working-class black female characters; it is his masculinist perspective that narrowly characterizes the women as "executioners,
all."[58] Link collapses his adulterous white lover, Camilo, elitist mother,
Abbie, and sensual black boarder, Mamie, into one castrating amalgamation, but his reductionism emphasizes the problematic of confining
women to either repressive models of middle-class white respectability
or racialized, "lower" class figures of lascivious desire. Concomitantly
Abbie's privileging of the configured image of middle-class white femininity inherently negates her black female subjectivity, as it undermines
her equitability with white women and inhibits her kinship with other
black women. Whereas *Seraph* concludes with Arvay's commitment to
the white patriarchy that stymies her homosocial bonds, *The Narrows*'s
denouement gestures toward building the interracial, cross-class female
partnerships critical for upending the union of Jim and Jane Crow.

Toward this end Petry connects Abbie and Camilo thematically,
although their differences in race, class, and age presuppose the near
impossibility of their becoming proto-feminist allies. The women are
yoked together as toxic models of femininity as well as the twin loves
of Link's life. He proposes to Camilo at twenty-six, but Abbie is the first
woman the eight-year-old wants to marry when she and her husband,
Major, adopt him. With her market basket, polished oxfords, dainty
gloves, and erect figure, Abbie "had New England aristocrat written all
over her." Her elegant femininity is a "lost art," and Link classifies her
as "one of the last of the species known as lady." She projects the airs
of white propriety even though her husband readily claims "his people
were swamp niggers." Abbie articulates her double consciousness while
living in the segregated black section of Monmouth, Connecticut (which
is pointedly dubbed "the Narrows") by constantly asking herself, "What
will people think?"[59]

Abbie's faithful deference to the gospel of whiteness allows her to construct a respected image of black femininity. However, it is not without
consequence, as her propriety alienates her from her family and the por-
tents of history. Because she fears that her husband's indecorous behavior will damage her carefully crafted persona, Abbie mistakes Major's
fatal stroke for drunkenness. Likewise she burdens a young Link with
"The Race," which includes teaching him that light skin and straight hair
are "good" and African Americans "had to be cleaner, smarter, thriftier,

more ambitious than white people, so that white people would like colored people." Abbie's code of respectability makes Link ashamed of his
race, until he is taken under the wing of Bill Hod, a local bar owner who
becomes Link's surrogate father, guide to the street, and model for racial
pride. Bill educates Link that "black could be other things, too. . . . The
rarest jewels were black: black opals, black pearls."[60] Abbie idealizes
codes of conduct esteemed by white New England matrons. Yet *The Narrows* qualifies, as Petry explains in an interview with Mark K. Wilson,
that Abbie's racial identity supersedes her northeastern setting: "Though
we take on all the—what shall I say?—the speech patterns, we accept the
kind of food, the cooking, the houses, and so forth, nevertheless truly
we're not New Englanders." Just as the writer's experience being pelted
with rocks and profanity on the first day of school in Connecticut differentiates her from white New Englanders, Abbie's life in the Narrows,
to use Petry's words, "does not a New Englander make."[61]

Abbie's deluded assimilationist elitism deconstructs myths of true
white womanhood as well as the politics of the black middle class. The
gospel of whiteness Abbie touts most obviously affects Link's subjectivity
in the novel, but arguably her psyche, as Sybil Weir asserts, is the most
impaired.[62] Abbie's private and public identities are proscribed by the
standards and symbols of femininity coded as white. Consequently her
liminal performance of middle-class black subjectivity ideally facilitates
interracial bonds but actually sabotages cross-class coalitions among
women.[63] Abbie may play the part of middle-class white subjectivity with
her speech, clothes, posture, and conflicted relationship to "The Race,"
but her white counterpart, Camilo, is born-and-bred New England aristocracy. The latter's whiteness and wealth legitimates her as a New England lady, just as her New England–ness substantiates her race and class.

Even as Petry gestures toward the possibility of black and white
women building proto-feminist bonds, Camilo's and Link's roles in their
interracial drama are overdetermined. When Link attends a minstrel
show with Camilo, he recalls being assigned the role of a minstrel in a
school play, which inspires his white classmates to rename him Sambo.
Link admits that, if not for Bill's mentoring, "the color of [Camilo's] skin
would disturb me as I watch [her] laughing at Sambo sittin' in the sun."
Still, Camilo's ignorant enjoyment of the racial spectacle exacerbates
Link's angst that his lover has cast him as the black plantation buck to her
chaste white lady in their romantic production. Cesar the Writing Man,
who is the Narrows' urban prophet, warns readers with biblical foresight
that the couple's relationship is doomed from the start. He writes on the

sidewalk, "Is there anything whereof it may be said, See, this is new? It hath been already of old time, which was before us. Ecclesiastes 1:10."[64] Beyond the universal boy-meets-girl, boy-loses-girl scenario, Link's race and Camilo's marital status complicates their liaison. When Link ends their extramarital affair, Camilo punishes him with the privilege afforded her in the gospel of whiteness, and her mother and husband enact its wrath. Link's murder is the result of his profession of love rather than his confession of rape, and his death is unsettling because of its implications for the civil rights politics debated during *The Narrows*'s publishing moment.

Unlike Link and Camilo's love story, the novel's deliberation about whether homosocial bonds between black and white can be fostered and sustained remains undetermined. Camilo and Link's affair is not the only interracial relationship in the text. Comparable to the social relationships Jim Meserve develops with minority laborers in *Seraph*, Malcolm Powther and Al build a tentative friendship working at the Treadway estate, where they are the butler and chauffeur, respectively. Bigoted Al eventually recognizes Powther's humanity and compliments, "You're just like a white man, Mal." Similarly Link seems oblivious to the supposed rigid boundaries that distinguish white women from black women, and he demonstrates that race and pedestal femininity are socially constructed when he confuses Camilo with a light-skinned African American. He first meets Camilo on a late foggy night on the Narrows' docks, and he is "fairly certain she was one of the clinker tops from China's Place," one of Bill's brothels.[65] Camilo's presence in the Narrows racializes and classes her, while Link's Connecticut upbringing and Brown University education make it difficult for him to detect her whiteness. Because he has seen black women with blond hair, blue eyes, and white skin, "the Vassar-Wellesley-Bennington colored ones," he does not initially note the condescension in Camilo's voice, which he categorizes as "a special characteristic of the female Caucasian." Link's black friend, who realizes that "his life would depend on his ability to recognize a white woman when he saw one" in the South, immediately looks upon Camilo with hostility.[66] In reality Link's life also depends on acknowledging the social construction of white femininity as well as the consequences of his misrecognition and miscegenation.

Link's centrality to *The Narrows* makes it difficult for the women in his life to form a feminist camaraderie. He identifies similarities between Abbie's bourgeois brand of racial uplift and Camilo's white elitism, but he is the racial break between them. When Abbie catches the couple in bed, she feels that they violate her respectable domestic space: "A white girl. How dare he? In her house, her house." Because Camilo transgresses the interracial taboo policed on both sides of the color line, Abbie deems her a prostitute. "In my house, hussy, plying your trade," she accuses, "get out, get out of my house."[67] As Melina Vizcaíno-Alemán argues, Camilo's character serves as an "ideological fissure" that disrupts the boundaries between Abbie's domesticated morality and Bill's businesses, which profit from vice.[68] In *Seraph* Arvay's policing of feminine boundaries ejects the prostitute Fast Mary from estimable womanhood. Similarly Abbie's discriminating glower marks Camilo as licentious. The latter is not the pedestal figure of white womanhood but a "tramp of a white girl," whose blond hair desecrates Abbie's treasured bridal pillowcases on Link's bed.[69] While Link walks the line between beau and plantation buck, Camilo treads the line between lover and loose woman. She nearly forfeits her white privilege because she has a sexual relationship with a black man.

Camilo's violation of middle-class black respectability impresses that she is a doppelganger for Mamie. Both are undesirable women of "the street" intruding upon Abbie's domestic space and unsettling her carefully cultivated image of civility. Abbie aspires to New England aristocracy, but "Mamie Powther was Dumble Street," the epitome of the working-class Narrows. Mamie is no lady but a woman of excess in Abbie's esteem. She reveals her abundant figure, uses too much lipstick, wears a pair of dirty white gloves over red-painted nails, and, in Abbie's imagination, invites the wind under her skirt "again and again for another look." Although Mamie is married to Malcolm Powther, Abbie criticizes that she is "not a man's wife, permanently attached, but an unattached unwifely female."[70] Abbie polices the borders of respectable femininity while Mamie disregards its edicts. She emasculates her husband with her ongoing affair with Bill and neglects her son, J.C. As a result Abbie cannot appreciate the women's shared interests: Mamie sings the blues while an idle Abbie enjoys making up jingles in her head. Abbie's patriarchal notions regarding gender complement Link's masculinist conceptualization of the enticing yet treacherous figure of "woman."

Link's amalgamation of desirous female bodies stigmatizes women excluded from the feminine ideal as prostitutes and castrators. Inverting *Seraph*'s series of black, ethnic, and white women wedded together by their sexual vulnerability, Link equates Camilo, Mamie, and a prostitute named China in a signifying chain of destructive desire. Camilo "is a younger fairerskinned thinner more beautifully put together edition of Mamie Powther"; Mamie is "a younger shapelier browner edition of China"; and China has left "such a mark on her profession that . . . no matter what their names or what they call themselves . . . [all prostitutes are known] as China's girls." Camilo and Mamie are also China's girls, since Link's sexual history with each of the three women is "just another variation on the theme." Bill beats a teenage Link for visiting China's Place against his orders. Later Malcolm Powther erroneously suspects Link and Mamie are having an affair and thus points him out to the Treadways. And Camilo's husband murders Link on account of his wife's lie. "It's MamiePowtherChinaCamiloWilliams that has me by the throat," Link broods. "She is what all men chase and never capture."[71] In joining their names into one composite woman, he implies that all women are essentially the same femme fatale. The women are responsible for his fatal downfall, not their male counterparts who execute the violence.

Link's masculinist, pseudo-scientific perspective on women may dominate *The Narrows*—for it is his victimized, eroticizing lens that frames the novel's female characters—but his subjective viewpoint is not the only one theorizing "woman." Link conjectures, "The human female is a predatory animal like the cat, because the hunting instinct is congenital too." Yet Mamie and Abbie demonstrate less rapacious qualities in the context of women's potential interracial and cross-class bonds. Mamie assesses, for example, whether she should correct Camilo's misconception about her platonic relationship with Link, but she concludes, "Aw, she's white. It's no skin off my back. . . . A rich white girl. She don't need no help." Mamie decides not to enlighten her because Camilo is authorized traditionally with resources and access to knowledge. "When you thought about all the white men there were for this girl to climb in bed with," Mamie justifies, "it wasn't fair that she should cheat some colored girl out of the chance to go with [Link]."[72] Mamie does not share her privileged information with Camilo because hegemonic culture affirms white beauty aesthetics over her blackness. Mamie's decision temporarily makes her feel superior to Camilo, but the misunderstanding between the two women becomes another incident in a chain of events leading to Link's death. While Link is the catalyst for this disjuncture, the lack of common ground between Mamie and Camilo is due to the race and class tensions inhibiting open dialogues between black and white women.

In the end Petry does not realize a feminist movement but establishes a foundation for forming mutually beneficial relationships between middle-class black women and their racial and class others. In *Seraph*

Arvay clings to her hierarchical position in relation to black, ethnic, and working-class women, but in *The Narrows* Abbie's realization that she is culpable in the death of her son allows her to embrace her kinship to Camilo and Mamie. Abbie's middle-class chauvinism first encourages her to blame Mamie for Link's murder because "a woman like that starts an evil action, just by her mere presence." Of course, the same can be said of Camilo, whose presence in the Narrows begins the ill-fated sequence of events. Abbie's internalized patriarchal understanding of female subjectivity dictates that "woman," as exemplified by the adulterers, is responsible for Link's death: "It started when the first married woman whoever she was took a lover and went on living with her husband." Abbie concludes, however, that "It was all of us, . . . we all had a hand in it, we all reacted violently to those two people, . . . because he was colored and she was white."[73] She acknowledges her prejudice toward interracial couples and concedes her culpability in Link's cultural alienation and symbolic death in his youth. Abbie shares the blame with the Powthers and Treadways who bring about her son's literal death.

Petry's classic storytelling, which references biblical themes and repeating histories, seemingly recapitulates white supremacy and patriarchal dominance. The text, however, tentatively imagines a radical feminist consciousness. In the essay "The Novel as Social Criticism" (1950), Petry explains that her fiction is founded on the belief that individuals are their brothers' keepers. She draws on this adage in *The Narrows*, but she does not realize historical change for black male subjects in light of blacks' institutional oppression.[74] Link's murder is overdetermined by a series of falsehoods and misunderstandings, and at the hour of his death he learns that the course of a black man's life was decided "ever since that Dutch man of warre landed at Jamestown in 1619 and sold twenty 'Negras' to the inhabitants."[75] Yet in encouraging women to be their sisters' keepers, *The Narrows* envisions rewriting history through Abbie's acts of reconciliation. When she warns the police that Bill will avenge Link's death by harming Camilo, Abbie does not remain fixed in her racial identity but privileges her developing gender consciousness. She also takes Mamie's son, J.C., with her to the police station; his presence conveys that Abbie has a second chance to redefine motherhood in the wake of Link's death. Additionally her "adoption" of J.C. implies that she will abjure the class elitism that alienates her from Mamie. Petry's twofold denouement intimates that individual acts precipitate interracial, interclass women's coalitions. Camilo's salvation comes at Abbie's behest, while Abbie achieves redemption by way of Mamie.

This triangular relationship between elite white, middle-class black, and working-class black women presages future feminist alliances.

The Legacy of the White Plot and Integrated Text

There is no sorority of white and black, rich and poor women embracing each other at the conclusion of *The Narrows*, but the novel's resolution suggests that Abbie Crunch will redeem herself by forgiving and saving wealthy white Camilo Treadway, on one hand, and fostering a relationship with working-class black Mamie Powther, on the other. Petry's text foregrounds the subjugation of black masculinity, which connects Link Williams to Wright's string of disenfranchised black male protagonists, from Bigger Thomas in *Native Son* to Damon Cross in *The Outsider*. Yet Farah Jasmine Griffin notes that Petry's novel also anticipates some of the most extraordinary figures in the black women's writing tradition: "Before China, one of the whores in Toni Morrison's *The Bluest Eye*, there was China the whore who lived in the Narrows. Before Alice Walker's sexy blues singer Sugg Avery, there was Mamie Powther the busty, sensual, blues-singing woman desired by all the men of the Narrows and beyond."[76] Petry refigures the historically censured bodies of the prostitute and the blues singer as counterweights to Abbie's moralizing and Camilo's privilege. From a masculinist perspective, *The Narrows* implies that strictures of middle-class respectability and figures of lascivious desire contribute to the unmanning of black male subjectivity. More provocatively the novel demonstrates that patriarchal constructions of respectability bind all women. *The Narrows* prefigures a renaissance of literature influenced by a black feminist agenda that affirms African American women's responsibility to other women. The novel promotes gender allegiances despite black women's racial loyalty (as it relates to interracial homosocial bonds) and in spite of the race's class stratification (as it relates to middle-class and working-class African American women).

In Petry's critique of the black bourgeoisie, the specious ideals of middle-class white femininity damage the esteem of black female subjectivity. Abbie embodies neither the image of a supportive wife for Major nor the portrait of a nurturing mother for Link. Equally destructive is her rebuff of Mamie, since pedestal femininity is intrinsically defined by the oppression and policing of the Other: what is black as well as what is female. Abbie and Mamie's commensurability as black women momentarily manifests in their mutual rejection of Camilo from their shared domestic space. Transposing black women's expulsion from the cult of true womanhood onto white women, Abbie puts Camilo out of her house while an amused Mamie watches. Black women's exclusion from true womanhood hits home in this moment, and the authority to reject as well as the power of the gaze provisionally resides with Abbie and Mamie.

The Narrows unravels the homosocial intricacies of Jane Crow oppression with its depiction of elite white women's and middle-class black women's mutual investment in regulating racial and class boundaries. Although Petry aligns distinctly raced, differently classed female bodies into one fetishized body of dangerous female desire, she can only gesture toward amity between black and white women at the end of the novel. Anticipating but not quite actualizing this conciliation, *The Narrows* facilitates this tête-à-tête by exposing white women's complicity in racism, middle-class black women's dogged classism, and black men's patriarchal gaze. To be clear, Petry's promotion of interracial and cross-class female bonds does not refute the specificity of black women's disenfranchisement. Her juxtaposition of black and white women instead highlights racist society's sexism, which includes black men's participation in black women's Jane Crow oppression. While Link collapses desirable women into an emasculating MamieChinaCamilo amalgamation, domestic abuse reveals the gravity of failing to recognize the specificity of black female subjectivity in Petry's short story "Like a Winding Sheet" (1945). In the latter, the black male protagonist returns home to hit his wife after he feels enervated in the public sphere. His injured gaze substitutes his black partner for the two white women who are the actual perpetrators of his emasculation.[77] One must interrogate the displaced anger in "Like a Winding Sheet" just as one must question Link's negligence in differentiating black and white female bodies given his knowledge of African American history.

Hurston's novel *Seraph on the Suwanee* creates a comparable duality by not only challenging white publishers' promotion of black stereotypes but also by exhibiting whiteness as an equally empty cipher. In "What White Publishers Won't Print" Hurston reports that white publishers desire only limited characterizations of African Americans as "mechanical toys . . . built so that their feet eternally shuffle, and their eyes pop and roll."[78] Accordingly in *Seraph* Arvay Meserve's covetousness of whiteness blinds her to the fact that her marital subjection parallels the social oppression of her raced and classed Others. Arvay shuffles her feet and rolls her eyes at other women, to employ Hurston's imagery, because of her racial insecurities. Yet Hurston ties white, ethnic, and black women together by their lack of underwear, which symbolizes their lack of safe space, in order to illustrate the intersectionality of sexism, classism, and racism. Hurston and Petry employ different plots to survey these crossroads, but both writers explore the same question: What are the potentialities and impossibilities of building feminist coalitions? *The Narrows* forecasts an emergent black feminist consciousness in response to black women's multivalent oppression, and *Seraph* foreshadows black feminist critiques of early feminism's racism due to its refusal to confront that oppression.

Whereas Hurston's and Petry's proto-feminist discourse is a subplot in their novels, Alice Childress directly addresses the silences between black and white women by portraying literal conversations between the two. Schultz argues that it is not until Alice Walker's novel *Meridian* (1976) and Toni Morrison's novel *Tar Baby* (1981) that black women writers "establish the open confrontation of racial stereotypes as the necessary basis for an interracial friendship."[79] Yet Childress does exactly that in literary genres other than the novel. Her play *Florence* (1949) and vignettes in *Like One of the Family . . . Conversations from a Domestic's Life* (1956), which compiles her *Freedom* newspaper column "Conversations from Life," resonate thematically with the multiple forms of oppression treated in Hurston's and Petry's work. In *Florence* Childress symbolizes Jim Crow segregation with a railing that divides two conversing women into their respective white and "colored" sections at a southern train station. Moreover the out-of-order bathroom designated for "colored women" signifies upon Jane Crow oppression, as the play's black female protagonist cannot use the bathroom labeled "white ladies" and must use the facilities reserved for black men. *Florence* ultimately shows the limited economic, social, political, and psychic options for performing black female subjectivity when the play's protagonist leaves the station piqued by the white woman's arrogance. Rather than travel north to bring her aspiring actress daughter Florence home, the protagonist sends a brief encouraging note: "Keep trying."[80]

Childress also explores the dynamics between black and white women through her character Mildred, the witty domestic in *Like One of the Family*. Mildred's first-person narration details her frustrations as a dayworker, which draws on the writer's own trials laboring as a maid. For example, in "The Health Card" Mildred's white female employer requires her to show proof of a clean bill of health until Mildred asks the same of her employer. In "Mrs. James" the eponymous white employer refers to herself in the third person and attempts to get Mildred to work on the weekends. Mildred's telling of her experiences with racial prejudice and economic exploitation is cathartic, as Trudier Harris argues, for Mildred, her listening friend Marge, and Childress's readers. Mildred's direct confrontation with a narrow-minded white domestic worker in the episode titled "In the Laundry Room" forces the latter to acknowledge the myths of pedestal white femininity. "Tell me, young woman . . . does she cram eight hours of work into five and call it *part time*?" Mildred asks after the woman clutches her employer's wash. When the woman nods yes, Mildred continues, "I am not your enemy, so don't get mad with me just because you ain't free!"[81] Her final comment reveals the potential as well as the limits of women's alliances across divides of race and class. Like Hurston and Petry, Childress is another example of a black woman writer whose work, though successful in her cultural moment, is deserving of more critical attention.

More specifically *Seraph*'s critical and commercial "failure" speaks to Hurston's collision with the Jane Crow politics of black literary production. In her novel the black female writer draws upon white women's romantic fiction and eschews "the Negro problem" characteristic of protest fiction. She also circumvents the literary segregation decreed by white publishers and enforced by literary critics. However, *Seraph*'s continued obscurity in the African American literary tradition, despite black feminists' recovery of *Their Eyes Were Watching God* and the writer's later mainstream canonicity, attests to her inability to fully surmount the double jeopardy of racism and sexism. Hurston's supposed decline during the period of social realism was not unlike the waning of other Harlem Renaissance artists after the Depression, yet black women's mid-twentieth-century literary contributions received criticism that belied male chauvinism and racial provincialism. Hurston and Wright published harsh reviews of each other's classic texts, and their public dust-up is yet another factor in why critics have so often overlooked the connection between her fiction and social realism. As late as 1954 Hurston continued to criticize how her contemporaries' inferiority complexes and communist affiliations compromised their work. "On the occasions when I was solicited to join up, with the usual bonus," she writes in a letter, "I went right to the heart of the matter without beating around the bush and told them that I could get all the White men I wanted without any help from them and pick from a higher bush for a sweeter berry."[82] In spite of her bravado, Hurston's career is summed up as reaching its peak with the publication of *Dust Tracks*, and she worked as a maid just seven years later to support herself.

Critics' attenuation of *Seraph*'s significance to Hurston's oeuvre reflects the perceived truancy of the black female writer who traverses the tacit mandates of black literary production. *Dust Tracks* is identified as the apex of her writing career before its decline. Yet the memoir's negotiation of the complexities between artist and patron—both deliberate and latent—reinforces traditional roles between Hurston and the white woman writer Fannie Hurst. Hurst's novel *Imitation of Life* (1933) examines an interracial female friendship. The black female character in the novel, Delilah, is the secret talent behind the white female protagonist's successful chain of restaurants, while Delilah's daughter, who passes for white, denies her as a mother. In *Dust Tracks* Hurston discusses her friendship with Hurst, whom she portrays as part eccentric artist and part infantilized adult. Hurston works as Hurst's assistant while in college, but she serves as an indulgent maternal figure in the white writer's flights of playful whimsy, which include "behaving like a little girl, teasing her nurse to take her to the zoo, and having a fine time at it."[83] Hurston's double-voiced autobiography further implies her racial objectification when Hurst parades her around dressed like an African princess. *Dust Tracks* blurs the lines between interracial friendship and exploitative patronage, but the autobiography's place in Hurston's oeuvre is evident, though certainly conflicted.

Reclaiming Hurston as a black literary foremother, however, seemingly requires a coherent narrative of the writer that excludes *Seraph*. In Walker's essay "Looking for Zora" (1975), the "lost" Hurston's unmarked grave as well as Eatonville residents' contradictory recollections of her signify on the black woman writer's fate. One contemporary believes Hurston died of malnutrition, while another recalls that the writer weighed two hundred pounds, loved to eat, and always ate well. Hurston's status as a "found" or recovered black woman writer is distorted similarly by what duCille terms the "precursor perplex," a critical mythology in which Hurston mothered herself as a writer without precursors like Frances Harper or contemporaries like Jessie Fauset.[84] At the same time catalogues of mid-twentieth-century African American social realism exclude Hurston as a Harlem Renaissance folklorist. This canon neglects *Seraph*'s interrogations of whiteness and gender violence. Hurston's peers dismiss her because she does not take up the proletarian figure dominating Wright's school of social realism, and later literary critics celebrate her only as the promoter of authentic black folk.

Ironically Hurston's visibility in the black literary tradition is as conscribed as Petry's relative anonymity. The Harlem Renaissance writer performed for publishers, patrons, and readers, and she eventually achieved an irrefutable iconicity. At the other end of the spectrum is Petry, who deliberately withdrew from the spotlight after her initial success in order to maintain her independence as a black woman writer. She moved from New York back to her hometown of Old Saybrook, Connecticut, after the publication of *The Street* in an effort to avoid becoming a consumable text. Throughout her writing career Petry turned down interviews and requests to write her biography so that she could guard her professional and personal space. "I decided I had a choice," she writes in her journal, "either become more or less a professional 'celebrity,' lose whatever privacy I had, be public property, or be a writer. I opted for becoming a writer."[85] She also expresses in a letter that her need for privacy was "maybe the result of having been born a female—for generations and generations women had no right to property or privacy."[86] Whereas Petry desired anonymity in order to retain authority over her own narrative, Hurston's paratext (defined by a blinding visibility) defines her writing authority. Both career trajectories reveal the personal and professional stakes of constructing a black female writing subjectivity during the Jane Crow era.

4 / "I'll See How Crazy *They* Think I Am": Pulping Sexual Violence, Racial Melancholia, and Healthy Citizenship

It just might be that after devoting so much of our energy to the unfulfilled promise of access through respectability, a politics of deviance, with a focus on the transformative potential found in deviant practice, might be a more viable strategy for radically improving the lives and possibilities of those most vulnerable in Black communities.
—CATHY COHEN, "DEVIANCE AS RESISTANCE: A NEW RESEARCH AGENDA FOR THE STUDY OF BLACK POLITICS"

Before Daisy Bates promised her dying father that she would not allow whites' racism to debilitate her, she nurtured a secret enmity against them. Bates became president of the Arkansas Conference of the NAACP in 1952, and she was an advisor to the Little Rock Nine during the integration of Central High School in 1957. At eight years old, however, Bates initiated a "private vendetta" after learning she was adopted. Three white men sexually assaulted and murdered her biological mother, and her biological father deserted the small mill town of Huttig, Arkansas, for fear of reprisals if he pursued criminal charges. In her autobiography, *The Long Shadow of Little Rock* (1962), Bates's adoptive father explains this traumatic familial history by disclosing to her "the timeworn lust of the white man for the Negro woman—which strikes at the heart of every Negro man in the South." Meanwhile Bates's depiction of her childhood illustrates the enervative effect the South's sanctioning of black women's rape and murder had on her as a mourning daughter as well as an always and already vulnerable black girl. The law did not prosecute her biological mother's murderers, but young Bates frequently visited one of the assailants at the town's commissary to punish him publicly with her accusing gaze. The child's condemning stare was daunting because she was "the living image" of her mother. Young Bates's reckless eyeballing drove the white man, whom she calls Drunken Pig, to cringe, beg, and deteriorate further in a constant state of inebriation. "I have read descriptions of the contest in staring which a bird and a snake will carry on. The two of us must have presented such a picture," she admits, "although considering my own feelings I don't know which of us symbolized the snake and which the bird." Seeing that Bates sustained her antipathy even after Drunken Pig died—presumably due to her relentless harassment as much as his poor health—it is difficult to differentiate between the torturer and the tortured in her memoir. Bates does not move past the loss of her biological mother or her anger toward the perpetrators until her failing father advises, "Hate can destroy you, Daisy. . . . If you hate, make it count for something. . . . Try to do something about it, or your hate won't spell a thing." Bates's vow to her father inspired the civil rights activism she painstakingly details in *The Long Shadow of Little Rock*. Nonetheless the brief moments of pleasure she savored as a grieving child casting daggers of justice at her mother's murderer are equally affecting in the autobiography. She recounts, "I had come to enjoy tormenting Drunken Pig. I felt as if I were making him pay for his sin."[1] His agony was worth the personal cost of her malice.

Wonnie Brown Anderson, the black female protagonist in Curtis Lucas's novel *Third Ward Newark* (1946), reifies the suffering caused by black women's sexual violation and subsequent desire for vengeance in Bates's memoir. Sixteen-year-old Wonnie barely escapes her abduction and rape by two white men, while her friend Mildred is beaten fatally when she resists her assault. Lucas's representation of interracial rape draws on black women's history of sexual violence. Moreover the writer provocatively explores the consequences for black women's psyches as well as the political, social, and economic repercussions during World War II for the northern black community. Similar to Bates, who grew up under the emotional weight of her mother's victimization, Wonnie is unable to cope with the loss of her friend, her inability to enact legal recourse for the crime, or the knowledge of her own physical and social vulnerability. She consequently develops a melancholic response to her trauma—remaining in a constant state of mourning and guilt-ridden anger—because she cannot forget the past and cannot ignore her ongoing political disenfranchisement under the institutional structures of racism and sexism. Wonnie too blurs the line between tormenter and tormented as an adult when she temporarily assuages her melancholia by publicly persecuting her assailant, Ernie Mihie, with her censuring gaze. Although she participates in various programs for social activism and economic mobility with her husband, Joe, such stratagems only momentarily abate her mourning. Wonnie cannot transcend her debilitating grief because such endeavors target abstract hegemonies, not her imminent emotional crisis. Nothing satiates her desire for justice more than her antagonistic surveillance of her attacker. However, her retributive efforts prove destructive for sustaining her marriage and for recuperating her sense of self-worth.

With its nuanced portrayal of black women's racial subjection and resulting psychological trauma, *Third Ward Newark* is a critical interlocutor in the rape rhetoric of mid-twentieth-century African American literature. In Wright's novel *Native Son* rape is an expression of Bigger Thomas's rage against oppressive white society. Bigger explains, "Rape was what one felt when one's back was against a wall and one had to strike out, whether one wanted to or not, to keep the pack from killing one." If rape is the violation Bigger experiences in oppressive white society that provokes his murderous response, then the body of his girlfriend Bessie Mears is figuratively unrapable in racist and patriarchal culture. Bigger sexually assaults and fatally beats Bessie, but the court prosecutes him for raping and killing white Mary Dalton, though he does not rape her. Bessie's abused black body is "merely 'evidence'" in the trial enumerating his crimes against Mary, and it is peripheral to his defiant reckoning with white supremacy.[2] In contrast, Lutie Johnson's assault in Petry's novel *The Street* employs intraracial sexual violence, as Sabine Sielke argues, "not merely as an event that triggers narrative development, but as a consistent structural device corresponding to an acculturated dynamics of desire."[3] Lutie's resistance to Boots Smith's attempted rape signifies upon her struggle against sexual and economic exploitation. Her would-be rapist is a procurer for the white bar owner Junto, who tries to coerce Lutie into a sexual relationship and uses vice to profit from the impoverished black community. When Lutie lashes out at Boots during his attack, she also strikes back at an "anonymous figure— a figure which her angry resentment transformed into everything she had hated, everything she had fought against, everything that had served to frustrate her."[4] Petry inextricably links intraracial sexual violence to white patriarchal culture's subjection of African American women and men's material and erotic desire.

In *Third Ward Newark* Lucas's literal and figurative representation of rape unevenly articulates the proto-womanist perspective in *The Street* while reiterating the masculinist privilege in *Native Son*. More specifically Lucas's novel concomitantly evinces black women's double jeopardy and invalidates their melancholic response to this trauma. Wonnie's repeated confrontation of her attacker with her menacing gaze is compensatory and threatening, as historically interracial rape was condoned and black women's accusations were unspeakable. Yet the narrator also describes

Wonnie's gaze as "wild and *insane*, and red-hot with hate," which suggests that her damning stare is both feral and pathological.[5] Lucas formu-
lates his novel as a Freudian textbook case of melancholia. In the essay
"Mourning and Melancholia" Freud differentiates the two emotional
states as successful and failed responses to loss. Mourning is the natural
reaction to the loss of a loved person, ideal, or abstraction; it is finite,
as the lost object is merged into the ego. In contrast, melancholia is the
inability to put closure to one's mourning; the melancholic experiences a
diminished ego as his or her persistent obsession with remembering the
lost object becomes the foundation of a self-denigrating psychic identity.
Thus in *Third Ward Newark* all-consuming "thoughts of a colored girl
begging to be left alone, while a white man beat her to death, were ever
with [Wonnie]."[6] Still, there is sense and sensibility to her neurosis. She
does not forget her friend Mildred's murder because it represents the
lack of parity between black womanhood, traditionally deemed wanton
and inviolable, and the pedestal figure of white femininity, convention-
ally heralded as chaste and worthy of protection.

Wonnie, then, mourns Mildred inasmuch as she grieves the lost ideal
that black women can attain pedestal femininity. As Anne Anlin Cheng
theorizes, "The entire process of racialization, of configuring visibility
(who is white, who is black; who is visible, who is not), must be considered as itself melancholic."[7] David L. Eng and Shinee Han likewise
define racial melancholia as a response to the loss of social ideals in the
minority assimilation process, during which preserving the lost abstraction is a "*social* threat" revealing the "social truth" about racial injustice.[8]
Wonnie's incapacity to "get over" her friend's death, overlook her own
violation, and turn a blind eye to her social powerlessness undermines
her emotional well-being. Every white man is her would-be rapist, who
is "always before her, a symbol of all that was wrong, a personification of
all the prejudice and ugliness and grief she had ever known."[9] Wonnie
survives her physical trauma, but she struggles to psychically reconcile
it with her perception of self. Hence she is both the melancholic subject,
whose loss of self-esteem prohibits her from productively mourning the
elusive ideals of racial equality, and the melancholic object, which cannot assimilate into the racist and sexist body politic.

Third Ward Newark's employment of conspicuous psychological
tropes and lay psychoanalytic language signals the gendered as well as
generic tensions in the novel. The text's titillating characterization of
individual neurosis, which is readily featured in romance, mystery, and
pulp novels, attenuates the narrative's realist critique of black women's

multivalent oppression. In other words, racial melancholia is both the source of the text's voyeuristic drama and the material for its social commentary. In the novel's melancholic matrix, black women's subjugation is commonplace and institutionally structured in Newark's Third Ward, which is the segregated African American section of the city. "Yeah. A colored girl is too black to work in their offices, or in their department stores downtown," the collective community voice complains. "But she ain't too black for one of them to go to bed with on Saturday night." While whites stereotype black women as always sexually available, the discriminatory labor practices of war factories and low-wage domestic work force black women into prostitution. At the same time *Third Ward Newark*'s sensationalizing of Wonnie's racial melancholia tempers the novel's naturalist critique of systematic urban oppression and problematizes her desire for redress as personal psychosis. Readers are prompted to empathize with Wonnie, but even her family and friends repeatedly question whether she is sane or "mentally deranged."[10] Lucas's depiction of Wonnie's psychic trauma critiques black women's exclusion from the cult of true womanhood, but the black male writer also pathologizes her despairing response to her Jane Crow oppression.

Such faddish conventions and conflicting objectives might account for *Third Ward Newark*'s lack of scholarly engagement in literary histories of mid-twentieth-century African American social realism. Routinely critics perceive fiction responding to the marketplace's bids and readers' interests as having little social relevance or academic legitimacy; they undervalue this literature by way of canon gatekeeping. However, as Susanne B. Dietzel elucidates, early twentieth-century African American popular fiction's significance to the literary tradition is founded on its efforts to balance audience demand with genre conventions.[11] Chester Himes and Frank Yerby, for example, have gained increasing critical attention from contemporary scholars for their popular fiction's contributions to the tradition. Although his first novel, *If He Hollers Let Him Go* (1945), is a social protest novel, Himes shifted to publishing a series of detective novels later in his career in order to make money. Comparably Yerby, one of the most prolific and commercially successful African American writers of this period, wrote historical romance sagas he referred to as costume novels. On his preference for producing popular fiction rather than protest fiction, Yerby explains, "I honestly believe that thumbing through an occasional detective yarn, science-fiction tale, or costume novel, is rather better preventive therapy than tranquilizers, for instance."[12] The escapism popular fiction provides, he reasons, has both a psychological and a social function.

In addition to *Third Ward Newark*'s 1952 reprint by the well-known pulp publisher Lion Books, the contemporaneous critical response to the hardback publication implies that Lucas engaged social realist conventions but was also a relatively successful popular fiction writer like Himes and Yerby. A *New York Times* review invokes Lucas's protest themes and surmises that *Third Ward Newark* "is motivated by a genuine awareness of social injustice, an acute sensitivity to the nuances of the bitter racial conflict in an industrial society."[13] Interestingly a review in the *Chicago Defender* provides a less idealistic summation of Lucas's work: "[It] is not an extremely ambitious novel, but within its somewhat limited scope it is an impressive and entertaining one."[14] In an interview for *Third Ward Newark*'s release, Lucas legitimated both the mainstream and black newspapers' evaluations of his text as polemical and cursory. "Naturally, I hope to make some money out of the book," he concedes, "but if the story does any good at all in relieving such conditions as exist in the Third Ward, I'd gladly give up the profits."[15] The Negro Book Club's adoption of the novel for its January 1947 reading selection substantiated the text's commercial appeal. Also Lucas's production of several original paperbacks in a short time period for pulp publishers Lion and Beacon attests to his penchant for using efficient language to render spectacle. There is still little to no literary criticism on Lucas's oeuvre, which includes *Flour Is Dusty* (1943), *So Low, So Lonely* (1952), *Angel* (1953), *Forbidden Fruit* (1953), and *Lila* (1955).[16]

Notwithstanding popular fiction's understood generic compromises, Lucas's foray into pulp fiction informs one's reading of *Third Ward Newark* but does not supersede the work's biting social critique. The novel's apparent profitability and entertainment value intimate that the text is a social barometer for the heightened racial politics, shifting literary conventions, and changing gender roles occurring during this publishing moment. As C. L. R. James gleans more broadly about "the tremendous social manifestation hidden behind what is called 'entertainment,'" Lucas's novel is telling of the larger cultural implications of Jane Crow oppression because of "what it is and what it is *not*."[17] Categorizing *Third Ward Newark* as pulp fiction assumes that readers pruriently enjoyed its depiction of sexual trauma, and yet the genre's commodification of historically taboo sexuality (which included interracial and homosexual relationships) allowed Lucas to address explicitly black women's racial and sexual subjection. In fact, as Paula Rabinowitz affirms about postwar crime and film noir, pulp is "prefigurative, a kind of political theory of America's problematic democracy disguised as cheap melodrama."[18] Lucas's "pulping" of white men's violent transgressions against black women challenges what had been regarded as unrepresentable. The black male writer's personification of race, class, gender, and sexual subjection in *Third Ward Newark* bares the psychological repercussions of Jane Crow oppression, and his blurring of political discourse and cultural entertainment evidences the critical value of popular fiction's contribution to mid-twentieth-century social realism.

However, *Third Ward Newark* manifests a masculinist perspective that mitigates the authority of its protagonist's castigating gaze and climactically usurps black female subjectivity. Despite its intense examination of interracial rape, Lucas's Jane Crow text does not advance a proto-womanist political agenda. The novel's popular conventions gesture toward the work's potential to reject the mandates mainstream white publishers imposed on mid-twentieth-century African American fiction. What is more, the novel's explicit psychological framework seemingly models a process of critical self-inquiry that speaks productively to issues of race, an assertion Hortense J. Spillers makes about the possibilities of psychoanalysis for recognizing blacks' interior intersubjectivity.[19] Yet in the end Lucas reiterates black women's subjugation in the novel by hemming his portrait of black female subjectivity in hegemonic racist and sexist proscriptions.

As a result *Third Ward Newark* exhibits the literary inscriptions conscribing mid-twentieth-century representations of black women, as Lucas ambivalently acknowledges their Jane Crow oppression but denies them resolution. It is only through "a politics of deviance," which Cathy Cohen defines as practices outside of dominant norms and racial-uplift agendas, that Wonnie asserts a degree of personhood in spite of the narrative's censure.[20] In the context of contemporary understandings of resistance, deviant protest is a valid strategy for expressing the social power of those with limited agency. However, *Third Ward Newark* is invested in interwar politics of respectability, and Wonnie's manic measures remain heretical. Lucas's description of black women's physical and psychological abuse is effective, then, for mapping Jane Crow's social and mental extremities. In foregrounding the psychological exigency of racial and gender oppression, *Third Ward Newark* contests white male hegemonies, explores various kinds of gendered and racial protest, and presents a rare depiction of a black female protagonist as imagined by a black male writer. Unfortunately Wonnie's demise due to Jane Crow's political circumscriptions and textual delimiters concretizes black women's overdetermined abjection and the hegemony of black masculinity in the novel.

What She Says: Black Women's Melancholic Matrix

Third Ward Newark deconstructs the fiction that black women are unassailable by portraying them in a constant state of about to be raped. Stereotypes of black women's promiscuity, as Angela Y. Davis argues, are the "inseparable companion" of myths of the black male rapist.[21] Lucas counters such defamation by overdetermining black women's economic and sexual vulnerability in the Third Ward, with its roach-infested houses and pimp-lined streets. Wonnie's melancholic matrix consists of a series of lost loved ones: her mother, who is underpaid and essentially worked to death; her cousin Hattie, who is exploited sexually and sentenced to reform school; and her friend Mildred, who is murdered during an attempted rape. All three figures epitomize the limited agency available to black women in Newark's segregated black community. The novel illustrates black women's double jeopardy and tersely summarizes, "Some colored women took domestic jobs or worked in the laundries. Others went up on Broome Street and sold their bodies. They all got along somehow." Teenage Hattie initially replaces Wonnie's mother as a domestic worker, but the narrator explains, "It did not take long for Hattie to learn what men would do for a girl like her."[22] Low wages and high living expenses coerce Hattie into commodifying her sexuality, including soliciting white men. Hattie's neighbors, who share her abject poverty but view interracial sex as the ultimate degradation of black female subjectivity, inform the police of her delinquency. The system subsequently sentences Hattie to a home for wayward girls and sends twelve-year-old Wonnie to foster care.

Wonnie's series of lost maternal figures precipitates the perpetual mourning that structures her life. Her sexual assault and friend's murder do not initiate her racial melancholia; these traumas only exacerbate her existing despondency. When sixteen-year-old Wonnie and Mildred run away from their foster home, the latter becomes another substitute maternal figure for Wonnie. "Don't worry, kid," an older-looking, more mature Mildred repeatedly tells her, "I'll take care of you."[23] Mildred's constant insistence that she can safeguard Wonnie reveals her naïveté, and her murder demonstrates her inability to protect them both from the predations of white men. Nevertheless Mildred attempts to negotiate the fact that her sexuality is commodified already for her. Whereas Wonnie is the ultimate ingénue in the novel, Mildred and Hattie are foils as "bad" girls. They embody the palpable sexuality characteristic of popular fiction as well as the novel's critique of white society's sexual exploitation. Mildred's suggestion that she is willing to exchange sex-ual favors for money mediates the continuum Elizabeth Alice Clement argues emerged between courtship and prostitution in the interwar era; such liminality permitted working-class women to profit from sex without forsaking respectability.[24] Mildred specifically takes advantage of older men who try to exploit young girls, but unlike Hattie, she does not consummate any of her implied promises with men outside the race. "Are you kidding?" she clarifies for a guileless Wonnie. "I wouldn't have nothing to do with a white man for a thousand dollars."[25] Mildred cajoles every man, but her erotic desire is discriminate.

As the dialogue in *Third Ward Newark* is unencumbered with esoteric language, Mildred's refusal to consent to her sexual exploitation via aus-tere speech-acts unequivocally exposes the legal and cultural implica-tions of interracial rape. Two white men force Wonnie and Mildred into a car at gunpoint and drive them to the outskirts of the city, but Mildred is certain that invoking the law will protect the teens from sexual assault. Their assailant, Ernie Mihie, offers to buy the girls' sexual consent, as if the abduction and strong-arm tactics connote an equitable business transaction. "Now listen . . . you girls be nice to us, and everything'll be all right," he speciously explains. "We're gonna give you some money and take you back to town after a while. But you got to be nice to us. See?"[26] In response Mildred threatens the men with the police and the fact that she and Wonnie are underage. Her identification of Ernie and his bar, the Gin Mill, by name further strengthens her verbal assertion of what Lauren Berlant calls "Diva Citizenship."[27] "We ain't but sixteen, and the law'll handle you if you bother us," Mildred warns.[28] She attempts to claim the rights of subjecthood, but rape laws, as feminist legal scholar Catharine A. MacKinnon contends, deny the power inequalities created by social hierarchies.[29] Jurisprudence recognizes power inequality in regard to the age of sexual consent, but Mildred and Wonnie's class and racial difference debases the girls and overrides their youthfulness in the white males' gaze rather than criminalizes the men's solicitation of the minors. Ernie bluntly confirms, "There ain't much use in stopping now."[30] The girls are in a constant state of about to be raped in white patriarchal culture, and extant statutory rape laws do not guarantee their security.

In her second attempt to stay her rape, Mildred's interlocution keenly registers the cultural signification that discredits black women as sexual victims and white men as sexual perpetrators. "Let us go, mister," she begs. "You don't want me. I'm—I'm sick. Let me go, and I'll give you all the money I got." She offers Ernie money in exchange for her safety in an effort to invert the power inequality intrinsic to his solicitation. Her equivocating claim to be sick plays on stereotypes of sexual pathology purportedly evident in black women's licentious, diseased bodies and seemingly justifying white male predation. Hence her rejection of her would-be rapist not only racializes him but also emasculates white masculinity traditionally configured as privileged prowess. "Take your hands off me, white man. Go get a white girl," she demands.[31] Mildred belittles Ernie and reduces him to his race. She further usurps his presumed authority by alluding to his impotence. She differentiates her sexually exploited black body from his entitled white one and demotes white male desire as true sexual pathology. Her demand that Ernie direct his rapaciousness toward white women presumes his inability to do so: his wife is an invalid, and earlier in the evening two white women stood up him and his partner. The men's impotence in addition to their bigotry reveal them as the black, working-class, teenage girls' social inferiors.

Third Ward Newark further demythologizes the denigration of black femininity and the enabling of white masculinity by telling Mildred's murder from two disparate perspectives. The novel's third-person narration juxtaposes a version from Wonnie, who only hears the attack, and a version from Ernie, who perpetrates it, in lieu of invoking Mildred's viewpoint. To an extent, black women's rape remains unrepresentable in Lucas's text, while white men's transgressions are ineludible. Wonnie bears witness to the violent struggle as she herself is restrained. Lucas relays exposition through Mildred and Ernie's dialogue, during which Mildred threatens him with a knife and Ernie retaliates by calling her a "dirty black bitch." The text escalates this drama by describing Mildred's death in hurried, concise details: "There was a blow, a muffled scream, then another blow. After that came a solid *bop*—dull, sickening, terrifying. After that—silence." Given her vehement physical and verbal resistance, Mildred's deafening silence speaks to the literal and symbolic negation of black women. Lucas then revisits the night's events in the novel from Ernie's point of view, which reveals the intoxicated men's futile attempts to woo several black women before one threatens them with a knife. "The best colored girls are usually like that," Ernie reasons. "They won't have anything to do with white men. Same as the best white girls won't have nothing to do with colored men." Ernie appears appreciative and affirmed, respectively, by black and white women's prejudice, but the murder proves his impotence and emasculation. His irascibility during his vicious attack dissolves into doubt in its aftermath; this transition prefigures his suffering under Wonnie's relentless harassment.

"Who would have thought the girl would have fought him like she did?" he angles his rationalizations. "How was he to know that she was another one of those colored girls who wouldn't have anything to do with a white man?"[32] It is not until his partner reminds him that the police do not investigate black women's deaths because authorities are apathetic about such crimes in the Third Ward that Ernie ceases to question his felony.

Mildred's abduction results in murder and not rape, but Wonnie escapes both crimes only to be violated by the natural environment and pathologized by the two white men who later find her abused body. Wonnie flees into the woods and suffers the emotional agony and corporeal violence of sexual violation even though she does not experience physical rape.[33]

> She ran on through the tall reeds, letting out long, loud, terrified screams. One of her shoes came off, and she ran on without it. Something sharp, a broken reed or stick, stuck into the bottom of her foot, hurting her cruelly. She gave a loud, agonized wail and stumbled on. Her skirt caught on something and tore from her body as she fell. . . . She started crawling on her hands and knees, and reeds and sticks raked at her body like spurs, tearing her underclothes from her body and scratching her flesh.[34]

Wonnie's metaphorical rape is emblematic of the pervasiveness of black women's sexual exploitation, and the terrain's assault makes plain *Third Ward Newark*'s naturalist critique. Mildred's brutal murder and the extenuating circumstances of Wonnie's survival magnify the drama in the novel and delineate the systematic violation of black female bodies in racist and patriarchal culture. This is again demonstrated when two white truck drivers discover Wonnie's nude and bruised body on the highway. Because her blackness apparently explains her victimization, Wonnie's obvious trauma is virtually invisible to the white men. They muse, "You can't never tell about colored girls. Something's always happening to them." Weeks later the police discover Mildred's body in the river with a fractured skull and broken jaw, but she is "fully dressed, except for a tear on the skirt."[35] The novel precludes both girls' physical rape, but both of their bodies show the evidence of sexualized interracial violence.

Lucas balances hegemonic discourses with the impassioned voice of the disenfranchised African American community in order to make evident the social, political, cultural, and psychic violence directed at black women. Just as the truck drivers blame Wonnie for her victimization, white health care professionals, privileged with the authority to evaluate and diagnose trauma, suspect that Wonnie is an escapee from a mental institution. In her delirious state she "kept mumbling something about two white men, and she seemed afraid of all white faces. At times she would call for someone named Hattie, then she would change and call for someone named Mildred."[36] The nurses' misunderstanding of Wonnie's recurring psychic injury as psychosis highlights what Karla F. C. Holloway argues about the right to privacy as "a socially selective privilege": the individual personhood of racialized and gendered bodies "is either subsumed into this nation's social history or extracted from it," whereas white bodies are entitled with "a normative protection that extends from their citizenship."[37] The nurses' misdiagnosis maintains American epistemological hierarchies between white and black, male and female, privileged and oppressed by denying Wonnie's traumatized interiority and right to privacy. In turn Wonnie's fear of whiteness extends to the nurses and the police in addition to her attacker, and it prevents her from narrating her trauma. The black community, however, effectively names all white men culpable in her assault as well as the Third Ward's collective subjugation. The neighborhood is critically aware that black women's economic exploitation engenders their sexual vulnerability at the same time that their sexual exploitation compounds their economic vulnerability. The community angrily denounces, "White bastards! Pay a colored girl fifteen dollars a week to scrub their floors, and fifteen dollars a night to sleep with them." Mildred and Wonnie's ordeal is an "old story," and the riotous black residents deface white-owned businesses with the warning "KEEP YOUR HANDS OFF COLORED GIRLS."[38]

The Third Ward reacts to Newark's history of interracial sexual violence and police brutality with an urban insurrection, but Lucas's novel promotes voting and education as long-term alternatives for opposing institutional oppression. Historian Clement Price esteems *Third Ward Newark* as "a prophetic novel," as Lucas's depiction of vandalism, looting, and physical violence forecasts the 1967 Newark riots.[39] The 1943 New York riots, which are the first incited by African Americans because of an altercation between a white policeman and a black soldier, and the Detroit riots of that same year, which were inflamed by the rumor that white men had forced a black mother and her infant off the Belle Isle Bridge, probably inspired Lucas's representation of an uprising.[40] In the novel lawyer and politician Otis Evans employs both Hattie's and Wonnie's stories of sexual coercion to mobilize the Third Ward to unseat the police chief in the upcoming election. "All I know is that [Hattie] tried to keep going. She tried to feed her little cousin," he beseeches. "Now, for the life of me, I can't see how a girl like that can be bad."[41] Otis also organizes a community fundraiser to finance Wonnie's out-of-state education; the opportunity saves her from the state's efforts to place her in a home for wayward girls. Yet her leaving does not change the status quo for blacks in Newark. Her absence allows everyone to forget, and her family—like her attackers—hope she does too.

Wonnie's return to Newark five years later reveals that time, distance, and erudition do not resolve the social and psychic crises triggering her racial melancholia. In Wright's novel *Native Son* education actually exposes the depth of African Americans' disenfranchisement. The ranting man who shares Bigger's jail cell "went off his nut from studying too much at the university."[42] Comparably vocational schooling does not suppress Wonnie's memories or her evolving awareness of black women's systematic subjugation. A "slender, mature, poised, and thoughtful" Wonnie comes home, but her "warm, mellow voice" turns "sharp, taunting, with a suggestion of fury in it" and her eyes become "hard and smoldering, with an insane light in them" when she confronts Ernie in his bar. Similar to the pleasure and suffering Bates experienced harassing Drunken Pig in *The Long Shadow of Little Rock*, Lucas's narrator notes that Wonnie feels "a crazy kind of joy" facing Ernie's "pig eyes." Her compulsion to punish him with her tormenting gaze proves emotionally satiating and yet psychologically destructive, since Ernie first misrecognizes Wonnie and then cowardly dismisses her as mentally unstable. "Maybe I am crazy, Ernie. I wouldn't know," she threatens. "I'll see how crazy *they* think I am." Wonnie tries to intimidate him with the police, but the repeated failure of jurisprudence intensifies her racial melancholia. The police become fellow accomplices in her melancholic framework. "You've thought about this thing too much. . . . It's become an obsession with you," an officer placates. "I'm sorry to say this, but if you keep thinking about it, it could drive you insane. Now if you doubt what I'm telling you, just go to any reliable psychiatrist and he'll tell you the same thing." With no avenue for legal recourse, Wonnie visits the Gin Mill to enact her own justice. "You're a murderer, and I don't want you to forget it," she pledges. "I want you to suffer. I—I want you to feel that girl is chained to you, you—you murderer!"[43] She frequents the establishment to accost him publicly as the living evidence of his crime. In Mildred's absence, Wonnie functions as the return of the repressed.

Wonnie's haunting gaze is an affecting form of torment because her recondite confrontations with Ernie repeat and revise the novel's earlier trauma. Their contests also mark Ernie as a melancholic subject. Whereas his partner meets his comeuppance with a brutal death in the numbers racket, Ernie's apologist stance makes him susceptible to consuming regret and debilitating fear. He does not mourn Mildred, but he has never forgotten the murder. Mirroring Wonnie's melancholic tone, Ernie confesses, "It's always with me. Sometimes I can't eat, and sometimes I can't sleep."[44] Wonnie perpetually laments Mildred as the lost loved one, but Wonnie is also the melancholic object to Ernie's plagued subject. As Cheng posits, the minority Other simultaneously operates as the subject of loss and the lost object in the melancholic processes of American racialization, while hegemonic white subjectivity is "an elaborate identificatory system based on psychical and social consumption-and-denial" of the Other.[45] Both whites and people of color are defined through practices of racial inclusion and exclusion. In *Third Ward Newark* an increasingly suicidal Ernie acquiesces: "Little by little the girl was punishing him; little by little she was driving him mad."[46] Ernie loses his sense of white male supremacy along with his mental well-being because he can neither subsume Wonnie nor negate his past transgressions under her unyielding gaze.

Wonnie and Ernie agonize over discordant abstractions, but the two are charged with remembering Mildred's grim murder. Wonnie's constant presence tortures Ernie, and, in this way, his loss of self-esteem more than his guilty conscience inundates him. Wonnie's girlhood is saturated with lost loved ones, her coming into womanhood devastated by sexual trauma, and her adulthood consumed with desire for retribution. Her need to persecute Ernie continues to burden her the most, as her outrage inhibits her from pursuing more generative desires. "What happened to us, what we did, would have happened to anybody else in our place," Hattie tries to persuade Wonnie. "It just happened, that's all." A model of redressed black womanhood, Hattie reconciles her economic and sexual exploitation with her later marriage to Otis. Joe Anderson also ostensibly emerges heroically in the novel as Wonnie's talking cure. She builds romantic intimacy with him by unabashedly sharing her past: "She left out nothing. She told him about her mother's death, about Hattie's getting into trouble, and about herself and Mildred, and the white men." Joe becomes the object of Wonnie's affections, and she adopts his economic coping strategies for racism and discrimination. However, Joe does not understand the gender dynamics undergirding Wonnie's racial melancholia. He proposes, "I'll guess we'll get married right away. . . . And—and you can just—just forget about what you told me. Just forget it ever happened."[47] Neither marriage nor the accoutrements of respectability can reconcile the way Mildred's murder razes pedestal femininity for Wonnie. Her life with Joe, then, is only a short-term cure that entrenches her social and psychological vulnerability under Jane Crow oppression.

What He Says: Black Economic Independence as Cure-All

Joe Anderson manifests the dominant masculinist perspective that subverts Lucas's potentially proto-womanist sensibility in *Third Ward Newark*. The character is also the writer's alter ego. Both are Georgia-born southern migrants who moved to New Jersey (also known as "the Georgia of the North," according to Price) for the economic opportunities created by World War II's labor demand.[48] Lucas attended high school in Eatonville, Florida (the hometown of writer Zora Neale Hurston), and then went to night school while working in Atlantic City. He initially aspired to a career in medicine, but he studied creative writing at the Columbia University Extension School before he settled into a series of jobs at Newark's Federal Shipyards. He was employed as a sheet metal mechanic during the war, and he worked as a food processor at the time of *Third Ward Newark*'s publication with the hope that his novel's success would allow him to open a bookstore. Analogously Joe is "a big country boy" who offsets Wonnie's nightmarish past with his dream to open a grocery store in the Third Ward. Also a shipyard sheet metal worker during the war, college-educated Joe plans to force white-owned establishments out of the black community with his saved earnings. "We have to go into competition with them and drive them out of business. When we do that, we can start going places," he explains to Wonnie. "If we don't do that, we can hate all our lives, and it won't get us any place."[49] Reminiscent of the fatherly advice that frees Bates from consuming bitterness in *The Long Shadow of Little Rock*, Joe promotes economic strategies for black collective empowerment. Moreover his marriage to Wonnie is the paragon of what Ruth Feldstein calls "healthy and productive citizenship."[50] Joe restores Wonnie's faith in her ability to attain the ideals of respectability in his role as protector and provider. Yet his authority in her narrative complicates the text's Jane Crow politics because he fails to recognize black women's double jeopardy. As a result he forecloses a womanist agenda and cements the narrative's masculinist politics.

Lucas employs Joe's character to demonstrate the benefits of World War II labor for bettering interracial social relations. When Wonnie joins her husband working at the shipyard, she witnesses democracy in action. Joe instructs Wonnie to reject the janitorial job the shipyard will initially offer her and demand the welder's job for which she has been trained.[51] Historian Karen Anderson specifies that black women were at the bottom of the hiring hierarchy despite the labor shortage during World War II, as most companies employed them in domestic service or other low-paying, unskilled positions, if at all. Wonnie's new employment is crucial because she works in a skilled, high-paying position alongside her husband, and her job allays her phobia of whiteness by way of the friendship she develops with the white female welder Mary. The equitable triangular relationship between Mary, Joe, and Wonnie is an American leftist ideal. White women, black men, and black women are all oppressed in a white male capitalist society, and the war provides all three constituents an opportunity to unite under worker solidarity. Wonnie is originally uneasy about Mary's whiteness, but Joe claims, "Out here in the Yard they don't pay much attention to all that stuff. Everybody is too busy trying to get their work done. The Union did a pretty good job out here, and a man is a man."[52] Mary treats Joe like a peer and vice versa, despite their racial difference; Wonnie and Mary bond as women within the male-dominated labor force. Their interracial homosocial bond is particularly significant, as white women historically exhibited hostility toward black women in such labor settings. Black men were employed in industry before the war, so it was their promotion and not their hiring that was a source of conflict for white men.[53] In contrast, white women's desire to maintain social privileges rather than economic appurtenances caused work conflicts between black and white women because the latter felt less entitled to their nontraditional labor.[54] However, in *Third Ward Newark* Wonnie and Mary grow so close working together at the shipyard that Wonnie shares her past sexual trauma with Mary, who is "genuinely touched by her story."[55]

The war's unprecedented open labor market improved race relations as well as expanded women's roles in the public sector, but the social and economic benefits awarded black women on their jobs did not necessarily change their roles in the home. In *Creating Rosie the Riveter* Maureen Honey illustrates that even though contemporaneous media images depicted women's importance to war industries, they maintained traditional views of women's roles within the family. Black women's increased financial independence was particularly contentious for disenfranchised black men, who wanted to achieve and maintain their status as breadwinners and their wives' identities as homemakers. "I'm a man, Wonnie, and I can take care of my wife," Joe insists. "I let you come out here to work because you said you wanted to. But what money you make out here I want you to put into bonds. All of it. I'm taking care of you."[56] His decision upholds his masculine authority as financial provider, and it conveys, to use Lawrence R. Samuel's words describing Americans' engagement with the bond program, Joe's commitment "to literally and figuratively buy into the war."[57] The bond campaign was a nationalist rally to sell the idea of the war to all Americans—including African Americans excluded from the rights of citizenship—with the promise of prosperity in postwar life. Blacks' participation in the bond drive indicates that the *Pittsburgh Courier*'s Double V campaign was at the beginning of the modern civil rights movement, during which African Americans mobilized for victory over racism at home in addition to victory over fascism abroad. To purchase a war bond meant funding the war and investing in blacks' economic independence, and Joe's labor and monetary investment exemplifies patriotic citizenship. Furthermore single ladies as well as hustling women in the Third Ward recuperate black female respectability by ending their patronage of the Gin Mill and securing factory jobs. White men's economic and sexual exploitation does not dictate black women's industrial labor the same way it controls black women's domestic work or prostitution at Ernie's bar.

Third Ward Newark points to the social, economic, and civic advantages of African Americans' war labor. However, the novel ultimately deconstructs affirmative nationalist politics with two popular plot contrivances: a rat (a familiar symbol of mid-twentieth-century oppression) and a dream (a classic psychoanalytic trope). Bigger's memorable killing of a rat in the opening pages of *Native Son* introduces readers to the subjugation driving his actions and subsequent execution. In *Third Ward Newark* the rat symbolizes the intersection of black women's racial and gender subjection. Men at the shipyard act out a war fantasy and pretend that the rat they chase is a "Jap" they must kill in his foxhole. They are confused as to why Wonnie goes "nuts" after witnessing the scene, and they use her emotional response as evidence that women have no business working there.[58] Connie Field corroborates this chauvinistic sentiment in her documentary *The Life and Times of Rosie the Riveter*. As white female World War II welder Lola Weixel explains in the film, "To a man, when a woman walked in, it meant that a man went to war." Unsurprisingly Wonnie identifies with the rat's torture instead of the men's bravado; rats, Japanese soldiers, and black women are all comparable targets of white American male antipathy. This chain of signification is made more explicit in Wonnie's later nightmare, during which the persecuted rat transforms into Mildred. In the dream Ernie puts a blowtorch to the pipe in which Mildred is hiding, and he has the long and yellow teeth of a pernicious rat. When Joe wakes Wonnie from this night terror, he inadvertently interrupts his wife from processing the dream with his well-intentioned though paternalistic concern that Wonnie works too much. He does not address her fears but perpetuates the melodrama regarding her mental instability.

Thus Lucas employs Joe for two primary narrative functions: to demonstrate the benefits of war labor for black workers and to endorse black economic independence for the Third Ward's collective wealth and self-esteem. Wonnie buys into Joe's dream and reconfigures herself into the kind of activist Lizabeth Cohen calls "citizen-consumer ideal types," who "put the market power of the consumer to work politically, not only to save a capitalist America in the midst of the Great Depression [and World War II era], but also to safeguard the rights of individual consumers and the larger 'general good.'"[59] Wonnie practices socially conscious consumption and revitalizes Joe's favorite restaurant. She not only improves the black-owned establishment's quality in terms of food and service, but she also opposes the Third Ward's economic exploitation by taking the nearby white competitor's black customers. Her efficacy as a consumer-citizen kindles her hope that she can end white men's predation of the Third Ward: "She was doing something, she was fighting back. At times she was elated, jubilant. At other times she became bewildered, frightened at the things she could really do."[60] Historically, black women participated in economic racial-uplift strategies through organizations like the Detroit Housewives' League, whose motto, "Buy, Boost, Build," encouraged consumers to boycott the stores that did not carry black-produced brands and to patronize the black-owned businesses that promoted jobs for blacks. Members also educated black women, as the managers of household incomes, about economic issues such as war rations, their spending power, and new products. Wonnie's work at the restaurant fulfills her commitment to blacks' economic progress, but Joe worries that this second job will cause her to fall sick.

Institutional racism devitalizes the Third Ward's economic determination by impeding African Americans' social mobility through Jim Crow segregation. Wonnie realizes the limitations of the black community's economic independence when a white man sexually propositions her outside the door of her rented room. She and Joe are aware that their landlord manages a gambling and prostitution enterprise, but Joe advises his wife to "be a good girl and play blind for the time being," until the newlyweds can move.[61] In short, he asks Wonnie to deny what she sees and to forget what she knows. Her racial melancholia rebounds with the white john's threat of rape and his epidermalization of her within the supposed sanctity of her domestic space. As Charles Johnson theorizes, African Americans' encounter with white society's gaze denies their interiority and reduces black subjectivity to "black-as-body."[62] In *Third Ward Newark* Wonnie's epidermalization relegates her humanity to *black-as-sexed-body*. Racial and sexual difference eroticizes white men's perception of black women's bodies; thus the john's gaze surveys Wonnie's blackness as lascivious sexuality. The encounter sabotages Wonnie's psychological gains and reminds her of her economic and sexual vulnerability. She encourages Joe to work all the overtime he can so that the couple can rent a suitable apartment, but she informs him, "I'm not going out to the shipyard any more, and I'm not buying anymore bonds, Joe. Democracy. Huh!"[63] Beginning to lose faith in the American Dream and the cult of pedestal femininity, she reverts to her fears that she cannot access the privileges of healthy citizenship due to this new, yet familiar crisis.

Wonnie's return to the Gin Mill portends the demise of her promising marriage, precipitates the end of World War II prosperity, and predicts her physical death in addition to her psychological decline. The concluding war makes little long-term impact on the quality of African American life in the Third Ward. The shipyard executes mass cutbacks and layoffs; the union uses seniority as an excuse to exclude black workers; and black consumers can no longer support black-owned businesses. In *The Life and Times of Rosie the Riveter* Wanita Allen recalls that in Detroit in the postwar years black women were forced to return to custodial work. "Anytime there is a restaurant job, or a dishwashing job, or a cooking job," she concludes, "I always felt like blacks could always get those 'cause they save those jobs for us." In Lucas's novel single black women return to the Gin Mill in order to solicit men when they lose their factory jobs, and Wonnie revisits the bar to await official word of the war's end. This time her confrontation with Ernie relapses into prevailing power dynamics between black women and white men, and her despair makes her defenseless against his predation. Ernie instigates a commotion between a white soldier and a black female customer that echoes the novel's original scene of trauma. While the rebuffed soldier angrily proclaims, "I been overseas fighting for you," the woman dismisses him as a drunk "white boy."[64] Their exchange demonstrates that the ideologies regarding race, class, gender, and sexuality existing before the war are the same afterward. The soldier's racist profanity incites the

bar into a bottle-throwing riot, and Ernie seizes the opportunity to murder Wonnie with a blow to her head. Dominant discourses frame urban
riots as lawless assertions of black manhood and black women as loot-
ers or culpable victims.[65] Therefore, upon discovering Wonnie's body,
the police believe she is a casualty of black criminality and not white
male predation. Lucas adds further insult to Wonnie's murder by briefly
informing the novel's readers that the white soldier provoking the race
riot is a recent escapee from a psychiatric ward.

Third Ward Newark's preemptory masculinist perspective usurps
the text's portrayal of black women's economic and sexual exploitation.
Joe achieves his dream of opening a grocery store in the denouement as
well as Lucas's moral regarding proper grieving. Together Joe and Otis
deduce Ernie's collusion and torment him with their suspicions, despite
not having a full understanding of the events culminating in Wonnie's
death. Reminiscent of Wonnie's conviction when tormenting Ernie, Joe
pledges his commitment to solve his wife's murder. "If I don't find out
tonight, I'm gonna find out tomorrow, and if I don't find out tomorrow
I'll try the next day," he declares. Otis arouses such suspicion that Ernie
loses his liquor license and hastily confesses to all of his crimes before
committing suicide. Joe's grocery store, Anderson & Anderson, replaces
the Gin Mill anon. The new business promises an end to white economic
exploitation in the Third Ward, but Joe's store also stands as a memorial to Wonnie because, as Otis states, "all he'll ever do is remember her
now."[66]

Lucas charges Joe to never forget, but the writer differentiates between
Wonnie's pathological melancholia and Joe's productive mourning.
Monuments theoretically negate death as extensions of or substitu-
tions for the absent body, and consequently they often arrest memory
work.[67] Lucas's widower specifically finds closure to potentially consuming bereavement by incorporating his beloved into his ego—his store.
However, Joe's mourning process does not necessarily preclude him as
a remittent melancholic since the best mourner is in fact a more refined
melancholic that can capably displace the lost loved one.[68] Wonnie essentially dies for Joe's dream to materialize, but he is confident he has not
completely lost her. "Maybe I'll feel her again, like I used to feel her before
I met her," he speculates.[69] Joe envisages his wife before their paths cross
just as he imagines his business before he can make it a reality. Hence
for Joe, Wonnie is less a person than an abstract ideal complement-
ing his collective goals. The narrative privileges his perpetual grieving
because he is an agent that empowers the community without repeating

its debilitating trauma. Joe bests capitalist enterprise while Wonnie's acts are considered deviant and threatening in relation to the community and the state. She is an inevitable casualty of the contest between black and white men, and her stake in the store is symbolized by her married name only.

Lucas presents his fictional counterpart as a model of healthy citizenship, and he sacrifices his black female protagonist for the benefit of the entire Third Ward. In an effort to restore domestic intimacy as an inviolable space for desire, *Third Ward Newark* fulfills what Candice M. Jenkins terms the "salvific wish," by which black women pay the cost of the black community's safety with the restrictions placed upon their bodies.[70] Correspondingly one contemporaneous review praises the novel as "an effort to lead the white man to [a] better understanding of his black brothers—something that probably would bring about the equality so lacking at present."[71] For Lucas, black women's rape stages black men's mourning, and black women's death serves to emancipate black collective identity. As the most marginalized subject in *Third Ward Newark*, Wonnie, who seeks restitution through looks of condemnation, never sees justice. The novel's latent conflicts between its male writer and female protagonist vividly demarcate mid-twentieth-century Jane Crow politics, as the male-female dichotomy maps onto the differences between privileging the demands of the community over the needs of an individual, between economic security and psychic stability. The text's affirmation of communal salvation versus individual psychosis forfeits Wonnie's subjectivity.

What the Market Demands: Commercializing Black Women's Subjugation

Third Ward Newark intimates the disconnection between the needs of the race and the supposed inferior sex by making Wonnie collateral damage in Joe's achievement. World War II labor, patriotic war bonds, and black economic independence resolve his subjugation but not her constant anger about her sexual abuse. The text fails to reconfigure social protest for its black female protagonist, since Wonnie's putative recklessness precipitates her murder. It also falls short in conceiving constructive ways for black women to dismantle racism, sexism, and the expectations of middle-class respectability, given that Wonnie is affirmed as Mrs. Anderson only after her passing. Lucas implicates two perpetrators complicit in black women's disenfranchisement: white men who assault their bodies and institutional structures that condone this oppression. However, *Third Ward Newark* also inadvertently indicts the novel's black male actor in its Jane Crow discourse. Wonnie's death critiques Joe's efforts to utilize solely economic strategies for structurally constituted crises. Moreover Lucas underestimates Wonnie's self-determined desirous pursuits as subversive resistance. She is predisposed to construct black female subjectivity outside the politics of respectability, but Lucas limits her subjectivity to the fear and vulnerability Joe chauvinistically associates with femininity.[72] With this feminine archetype, Lucas suggests that black women's physical violation is overdetermined and black women's anger in response to such oppression is psychologically devastating.

While Lucas's plot contrivances circumscribe black women's social, political, economic, and psychic concerns within the reductive boundaries of black masculinist discourse, *Third Ward Newark*'s evolving cover art exemplifies the commodification and consumption of black women's intersecting oppressions. The differing visual interpretations of Lucas's narrative by Ziff-Davis Publishing and Lion Books vividly illustrate the Jane Crow politics of the novel's cultural production. The Chicago-based Ziff-Davis established its catalogue in the 1920s by producing magazines for hobby activities such as radio and aviation, and in the 1940s the publisher expanded its brand to include pulp fiction magazines, such as the science-fiction *Amazing Stories*. In 1943 Ziff-Davis acquired the New York–based imprint Fingerprint Mysteries, whose logo featured a fingerprint in a magnifying glass on the books' dusk jackets. Titles for the series' novels were suspenseful, and their covers often used literal imagery to catch the reader's eye. For example, Helen Farrar's novel *Murder Goes to School* (1948) shows a skeleton holding a pointer to a chalkboard on which the book's title is written. In 1948 Ziff-Davis ended the mystery series but continued to produce pulp magazines and nonfiction on such varying subjects as sports and photography.

Ziff-Davis distributed the original hardback edition of *Third Ward Newark* under its main, flying horse logo. Unlike the Dali-esque dust jacket for Murray Forbes's contemporaneous psychological suspense novel *Hollow Triumph* (1946), the illustration for Lucas's cover gives a realist representation of Wonnie as a middle-class lady (Figure 3). The dust jacket affords the character more agency than the plot; the artwork does not hint at the psychological pathology exhaustively debated in the novel. Instead the cover presents a pedestal portrait of African American womanhood, with Wonnie's perfectly coiffed hair, feminine dangling earrings, modish red lipstick, and chic red dress. Red accents often

FIGURE 3. *Third Ward Newark* by Curtis Lucas,
1946 edition, dust jacket. (Special Collections and
University Archives, Rutgers University Libraries)

intimate sex or danger, but Wonnie's sideways gaze and angled body
position convey a demure, not an impudent air. Interestingly her hair
takes on the gold tones of the cover's background and gives her an almost
white appearance, while the summary of the novel complicates this fair
image of refinement. The inside flap relates that Wonnie "sprang" from
the "tough, turbulent, and overcrowded" Third Ward with "her haunting
beauty, her rebellion against injustice, and the story of the vengeance she
swore against the white man who nearly ruined her life." On the back
jacket details about Lucas's migration north and attainment of education
lend credibility to this drama. The biographical information markets the
novel as a sociological analysis of urban black disenfranchisement, as

Lucas's various working-class jobs "giv[e] him a firsthand opportunity to study the social and living conditions of the Negroes in Newark." The cover's script spotlights the community, but the illustration exhibits Wonnie's composed subjectivity as a decorous representative of the black community—even though the plot contends otherwise.

The 1952 paperback reprint of *Third Ward, Newark* has the same narrative content, but its cover reflects a transition in the text's cultural production. The artwork for the Lion Books edition luridly pushes race and sex in vintage pulp paperback tradition. Initially mid-twentieth-century publishers produced paperback reprints of classic works on cheap wood-pulp paper so that they could be inexpensively priced and mass-produced. As the industry expanded in the 1940s, pulp paperback publishers such as Avon, Bantam, and Dell began to produce original content containing more sex and violence. Editors at Lion even wrote and handed out synopses of novels as assignments for writers, and as the king of noir and hard-boiled paperback publishing, Lion concentrated on themes of despair, crime, rage, and revenge.[73] Easy to buy, easy to read, easy to discard, pulp paperbacks provided readers with fantasy as well as postwar realism. The novels sensationally flaunted race and sex in provocative titles and even more suggestively illustrated cover art. Such artwork marketed the racy narratives like a peep show, a stylized performance in which its iconography is explicit and often symbolic.[74] The covers were important for merchandising the popular fiction, though there was little creative distinction among illustrators.[75] Scantily clad women, for example, were commonly displayed, regardless of the work's content.[76] Branding all of its books with its eponymous logo and a publishing number, Lion produced three novels shortly before and after *Third Ward Newark* that feature virtually the same woman on their covers. James Gordon's *The Lust of Private Cooper* (number 77) baits consumers with a blonde in a pink negligee and a seductive pose; Jeff Bogar's *My Gun, Her Body* (number 79) shows a blonde standing in a pink robe that nearly reveals her bosom as it slides off her shoulders; and Gerald Butler's *The Lurking Man* (number 81) suggests subterfuge with a blonde's downcast gaze and pink dress, whose neckline hardly covers her cleavage.

Lion's cover art for *Third Ward, Newark* (number 80) literally and figuratively cheapens Lucas's rape rhetoric. The novel is priced at a quarter, and the illustration amplifies the racial and sexual tension of the text (Figure 4). With the paperback reprint, the text's written and visual narratives jointly thwart Wonnie's efforts to attain subjectivity. Curiously the cover emphasizes the novel's racial conflict with the subtle addition

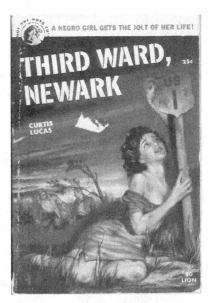

FIGURE 4. *Third Ward, Newark* by
Curtis Lucas, 1952 edition, cover
illustration. (Private collection)

of a comma to the title, which grammatically separates the Third Ward
from greater Newark. Above the title an introductory blurb teases, "A
Negro girl gets the jolt of her life!" Yet the front cover's most salacious
aspect is its depiction of Wonnie's metaphoric rape. In contrast to contemporaneous Lion pin-up figures, Wonnie is a light-brown-complex-
ioned, dark-haired beauty in red lipstick, a torn skirt, and a red shirt
barely covering her breasts. Ernie and his partner search for Wonnie
in the distance, while she, bruised and dirty, clutches a U.S. 1 highway
sign. Her kneeling position and pleading gaze in relation to the sign—
an unmistakable symbol of nationalist discourse—epitomizes her low
subject position in the racist and sexist hegemony of the state. The Lion
cover gestures toward the social commentary of the Ziff-Davis version,
but the paperback visually grabs the voyeuristic reader. The illustration
eroticizes the novel's violence in lieu of portraying Wonnie's retributive
gaze. Moreover the back cover advertises black and white men's competing desires for Wonnie with two more sensational images. "Wonnie
Brown ripened on the filthy, teeming pavements of Newark's slum—
young, beautiful, Negro," the summary tantalizes. "Then Ernie Mihie,

white, saw her, wanted her, brutalized her on a lonely road outside the city." A picture of Ernie forcing Wonnie into a car is juxtaposed with a romantic sketch of Joe and Wonnie sharing a loving embrace, but the précis forewarns readers, "Not even a bone-aching hunger for love could stop her thrust to revenge." Sexual innuendo saturates this script and implies Wonnie's wanton desire despite her sexual assault on the front cover. In hypersexualizing the black female body for the presumed male (and perhaps white) reader, the illustration echoes the novel's sacrificing of Wonnie for the benefit of the black community at the novel's climactic end.

The covers for Lucas's subsequent paperbacks continue along these thematic lines, but they distinctly market black men's and white women's interracial desire. *So Low, So Lowly* touts its risqué subject matter with the introductory blurb "A Negro searches for love in an alien world" and an image of a frustrated black man sitting in a dilapidated kitchenette with a pensive-looking blonde. *Angel*'s cover shifts subject positions by declaring, "A white woman shocks the whole city." An interracial couple walks down the street in the foreground, while a series of gazes draw the reader in: the black man looks dubiously at the white woman; she looks flirtingly at the reader; and a white male in the background throws a furtive look at both of them. The cover of *Forbidden Fruit* centers on a cigarette-smoking, shirtless black man with his head in the lap of a sultry redhead in an unbuttoned dress. The cover's caption underlines their postcoital repose: "A compelling novel of a boy and girl in love—facing the great question of racial segregation." The interracial affairs paraded in these three novels are very different from the racial and sexual intrigues of Joe, Wonnie, and Ernie, whose triangle of desire, so to speak, is romantic on one side, vengeful on another, and finally predatory. "That first novel was a crusading sort of book. . . . I guess I was naive, but I thought the book might help to remedy some of the conditions," Lucas admits in a 1949 interview. "I was wrong about that. This time, I'm not writing on a social or economic theme. The new novel is a love story."[77] The liaisons between black men and white women apparently fulfilled the writer's ambition for romance. However, before Lucas wrote about love and consensual sex, he wrote about rape and hate. The respective artwork for the Ziff-Davis and Lion productions of the novel reflects the Jane Crow politics shaping popular mid-twentieth-century imaginings of black female subjectivity. Black femininity is venerated on the hardback's dust jacket, but black women's economic and sexual exploitation is realized and then becomes disposable on the cover of the paperback reprint.

The representation of black female subjectivity in Lucas's novel and publishers' pictorial interpretations of it archives the period's jockeying between race and gender politics. The covers' depictions of pedestal black womanhood and black women's abject subjugation document the publishers' contrary desires to champion black women's agency and to codify their victimization—just as Lucas's fictional alter ego loves his wife but benefits from her death. As Lucas likely had no control over *Third Ward Newark*'s production, the illustrations also pointedly reveal the publishers' efforts to shape and respond to readers' desires. In effect the paperback reprint recapitulates the lack of long-term change in postwar interracial relations that black women lament at the conclusion of *Third Ward Newark*. The cover's selling of race and marketing of sex effectuate the gendered violence critiqued in the novel, and its commercial exploitation of black women's sexual trauma is displayed gratuitously.

5 /   Rereading the Construction of Womanhood
in Popular Narratives of Domesticity

And now as I walk through the valley of despair;
I am surrounded by evil, for thou art with me;
Thy policy and thy staff they confuse me.
Thou preparest a table for my enemies in the presence of me;
Thou anointeth my head with baloney and thy cup runneth over.
                                    —JOHNNY DIRTHROWER, "NEGRO PRESS"

Signifying on the Bible's Twenty-third Psalm, Johnny Dirthrower's impassioned 1950 letter to the editors of *Negro Digest* criticizes Johnson Publishing Company's exploitation of black readers. The letter translates biblical piety into a condemnation of print discourses produced by, about, and for African Americans. The psalm's opening verse, "The Lord is my shepherd; . . . he leadeth me in the paths of righteousness for his name's sake," is the antecedent for Dirthrower's detraction of the black press, which "leadeth me into the path of complacency for advertisement sake."[1] Dirthrower believed the materialistic "baloney" inundating black readers delivered neither the spiritual salvation exalted in the Bible nor the social justice for which black publications historically mobilized. John H. Johnson established *Negro Digest* as well as a series of successive magazines as counternarratives to hegemonic discourses' systematic whiteout of African American subjects. However, product endorsements from companies that profited from black consumer markets yet practiced Jim Crow advertising saturated black media. Thus Dirthrower (whose name appears to be a pseudonym highlighting Johnson's transgressions) castigates black publications that "preparest a table for my enemies in the presence of me" by colluding with white hegemonies under the auspices of racial integration. "Surely evil and injustice shall follow me all the days of my life," he prophesies, "And I will not even be permitted in Hell in the Hereafter." In the profitable collusion between white advertising and black publishing, black consumers' subjectivity suffered the damnable costs. "I am sure you will not publish this anyhow," Dirthrower closes, "but I had to get it off my chest." *Negro Digest* printed the letter, but it did so without offering a defense to Dirthrower's attack, restitution to beguiled black readers, or strategies for reforming the black press.

Comparably Gwendolyn Brooks attends to print discourses' betrayal of black readers in her novel *Maud Martha* (1953) by exploring the influence of hegemonic and nonhegemonic discourses on black female subjectivity. Brooks's text reveals the mounting effect popular conceptualizations of race, gender, and class have on her titular black female protagonist's self-esteem, but Maud Martha Brown Phillips rarely articulates her grievances in the narrative. Slighted by her family's preference for her light-skinned sister, a resigned, dark-skinned Maud Martha recalls hiding in the kitchen pantry to shed tears, "now dried, flattened out, breaking into interesting dust at the merest look."[2] Contemporaneous black publications like *Negro Digest* perpetuated the intraracial caste between African American women with titles questioning "What Color Will Your Baby Be?" (1946) and "Are Black Women Beautiful?" (1951). Meanwhile the absence of black beauty images from white fashion magazines like *Vogue* and *Harper's Bazaar* confirmed interracial hierarchies. Hegemonic discourses excluded black women from the cult of true womanhood because the media aligned mainstream beauty standards with the social boundaries defining whiteness. As a result black counterdiscourses equated beauty with skin color, by which black women's proximity to whiteness helped them attain the privileges of pedestal femininity. Brooks's novel demonstrates that both hegemonic and nonhegemonic discourses prescribe Maud Martha's belief that she has "ordinary allurements" in comparison to her sister Helen's "heart-catching beauty." Thus Maud Martha concedes to "work miracles" on her alleged comeliness with the hope that she will be prized by her husband, whose skin tone is described as "low yellow."[3]

Brooks illustrates the exigency of cultural literacy for black women's self-definition during the Jane Crow era, as race, gender, and class politics determined the content and circulation of African American representation in mid-twentieth-century popular culture. Maud Martha's critical perception of herself throughout her narrative recapitulates the interwar media's ideological discourses. Together the news articles, entertainment features, gossip columns, advertisements, and photographs targeting black readership lionized black women's beauty. Yet such media coverage delimited black women's performance of subjectivity to middle-class domesticity. Black newspapers and magazines promoted racial-uplift rhetoric, but Maud Martha constantly finds herself inferior. The references to reading in Brooks's novel expose the privileged media images of beauty, domesticity, and chaste sexuality as configured fictions. "You'll never get a boy friend . . . if you don't stop reading those books," teenage Helen warns her younger sister while dusting her face with Golden Peacock powder.[4] For passive consumers like Helen, critical reading and achieving true womanhood are mutually exclusive. However, critical reading is imperative for black women's self-authorized construction of subjectivity in *Maud Martha*. The black press's portraits of pedestal African American womanhood are in stark contrast to the realities Helen and Maud Martha face in adulthood. Helen's consumption of beauty products—which promise eye-catching appeal—does not exempt her from desperately having to market herself to an older man for financial security. Analogously Maud Martha dreams of emulating the lifestyles of the rich and famous featured in black newspapers, only to discover economic poverty and a lack of luster in her marriage during World War II. In *Third Ward Newark* Curtis Lucas characterizes the war as a boon for the black community's economic opportunities. In *Maud Martha* the war's economic hardships disabuse black women of their romantic ideals about domestic luxury.

Maud Martha is thus a metafiction that purposefully excogitates how black women read, internalize, and embody hegemonic and nonhegemonic discourses. As Madelyn Jablon explicates in her study of self-consciousness in African American literature, metafiction "focus[es] on [its] own production and often suggest[s] that the production of this text is parallel to the creative process that we are involved in in the creation of the world."[5] Implementing themes of fictionality, intertextuality, and formal innovation, metafiction proposes its text as a metaphor for the self. In *Maud Martha* Brooks assays black women's private and public performance of subjectivity by subversively deconstructing contemporaneous popular cultural narratives with scenes of reading. The novel's symbolic self-reflectivity demonstrates that the construction of black female subjectivity is dependent upon critically reading written texts as well as social contexts. *Maud Martha* explicitly examines how black women read, but the novel also intrinsically considers how black women are read—that is, negated—by white society and commodified by black publications. The coming-of-age tale, written during the emergence of a post–World War II periodical culture, recognizes the significance of black women's representation in print discourses. Brooks deliberates mass media's portrayal of black womanhood as well as the ways processes of reading inform black women's self-awareness and social consciousness during the Jane Crow era.

In effect *Maud Martha*'s metafictionality challenges the publishing mandates typifying mid-twentieth-century African American social realism. The nuanced structure of the text, in addition to its almost quiescent plot, marks an aesthetic shift in the tradition. Brooks organizes the novel into a series of vignettes ranging in length from two to eighteen pages (with most chapters consisting of four or five pages) that detail episodes in the protagonist's life. These collated portraits sketch Maud Martha within economic—though poetically rich—prose requiring readers to weigh every word. Also the novel is, to borrow Ira Dworkin's term, "transgeneric" due to its slippage between the conventions of fiction and memoir.[6] In her autobiography *Report from Part One* (1972), Brooks explains, "Much in [*Maud Martha*] was taken out of my own life, and twisted, highlighted or dulled, dressed up or down." Unlike her protagonist, Brooks did not have a sister growing up. Yet the writer admits, "True in the chapter ['Helen'] . . . is the little catalogue of childhood memories," including a male playmate's "phobia" of dark-complexioned girls and Maud Martha's secret tears in the pantry.[7] While *Maud Martha*'s realistic elements are altered versions of Brooks's life, the text elides the precepts of fiction driven by social conflict by narrating an ordinary life set within the domestic space. The novel's third-person narration relays Maud Martha's childhood, courtships and marriage, creation of a home and familial traditions, and experience in childbirth. With few events outside the rituals of domesticity, Brooks's work concludes with Maud Martha anticipating a second child at the end of the war.

This domestic focus distinguishes *Maud Martha* from critically acclaimed and commercially successful reiterations of the protest novel, whose aesthetic conventions, plot formulas, and social polemics dominate mid-twentieth-century African American social realism. Fellow poet Langston Hughes declared Brooks's work a long-awaited reprieve from the period's dearth of creativity: "For years, and years, AND YEARS now we have had novel after novel AFTER NOVEL about Negroes who went to the dogs, went to jail, went to the death chair, never amounting to anything, lynched, hung, burned, . . . never escaping from the slums, miserable passing for white or miserable being colored." In contrast to this cadre of oppressed black protagonists, Hughes's review describes Maud Martha as "a normal Negro girl growing up into a normal woman finding love and being happy in it."[8] The narrative is an obvious departure from the naturalist conventions in Wright's novel *Native Son* (1940), whose protagonist Bigger Thomas murders a white woman in a panic because of the violence he faces if he is found in her bedroom; he is later sentenced to death, the fate he sought to avoid by committing his crime. Brooks rejects and rewrites *Native Son*'s violent masculinist premise with *Maud Martha*'s domestic focus. The black female writer reimagines Bigger's brutal killing of a rat (which symbolizes his economic, spatial, and psychological oppression) and renders Maud Martha quietly saving the mouse that wanders into her home. The brief sketch alludes to Maud Martha's economic despair, spatial confinement, and social powerlessness, but it affirms her "godlike loving-kindness" in lieu of reenacting the wrath of oppressed black subjects like Bigger Thomas.[9] As Patricia H. Lattin and Vernon E. Lattin point out, "Maud's rites of passage are not heralded by trumpets and fanfare, but they are nevertheless real and meaningful."[10] Maud Martha may be "normal," as Hughes contends in his *Chicago Defender* review, but her narrative only domesticates her conflicts and frustrations. Brooks does not ignore the racial and gender politics of Maud Martha's cultural moment; rather the writer pointedly resituates such social concerns in the novel.

Maud Martha's textual subtleties intimate the discursive dilemmas underlying black women's relationship to hegemonic and nonhegemonic culture as theorized in late twentieth-century African American literary criticism.[11] In Petry's novel *The Street* (1946), domestic worker Lutie Johnson receives "a college education free of charge" by reading her white employers' subscriptions to the fashion magazines *Vogue* and *Harper's Bazaar* and the lifestyle manuals *Town and Country, House and Garden*, and *House Beautiful*. Lutie is critically aware that the popular cultural scripts in movies "had nothing to do with her, because there were no dirty little rooms, no narrow, crowded streets, no children with police records, no worries about rent and gas bills."[12] However, the disparity between Lutie's working-class Harlem apartment and her white employers' suburban home spurs her desire for the hegemonic fantasies projected in films and consumer magazines. In *Maud Martha* Brooks exhibits this discursive dilemma with the black and white media inscriptions compromising Maud Martha's voice both literally and figuratively. Hegemonic and nonhegemonic publications relegate her to what Dworkin and Mary Helen Washington, respectively, conceive of as "untalk" and "muted rage."[13] Maud Martha tacitly communicates her anger, but she never actually speaks it.

Moreover the narrative's discursive dilemma nods at black women writers' struggle to gain critical recognition during the heyday of social protest fiction. Brooks's novel virtually disappears in mid-twentieth-century critical discourse, which reduced African American literature of the period to an intertextual dialogue between Wright, the literary father; Ellison, the heir apparent; and Baldwin, the prodigal son. Washington notes that roughly 600 words were devoted to reviewing *Maud Martha*, whereas 2,100 words were dedicated to reviewing Ellison's *Invisible Man*. Ellison's unmatched critical attention led Washington to conclude, "The real 'invisible man' of the 1950s was the black woman."[14] Similarly Baldwin's Bildungsroman *Go Tell It on the Mountain* (1953) became a major work in the tradition, in part because of its distinction from the protest novel. However, literary histories essentially displaced *Maud Martha* although it was published the same year. The obscurity of Brooks's novel in comparison to the work of her male writing peers epitomizes mid-twentieth-century black woman novelists' anonymity during the Jane Crow era.

In *Maud Martha* Brooks acknowledges the gendered processes of reading—and prefigures a model of literary criticism that recognizes black female utterance—by differentiating black women from their representation in post–World War II print culture. To this end she associates black men in the novel with hegemonic discourses. Maud Martha recalls that one of the few public facts known about her deceased uncle is that he "was a man who had absorbed the headlines in the *Tribune*, studied the cartoons in *Collier's* and the *Saturday Evening Post*." Correspondingly a teenage beau uses his literary mastery of "those Goddamn Greeks" to gain cultural capital.[15] In contrast Maud Martha's relationship to popular cultural texts reveals her efforts to navigate public discourses in order to actualize her subjectivity. Tellingly an early draft of Brooks's work contained a scene in which Maud Martha partakes in a literary club discussion that was omitted from the final manuscript. Brooks's editor Elizabeth Lawrence questioned the character's consistency in light of Brooks's revisions to the manuscript: "How did Maud Martha suddenly acquire this aura of 'culture'? A false note."[16] Instead the novel engages Maud Martha's interiorized, intertextual dialogue with the idealized construction of black womanhood in contemporaneous magazines' literary culture. The *Chicago Defender* chronicles black celebrities' glamorous marriages; an *Ebony* editorial implies that buying a Cadillac will bring about racial equality; and *Tan Confessions* frames stories of illicit sex with extensive homemaking coverage. Maud Martha's discontent in the domestic space, however, problematizes these fantasies. The discrepancy between her life and how popular culture portrayed black women suggests the incongruity between the real and imagined black female body as text. Deconstructing periodical culture's depiction of black women, then, is critical for Maud Martha's self-definition as well as for Brooks's readers to decipher the novel's complex portrait of black female subjectivity.

Reading *Maud Martha* alongside contemporaneous black publications highlights the processes of mid-twentieth-century black woman-making—cultural practices that evince and shape commonly held understandings of race and gender. Looking at Brooks's fiction in conjunction with popular cultural scripts uncovers the ways that marketing race, selling sex, and advertising middle-class consumption helped dictate the interests and investments of texts produced under Jane Crow oppression. *Maud Martha* explicitly refers to the *Defender* newspaper, as both are set and produced in Chicago. The city is also home to Johnson Publishing Company's series of magazines: *Negro Digest*, started in 1942; *Ebony*, 1945; *Tan Confessions*, 1950; and *Jet*, 1951. Unlike the *Defender*, Johnson's ventures are not named in Brooks's work, but their high circulation among black readers locally as well as nationally attests to the publications' influence on the novel's cultural context. Hence Maud Martha struggles to develop a critical consciousness in relation—and in opposition—to this literary culture, while Brooks's work encourages readers to reconceptualize black womanhood. "What difference did it make," Maud Martha asks when she quits a domestic job without notice, "whether the firing squad understood or did not understand the manner of one's retaliation or why one had to retaliate?"[17] An example of her critical self-talk, the rhetorical question speaks to the consequences of misinterpretation for black women. *Maud Martha* intimates a model for reading the public and private constructions of black womanhood, and it gestures toward a methodology of black feminist criticism.

Scripting and Staging Good Housekeeping

Maud Martha manifests its metafictionality by signifying on interwar racial-uplift narratives proclaimed in black newspapers and magazines. When mid-twentieth-century hegemonic discourses represented African Americans, they stereotyped them in whites' imagination as morally questionable, socially reprobate, and pathologically sexual in order to reinforce white supremacy. The black press articulated a counterdiscourse that documented the black community's professional successes and worked to secure its economic and social mobility with idealized representations of middle-class domesticity. With product advertisements and celebrity features, black media discourses courted a "consumers' republic," which Lizabeth Cohen defines as an imagined democracy founded on the promise of greater freedom through mass consumption.[18] African American publications specifically assured the black reading public that it could realize economic gains and racial equality with material goods and commensurate status symbols. Accordingly in Brooks's novel Maud Martha and her husband Paul's desire to emulate celebrated media models of domesticity rivals the couple's affection for each other. Maud Martha aspires to the pedestal femininity depicted in hegemonic and nonhegemonic discourses, by which a woman's fashioning of her home, devotion to her spouse, and kitchen skills are as integral to achieving the American Dream as proving the venerability of black womanhood. However, Maud Martha's economic realities and marital compromises temper this romanticized image of housewifery. Her increasing disenchantment with consumer fantasies precipitates her social as well as domestic alienation. As a result her gendered processes of reading conscribe her public and private performances of subjectivity.

Maud Martha first encounters fantasies of consumerism by reading hegemonic discourses, which customarily defer African Americans' attainment of the American Dream by barring images of blackness from their portraits of the "good" life. As Nancy A. Walker observes, "From the editorial content to the images in advertising, there is scarcely a hint of any appeal to or recognition of the African American woman" in mid-twentieth-century women's magazines.[19] Yet these hegemonic discourses initiate Maud Martha's material fantasy that she can accrue social capital through coveted cultural objects. New York newspapers and magazines, the flagships of mainstream American publishing, seduce a teenage Maud Martha with a cornucopia of advertisements marketing Chinese boxes, Italian plates, French figurines, and Russian caviar. In actuality urban cosmopolitanism is the symbolic object of her consumer desire, "for—for—Her whole body became a hunger, she would pore over these pages." Although the text illustrates with excited dashes and interjections that this desire is not yet completely realized, Maud Martha fully internalizes the New York papers' narratives of wealth and culture. Furthermore she interpolates herself as a part of New York's sophisticated elite: "*She was* on Fifth Avenue whenever she wanted to be, and *she it was* who rolled up, silky or furry, in the taxi, was assisted out, and stood, her next step nebulous, before the theaters of the thousand lights, before velvet-lined impossible shops; *she it was*."[20] The text's repetitive phrasing conveys Maud Martha's efforts to materialize her dream-self in a reality traditionally exclusive to white socialites. She fantasizes about inhabiting this portrait of privileged white womanhood by obtaining the accoutrements that beget social status and recognition.

Significantly Maud Martha's New York fantasy is not inspired by popular counterdiscourses that affirm black subjectivity, as she envisions her dream-self in Manhattan, not Harlem. At the center of the early twentieth-century black imagination, Harlem was the cultural mecca in which the "New Negro"—especially the African American writer and reader—was esteemed and recognized. Yet Harlem is not Maud Martha's cultural muse, though she could benefit from its epistemology of negritude. To her detriment she accedes to the white supremacist belief that "pretty would be a little cream-colored thing with curly hair. Or at the very lowest pretty would be a little curly-haired thing the color of cocoa with a lot of milk in it." At the other end of the color spectrum, Maud Martha incriminates her dark skin: "I am the color of cocoa straight, if you can be even that 'kind' to me."[21] In contrast Hughes's poem "Harlem Sweeties" expresses appreciation for the diversity of black women's beauty. From the "Rich cream colored / To plum-tinted black," the poem weighs, "Feminine sweetness / In Harlem's no lack."[22] Maud Martha's conceptualization of black female subjectivity is not anchored in or limited to an imagined Harlem; she expansively dreams that "the world waited. To caress her."[23] Brooks's novel nonetheless laments the question left pending in Hughes's poem "Harlem": "What happens to a dream deferred?"[24] Given hegemonic discourses' denial of black subjectivity, the absence of a real or imagined Harlem in *Maud Martha* suggests the extent of blacks' negation within mid-twentieth-century dominant culture. Maud Martha's isolation from Harlem also indicates her symbolic withdrawal from black cultural spaces.

While hegemonic discourses disregard black subjectivity, African Americans' hypervisibility in Chicago's black newspapers and magazines further defer Maud Martha's dreams for economic mobility, social recognition, and personal esteem. Because the black press deifies celebrity as the emblem of the American Dream, Maud Martha remains estranged from it. In response she constructs a private identity in order to validate her ordinariness and to protect herself from being commodified and consumed publicly. The black press's substantive news coverage of African Americans, as Juliet E. K. Walker contends, "represented a collective effort, and contributed to the development of a national black communal consciousness."[25] The *Chicago Defender* helped mobilize African Americans' exodus from the Jim Crow South to the industrial North during the first and second phases of the Great Migration, and the *Pittsburgh Courier* initiated the Double V campaign, which concomitantly galvanized blacks' domestic struggle for racial equality and fight overseas against fascism during World War II. However, in *Maud Martha*'s self-reflexive gendered reading, the *Defender*'s sensationalized gossip pages drive Maud Martha to create an individual, bifurcated consciousness. When she equates a singer's stage performance with his overexposure in the newspaper, she questions how people "exhibit their precious private identities." More important, she recognizes that her performance of black female subjectivity is also a public construct. She rejects the audience's engrossing gaze and resolves to "keep herself to herself" in an attempt to control her own text. Because nonhegemonic discourses do not value her ordinariness, she concedes to "donate to the world a good Maud Martha."[26] By differentiating between an accessible and a concealed identity, she presents to the public a configured object of gendered art that she will "polish and hone" while safeguarding her privacy and remaining self-contained.

Maud Martha critically reads popular cultural scripts, but she is powerless to rewrite her public text, so to speak, in order to circumvent conventional ideals of beauty and domesticity. The black press blurs the lines between black women's public performance of subjectivity and private construction of self by obscuring the difference between readers' bodies and bodies of text, between consumers and objects of consumption. Consequently newlyweds Maud Martha and Paul succumb to the allure of public commodification and imagine creating a domestic space filled with objects of envy as advertised in newspaper circulars and celebrity features. In turn the couple hope their marriage will become the object of consumer desire they themselves aim to possess. "Your apartment, eventually, will be a dream," Paul promises Maud Martha. "The *Defender* will come and photograph it."[27] Paul's verbalized ambition draws attention to the newspaper's stylization of domesticity. The lavish lifestyles depicted in articles and, most strikingly, in photographs of celebrities stimulate, Deborah Willis theorizes, the "reflected desire" motivating readers to yearn for material objects and identify with featured subjects.[28] Susan Sontag argues that photographs "are grammar" similar to prose, but she specifies that photographs are a testament to "an ethics of seeing."[29] Their visual language is interpreted mistakenly as unmediated, though their veracity is as constructed as fiction because the photographic image transforms subjects into objects that presumably can be consumed and possessed. In *Maud Martha* the *Defender* photographs seemingly guarantee the married couple's ability to attain affluence and satiation through consumerism. Yet being photographed for the newspaper would not simply document Paul and Maud Martha's social mobility; it would also configure them as consumable objects.

Brooks discredits the *Defender*'s specious photographic domestic fantasy with Maud Martha's inability to model middle-class mores as a working-class black woman. Interestingly Brooks initially envisioned *Maud Martha* including thirty "captionless" and "unposed" photographs that might have reified her commentary on reading with regard to both words and images.[30] Graham Clarke's contention that formal portraits conceal subjects, unlike the exposure of the authentic self in candid shots, implies that media images staging glamorous domesticity likewise "reassert and reaffirm the extent to which we *show* rather than *reveal* a face in any public context."[31] The *Defender*'s photographs are manufactured material fantasies as well as scripted narratives of gender performance. For example, the article "Mrs. Bill Robinson Stars in Important Role—'A Wife'" (1940) features Fannie Robinson, spouse of the famed actor and tap dancer "Bojangles," as an unknown leading lady worthy of acclamation. The article depicts the conventional role of the dedicated housewife as a rewarding identity that black women should envy and duplicate. "One could say the Robinson residence in California is like a dream," the story gushes. "But it isn't really. It's like 10,000 of your most pleasant dreams all tied up together." The article's brief tour of the Robinsons' home raves about the den, game room, and sleeping chair that serve as Bill's masculine sanctuaries, while applauding Fannie's devotion to "the career of 'being a good wife.'" The piece announces that her "every thought is to please her husband," and it describes her doing so while "quite admirable in her selections of beautiful costumes."[32] Both Fannie and the house are complementary symbols of Bill's luminary status.

The two photographs accompanying the article under the subtitle "The Other Robinson—'Mrs. Bill'" tout the "good wife" construct as both the subject and object of consumer desire. Whereas the headline suggests a kind of intimacy between the subject and the reader, the pictures preclude the domestic ideal for aspiring homemakers like Maud Martha. The first photograph is cropped and framed, but the hem of Fannie's gown exceeds the picture's bottom border just as the high-backed chair in which she sits crowns the picture's top border. Both dress and chair are markers of material excess dominating the composition of the picture. Moreover Fannie appears to gaze down at readers (not at the picture book in her lap), as if evaluating their social status. The second photograph connotes similar regality, with Fannie standing in a dress suit with her hands in her jacket pockets. This picture displays several home furnishings, while the caption discloses that Fannie is "relaxing" in Chicago, not in her California house.[33] The "good housewife" construct is configured with surrounding props, but the photograph shows Fannie neither in her real dream house nor in actual acts of domesticity. The newspaper represents her as a constructed object; it does not reveal her as a subject to readers.

The *Defender*'s ample coverage of Mr. and Mrs. Joe Louis similarly complicate the interplay between notions of fact and fantasy, domestic work and leisure inscribed in the newspaper's visual narratives of domesticity (Figure 5). For example, the article "Marva Draws Up 5-Point Plan for Reconciliation" (1941) exposes the legendary boxer's abuse of his spouse. Marva's plan boldly headlines the *Defender*'s front page, which includes a series of concordant texts: an editorial contemplating African Americans' participation in World War II, an article delineating an NAACP lawsuit for equal pay, and a brief report of three lynchings. However, the Louises' story of marital conflict appears paramount. Marva's five-step strategy requests that Joe refrain from hitting her, be more attentive, take her on business trips, arrange joint vacations, and share his interests with her. The plan enumerates her desire to reunite with her husband, but the article also details her petition for divorce and spousal support.

The photo collage appearing twelve pages later sentimentalizes the Louises' relationship and beatifies Marva's ascent from girl to wife by ignoring her plateau as an incipient divorcée. Titled "Camera Record of Married Life of Joe and Marva," the photo-essay connotes happily-ever-after marital bliss as a stand-alone visual narrative of the celebrities' union. The sixteen pictures covering their six-year marriage (including a photo of the couple outlined in a heart at the center of the pictorial) is as much about documenting an idyllic relationship as it is about idealizing a woman's evolution into her public identity as a housewife. The caption notes that the photographs trace the "development of Marva from average city girl to a well poised lady of wealth and position."[34] The photo-essay consists of nine pictures of Marva, six of the couple together, and only one of Joe alone. As a result Marva's representation as the "good wife" in the montage supersedes the previous text's depiction of Joe as the "bad husband." Pictures show Marva at home posing in furs and looking chic with a vacuum cleaner (Figure 6). Her gender performance is staged also within the public sphere of consumption; several photographs show her shopping, traveling, and socializing with as well as without her husband.

FIGURE 5. Joe and Marva Louis, circa 1942. (Courtesy of the *Chicago Defender*)

The *Defender* seemingly vouches for this lifestyle of leisure, mobility, and glamour, but two years later the newspaper's front page discloses that Marva and Joe are proceeding anon toward divorce. "Too much glamour—the glare of publicity—the tragedy of belonging to an adulating public—all have combined to wreck the glittering romance," the paper laments.[35] The story self-consciously indicts the black press (its values as well as its audience) as the source of the marriage's ruin only to exploit the couple—again—as a desirable object of consumption to titillate the *Defender*'s readers.

In *Maud Martha* Brooks elucidates working-class black women's disillusionment due to the domestic fantasies belying their economic and

FIGURE 6. Marva Louis, circa 1935.
(Courtesy of the *Chicago Defender*)

interpersonal realities. In the chapter "Everybody Will Be Surprised,"
Paul voices his dream that the *Defender* will photograph the couple's
apartment, but Maud Martha is taken aback with the realization that
his consumer fantasy will never be achieved on his meager income. Paul
decides that their kitchenette, a financial compromise, is "'cute and cozy'
enough." But Maud Martha's critical reading of literary texts as well
as social contexts informs her curt, unspoken thought, "The *Defender*
would never come here with cameras."[36] Although less astute readers

perceive their world exactly as the camera frames it, one's understanding of a photograph, as Sontag clarifies, "starts from *not* accepting the world as it looks."[37] Maud Martha learns to differentiate her public and private selves by reading the *Defender*, and her lived experience with roaches and secondhand furniture demystifies the newspaper's elite domestic fantasies. This ruminative moment registers the transgeneric characteristics of the novel, as Maud Martha's disillusionment reflects Brooks's own disappointment with romanticized narratives of domesticity. In her autobiography *Report from Part One*, Brooks writes, "I remember feeling bleak when I was taken to my honeymoon home, the kitchenette apartment in the Tyson on 43rd and South Park, after the very nice little wedding in my parents' living room." She goes on to qualify, "Even in the cramped dreariness of the Tyson there was fun, there was company, there was reading, mutual reading."[38] Maud Martha is not Brooks, however, and she and Paul do not share the intimacy or companionship of escapist reading in their confined kitchenette. Maud Martha's disenchantment structures her solitary way of reading and experiencing domesticity, in that her neighbors' audible speech and overwhelming bodily smells impress grayness upon her.

Maud Martha is critical of her domestic space, but she suppresses her insights in order to maintain a traditional image of true womanhood. During the interwar period many black women reassessed conventional gender roles in the private sphere as a result of their economic and social progress in the public sphere. Maud Martha fitly expresses her disagreement with Paul's compromises for their household. Yet ultimately she questions, "Was her attitude unco-operative? Should she be wanting to sacrifice more, for the sake of her man?"[39] She replaces her dream of middle-class consumption with a vision of herself embodying a pioneering woman's forbearance. A contemporaneous letter to the editor published in the *Defender* similarly subscribes to women's surrender to the patriarchal domestic roles championed and challenged in prairie novels. "It isn't a very easy job to be a good wife and mother. It is confining. It is founded on sacrifice and constant devotion to duty. It means work," a married mother writes. "But for every outside pleasure one sacrifices an acquisition in some new happiness is made."[40] Maud Martha echoes this conviction when she parallels her Depression-era urban life to that of early homesteading wives, whom she admires as "women who could stand low temperatures. Women who would toil eminently, to improve the lot of their men. Women who cooked."[41] Women's sacrificial and laborious domesticity becomes "a beautiful thought" to her. At the same time, eulogizing the idea of "dying for her man" silences her until she gives birth to her daughter, whose cries momentarily restore Maud Martha's own voice.

Notably Maud Martha's performance of sacrificial domesticity is not always in service to her husband; sometimes it subtly advances her quiet declarations of agency in the novel. The chapters "Maud Martha Spares the Mouse" and "Brotherly Love" show her transition from disillusioned newlywed to adroit housewife. In the first chapter Maud Martha traps and frees a mouse because she empathizes with the animal's apparent understanding "that there was . . . no hope of reprieve or postponement—but a fine small dignity." She projects women's domestic trappings (summed up in housecleaning and child rearing) onto the caught mouse, and she imagines it "might be nursing personal regrets." Hence she feels empowered by her ability to destroy the mouse, but she is bolstered more by her decision to save it. "Why, I'm good! I am *good*," she asserts. In sacrificing her comfort, she becomes a domestic goddess. Her morality validates her as a "good housewife" just as her benevolent act demonstrates her superiority in the domestic space. She finds similar satisfaction in the chapter "Brotherly Love" when she expertly cleans and quarters the "vomit-looking interior" of a chicken.[42]

Maud Martha's confrontation with the "nasty, nasty mess" of poultry parts is in conversation with *Ebony* magazine's paradigm for performing true womanhood. Brooks does not specifically reference *Ebony* in *Maud Martha* as she does the *Defender*, but the magazine's large following, contemporaneous Chicago production, and discourse regarding black female subjectivity permit an intertextual reading. The magazine exhibits the black beauty shunned in hegemonic discourses with photographs of bathing glamour girls and celebrity pin-ups on its covers. Conversely the display of black female bodies in Johnson's picture magazine exemplifies their double jeopardy during the height of Jane Crow oppression as objects of consumption. "Why not be a little more careful of the low cut dresses on your women," one female reader criticizes in *Ebony*'s first "Letters and Pictures to the Editor." "It is one phase of the white woman's fashion that the colored woman might well eliminate."[43] A reader would be remiss, however, to oversimplify *Ebony*'s gender discourse by focusing solely on the way the magazine sells sex to market the race. In contrast to the magazine's eroticizing of black female bodies, the installment of the "Photo-Editorial" section titled "Goodbye Mammy, Hello Mom" (1947) endorses conventional middle-class respectability. The editorial commends the post–World War II "kitchen revolution," when black women returned to their homes for the first time after toiling

as domestic workers for white women and drudging as factory workers during the war's labor shortage. "The cooking over which the 'white
folks' used to go into ecstasies is now reserved for [the black woman's]
own family and they really appreciate it," the editorial cheers. "Domestic
peace seems to be the order of things since she came home."[44] The piece
does not begrudge black woman's choice or need to work outside the
home, but it privileges the housewife's commission. Such expectations
did not necessarily match the reality or stifle postwar anxieties about
women's place.

Ebony also makes known its investment in "good housewifery" with
Freda DeKnight's column "Date with a Dish." The monthly feature monu-
mentalizes cooking with recipes as easy as spaghetti and as sophisticated
as boning a leg of lamb, and thus it addresses frustrated homemakers
like Maud Martha. Historian Adam Green recognizes DeKnight's key
contribution to *Ebony*'s success as her intuitive framing of cooking "as a
site of voluntary pleasure—leisure more so than self-sacrificing labor."[45]
The food editor was an interlocutor in the publication's gender discourse
in addition to managing editor Era Bell Thompson and librarian Doris
Saunders, who built the private book collection supplementing Johnson
Publishing's articles and studies. Given black women's history of undervalued and underpaid domestic work, DeKnight's espousal of the joys
of cooking played a pivotal part in black women's "kitchen revolution."
A white librarian at a corrections facility, inspired by the effect the food
column had on her black female patrons, encourages *Ebony*'s editors,
asserting "that it is an infinitely superior idea to have such features written by a Negro rather than the usual syndicated series."[46] With its written
instructions and photographed demonstrations for each recipe, "Date
with a Dish" extolled the culinary arts for the black celebrity, career
woman, and ordinary housewife alike. The column was so popular
that cartoonist Jackie Ormes parodied it in her comic *Patty-Jo 'n' Ginger*, published in the *Pittsburgh Courier*. "It's one of your recipes, Miss
DeKnight, an' time's runnin' out," Ormes's precocious child protagonist
complains into the phone. "We got the cake baked for Mother's Day but
it's been in the 'frigerator since noon. . . . Now how come it isn't frosted
yet?"[47] The humor lies in Patty-Jo's belief that the appliance, not she, has
to ice the cake. Lena Horne cements the cultural currency of "Date with
a Dish" when she extends her star appeal from *Ebony*'s covers to a Valentine's Day edition of the column, in which she makes curry chicken.
(Her daughter is featured in a later issue making cookies for Horne's
birthday.) "Date with a Dish" recasts Horne and fellow actress Dorothy

Dandridge, known for their beauty and desirability, in domestic roles. In "Quick Coffee Breads for Sunday Morning" the pastries "prove perfect for a busy career girl like Dorothy, who is also a perfect mother and a good housewife."[48] Such celebrity features perpetuate what Green labels "the cult of black stardom" hailed throughout *Ebony*, while typical monthly installments declare that the everyday women too can gain stature in the kitchen.[49] "Hot Roll Mix" lauds a black female entrepreneur manufacturing and marketing her own product, and "Buffet Bridge Luncheon" honors African American clubwomen's middle-class respectability.

Despite the fact that Maud Martha is not a starlet, socialite, or career girl, her disgust at cleaning a chicken commiserates with the less fortunate, inexperienced, and discouraged housewife whom "Date with a Dish" also addresses. One of the column's first published recipes utilizes the everyday apple and indirectly compliments the efforts of the average housewife: "Apples need never be commonplace. Do your best to glorify them."[50] "Tamale Pie for New Year's Eve" spotlights singer Nat King Cole enjoying his favorite meal, but DeKnight promises that the recipe is "simple enough for any housewife yet fancy enough for the best of chefs."[51] In "Fruit Pies" the food editor acknowledges that the "bane of many younger housewives' kitchen existence is the ubiquitous fruit pie, which, however, when once mastered inevitably merits hearty grunts of approval from the dining room table."[52] The installment "Budget Meals for Vet Wives" offers garlic and sage as strategies to help women "beguile steak appetites" with "hot-dog" allowances.[53] In another issue dedicated to the less seasoned cook, DeKnight declares, "The days when cake making was an accomplished art are over. Today any housewife with common sense and the ability to read a recipe can have her cake and eat it too."[54]

Brooks tests DeKnight's recipe for culinary pleasure and uses the messy image of preparing a chicken to connect black women's domestic unease to their social unrest. The chapter "Brotherly Love" describes Maud Martha "fighting" with the bird and looking forward to the "praise coming to her" for the effort.[55] The struggle exemplifies what Valerie Frazier identifies as Maud Martha's "domestic epic warfare."[56] Brooks contextualizes the kitchen contest with direct reference to military battle. Unlike in the days before World War II, Maud Martha is cognizant that "now meat was jewelry," and no housewife can afford to abandon her duty.[57] DeKnight notes this historical shift in "Dinner of Leftovers," in which she rallies that "Monday morning's refrigerator, dotted with ... [the] odds and ends of Sunday's roast, is a sight to make inexperienced housewives burst into tears. . . . But in 1947 food is neither so plentiful nor so inexpensive that a real housekeeper can in good conscience throw away even a scrap."[58] Almost out of ration points, Maud Martha toughs out her dirty prep work with similar self-talk. "You were lucky to find a chicken," she tells herself. "She had to be as brave as she could," the novel's narrator prompts. Brooks makes concrete her comparison between women's domestic conflict and men's military combat when Maud Martha imagines the butchered chicken as a headless man worthy of dignity. Maud Martha's commentary on domestic warfare is reminiscent of the sacrifice she makes saving the mouse, but her critical reflection is short-lived. The vignette ends with her smacking her lips in anticipation of her meal; she returns to a positive perspective on her domestic role that stresses her pleasure and measures her frustration.[59]

Maud Martha finds self-worth in being a "good wife" even as she resigns herself to compulsory acts of domesticity. Although her interventions are seemingly insignificant, saving a mouse and cooking a chicken are allegories for her attempts to claim a degree of agency in the domestic space. She masters another rite of passage by standing firm in her preference for nutmeg over cinnamon when her mother criticizes her gingerbread recipe. Still, her growing confidence in the kitchen does not confirm per se that she embraces *Ebony*'s representation of domesticity as voluntary pleasure. The magazine advertises DeKnight's recipes as "an invaluable guide to the pot and pan pilot from the honeymoon type to the golden anniversary wife," but *Maud Martha*'s chapters dedicated to a mouse and a chicken are succinct critiques of black women's domestic oppression.[60] Maud Martha magnanimously frees her mousy alter ego only to later swallow the insights she makes about her place in the world beyond the home front. She does not wholly consume the domestic fantasies print discourses perpetuate, though she commits to the public performance of "good housewifery." As she distinguishes her public self from her private self, she often reads in opposition to hegemonic and nonhegemonic discourses while staging her gendered art for others.

Readers' Response to True Romance and Taboo Sex

Brooks not only interrogates black women's engagement with public discourses; she also theorizes black female subjectivity as text. That is to say, *Maud Martha* attends to how black women read and are read—or misread—by others. Maud Martha's marital disconnections are predicated on black women's misrecognition, as she shares neither social interests nor sexual desire with her husband. In response to hegemonic culture's pathologizing of black sexuality, black counterdiscourses contrived expressions of female sexuality as permissible only within the confines of wedded bliss. Therefore marriage rewards Maud Martha with the mores of middle-class respectability, but the union stirs her displeasure, not her conjugal satisfaction. Brooks foreshadows Maud Martha's marital frustrations in the *Negro Digest* article "Why Negro Women Leave Home" (1951). The exposition likely replied to Roi Ottley's incendiary reading in "What's Wrong with Negro Women" (1950), which was published in the magazine three months earlier. In her rebuttal Brooks cites couples' financial conflicts and sexual incompatibility as two reasons driving women to escape wedlock. Additionally some women "have married men whom they consider inferior, in education or intelligence or in breeding," she enlightens, "and the honeymoon is hardly over before they realize that they were in error, that the thing will never work."[61] In Brooks's novel Maud Martha feels she must ensnare lighter-skinned, better-looking Paul into marriage, but the lack of sophistication he displays wearing a food-stained blue work shirt to the theater insinuates that Maud Martha is the one bamboozled by her efforts.

Brooks's demythologizing of marital desire, then, is a counterpoint to the commodification of romance and sex in *Tan Confessions*. Johnson's confessional romance magazine lured black female readers with innocuous stories about marriage proposals in addition to scandalous tales of passion. The combination briefly subverted the politics of respectability, but the magazine's duality basically reinforced those gendered and classed social strictures. Consequently Maud Martha's marriage does not yield forbidden passion or proper romance. Whereas reading *Maud Martha* alongside *Ebony* unveils the media's sophisticated staging of domestic rituals, reading the novel and *Tan Confessions* in tandem accentuates black popular texts' regulation of black female sexuality. The discursive management of black female desire occurs within the privacy of the bedroom as well as in the public sphere's racial-uplift rhetoric. Maud Martha rarely verbalizes her chagrin to her husband, but her literal and symbolic relationship to literary texts and cultural contexts articulates her desire—or lack thereof.

Like her illusions about glamorous domestic spaces, Maud Martha's reverie about matrimonial romance is another fantasy that dissolves due to her husband's abiding obtuseness. In "Why Negro Women Leave Home" Brooks writes that many black women remain married despite their increasing financial independence "because they love and/or are loved."[62] Yet Maud Martha relies on neither adoration nor companion-ship to sustain her marriage; she settles for the fleeting moments in which her husband demonstrates his respect and affection for her. On one occasion when Paul opens the door for her, Maud Martha welcomes this chivalrous "way of calling her 'lady' and informing her of his love" because it makes her feel "precious, protected, delicious." His consistent inattention to her needs, however, leads her to conclude that a woman can only depend on "the marriage shell, not the romance, or love, it might contain." Brooks exacerbates Maud Martha's acute resignation to the paucity of emotional intimacy in her marriage by juxtaposing the couple's austere connection with the palpable love shared by their neighbors the Whitestripes. Paul's public faux pas garner Maud Martha pitying looks from passersby, but she reasons that being in the presence of the Whitestripes assures that "you were embarrassed, because it was obvious that you were interrupting the progress of a truly great love." She longingly observes the elderly couple's "love story," but a sophomoric and indolent Paul rejects the august romance. "You can stop mooning," he instructs his wife, "I'll never be a 'Coopie' Whitestripe."[63] His ridi-cule substantiates the derision Janice Radway discerns in her analysis of middle-class white female readers of romance; Radway apprehends that contempt of such gendered reading practices often come from "men who claim superior taste."[64] While Maud Martha pines for her own love affair, Paul devalues the symbolic text of her subjectivity. The Whitestripes are an unattainable fiction for pragmatic Paul, but the couple's name also implies the "white" aspirational nature of Maud Martha's fantasy.

As there is little romance between Maud Martha and Paul, it is no sur-prise that the novel does not disclose their sex life. Other than references to the couple's children, *Maud Martha* modestly engages sexual discourse by associating the aloof spouses with conflicting texts. The chapter "The Young Couple at Home" portrays black female sexuality as a readable text: Maud Martha strategically expresses her lack of desire for her hus-band with her pleasure reading, while Paul demonstrates his inability to read his wife's signals with his proclivity for sex over romance. After he uncouthly falls asleep in the theater, Paul engages in clumsy, childish public affection in expectation of sex at home. Because Maud Martha is disappointed with his disinterest in the play as well as his lack of "grace" in seduction, she directs her attention to a book instead. He kisses her neck to heat things up; she uses *Of Human Bondage* to shut things down. "Snuggle up," Paul invites. "I thought I'd read awhile," Maud Martha responds. Undeterred, Paul picks up *Sex in the Married Life* and urges his wife to read a chapter each night before bed. His request reflects his conspicuous efforts to spark his wife's sexual interest and perhaps his mistaken confidence that he has mastered the subject. In a definitive move, Maud Martha distracts Paul with an offer to make cocoa and sandwiches.[65] As Frazier contends, Maud Martha "subverts the domestic role by enacting *her own* version of the role of ideal wife—cooking as a decoy to retain her sense of self while superficially upholding the domestic position."[66] Cooking deposes Paul's sexual desire in favor of domestic propriety, which allows Maud Martha to maintain dissemblance in the bedroom yet profess her role as the "good housewife" with the dainty fare.[67] Shortly after Maud Martha's maneuver, a satisfied Paul falls asleep and Maud Martha makes no effort to retrieve his book from the floor.

Brooks's depiction of marriage's banalities does not exhibit the fierce love or sexual fervor saturating the stories published in *Tan Confessions*. Maud Martha's and Paul's opposing ideas about desire, however, manifest the magazine's synchronous promotion of middle-class respectability and sexual laissez-faire. Paul's misreading of Maud Martha causes her reticence in the bedroom, while the seemingly progressive sexual discourse of *Tan Confessions* reiterated black women's Jane Crow oppression. In fact Paul's book *Sex in the Married Life* resembles the manual *Sex Life in Marriage* advertised in *Tan Confessions* with a money-back guarantee. "In all too many cases," the endorsement counsels, "[the wife] is cheated out of her sex rights. The sex act becomes a one-sided affair. The husband thinks his wife is at fault. The wife thinks her husband is to blame. The marriage itself is in danger!"[68] Beyond such suggestive advertisements, the racy testimonies in *Tan Confessions* made private sex acts daringly public given the proscriptions placed upon black women's expression of sexuality. The publication's short story titles palpitate with traditionally unsanctioned exploits: "I Sold My Baby," "You're Not the Father," "I Fell for My Father," "I Took My Mother's Man," "The Most Dangerous Kind of Love," "I Wanted a Thrill," "I'll Never Pass Again," "Our Mixed Marriage Didn't Work," "Backstreet Wife," and "I Married a Thief." The blurb in the table of contents for the confession "Three of Hearts" tantalizes, "It was a strange three-cornered love affair until Roy married Phyllis but he was in for a surprise when she sent him out for Tony on their wedding night."[69] With covers featuring couples in sensual embraces or risqué repose, *Tan Confessions* fleshed out its testimonials with photographs dramatizing undeniable lust, furtive gazes, and agonizing suffering. The prurient images and true-to-life stories simultaneously accede to black women's prerogative to act on their sexual desires and undermine their ability to do so.

Tan Confessions censured black female sexuality by reminding readers of the inevitable punishment succeeding erotic fancies. To this end the "true" confessions restore marriage as black women's real-life salvation. For example, the blurb for "Strange Love" reveals the magazine's acquiescence to compulsory heterosexuality: "An exotic woman stole this wife from her husband but true love finally won out over this tainted affair."[70] Similarly the teaser for "Hell's Greatest Fury" warns, "When Sally hesitated in accepting Stu's proposal of marriage, she showed that hell's greatest fury is a suitor scorned rather than a woman scorned."[71] The teaser betrays *Tan Confessions*'s reproach of black women's unlawful desire with tangible repercussions. Moreover the magazine restated the importance of holy matrimony in its monthly features extolling domestic fantasies. "How He Proposed" concentrated on celebrity couples like Hazel Scott and Adam Clayton Powell Jr., and "If You Married . . . " filled in the title's ellipses with the likes of Sidney Poitier. Meanwhile "Just Married" detailed everyday couple's wedding ceremonies, and "Dearly Beloved" offered marital advice to inquiring readers. *Tan Confessions* also contained a home service magazine directed by *Ebony*'s food editor Freda DeKnight, which included sections on hair, cooking, shopping, decorating, beauty, childcare, health, and fashion. The segments created a narrative whole that conveyed the inimitable benefits afforded black women who performed middle-class respectability. As Noliwe M. Rooks argues, "It was only within the confines of committed domesticity, readers were told, that they would ever be able to enjoy the full privileges of product consumption and find sexual satisfaction and personal happiness."[72] *Tan Confessions* reverberated with consequences for rejecting conventional domesticity. Alternatively the magazine encouraged black women to transfer their erotic desire to consumerism.

Though binding black female sexuality to the politics of respectability, *Tan Confessions* flaunted black female desire as an object of consumption. Reader surveys identifying white confessionals as the biggest selling magazines in black communities motivated Johnson to produce his own version. In the inaugural issue the editor and publisher delineates the magazine's aim to recognize the "emotional, intimate experiences of people who never make the headlines" and to disseminate "the most extensive home-making coverage in the Negro field." In other words, *Tan Confessions* deployed both sex and respectability to represent and sell black female subjectivity. Johnson's letter pitches the magazine's mission for readers and editors to "exchange true experiences for the benefit of all," and as such, he solicited letters and submissions from neglected African American readers who appreciated that "love and romance, marriage and the family are vital concerns of every colored man and woman, no matter what their status in life."[73] Readers' responses in subsequent issues proclaimed the demand for Johnson's new publishing venture. One black female reader rationalizes, "If they can publish that sort of literature, why can't we? Sex is what the world consists of—male and female—so why not talk and write about it?"[74] Johnson framed *Tan Confessions* as an apropos counterdiscourse to hegemonic media's disregard of black love and pathologizing of black sex. Thus the magazine allowed room for readers to parse its provocative focus as erotically empowering, but such proto-womanist interpretive strategies were moderated by the edicts of respectability dictating the lives of black female readers.[75] The magazine's popularity relied upon what Jane Greer terms "flexible moral realism," which permitted confessional magazines' working-class female readers "to accept the events portrayed in a narrative as a realistic depiction of the challenges of everyday lived experience and to resist the imposition of rigid moral standards when judging the actions of characters who move through such a mimetic narrative world."[76] *Tan Confessions*'s primarily teenage and young adult female readers embraced the publication's true-to-life salacious stories with letters giving characters advice, seeking story updates, requesting correspondence with protagonists, and asking that their tales too be represented. In keeping with this tractable moral code, one woman's letter to the editor is written to her fellow readers: "We should be grateful to the women who have courage enough to tell us about their mistakes and realize that their experiences may keep some of us from making the same mistakes by knowing beforehand."[77] While the publication might have operated as an erotic fantasy for a short time, it delivered the morals that readers supposedly needed and apparently expected.

Most readers' responses to Johnson's call applauded *Tan Confessions*'s didactic answer to Jim Crow publishing, yet several letters to the editor questioned the ethics of the magazine's erotic content. One female reader salutes the magazine but requests, "Please let's not have too many of those nude layouts. . . . Since TAN CONFESSIONS is our own, let's keep it high class."[78] More uncompromising critiques chided the confessions' implausibility and potential negative effect on impressionable readers. "Those stories that you call 'true-to-life' are simply impossible," a female reader complains. "No self-respecting woman, with an ounce of decency, would allow any of those things to happen to her that you have published as 'the truth.'"[79] Though the lesbian affair in the tale titled "Strange Love" is usurped by heterosexual marriage, a male reader disparages its inclusion in the magazine: "A story such as that is not accepted in our society, even if the facts are true."[80] For this reader, policing heterosexual borders is more important than the story's verity. In contrast, another letter gripes about the magazine's moralizing: "Why are all your stories about nice people? Don't bad people have a life story?"[81] Other letters question *Tan Confessions*'s various one-note formulas, which homogenized African American beauty, sensationalized interracial relationships, and privileged middle-class elitism.

Despite its racial-uplift agenda, the magazine unhesitatingly commodified black female desire and discussed taboo topics in order to influence the reader and consumer.[82] One letter to the editor criticizes, "There are those who prefer to believe the Negro to be motivated entirely by the sex urge, and your first edition bears them out heroically."[83] In all likelihood such concerns were warranted. When a white reader claims, "My husband has never approved of this type of reading material before, but let me tell you he bought this one for me," the letter substantiates the aforementioned anxieties.[84] *Tan Confessions* was a profitable business enterprise for Johnson Publishing because it attracted black and white audiences, but the purchase of the magazine did not necessarily mean readers approved of its content. Its thesis could have engendered racial voyeurism as easily as racial pride.[85] The predicament inspired one black female reader to admit, "I am a long time buyer of romantic magazines and while I know that they are trash I would much rather spend my money for 'colored trash' than 'white trash.'"[86] Langston Hughes satirizes this quandary in the sketch "Sex in Front," which features his popular character Jesse B. Simple serialized in the *Defender*. Simple ingeniously proposes to follow counterhegemonic magazines' model for exploiting sex to sell copy by producing a string of publications: "Ebony Sex," "Colored Sex," "Jet Sex," "Sepia Sex," "Tan Sex," "Brown Sex," and "Black Sex."[87] Three of Simple's titles are not so subtle reproofs of Johnson Publishing's penchant for naming its publications synonymously.

After almost two years of commodifying "black sex" in his confessional magazine, Johnson answered his critics and attempted to rectify his error by shortening the title to *Tan* and replacing some of the true-to-life stories with more obvious fiction. In 1952 *Time* magazine reported, "Though circulation grew to 300,000, Tan Confessions failed in another way. Said Johnson: 'Our magazines help the Negro to have a greater dignity and pride in his own accomplishments. I found I had to apologize for Tan Confessions. I had thought we could dignify even a confessions magazine.'"[88] The new and improved *Tan* published Brooks's short story "Luther" (1952) as the winner of its inaugural literary contest by way of a mea culpa. Described as an excerpt from Brooks's upcoming novel, "Luther" explores a working-class black man's feelings of inferiority in the face of his spouse's social refinement and intellectual sophistication. The participants in his wife's book club toss around the words "economic determinism," "aesthetics," "cultural morality," and "communism," which forces Luther to flee to the movies.[89] The short story inverts the focal point of *Maud Martha*: it is the husband who fears his inability to measure up in the marriage, while his wife must remind herself that "he's good, he's kind, he loves me." However, both works examine the well-read wife's dissatisfaction with her spouse. A vignette from an early draft of Brooks's novel, "Luther" augments Johnson's efforts to redress *Tan*. This notwithstanding, the magazine continued to publish stories with titles like "I Married a Playboy," "I Pay for Love," and "My Flesh Is Weak." The teaser for "Jilted" does not depict black women in any more dignified light: "Leda was heartbroken when Steve forgot their love and decided to marry Jean. She made up her mind to take him away from his wife."[90]

Brooks's short story does little to change the overall tone of *Tan*, but *Maud Martha* challenges the magazine's contradictory exhibition of black female sexuality and privileging of middle-class respectability. *Of Human Bondage* names Maud Martha's emotional disconnection from her husband, and through Maud Martha's reading of the text, Brooks criticizes the overexposure of black female sexuality as a consumable text in the popular culture of the Jane Crow era. In "Sex in Front" Simple's wife protests, "I am tired of hiding my magazine behind my pocketbook in the street cars and such places. Somebody sees me reading a colored magazine with 'Twenty Ways to Hold a Man' all over it and they will think I am a loose woman."[91] Hughes's black female character fears how the public will read her, while Maud Martha contends with those same racial and patriarchal discourses in her bedroom. Her husband not only becomes their mouthpiece, but he also tries to mediate her desire by directing her reading practices. Therefore Maud Martha concludes that love, "however good," was "a thing that varied from week to week, from second to second, but the parties to it were likely, for example, to die, any minute, or otherwise be parted, or destroyed."[92] The novel's ending is ostensibly happy, with Maud Martha expecting her second child, but Brooks proposed the marriage's later demise in an unfinished sequel, which she referred to as "Rise of Maud Martha" in a 1958 letter to her editor.[93] In a 1977 interview she explained that her eponymous protagonist would raise three children after her husband's death in a bus fire. "Wasn't that nice of me?" she asks. "I had taken him as far as I could. He certainly wasn't going to change. I could see that."[94] Perhaps because Paul constantly misreads Maud Martha, Brooks intended her sequel to envision black female subjectivity beyond his cursory gaze.

Toward a Black Feminist Critique

By deconstructing how black women read as well as how black women are read, Brooks helped usher in the methodologies of black feminist literary criticism that emerged two decades later. In this respect *Maud Martha* traces black women's multivalent oppression as well as their efforts to recover their voices within white, male, and elite hegemonies. The novel self-consciously contemplates the effect of gendered processes of reading on one's conceptualization of African American womanhood. *Maud Martha* indexes black female subjectivity as an often misread text in the novel's content and form. The vignettes create a fragmented whole that mirrors Maud Martha's divided identity and manifests in her internal, unspoken dialogue. Therefore Maud Martha's family cannot read her, but Brooks ensures that readers can interpret her. As Linda Hutcheon posits, "The point of *meta*fiction is that it constitutes its own first critical commentary, and in so doing . . . sets up the theoretical frame of reference in which it must be considered."[95] In *Maud Martha* Brooks challenges representations of black women in mid-twentieth-century popular culture by differentiating black women's public and private constructions of self. The novel's metafictionality moves toward a hermeneutics of active reading that gives agency to black women. Moreover it enables the audience to gain a broader understanding of Brooks's understated yet complex portrait of black female subjectivity.

Brooks establishes the necessity and immediacy of a theory of reading by depicting Maud Martha in private interpretive moments that lead to abject social and personal repercussions. The chapter "The Self-Solace" illustrates the consequences of reading passively, as Maud Martha unconsciously participates in her social alienation when she reads *Vogue* and *Harper's Bazaar* while waiting her turn at a black-owned beauty salon. The discordant discourses of African American beauty consumer culture surround her, but she reflects, "One was and was not aware of them. Could sit here and think, or not think, of problems. Think, or not."

Content "to let her mind go blank," she internalizes the contradictory media signs.[96] Yet these tensions become difficult to ignore when a white saleswoman marketing a lipstick branded Black Beauty casually uses a racial epithet in her conversation with potential black customers. The salon owner maintains her smile and does not respond. Likewise Maud Martha returns to reading *Vogue*, which, as Washington argues, "could certainly separate a black woman from her own cultural vocabulary."[97] Indeed Maud Martha parrots the language of racial hierarchies privileging white femininity over black beauty when she concludes that the white saleswoman is too "pretty and pleasant" to have uttered the racial epithet and that she herself is "too relaxed" to take on the "plain old ugly duty" of verbally confronting racism.[98] Racial-uplift rhetoric purported that African Americans could gain racial equality through accommodating acts of respectability, but Maud Martha's silence flags the importance of critical media consumption as well as socially conscious interpretative processes.

Brooks published *Maud Martha* on the cusp of the modern civil rights movement, and thus the novel stops short of actualizing the racial consciousness the writer exhibits in her later work. In her autobiography *Report from Part Two* (1996), Brooks admits, "I grew up to womanhood and went through early womanhood believing that the glittering white family on the screen *should* be my model."[99] The 1967 Fisk black writers' conference was the revelatory moment in which Brooks began to envision a new social order; it transformed her creative voice and marked a shift in the second half of her career. "I had been asleep. If I had been reading even the newspaper intelligently," she explains, "I too would have seen that [countenancing integration] simply was not working, that there was too much against it, that blacks kept exposing themselves to it only to get their faces smacked. . . . The thing to stress was black solidarity and pride in one's brothers and sisters."[100] As Brooks created her protagonist prior to her turn from modernist conventions to the aesthetics of the Black Arts Movement, Maud Martha desires to "be equal to being equal" and never verbally expresses the personal politics implicit in her configured performance of respectable femininity.[101] Brooks's proposed sequel, which would have sent Maud Martha to Africa after her husband's death, also never came to fruition. Hence Maud Martha does not vocally disrupt dominant discourses nor obviously revise them in her construction of subjectivity. She is not the black woman Brooks honors in the poem "To Those of My Sisters Who Kept Their Naturals":

You never worshiped Marilyn Monroe.
You say: Farrah's hair is hers.
You have not wanted to be white.
Nor have you testified to adoration of that state
   with the advertisement of imitation.[102]

When Brooks's novel concludes at the end of World War II, Maud Martha is far from a speaking agent in hegemonic culture, unlike her outspoken fictional sister Mildred, the protagonist in Alice Childress's 1950s newspaper column "Conversations from Life," whose undaunted voice reached a broad reading audience. Mildred tells her white female employer, "Don't be afraid to talk to me because if you say the wrong thing I promise to correct you, and if you want to get along you won't mind me doing so."[103] In contrast Maud Martha quits—without explanation—her domestic job with Mrs. Burns-Cooper, who talks at her.

This is not to say that *Maud Martha* does not forward a black feminist literary critique. The novel's final pages outline Maud Martha's inchoate social consciousness as she reads between the lines of black media discourses. News of southern lynchings dampens celebration of the war's end and effectively challenges the country's victory over fascism with African Americans' unsettled battle against domestic terrorism. Yet Maud Martha's reading also draws attention to black women's struggle against intraracial caste and patriarchal subjection, for she notes that "on [the newspaper's] front pages beamed the usual representations of womanly Beauty, pale and pompadoured."[104] Her brief comment on the black presses' beauty aesthetics is a parenthetical aside amid news about lynching, war, and her second pregnancy. However, the parenthetical interjection acknowledges the Jane Crow politics underpinning popular periodical literary culture. In regard to formal aesthetics, punctuation has an expressive materiality, and Brooks's specific use of the parentheses seems to mask but actually imparts Maud Martha's gendered critique of beauty. The parentheses also push Brooks's readers, like Maud Martha, to read literally between the lines. The novel's conclusion suggests that Maud Martha might become a critical reader who redirects her private self-reflections into commentary on public discourse. In the end Maud Martha surmises, "It was doubtful whether the ridiculousness of man would ever completely succeed in destroying the world—or, in fact, the basic equanimity of the least and commonest flower": ordinary women like herself. This veiled, creative articulation of feminine power rouses the reader to reconsider the boundaries of masculinist action.[105]

In spite of a predominant masculinist discourse and public sphere, Maud Martha treasures the quiet feminine heroism in black women's struggle against racism and sexism.

Black feminist literary critics like Mary Helen Washington, Barbara Christian, and Hortense J. Spillers recovered *Maud Martha* from the purgatory of mid-twentieth-century white male criticism and the canonization of the period's black male novelists. A contemporaneous *New Yorker* review claims that Brooks's "impressionistic style . . . is adequate for dealing with a kind of conventional sensitivity, but . . . it is not quite sharp or firm enough to do justice to her remarkable gift for mimicry and her ability to turn unhappiness and anger into a joke."[106] In faulting Brooks's form, the review surreptitiously undercuts black female subjectivity by deeming Maud Martha immaterial and her narrative insubstantial. Since *Maud Martha*'s domestic content and nuanced aesthetic charge readers to heed the voice of black female subjects, the review misses the point of Brooks's Jane Crow text. *Maud Martha* exemplifies the significance of critical reading to black women's self-definition given the narrow possibilities in the cultural imagination for black female art.

6 / The Audacity of Hope: An American Daughter and Her Dream of Cultural Hybridity

Usually an autobiography is written near the end of a long and distinguished career, but not taking any chances, I wrote mine first, then began to live.

—ERA BELL THOMPSON, 1967 FOREWORD TO *AMERICAN DAUGHTER*

Before semiretiring as the international editor of *Ebony* magazine in 1970 and receiving the prestigious Theodore Roosevelt Rough Rider Award in 1976, Era Bell Thompson recounted her coming of age as a black woman and a writer in her autobiography, *American Daughter* (1946). The memoir compellingly maps the rough terrain of her motherless girlhood among a family of men on North Dakota's predominantly white prairies. *American Daughter*'s success established Thompson's distinguished career with Johnson Publishing Company, first as an associate editor of *Negro Digest* in 1947, then as an associate editor of *Ebony* in 1949, and later as a co-managing editor of *Ebony* in 1951. During her tenure at Johnson Publishing Company, Thompson's articles frequently remarked upon her unique historical position as a mid-twentieth-century black woman writer. For example, in "Negro Publications and the Writer" (1950), she humorously recalls that while she was traveling cross-country for an assignment "hardly a passenger or trainman passed who did not stare at the spectacle of a Negro girl who could not only read reading, but type writing." A black porter confirms the specter of black female literacy by proudly announcing to white passengers, "Oh! You are that lady who writes! I've heard about you. . . . Yes, sir, I've done carried all the notorious women!"[1] Joining the esteemed company of actress Lena Horne and educator Mary McLeod Bethune, Thompson's stardom evinced the development of African American journalism. Nevertheless she illustrates in a 1950 installment of her *Negro Digest* column "Bell's Lettres" that her lauding was qualified by her gender. With self-deprecating wit, Thompson admits that she failed to meet the expectations of her readers, who were disappointed by her inability to "look like a lady at [her] first autographing party—gloves, girdle and all," while turning the pages of her speech. Moreover she confides to being misrecognized at her own speaking engagements. "I have even been called Miss 'Wright' (poor Richard)," she jokes.[2] Although honored with her own day in her hometown, Driscoll, in 1972 and a cultural center dedication as an alumna of the University of North Dakota in 1979, Thompson was humbled by being hailed as Richard Wright's wife or sister at the height of her career. The comparison to the most well-known African American writer of the period acknowledges Thompson's exceptionality as a black woman of letters, but the ineluctable misnomer also speaks to the mistaken identity of the black woman writer during the heyday of social realism.

As *American Daughter* predates Thompson's conspicuous journalism career and subsequent accolades of distinction, it documents the emergent writer's struggle to define black female subjectivity despite her Jane Crow oppression. Thompson contests both racism and sexism with her representation of her challenging yet winning maturation set in an isolating environment where all the blacks are men and all the women are white. With countless examples of her triumphs in interracial relations, she disputes overdetermined tropes of African Americans' institutional victimization and proves her indomitable spirit to conquer racism one person at a time. When called a racial slur by white classmates, she reminisces, "I didn't chase them, didn't cry, so they gave it up, because it wasn't any fun that way. And when they found that I could run faster, push the swings higher than most of them, I had many friends."[3] She credits North Dakota with fostering her personal agency as well as her identity as a writer. As a teen she finds her niche in regional writing for the *Chicago Defender*'s "Lights and Shadow" column under the pseudonym "Dakota Dick," whom she characterizes as "a bad, bad cowboy from the wild and wooly West."[4] Boasting that "the Mandan Chamber of Commerce could not have done better," Thompson not only spotlights her home state in the *Defender* but also affirms her authority over the rural landscape popularly configured as lawless, masculine, and white. Yet in *American Daughter* she depicts North Dakota as a racial utopia of white immigrants of various nationalities shaping the contours of her "nasal Midwestern accent . . . laced with Scandanavian [sic] and Hebrew phrases" as well as inspiring the "Negrowegian" she spoke with her siblings.[5] This syncretized American dialect, a playful mix of black vernacular and white immigrant lexica, is the official language of cultural hybridity and "the audacity of hope" promoted in Thompson's memoir.[6]

In *American Daughter* Thompson reimagines antagonistic mid-twentieth-century interracial relations while she argues that racism's most distressing repercussions are the segregated black community's cultural proscriptions. She was socially alienated within Chicago's black enclaves years after her migration to the city in 1933, and her descriptions of her cultural awkwardness during the Black Chicago Renaissance illustrate that her seemingly idyllic North Dakota upbringing isolated her from African Americans and black vernacular traditions. "I had trouble with the new words," Thompson writes in an Urban League newsletter. "I was slow to learn the inflections and to shift emphasis to new syllables. The music did things to me inside, but my body wouldn't respond. I stood rigid while others swayed."[7] Comparable recollections of communal longing and cultural lack in *American Daughter* complicate Thompson's construction of black female subjectivity, especially in the context of her avid promotion of cultural hybridity. "I was a racial misfit in Chicago," she confesses in a 1977 interview. "In a sense I was less accepted there by blacks than I was in North Dakota by whites. When I denied coming from the South, as Blacks did then [1930s], I was called a liar."[8] In *American Daughter* Thompson shares her difficulty defining her racial and gender identity during her childhood in the absence of her mother and a critical mass of African Americans, who made up only .001 percent of North Dakota's population.[9] The racial discrimination she experienced as an adult in Chicago further complicated her formative process. Her memoir highlights her frustrations being lumped together with the undifferentiated masses of black migrants segregated to the city's South Side. Black migrants' enmity toward prejudiced whites as well as their indifference toward blacks like herself, who lacked experiential knowledge of southern American oppression and black folk culture, also add to her racial estrangement.

Therefore Thompson constructs black female subjectivity in her narrative by embracing a western white utopia and rejecting conventional conceptualizations of blackness synonymous with southern subjugation. In these respects *American Daughter* effectively critiques and rewrites the predominant script of black male rage and white terrorism espoused in Wright's *Native Son* and fortified in his autobiography *Black Boy*. Whereas the title of her autobiography signifies on Wright's social realist novel set in Chicago, Thompson's representation of self as a nurtured "native" daughter offsets the themes of racial subjection and violence in Wright's southern memoir, published just one year prior to her text.[10] *American Daughter*'s response to Wright's famous novel and acclaimed autobiography reflects the frequent critical, generic blurring of these works. In "Richard Wright's Blues" (1945), Ralph Ellison parallels Wright's childhood self in *Black Boy* with his protagonist in *Native Son*: "Imagine Bigger Thomas projecting his own life in lucid prose guided, say, by the insights of Marx and Freud, and you have an idea of this autobiography."[11] As both Wright and Bigger were terrorized southerners and disenfranchised migrants, Katherine Fishburn employs *Black Boy* as an ur-text for Wright's fiction, and Valerie Smith contends that the writer and his black male protagonist shared a similar relationship to language.[12] Even Thompson conceded to a Belgian inquirer during her research trip to the Congo for her travelogue *Africa, Land of My Fathers* (1954) that Bigger was indeed a "composite picture" of real figures, just as Wright viewed his memoir as a collective autobiography for the "voiceless" black boys of the South.[13]

American Daughter, then, is a critical rejoinder to the racial and gender politics of Wright's oeuvre. Thompson reconfigures Wright's masculinist model of racial subjectivity by representing herself as a true American whose gender finesses her racial subject position. Ellison argues that the "blues" in *Black Boy* are the result of Wright's acrimony toward his disciplinarian mother and religiously fervent grandmother because they recapitulated southern whites' racial violence. This antipathy is prefigured in Bigger's resentment of his mother's emasculation of him, kowtowing to whites, and Christian complacency. Although Thompson's mother passed unexpectedly when she was twelve years old and left her to face the double jeopardy of racism and sexism alone, the writer maintained *"FAITH* in America because," she avows, "I AM A PART OF IT and IT IS A *PART OF ME."*[14] Thompson resisted the tradition of social protest in African American letters and its masculinist precepts by extolling interracial unity and endorsing cultural hybridity. Her portrait of "black hope" in *American Daughter* attests to the country's social progress and its racially inclusive democracy. "I know there is still good in the world," she encourages at the conclusion of her narrative, "that way down underneath, most Americans are fair; that my people and your people can work together and live together in peace and happiness."[15]

In the tradition of black women's autobiography, Thompson writes herself into subjectivity by championing an idealized portrait of an integrated nation that sustains its black daughters. As Joanne M. Braxton observes in *Black Women Writing Autobiography*, this vision is "central to the psychic wholeness of young women deprived of their connection with the primary source of their black and female identity."[16] Thompson's investment in projecting a nurturing and inclusive America is critical to her sense of self. Further, her gendered vision fulfills the social and political objectives of African American autobiography, a tradition distinguished by the fact that many of its writers published their accounts before their major accomplishments.[17] Since the earliest narratives written in bondage, African Americans struggled to authenticate their subjectivity through language mastery. Henry Louis Gates Jr. contends, "This connection among language, memory, and the self has been of signal importance to African-Americans, intent as they have had to be upon demonstrating both common humanity with whites and upon demonstrating that their 'selves' were, somehow, as whole, integral, educable, and as noble as were those of any other American ethnic group."[18]

With its reconfiguring of the Midwest, black migration, and urban life, Thompson's autobiography provides an anomalous representation of black exceptionalism previously undocumented in collective historical narratives. For this reason Braxton argues that *American Daughter* "embodies the black woman's continued quest for self-fulfillment and a self-defining identity—for recognition."[19] Thompson's reflections on her racial and sexual difference in North Dakota and Chicago evolve from lamenting her initial isolation to celebrating her eventual transcendence, which models her contemporary Zora Neale Hurston's autobiography, *Dust Tracks on a Road* (1942). Both black women writers approach life's struggles with humor, and each rebounds with the sustaining relationships they form with nature. Notably they construct their racial identities quite differently in their texts. Hurston grew up in the all-black town of Eatonville, Florida, and Thompson was socialized in North Dakota, where blackness was deemed more foreign than intrinsically inferior. Yet both women rejected the supposed tragedy of blackness through their emancipatory writing acts; to use Carole Boyce Davies's term, they also shed the conventions of femininity as "migrating subjectivities."[20]

Despite Thompson's portrayal of transcendent black female subjectivity, the literary inscriptions of Jane Crow oppression structure the creative and editing processes engendering *American Daughter*. Thompson does not escape the hierarchical power dynamics circumscribing the relationships between mid-twentieth-century black writers and white publishers. In fact she divulges in roughly thirty quarter-sheet memos chronicling *American Daughter*'s production that editors at the University of Chicago Press explicitly solicited her memoir as the antithesis of *Native Son*'s endorsement of racial protest and *Black Boy*'s depiction of despair. For instance, she records editor Joseph Brandt informing her, "You could write a book 10 times better than Richard Wright because you would be writing from a different angle, you have dignity and a feeling of enrichment!"[21] Thompson's notes reveal the stratagems various white cultural brokers exercised to canonize and censure African American literature. Hence her commentary draws attention to both *American Daughter*'s materiality (its published content) and its immateriality (the politics of its publication).[22] The memoirs of her more well-known contemporaries similarly exemplify that the mid-twentieth-century black writer's authorial intent was not the same as his or her authority over the text. As a case in point, Wright initially conceptualized his autobiography also including his experiences in the North under the title *American Hunger*, but the Book-of-the-Month Club requested that he end his memoir with his impending migration to Chicago. This ending exorcises Wright's Communist Party affiliations as well as his broader critiques of the United States.[23] Likewise Hurston's autobiography, to use Claudine Raynaud's imagery, is a "mine field of excisions, deletions, changes—sometimes willed by the author, other times imposed by the editor(s)."[24] In addition to expelling her views on foreign policy, sexual exploitation as a maid, and more sexually explicit folklore from *Dust Tracks on a Road*, Hurston's editors restricted the nuances of black orality, which are the hallmark of her oeuvre.

American Daughter is a comparable literary composite of the black writer's genius and the white editors' imposition. As a joint venture between Thompson and her editors, the autobiography realizes the cultural hybridity she privileges throughout the text. Yet Thompson's narrative also evinces the mediation of her distinct racial and gendered authorial voice in the hybrid sphere of publication. According to her notes on her writing process, Thompson's editors decided the title of her narrative as well as encouraged its race-themed social agenda. She discloses in her 1977 speech "Full Circle," given at Bismarck Junior College, that a memoir was not what she proposed to write when she applied for a Newberry Library fellowship for midwestern writers sponsored by the Rockefeller Foundation. Thompson intended "to educate those heathens who believed [North Dakota] was running over with buffaloes—and wild Indians, that it was the deep-freeze capital of the United States. . . . I wanted to write a book about my corner of the country, the real America." She goes on to clarify, "The committee, however, settled for an autobiography. They, too, were more interested in what I was doing 'way out there' than they were in what 'out there' was."[25] If Thompson had written the travel guide or historical study she proposed, *American Daughter* likely would not have included the affective racial experiences framing her juxtaposition of North Dakota and Chicago and undergirding her intertextual dialogue with Wright. Her acquiescence to the fellowship committee's interests and her alignment with the press's politics resulted in contemporaneous reviews questioning the authenticity of her narrative. For example, Nelson Algren calls *American Daughter* "a hopscotch autobiography, an amiable idyll presented with a kind of circuitousness which sometimes leaves the reader to wonder just what DID happen."[26] Perhaps recognizing Thompson's and her editors' efforts to neutralize Wright's school of protest, another review hypothesizes that somewhere between the "gay, often flip" *American Daughter* and the "stark, bitter horror" of *Black Boy* "lies the true, balanced, over-all picture of the race relations problem in contemporary America."[27]

American Daughter narrates Thompson's personal usurpation of Jane Crow oppression in white male hegemonic culture. However, the autobiography's cultural production and critical reception evidence the race and gender politics inevitably defining the writer and her work. Thompson boldly abandons Wright's literary blueprint, but she cannot fully circumvent the mandates of white publishers or the expectations of mainstream critics for mid-twentieth-century African American literature. Instead she fashions black female subjectivity by way of her memoir's favored daughter construct—an image that she continued to excogitate in subsequent autobiographical projects. As James Olney contends, "By its very nature, the self is (like the autobiography that records and creates it) open-ended and incomplete: it is always in process or, more precisely, is itself a process."[28] After years traveling internationally on assignment for *Ebony*, Thompson pursued publishing a second memoir centered on her career as a journalist. With the working titles "P.S. or the Rest of My Life" and "From Pokey to Palace," this follow-up report would have discussed the writer's night in a Johannesburg jail for thwarting apartheid laws; a stay in Rafael Trujillo's palace in the Dominican Republic; a response to the King and Kennedy assassinations; and personal letters from *Ebony* readers, 95 percent of which she claimed were addressed to Mr. Thompson.[29] Thompson also envisioned writing "'I Can't Cook Book' (You Can Read, Can't You?)," whose title emphasizes the workingwoman's adroit literacy despite her domestic ineptitude. She planned for the recipes to draw on her experiences as the only daughter of a widowed father, who was a cook, and her experiences as a career-driven single woman who loved to eat but had little culinary skill. Finally, Thompson considered writing a guide for white adoptive parents of black children and a study of black children raised in white homes; both interests were inspired by the writer's coming of age in predominantly white environments and pseudo-adoption by a white family while she attended college. These unfinished projects are seemingly unrelated, yet each intimates that Thompson protractedly theorized the unique racial and gendered identity she first represented in *American Daughter* but renegotiated throughout her life and writing.

From State Guide to Autobiography

American Daughter is a political treatise on racial tolerance and the real-life story of Thompson's racial and gender socialization. As a result it is difficult to distinguish in the text between the literal and the figurative. Thompson suggests as much thirty years after the publication of her autobiography, when she admits, "My book can be—and has been—embarrassing." She explains in "Full Circle" that she was obligated once to consume a plate of spaghetti ordered by a male dining companion. "I know you like it," he told her. "You said so in your book!" She concludes the anecdote by confiding, "So I ate the hated stuff, vowing to read *American Daughter*—which I had not—as soon as possible."[30] The tale is a joke told straight. Thompson's winking denouement acknowledges that she crafted a symbolic self in her narrative, which she differentiates from her private, authentic self in the story. By revealing that she did not like spaghetti and had never read her autobiography, she dispels any myths of full disclosure. Thompson also confesses in her personal notes that *American Daughter* is "about 75% imagination," and she is bolstered by the fact that there is "no way of proving it wasn't [real]!"[31] Perhaps undermining the validity of her autobiographical self as a racial ideal, her witty play in the aforementioned paratexts enriches one's reading of the published text. Moreover these paratexts beg further critical consideration of how the investments of various cultural brokers shaped the creation and reception of Thompson's work.

As head librarian at the Newberry Library, a member of its fellowship committee, and a mentor to novice autobiographer Thompson, Stanley Pargellis had a great deal of authority over her project's transition from an opus on North Dakota to an autobiography. In her letter of application for the Newberry Library fellowship, Thompson proposes to write an amusing account of her family's move from Iowa to North Dakota when she was nine years old. She relays, "I want to make people laugh a little. I want to write a book about a very urban American family which suddenly finds itself on a farm in the middle of nowhere; . . . I want the world to share with me the golden grain lands of Dakota, the honest friendliness that is Iowa."[32] Thompson's application reveals that her primary aim is to glorify North Dakota's utopian landscape, not theorize midwestern racial politics. Yet Pargellis recommended that an autobiography was a more "suitable vehicle" to expand upon Thompson's ideas and highlight the qualities in her writing that most interested the fellowship committee. "You seem to have learned a good deal about life," he encourages in a letter, "and to have come to sound conclusions of your own on a difficult subject."[33] Thompson's rural racialization intrigued the fellowship committee more than her romantic regional prose, and thus Pargellis advised her to foreground the edifying experiences of her life in her writing. He insisted that each event in her autobiography "must add something, and be seen to add something, to the development and maturing of one [Era Bell] Thompson, who has come to her own *personal* solution of a national problem."[34]

The fellowship committee and the University of Chicago Press shared a common objective: to employ the sanguine *American Daughter* to counter the supposed damaging effects of *Native Son* and *Black Boy*'s grim depiction of the race problem. From the outset the announcement for the fellowship discouraged manuscripts written in the propagandistic style of protest by requesting submissions dealing "primarily with human beings and not with sociological, economic or institutional forces apart from their effect on people."[35] Thompson's memos detailing her exchanges with the press illustrate that the intertextual dialogue between her and Wright was mediated by a matrix of white editors, advisors, and other writers. She records that W. T. Couch, director of the University of Chicago Press, appreciated her optimism regarding interracial relations and was "very anxious to have this *approach used in some* studies in the North as in the south—or something."[36] A couple of years earlier Couch was the director of the University of North Carolina Press, where he wrote an unconventional and conservative "publisher's introduction" to Rayford Logan's otherwise progressive compendium on integration titled *What the Negro Wants* (1944). "Booker Washington came nearer than anyone else to stating the problem of the Negro in its true terms," Couch posits. "Nothing is more needed in the South today than rebirth of his ideas."[37] The publisher seemingly "took his revenge" on *What the Negro Wants*, Lawrence P. Jackson contends, by later publishing *American Daughter*.[38] After meeting Couch, Thompson describes him in her notes as "all niceness. Sort of nondescript looking soul, whitish, talkative, trying very hard to be liberal sounding, nice. Hardly any southern inflection." She had an affinity for Couch's politics, which critiqued social programs that blamed "the white man" for blacks' disenfranchisement and failed to acknowledge blacks' social responsibility. "I told him people are too conscious of race, I'd rather get away from it, from writing solely about it," she surreptitiously concludes the entry. "He said he rather suspected he agreed with me, but if he said so, it would be called prejudice!"[39]

Thompson also transcribes informal reviews of Wright's work in her memos and juxtaposes them with praise of her mild temperament in regard to the race question. For example, she paraphrases Chicago writer and bookstore owner Max Siegel's criticism of Wright: "Black Boy: Wright seems to ignore fact thatt [sic] many Chicago white people befreinded [sic], helped him. Native Son was an awful book. He heard the repercussions there in his store after people read it. Did more to hurt race than help."[40] In contrast Thompson relates that others complimented her "lack of 'chip on the shoulder'"—another tacit critique of Wright.[41] Nonetheless Black Boy is on her reading list as she drafts her autobiography under the working title "I Found It Fun."[42] Editors constructively advised her to limit the history of North Dakota in her memoir as well as stories about her father in order to privilege her subjectivity. Yet her notes also imply that editors dictated her social commentary on race. Thompson reports that an editor asks, "What are you setting out to do? a—Write a series of humorous incidents of your life or b—prove a point." The same dated entry records only Pargellis's reply: "She is going to *SHOW by her own life* story, the *only way to solve the race problem*. That people of all colors can live and do live in harmony in America."[43] Whereas Thompson's fellowship application suggests that she might have chosen the less didactic option, she does not log her answer to the question.

Thompson's representation of this discussion in her transcripts—in which white editors and advisors virtually silenced the black female writer—effectively undermines *American Daughter*'s focus on amiable interracial relations rather than segregation and discrimination. From the autobiography's creative inception to its material production, Pargellis and University of Chicago Press editors strove to establish Thompson's text as an authority on the postwar civil rights agenda. As Raynaud points out, "The black American autobiographical text is both the stakes and the product of a racial ritual, repeating, at a historical remove, the relationship that united the black slave and the white abolitionist as guarantor of the authenticity of the slave's life story. The editor (the publisher, the guarantor, the patron) carries on, acting as authenticator; he or she actively competes with the author for control over the production of the text."[44] Thompson's cultural brokers advocated for harmony over protest, happiness over bitterness, and social unity instead of political partisanship. In compliance, Thompson declares at a tea hosted by the press and the Friends of the Negro Writer that *American Daughter* is "an attempt to *BALANCE THE LITERARY* picture of the Negro. If it is *light* and *gay* in places, it is because my life was light and gay—in places. If it lacks (the usual) *BITTERNESS & RANCOR*, it is because my life has been without (the usual) bitterness and rancor—in places. If it is *HOPEFUL*, then it is because I, too, am hopeful."[45] Stressing that she is not a southern-bred African American writer, Thompson distinguishes her narrative from the predominant script of social realism. She contends that her life story demands a generic shift in mid-twentieth-century African American literature, and she calls for more tempered racial politics.

Thompson's blithe narrative perspective purportedly proves blacks' ability to attain the American Dream, and the cover for *American Daughter*'s second printing manifests this racial ideal. The jacket represents western migration with a silhouette of a family traveling by wagon to a homestead in the distance. This imagery projects a pioneering spirit, which conveys that the autobiography is both a regional tale and a universal story of struggle and triumph. The blurb on the cover confirms, "This book is as American as *Tom Sawyer*."[46] Thompson comments in one of her publishing notes that a press salesman reassured her that with the Mark Twain "bit . . . they know classification book is in at start. . . . Just right, humanunderstanding [*sic*], element, about everyday people."[47] While her narrative is labeled quintessentially American, Thompson is characterized as thoroughly likeable. The jacket's description promises that her "infectious humor, her irresistible friendliness, and her deep understanding of people make her a person worth knowing." The innocuous packaging of American ideals and ecumenical values presumably marketed the autobiography to the hesitant white reader to the potential alienation of the socially critical reader. In his review "Stepchild Fantasy" Ellison dismisses Thompson's text as too lightweight: "'American Daughter' is amazingly lacking in political, sociological, economic, or psychological insights. Indeed one wonders at its publication by the very sociological University of Chicago Press—which does not usually publish autobiography." Finding Thompson's memoir "not nearly so worthy" as *Black Boy*, Ellison nods at the racial politics motivating her publication, and he accuses the black female writer of not only social accommodationism but also literary assimilation. He reminds readers that "writing, too, like the ointments with which some Negroes attempt to bleach their dark skins to a 'white' esthetic standard, can be a form of symbolic bleaching."[48] Ellison's criticism is particularly acerbic, but Thompson admitted years later, "Had I lived my early life among Blacks, perhaps my rage would have been much like his."[49]

Additional contemporaneous reviews imposed delimiting social conventions on *American Daughter*'s anomalous representation of black female subjectivity. Few reviews fail to compare Thompson to Wright, and an even smaller number credit her as the more cogent writer. Yet for that handful of critics, Thompson's winsome character encouraged the targeted white reader's sentimental response to provocative race matters. "Probably most critics would agree that Richard Wright has a more impressive talent for serious literary production than has Era Bell Thompson," one reviewer hypothesizes, "[though] certainly Richard Wright with a little less bitterness and a little more of Miss Thompson's humor and friendliness would be more easily read and more sympathetically received."[50] Another review praises *American Daughter* because it "sets forth in no unmistakable terms that discrimination is not confined to below the Mason-Dixon line. And she does it in a calm, logical case history, almost clinical in its objectivity, yet with an appealing individual presentation that we believe is more effective than Wright's rage against his environment."[51] Whereas these reviews praise Thompson's efficacy (at the same time that they fastidiously criticize her genius), others contend that her construction of subjectivity does not in fact exemplify a black perspective. One review celebrates Thompson's uniqueness by negating intraracial diversity and reducing blackness to racial antagonism: "*American Daughter* is distinctive primarily for what it is not. The autobiography of a Negro woman, it is not representative of typical Negro experiences, it is not essentially Negro in its viewpoint, and it is not bitter."[52] In contrast S. I. Hayakawa insightfully recognizes the double duty Thompson's autobiography performs for the segregated audience. For the white reader, "'American Daughter' may very well be the best possible introduction to the Negro world; . . . it is likely to scare no one." For the black reader, Hayakawa resolves, "the book is an object lesson in how to be a Negro without going nuts."[53] Thompson's psychic balance between black and white worlds assuages incidents of racial injury and refutes popular tropes of black pathology.

Since most reviews foreground Thompson's racial identity, they consequently ignore the significance of her gender in *American Daughter*. Louise H. Elder's review in *Phylon* acknowledges the autobiography's gendered conflicts only to recapitulate the critical discussion privileging race issues over gender matters. In response to criticism that Thompson was "too glad a Negro girl," Elder suggests, "Perhaps the problem of being a woman prevents her giving whole-hearted attention to the problem of being a Negro."[54] The review registers the difficulty for a mid-twentieth-century black female writer—and her critics—in addressing race and gender concerns simultaneously given their competing loyalties historically. For example, Margo Culley observes that of 710 entries in the bibliography *Black Americans in Autobiography* (1974), approximately 25 percent signal race in their titles.[55] Roughly a dozen black female autobiographers signal both race and gender in their titles, and just five solely reference gender, including Thompson and Maya Angelou. It is telling, then, that Thompson addresses only gender in her title and critics consider only whether she solves or exacerbates the race problem. Of course, race figures prominently in *American Daughter*, but reviewers' juxtaposition of Wright and Thompson limits the critical discussion of the latter's text to race and devalues its Jane Crow discourse.

Reading *American Daughter*'s immateriality (the way Thompson's advisors conceived, the press marketed, and the reviewers evaluated the autobiography) adds layers of meaning to the text. Yet tracing the politics of mid-twentieth-century literary production and its implications for *American Daughter*'s racial and gender tensions is more important than simply conjecturing about what Thompson's manuscript might have been had it not been shaped by white guarantors. Any authentic black woman writer was expected to focus on the race problem, and any major black writer was required to respond to Wright. *American Daughter* reflects the challenges burdening a black woman writer within a publishing moment culturally dominated by black male writers and economically controlled by white male editors. In rewriting Wright's alternately acclaimed and contested trope of embittered black masculinity, Thompson obtains symbolic enfranchisement through her transcendent representation of black womanhood. Her notes about the production of her text, however, mitigate her optimistic depiction of interracial relations by demonstrating her awareness of the black writer's limited authority within the public sphere of white publishing.

"If It Is Light and Gay in Places . . . ": In Search of Era Bell Thompson

Thompson explores the intricacies of black female subjectivity throughout *American Daughter*, but she privileges her racial and gender identities in different phases of the narrative. She directly confronts the gender conflicts of her childhood while she minimizes the racial tensions she experiences in North Dakota's predominantly white environment. Because she is "the First Black Child in a land that is still burying it's [*sic*] First White Children," Thompson represents her racial difference as no more foreign than that of the European immigrants settling the midwestern prairies—despite her differing status as a native American daughter.[56] With stories about her trials on her family's farm, Thompson broadens the masculinist western landscape and its limited racial scope for womanhood. However, in the final third of *American Daughter* she attenuates her gender discussion and centralizes the interracial and intraracial conflicts she experiences when she migrates to the South Side of Chicago. Seeking work and community in the black enclave, Thompson discovers for the first time how it feels to be surrounded by "colored people, lots and lots of colored people, so many that [she] stared when [she] saw a white person."[57] She struggles to establish kinship with Chicago's southern migrants, and she suffers under the segregation targeting the black masses. The racial tolerance she appreciates as a part of North Dakota's minuscule black population is vastly different from the lack of class and regional distinction she experiences under Jim Crow oppression. She challenges racism, then, more in *American Daughter*'s description of her adulthood than in her portrayal of her childhood. Meanwhile she considers her gender only in amusing Chicago anecdotes that highlight her lack of domestic skill when employed briefly as a maid. Although Thompson's racial and gendered concerns oscillate in terms of their preponderance in her text, she rhetorically frames both with humor and emotional distance. As a result she does not resolve the ambiguities of her racial consciousness or the consequences of her sexual difference for readers. Instead *American Daughter* demonstrates the nuances of the Jane Crow text by charting the social, spatial, and temporal locations constructing Thompson's autobiographical self.

The first chapter of *American Daughter* intimates Thompson's efforts to define black womanhood within a racist and patriarchal culture with the title "Go West, Black Man." Her father speaks the first words of the narrative at her birth: "My Lord, it's a girl!" Her sex is a surprise because, as she drolly writes, "my Lord had heretofore been very good to my father, for he had three sons: Tom, Dick and, Harry."[58] Thompson's birth meets neither her father's expectations nor those set up by the chapter's title for realizing black masculinity through migration. Thompson positions her birth as a feminine interjection in the summons to go west and launches her autobiography's break in this masculinist writing tradition.

She explains that her birth reclaims the family's racial ancestry, as her paternal grandfather was a white plantation owner, and, as a result, the first female child born to her parents "took back" with white skin and blond hair. In contrast to these markers of past miscegenation, Thompson relays that when she "lost the newborn pallor, [she] began taking on racial traits so quickly and decidedly that [her] Mother became alarmed." She quickly points out her dark skin in order to affirm there is no tragedy in being born a black girl. "Colored storks," Thompson jokes to account for the stark difference between her and her sister, who died before Thompson was born, "are notoriously inconsistent."[59]

Despite Thompson's insertion of herself in this familial and collective black history, the first chapter increasingly focuses on her parents' efforts to make enfranchised men out of her three siblings. As Michael K. Johnson observes, Thompson herself "almost seems an afterthought" in the autobiography's early chapters.[60] While Tom, Dick, and Harry constantly get into trouble at school, Thompson jokes that she becomes the carrier pigeon for their teachers' notes home at the same time that her own "propitious" education begins with failing kindergarten. She reports her brothers' rogue antics and expresses her hero worship of her father's floundering entrepreneurship, but she subtly refuses to the let the struggles of the men in her life eclipse her subjectivity. She concludes the first chapter by remarking that her family "left for far-off North Dakota . . . where there was freedom and equal opportunity for a man with three sons. *Three sons and a daughter.*"[61] The promise of her brothers' growing into manhood under less prejudice is the impetus behind the migration. Yet Thompson does not diminish her place in the family or exclude herself from their new western prospects. In conjunction with the opening description of her birth, Thompson's words closing the chapter present her as an equally endowed daughter and legitimate interlocutor.

Thompson claims her manifest destiny in North Dakota, but her mother is absent from the catalogue of the migrating family, though she does not die until three years after the move. Thompson excludes her mother from the family's western project because the latter is not present later to guide the twelve-year-old through the processes of black womanhood. The lost mother precipitates young Thompson's unfamiliarity with female ritual as well as adult Thompson's alienation from black vernacular traditions. Traditionally the initiation into African American womanhood starts with lullabies and girlhood games and graduates to shared recipes and sage adages.[62] Although Thompson must later relearn black rites by way of concerts and dance recitals with white friends, her mother's blues inaugurate her education in the performance of black female subjectivity. She remembers that her mother "would sit down at the deserted piano and play slow, sad things. She never played from music—I doubt if she ever had lessons—but, as she played, her eyes had a faraway look, her small fingers responding to the song in her soul."[63] The solemn song about a "downward road" conjures the mother's longing for distant places and intimate connections that is characteristic of the traveling blues. The mother's literal and figurative blues make young Thompson think of souls marching to heaven and prefigure the mother's passing. The blues imagery also displaces the writer's laconic mourning in her mostly entertaining account of her childhood. Finally, Thompson's association of her mother with blues intonations anticipates the writer's search for the lost mother manifest in her travels back and forth between North Dakota, her mother's final resting place, and Chicago, the location of cultural blackness.

The mother's death early in *American Daughter* suggests that she had limited influence over Thompson's construction of black female subjectivity. Still, the writer makes a point to detail her rejection of the traditional feminine conventions briefly enforced by her mother after the family's move west. As Braxton observes of African American women's autobiography more broadly, the initial chapters in *American Daughter* "reveal a growing sense of displacement that is geographic, cultural, and social; it is accompanied by a reevaluation and rejection of the traditional female role."[64] Just as Thompson's father requires her youngest brother to work on their new farm, she recalls that "Mother, too, began to make demands upon my time. She found tasks inside the house—little-girl tasks like setting the table, doing dishes, sewing my clothes, or endless pounding on the clabber in the stone churn. . . . My dislike of housework often brought me into violent conflict with Mother." When her mother whips her for shirking domestic duties, Thompson asserts her voice by defiantly exclaiming, "Damn it!" The repudiating speech-act is an expression of her individuality, a damning critique of her punishment for rejecting feminine domestication. Thompson's ingenuous desire to "run away from these colored folks and live with the Indians" demonstrates that she not only resists conforming to her mother's traditional femininity but also opposes domesticating the intractable land as her father and brothers attempt to do with their labor. For young Thompson, "colored folks" model obsequious womanhood and masculinist conquest, and she romantically associates Native Americans' relationship to nature as the epitome of gender freedom.[65]

In this way *American Daughter* reflects Thompson's obeisance to classic midwestern prairie fiction featuring tenacious pioneering women's challenges to traditional feminine conventions. In *Maud Martha* Gwendolyn Brooks's black female protagonist imagines that her work ethic as a housewife should model the self-sacrifice glorified in prairie novels, in which white female protagonists were "women who could stand low temperatures. Women who would toil eminently, to improve the lot of their men. Women who cooked."[66] By contrast, in a review of Willa Cather's novel *My Ántonia* (1918), Thompson expresses her admiration for "the story of pioneer women who worked like men in the fields, and of the 'hired girls,' the young farm girls of foreign birth who quit the farms for the small towns to work as domestics."[67] Cather's fiction elides racial tensions on the frontier and instead privileges the discord between Old World customs and New World opportunities for modern American women.[68] Thompson signifies on this script for transformation and naturalization in *American Daughter* when she explains, "Nearly all my friends were second generation; their parents spoke the mother tongue, wore the native clothes, had the ways of the fatherland, even the Indians. In a sense I was second generation, too." She identifies with the white children of immigrants because she also contests familial tradition and social convention. Thompson utters "Damn" again when her mother sees a rainbow after their stormy generational conflict, but Thompson realizes there is no pot of gold awaiting her.[69] Her version of the women's prairie novel demystifies fictions of privileged womanhood as well as fancies of western freedom. Both are fantasies limited by the politics of her race and gender.

Thompson is disillusioned when her mother unexpectedly succumbs to illness during a harsh winter and she is left with her father and brothers' well-intentioned though inadequate parenting. Young Thompson is so far removed from the epistemologies of black femininity that she "rudely" stares at a black female visitor because she had not seen another black woman in North Dakota besides her mother. In the chapter "Broken Dreams," the death of Thompson's mother describes the loneliness of the writer's journey into black womanhood as the mother's passing coincides with the fragmentation of the nuclear family. Thompson's father sends her to live with her uncle and his "bossy white" wife, but she shortly returns home with the understanding that she will have greater domestic responsibility. She recounts, "My first thought, after the shock of death was one of freedom: now I could wear what I wished and tie the ribbons on the ends of my braids like the other kids—but I was soon disillusioned." In actuality freedom means she must figure out the mysteries of hair care on her own: "I worked hard at the end-of-the-braid project, but it was no use—my hair was too short. The bow slid off as fast as we tied it on." The fact that she is left alone with the "burden of the house" while her older siblings run away from the farm also hampers the autonomy she hoped to gain. Despite these series of familial losses, Thompson manages to find humor in growing up as the only daughter of a widower. Her father encourages her to read articles in *True Story* magazine with such titles as "Is Your Daughter Safe from Temptation?" in lieu of having an explicit sex talk with her. Thompson amusingly shares her sympathy for her unsuspecting father by admitting that she had been reading the popular publication already.[70]

Most obviously the death of Thompson's mother brings to the forefront the writer's efforts to construct a gendered identity within her male-dominated family. However, the maternal loss also initiates the incipient insights Thompson makes about the performance of race. *American Daughter* primarily minimizes the psychological injury of whites' racism by demonstrating Thompson's providential fate to overcome such conflicts. Thus in the chapter "Broken Dreams" she offsets her mother's death by relaying a bigoted encounter with humor. When she asks her oldest brother if her teacher can blacken Thompson's face for a school play, he laughingly responds, "You crazy? Ain't you black enough now? . . . What kinda play is that you gotta be black? . . . Blacker." Thompson's account of this exchange focuses on the comedic irony of the situation, as she describes tearfully explaining to her brother that the production is about President Lincoln and all the children playing slaves will be in blackface. The joke, of course, is that she does not have to play the part in blackface because she is African American. Nonetheless her tale becomes less funny when her brother's critical racial consciousness clarifies the situation for his naïve sister: "They're white; they're not like you." Thompson ultimately triumphs over prejudice in this anecdote when the teacher allows her to choose any part she wants, and she takes the part of a taunting white male classmate, the role of the slave overseer. "Teacher excused the master and freed the slave," she writes. "If Lincoln could do it," she recalls the teacher saying, "then so can I."[71] Young Thompson's seemingly unwitting choice is quite amusing in its ability to empower black and white women alike, but this yarn is not metaphorically black and white. Thompson, the writer, does not fully engage the complexities of this episode, not even in retrospect. She refuses to comment critically on the performance's implications for interracial relations, and she leaves legacies of slavery, blackface minstrelsy, and racism unproblematized in this moment. Ellison's critique of Thompson's lack of self-reflection resonates in such tensions.

Thompson presumably naturalizes racial injury with humor in order to maintain a humanist image of her childhood. Hence any incidents of racial subjection addressed in the autobiography do not negate the acceptance the Thompsons receive from North Dakota's white immigrant community. With a mix of Scandinavian, Russian, Irish, Swedish, and German immigrants, the prairie is an ethnic utopia. The neighboring white farmers are friendly to the Thompsons: they offer advice to the novice farmers, lend tools and machinery, and gift pigs and chickens to help the new residents get established. When the family is left with only potatoes to eat after an unsuccessful farming season, a German neighbor gives them canned goods, meat, and other staples. "Nein, nein!" he tells Thompson's father, "I no vant money. . . . I got money, I your neighbor, I help you. Dot iss all." Thompson implies that the white residents' beneficence is reflective of the land, whose vastness poses few physical or social restrictions for the black family. "It was a strange and beautiful country," she writes poetically, "so big and boundless [one] could look for miles and miles out over the golden prairies and follow the unbroken horizon where the midday blue met the bare peaks of the distant hills."[72] Her descriptions of the open landscape and accepting white community promote the possibilities of the West for African Americans. Thompson positions North Dakota as an alternative to the prejudices of the South and urban North.

Thompson never lives in the South or experiences its abject oppression, but her autobiography's western chauvinism initially extends the South's racial horrors to Chicago. As Farah Jasmine Griffin observes of Wright's fiction, "Black bodies, exploited, dominated, and mutilated, are an indelible part of the Southern landscape."[73] Thompson equates southern lynching with urban riots after reading accounts of racial violence in the *Chicago Defender*. At first the prosperity her brother Dick achieves after migrating to Chicago rewrites the premise of *Native Son*. Dick has "a fine job chauffeuring . . . making good money, living a bright, colorful life," and his letters to the family incredulously ask, "How . . . can you folks stay out there in that Godforsaken country away from civilization and our people?" For Thompson, the *Defender* issue Dick sends to the family with an image of a southern lynching and coverage of the 1919 Chicago riots contradicts his auspicious lifestyle. "For a long time, I could see the lifeless body dangling from the tree," she writes. "To me it became a symbol of the South, a place to hate and fear." She concludes that "Dick's civilization was a riot, where black and white Americans fought each other and died. I wanted never to leave my prairies, with white clouds of peace and clean, blue heavens, for now I knew that beyond the purple hills prejudice rode hard on the heels of promise. . . . And I wondered where was God."[74] Dick perceives the West as God-forsaken because of its racial isolation, whereas Thompson presents her home state as the site of racial salvation given the social dystopia of the American South and the South Side of Chicago.[75] Since the prairies provide a spatial reprieve from the racial tensions she reads about in the *Defender*, Thompson renders them as a figurative state of spiritual and social peace.

Notwithstanding this romanticized image of the western plains, Thompson does not exorcise from her autobiography the estrangement she feels as "a fly in a glass of buttermilk" growing up in North Dakota's exclusively white towns. For example, in Driscoll the white children's curiosity forces her to question her racial difference: "For the first time I began to wonder about [the white palms of my hands] and about the soles of my feet and my pink toes."[76] She reveals in an interview that she gained her white peers' acceptance on an individual basis only. She explains, "Generally they forgot the color thing. They'd see a black person, and they would forget I was also black and they would call them a nigger."[77] When her friends make new alliances that exclude her, she writes in *American Daughter*, "they called me 'black' and 'nigger,' and I was alone in my exile, differentiated by the color of my skin." In the bigger city of Bismarck, Thompson claims that her race occasionally comes "in handy" because she can play the role of Mother Africa to raise funds for missionaries. "They didn't ask me to blacken my face," she recalls in regard to this racial performance, "all I had to do was put on a long white robe and follow Mother India and say: 'Help me, too. My people need you!'" Thompson repeatedly frames racial subjection with humor, joking, "Prejudice was a funny thing. It ran every way but out."[78] By recording her painful experiences as a fetishized Other, she also enlightens readers that the West imports the prejudices of the Jim Crow South.[79] For example, Thompson receives a standard Jim Crow education. Textbooks teach her that black people have "a thick skull that education could not penetrate," and a white classmate calls her "'a cute little coon' . . . without emotion and without malice."[80] She chooses not to editorialize the boy's offensive language and lets prejudice speak for itself. Her narration's constant textual masking—in both a literal and a symbolic sense—points to the layered processes of her self-conscious racial performance in *American Daughter*.

Thompson's narrative dissimulation manifests most clearly in her depiction of her pseudo-adoption by the Rileys, the white family with whom she lives and works while attending Morningside College. In Hurston's autobiographical works, whites' cultural adoption of an emerging black female artist is fraught with textual ambiguity. Hurston's young black female protagonist obtains a white patron for her folk performance in the short story "Drenched in Light" just as Hurston procures a white "godmother" and financial sponsor in her autobiography, *Dust Tracks on a Road*. Both texts depict whites' sincere admiration for black artists; they also intimate whites' misappropriation of black bodies of culture. In *American Daughter* Thompson portrays her adoption by Dr. Riley, the president of her college, with similar ambivalence. Mrs. Riley fears that Thompson is a stereotypical mammy and sapphire, "a big, black woman who would dominate her home, intimidate her child," but Thompson converts the most ignorant minds. She becomes such an integral part of the white family that she proclaims herself the "President's Daughter." In effect the writer flaunts the public recognition that no biological black child of a white president has ever received in fiction or real life, namely the descendents of Sally Hemings and Thomas Jefferson who inspire William Wells Brown's novel *Clotel: or, The President's Daughter* (1853). The black community, however, considers Thompson an exploited black body and not a beloved daughter. She discloses, "I remembered how Negroes looked at me as I walked down the street with Dr. Riley, looked at me as if I were a prostitute."[81] In the black community's gaze, Dr. Riley is not a legitimate father because any interracial coupling signals sexual illicitness. Thompson expounds later in an interview, "In fact, they went so far as to say that there must have been . . . well, they intimated that I was probably a real daughter rather than a foster daughter."[82] She critiques African Americans' censuring of her sexuality, but the black community's policing reflects its efforts to raise the esteem of black womanhood in whites' purview. Thompson later acknowledged the exclusivity of the cult of true white womanhood by admitting that "she might have grown to be far more 'straight' than she might have otherwise because she was fighting the stereotype that a black woman might be a prostitute."[83]

In spite of her seeming acculturation in North Dakota, white men are not sanctioned marital options for Thompson. She identifies Joseph Kolenski as "an ideal partner" for a church outing, but she does not shy away from articulating her racial dilemma: "I liked Joseph, and I knew he liked me, but Joseph was a white boy and I was black. Our side of the Thompson family didn't believe in miscegenation."[84] Thompson honors her deceased father's edict despite her uncle's interracial marriage and her own limited dating selection; most of the black men she encounters in North Dakota are "undesirables": gamblers, drifters, and reform school youths.[85] A white male college classmate presumptuously assumes that she will wed a white man because, as he puts it, "Where will you find a colored man to marry, one that is educated like you?" Thompson responds that a black professional class exists and that many black men work as porters to fund their schooling. "My problem isn't where I'll find an educated colored man," she playfully counters, "but where will an educated colored man find me?"[86] As Braxton suggests, here Thompson signifies on "conventional and/or 'white' notions of romance," in which a prince pursues and rescues the damsel from a hostile environment.[87] Her rhetorical question about her dating prospects not only speaks to her Jane Crow oppression but also qualifies romantic conceits of her cultural hybridity. Segregated socially from white men and distanced physically from black men, Thompson can neither reproduce the black community nor engender interracial relations. She is displaced geographically, culturally, and sexually in predominantly white environments.

Eventually Thompson leaves the plains to find intimate racial connections but discovers that she feels alienated within black communities. "Three times I came down from the prairies to live with 'my people,'" she confesses in her fellowship application, "and twice I returned to my plains; hurt, bewildered and a little bit afraid."[88] Upon her graduation from high school, the call of "the happy-happy land of [her] people" overrides her juvenile declaration never to leave North Dakota's "white clouds of peace." She answers this call by visiting her brother in St. Paul, Minnesota, for a summer, but the city's intraracial class hierarchies are off-putting. Thompson describes "rows of colored houses and colored people's gates—gates where I was still a stranger—and colored boys and girls who did not want me. . . . I felt hemmed in, apart from the rest of the world." Additionally she attends a disastrous dinner with a prominent black family during which she fidgets with her gloves and squirms in her girdle. This episode is one of the few to allude to her possible romance with a black man, but the writer's love life remains a latent plotline under the sartorial constraints of middle-class respectability. It is another event in her narrative's recurring interludes of loss and longing. When Thompson visits Chicago for the first time, she realizes that the city is "splendor and squalor, excitement and disappointment . . . black poverty, and black prosperity side by side."[89] She witnesses whites' economic exploitation of blacks' segregation, but the evolving writer also discovers the beauty of the Harlem Renaissance by working for a small magazine.[90] In contrast to the riotous violence reported in the *Defender*, Thompson "read[s] of black people beautified, Negroes exalted" in W. E. B. DuBois's novel *Dark Princess* (1928). She leaves "her people" this second time to care for her dying father. Similar to her response to her mother's passing, Thompson looks forward to constructing a new identity, beyond her domestic obligation, after her father's death. "My life now was my own choosing," she writes, "and there could be no more coming home."[91]

Thompson's desire for black community inspires her first two trips away from North Dakota, and her yearning for a racially integrated community motivates her permanent move to Chicago after her graduation from college. She remembers, "I rode away . . . eager and anxious; hating and fearing no one, confident now that I could make my way among the peoples of the world, black or white." She returns to Chicago with the hope of actualizing a true racial utopia where a critical mass of blacks as well as whites coexist. Instead her migration provides her with an experiential Jim Crow education. She learns that her white coworker pays the same amount for an apartment that she pays for a shabby room on the South Side. And she realizes that prejudice inhibits her interracial friendships: "I was ashamed for my white friend to know that white Chicago did not completely accept me. . . . I was ashamed for my white friend to know that black Chicago did not completely accept her." Black Chicagoans "return hate with hate, and hate with far more justification" by policing the South Side community with stares directed at Thompson and her white friend. To recapture some of the spatial freedom of her childhood and settle this racial dilemma, Thompson takes her friend to Washington Park, "where, under the pure blue sky and the whispering trees, no shadow of race would come between us."[92]

Thompson's literal and figurative lack of space underlies her biting critique of Chicago's black migrant community. She rewrites familiar tropes of racial kinship in black migration narratives by indicting urban intraracial politics. She is an outsider, and she initially finds it difficult to gain entrée into black Chicago. She lands a job interview with Robert S. Abbott, founder of the *Chicago Defender*, but learns "his recommendation no longer carried weight."[93] Moreover she is insultingly deemed "that black white girl" due to her limited knowledge of black vernacular culture.[94] Thompson, in turn, confides that she is not impressed with black Chicago: "I found it wanting; found myself hating the common Negro who had recently migrated from the South without benefit of freedom or education, who, having never had rights of his own, lacked respect for the rights of others." Her disgust with southern regionalisms mirrors black Chicagoans' elitist efforts to differentiate themselves from recent arrivals. "I hated his loud, coarse manners, loathed his flashy clothes and ostentatious display of superficial wealth," she upbraids an archetypal black stranger. "Yet by his standards, all of us were judged; for his actions, all condemned and imprisoned in a black ghetto, separated from all the other peoples of the city by covenants of prejudice and segregation." As she moves from a "boundless white world" to a tightly belted blackness, Thompson blames black southern migrants' complacency and crudeness for her cultural estrangement and racial segregation. She chafes under the Jim Crow directives demanding that blacks' show deference to whites as if still in the South, and she cringes at the thought of embracing "grits and grease" over "tea and toast."[95]

In order to fully extol the supremacy of cultural hybridity in *American Daughter*, however, Thompson must establish her place in black Chicago. Like her triumphs over white prejudice in childhood, she bridges the cultural gap between herself and the segregated black community and tackles social obstacles with persistence and charm. She learns how to snap her fingers rhythmically after a summer coaching a girls' dance team. She also undergoes a cultural conversion when she attends a black storefront church and recognizes that "[the congregants'] blood flowed in my veins, their color, their features were mine, but . . . theirs was a faith beyond anything I had ever experienced."[96] Chicago not only fosters Thompson's cultural identity; it also restores her soul. Integration for Thompson, then, does not mean assimilative white-washing, as Ellison's review suggests; it is what Johnson describes as "a mixing of cultural elements."[97] Having lived on both sides of the color line, so to speak, Thompson feels that she is "fighting the world alone, standing in a broad chasm between the two races, belonging to neither one." Yet in the face of this abyss she maintains hope that, "somewhere . . . between the white and the black there must be a common ground."[98] She finds racial communion through domestic travel and a job with the Works Project Administration (WPA), which allow her to practice cultural hybridity.

Thompson participates in a diverse America by way of her privileged physical and social mobility. Wright ends *Black Boy* with his imminent migration to Chicago and the awareness that critical reading "created a vast sense of distance between me and the world in which I lived and tried to make a living. . . . My days and nights were one long, quiet, continuously contained dream of terror, tension, and anxiety."[99] In contrast Thompson's concluding chapter, "My America, Too," celebrates the leisure and labor that enable her to make interpersonal connections within the country's metaphorical melting pot. Her work as an employment counselor provides her with a stage on which to perform cultural hybridity; with no racial qualifier, employers compliment her for "sound[ing] like a real American girl" over the phone. Her job positions her at "the crossroads of America. From the East and West, the North and the South, they come—rich man, poor man, black man, white; the foreigner, the old-timer, the young, the intellectual, the illiterate—restless, changing jobs." Unemployment is the great equalizer, and Thompson's indiscriminate compassion for the itinerant is in concert with her faith in the Union. She solidifies this ideal by traveling the country's disparate regions. On a bus trip to Washington, D.C., the writer muses that she is accompanied by southern whites "who out-accented Amos and Andy."[100] During a train trip from California to Arizona, she observes Native American communities replacing Asian American communities and Joshua trees supplanting orange groves and palms. Her exposure to the country's diverse domains affords her a rare perspective. Because Thompson shares her extraordinary insights with her readers, *American Daughter* symbolically produces the common ground between black and white for which she advocates. The text's final lines contend, "The chasm is growing narrower."[101] Hence Thompson concludes her narrative confident that America will fulfill its promise to its native and adopted progeny.

Thompson's bearings within various geographical and cultural locations influenced her coming of age as well as her maturation as a black woman writer. Whereas she initially presents North Dakota as an ideal environment for constructing black subjectivity outside of southern racism and urban plight, she ultimately demonstrates that Chicago is the ideal space for the black migrant's cultural sustenance. Her experiences in both places fuel her longing for a united America, a model of cultural diversity that accounts for her "white" childhood and "black" social existence. As a result the autobiography is a self-conscious composite of the writer's real and imagined selves; she attempts to literally write herself into subjectivity. Thompson began her writing project to educate others about North Dakota—to let people know where she came from—but the final product is an autobiography that depicts her straddling racially divided worlds. Thus her personal efficacy and writing subjectivity were constantly evolving texts, and she continued her journey of self-discovery long after the publication of *American Daughter*. In her foreword to the 1967 edition, she admits, "When offered an editorial job with *Ebony Magazine*, I was advised to take it for a few months 'to learn about Negroes.' That was 20 years ago, and I am still writing for *Ebony*, still learning about Negroes."[102] She accepted the job to further her education about black people and black culture, but the foreword, written during the height of the modern civil rights movement, suggests that her performance of cultural hybridity was still a work in progress.

Ebony Daughter

Thompson's employment with Johnson Publishing Company is an equally intriguing narrative for exploring her performance of black female subjectivity. She struggled to overcome the obstacles of race and gender in her life as well as while writing her autobiography. As a journalist, she continued to deliberate issues of race, class, and gender as well as expand her memoir's discourse on the politics of Jane Crow. For example, in *American Daughter* her cross-country travels are a source of racial insight, but she admits in her March 1950 edition of "Bell's Lettres" that envious WPA coworkers called her "Miss Rich B." for months after her return.[103] Her column's September 1949 installment relates her fears that she will be misread as a prostitute while on assignment if she meets her white photographer upon his arrival. Thompson's concern in the article is reminiscent of her frustrations with the black community's censure of her familial relationship with Dr. Riley. Comparably in June 1950 "Bell's Lettres" draws upon her difficulties coming into black womanhood in a white cultural hegemony. In her autobiography she shares her disillusionment with independently styling her hair. However, in *Negro Digest* she reveals that she has "led a deceitful life" by hiding from her white surrogate family the fact that she straightens her hair. The essay's facetious social message is Thompson's hope that "hair, the Negro's most defiant problem, . . . will someday emerge from the realm of the hush hush and cease to be a phenomenon, a thing of shame."[104] Her work at Johnson Publishing evinces her extensive efforts to theorize her black cultural identity. Although she knew little about "her people" when she started working at *Ebony*, she furthers her racial education through her domestic and international travels. Her *Ebony* articles explore interracial adoption in the United States, biracial black American and Vietnamese children, and Australia's racial codes in light of its indigenous population.[105] These related projects suggest the writer's lifelong objectives to understand her American racialization through her development of a global perspective and to find acceptance for her multicultural identity through her travel writing.

Thompson's growing racial insight, however, does not necessarily lend itself to proto-womanist posturing in her early writings. For example, *Negro Digest* executive editor Ben Burns solicited Thompson to highlight the positive attributes of black men in response to Ann Petry's critique of patriarchy published in the magazine. In "What's Wrong with Negro Men?" (1947), Petry points out, "The average Negro male likes to think of himself as a creature of the Twentieth Century. . . . Yet his attitude toward women comes straight out of the Dark Ages." While they work eight-hour jobs like black men, black women also labor additional hours in the home. Petry contends that the married man believes domestic chores "are performed by sleight-of-hand tricks known only to the female," and he expects to live "as though he had in his employ a first-class cook, chambermaid, waitress, cleaning woman, valet and butler."[106] Anticipating the critique of black women's Jane Crow oppression articulated in Pauli Murray's *Negro Digest* article published just four months later, Petry's article "What's Wrong with Negro Men?" exposes the male privilege typifying mid-twentieth-century black heteronormativity. In contrast Thompson's rebuttal, "What's Wonderful about Negro Men?" (1947), praises the comforts black women provide black men, as the former are the indispensible foundation of the latter's success. Thompson's initial reply to the question in the article's title is a resounding "Everything! They are men, aren't they?" Then she qualifies that black women are "the answer, for whatever men are, women have made them, and there is nothing so wrong about any man that a woman can't right. And usually does!" She acknowledges the mamas raising, teachers educating, girlfriends socializing, wives supporting, and even the waitresses serving men as critical to the processes of black men-making. "They are *ours* and we love all of them," she encourages, "for they are *our* husbands and brothers, the fathers of *our* children. And that's wonderful!"[107] By claiming ownership of black men, Thompson co-opts their accomplishments as black women's successes. The upbeat article, which was likely inspired by Thompson's experiences growing up with three brothers as a widower's daughter, foregrounds black women's positive effect on black men. The piece playfully elides the tenet of Petry's critique, that black men are complicit in black women's oppression.

Nevertheless the never-married Thompson seemingly performed the sleight-of-hand tricks masking black male privilege as the woman behind *Ebony* magazine. If one critically reads her career at Johnson Publishing as a Jane Crow text, it is not surprising that intersecting racial and gender oppressions affected her professional pursuits, just as they shaped her account of her life. For example, a thirtieth-anniversary retrospect attributes *Ebony*'s early sensationalism to white executive editor Ben Burns, while it applauds Thompson and her coeditor Herbert Nipson for elevating the magazine to a "family-interest" publication.[108] For Harlem Renaissance poet and Washington, D.C., salon hostess Georgia Douglas Johnson, Thompson's tenure at *Ebony* "struck a new high, both in subject matter and in the deeper and far reaching business of heartening its many readers who are so much in need of a word of encouragement and cheer."[109] Thompson earned recognition from her highly esteemed female contemporary, but Johnson Publishing's black male founder, John H. Johnson, neither recognized nor rewarded her contributions to his media empire consistently or equitably.

In Thompson's 1952 letter to Johnson, she expresses her resentment with the glass ceiling enforced by the editor in chief among his editorial board. In fact it was Johnson's criticism of Thompson in an unexpected review that prompted her scathing evaluation of his sexism and intraracial politics. "My production work habits are as unsatisfactory to me as they are to you," she counters. "For the past three years I have taken work home with me every week-end and practically every night. Recently I have been working on part of my lunch hour. . . . My health is worth more to me than any job."[110] Thompson protests that she is the only managing editor working on all three of Johnson's publications (including *Jet*, which was established in 1951). As such, she wrote unsigned editorials for *Ebony*, but she had only one byline in the flagship magazine.[111] Thompson not only accuses Johnson of paying her merely five dollars more than her co-managing editor Nipson (who had less seniority), but also that Johnson intimated to his staff that "a white man is worth more than a Negro." This latter claim is a reference to Burns, whom Johnson fired two years later and subsequently blamed for *Ebony*'s sexual sensationalism policy and its political conservatism.[112] With Johnson also reducing the travel assignments she coveted, Thompson contends that she gives more than she gets at the company. "If I hear nothing from you on this matter by Friday," she boldly closes the letter, "I shall assume that my job here terminates with the end of this pay period." Whether Johnson formally responded to these charges is not clear, but he apparently addressed one of Thompson's grievances by sending her on a three-month tour of the African continent as a foreign correspondent. By 1954 *Ebony* had published seven articles on Africa—two bearing Thompson's byline—that echo her travelogue *Africa, Land of My Fathers*. Notwithstanding her advancement from associate editor of *Negro Digest* to the editor of the short-lived *Ebony Africa*, Thompson faced Jane Crow politics in the black male–dominated publishing industry despite Johnson's commitment to African Americans' social mobility and racial uplift.

As an enigma of the Jane Crow epoch, Thompson had to renegotiate her racial and gender identity in the wake of second-wave feminism. In "What's Wonderful about Negro Men?" she attempts to affirm black women by celebrating their value to the other, supposedly superior sex while she suffered gender discrimination in the workplace. Yet in a 1979 interview she was more forthcoming in her reflections on her extraordinary historical position as a mid-twentieth-century black woman writer. Whereas her race, gender, "short stature and plain looks presented writing obstacles" for her, her traveling lifestyle proved difficult for her romantic prospects.[113] Thompson explains in the interview that men had the "feeling that they owned you, [laughs] and they wanted to tell you what to do, and what not to do."[114] At the same time, she admits that she did not like opening doors for herself, pulling out her own chairs, or being referred to in the press simply as "Thompson," without a gendered prefix in this new era of gender equality. Under Johnson's management and in spite of Wright's critical predominance, Thompson accomplished her major professional endeavors during the height of Jane Crow oppression. Her acclaimed international journalism in addition to the popularity of *American Daughter* illustrates that she could do anything she set her mind to achieve. Her autobiography and subsequent life-writing reportage exhibit the tacit, exigent diplomacy of the black woman writer.

Epilogue: Refashioning Jane Crow
and the Black Female Body

*C'mon Ginger ... Let's have the rest of that story! I sure will be glad when
I can read MYSELF out of these gosh-awful predic-a-mixes!*
—JACKIE ORMES, *PATTY-JO 'N' GINGER*

While the previous chapters favor portraits of black female subjectivity in
mid-twentieth-century African American novels, I round off my discussion
with Jackie Ormes's contemporaneous illustrations of black womanhood.
This epilogue ends *Writing through Jane Crow* in the manner in which the
book begins: with my resistance to reinscribing old, reductive critical frameworks and to imposing new, tidy literary histories of the period. Instead of
summing up my study, I continue its exploration of disparate yet related
episodes in mid-twentieth-century black literary production by looking at
the oeuvre of the first black female cartoonist to draw her own syndicated
comic strip.[1] Jackie Ormes's comics thus extend rather than curtail my reading of black female subjugation and protest during the Jane Crow era. Their
nuanced depiction of black female subjectivity richly complicates my reading. This refinement notwithstanding, her work also reaffirms my central
claims in this book about black women's distinct contribution to the period's
realist portrayals of their multivalent oppression. In mapping the processes
of black woman-making, I situate the Jane Crow text historically between
the Harlem Renaissance and the Black Arts Movement, between World War
II and the modern civil rights movement. Hence this historical juncture's
discursive registers ensue from heightened cultural tensions between black
women's race and gender concerns, between their desire for middle-class
respectability and disillusion with domesticity. As a result the Jane Crow
text wrestles with refining the conventions of the protest novel, theorizing
the intersections of racism and sexism, and resisting black women's double
jeopardy as both subjects and writers. These contentions also hold true for

Ormes's comics, as the black female cartoonist pushed against the textual as well as the social boundaries of Jane Crow oppression by providing additional interpretive possibilities for black women. Her protagonists usurp the traditional power hierarchies between black and white women, and they assert their sexual agency despite their sexual vulnerability. In this way my examination of Ormes's work is a culmination and counterpoint to the circumscriptions I trace in the mid-twentieth-century women-centered novels negotiating Cleo's dissemblance, Lutie's resignation, Wonnie's violation, and Maud Martha's silences.

Ormes's stylishly eroticized figures enact an empowering selfhood though they are subjected to the same race, gender, and class politics as their fictional black female counterparts. Published in the *Pittsburgh Courier* and *Chicago Defender* from the 1930s to the 1950s, Ormes's comics refute stereotypes of the asexual Mammy, benighted Topsy, and promiscuous Jezebel—perpetuated to justify the social, economic, and sexual oppression of black women—with the fashionable, estimable, and desirable black female subject. In Ormes's first comic strip, *Torchy Brown in "Dixie to Harlem"* (1937–38) the titular southern migrant turned Harlem Cotton Club dancer encounters both danger and opportunity following her dreams in the city. In the series *Candy* (1945) a black domestic worker borrows her white employer's clothes and boasts that she looks better in them. The single-panel gag *Patty-Jo 'n' Ginger* (1945–56) features a little sister and big sister comedic duo criticizing racist apologists' claims that the murdered Emmett Till whistled at a white woman by scolding a white tea kettle for whistling at *them*. Finally *Torchy in Heartbeats* (1950–54) reconfigures the black female protagonist in Ormes's first comic strip as a nurse turned environmentalist who fights off sexual predators and bigoted industrialists. This last strip also allowed readers to outfit an accompanying paper doll cutout of Torchy in elegant dresses and smart suits. These portraits of black female subjectivity differ from the commodification of Wonnie Brown's sexual trauma on the pulp cover of Curtis Lucas's novel *Third Ward, Newark* (1952). Ormes similarly acknowledges the constant threat of black women's sexual violation, but her illustrations decidedly authorize black female sexuality and idealize black female bodies as figures to be respected, modeled, and envied. Her protagonists face black women's double jeopardy, yet they transgress historical and cultural strictures as witty, mod heroines.

By providing rare sketches of black beauty and sexuality via black newspapers' counterhegemonic discourse, Ormes's comics at once contributed to mid-twentieth-century objectives for racial uplift and challenged the

prescriptions of middle-class respectability. In the *Chicago Defender* column "Second Thoughts" subtitled "Why Art Matters" (1945), S. I. Hayakawa
explains visual texts' influence on African Americans' conceptualization of
self. The critic contends, "The way in which we, subconsciously and at the
moment of impact, evaluate experience depends on the way in which our
perceptions have been trained. The way our perceptions are trained is by the
kind of music, fiction, comic-strips, paintings, and other arts to which we
have been exposed. The visual arts are perhaps more powerful than any of the
others in determining the quality of our experience." Hayakawa encourages
readers to support *Ebony* magazine and the South Side Community Art Center in lieu of emulating advertisements that privileged white women as the
ideal image of beauty and prompted black women to preserve "a dim hope
of some day getting to look like Veronica Lake." He also condemns films that
"say to the Negro, 'You can't be an ideal anything, except possibly an ideal
servant.'"[2] In justifying "Why Art Matters," Hayakawa rouses the black community to assert its agency as critically conscious readers and consumers.

Ormes's single-panel comic *Candy* seems to answer Hayakawa's call
on the very same page of the *Defender*, as the series' domestic worker
dismantles pedestal figures of white women professing superior beauty.
"So that's the great Swoona Stagrow!" Ormes's eponymous protagonist
muses. "Hmmph . . . I've seen gals with more by accident than she's got
on purpose!"[3] Candy prides herself on black women's effortless beauty,
which is equal to if not preferable to the contrived allure of the white
starlet she references. More broadly she takes to task dominant white
and assimilationist black beauty standards with her sideways glance at
the reader (Figure 7). Candy's model-like pose intrepidly steps out of the
panel's frame as well as any boundaries delimiting black women. The
portrait's bravado is antithetical to the fetters hegemonic and counterhegemonic discourses place upon black female subjectivity in Gwendolyn
Brooks's novel *Maud Martha*, in which a prejudiced white saleswoman
peddles Black Beauty lipstick in the seemingly safe space of an African
American hair salon. Ormes's work utilizes the interplay between words
and images to eclipse the disenfranchised social and economic status of
the domestic worker. Candy confidently exercises her voice at her job
and capitalizes on her attractiveness for her own ends. Her white female
employer's absence—or silence—is significant for authorizing her speech
and body outside of white scrutiny. Thus the illustration shows off Candy's shapely profile despite her maid's uniform when she alludes to "the
great Swoona," and she beautifies herself with lipstick all the while cognizant of the black reader's presumably appreciative gaze.

FIGURE 7. Caption: "So that's the great
Swoona Stagrow! Hmmph . . . I've seen
gals with more by accident than she's got
on purpose!" *Candy, Chicago Defender*,
national edition, April 21, 1945, original
artwork. (Tim Jackson Collection;
reprinted by permission)

    Ormes's representation of a style-conscious, self-possessed black female
agent exhibits her efforts to write and draw herself into subjectivity. It is as
if Ormes's young character Patty-Jo articulates the cartoonist's own frustrations when she declares, "I sure will be glad when I can read MYSELF
out of these gosh-awful predic-a-mixes!"[4] The comment reflects the child's
dependence on adults to read her a bedtime story, but her language intimates a mature self-reflexivity. In fact all of Ormes's protagonists resemble
her own countenance, physicality, and vogue. Her work as a reporter for
the *Chicago Defender*'s society pages suggests her long-standing interest
in the glamorous depiction of black female subjectivity, just as her later

work training fashion models and producing fashion shows for the Chicago Urban League evidence her investment in its performance. Comics were an effective artistic medium for Ormes to continue to engage in this kind of cultural work, as their popularity was a part of the mass media production arising after World War II.[5] Her pictorial narratives—visual texts that are part autobiographical and part creative invention—externalized her performance of subjectivity and paralleled her upward mobility as a part of Chicago's Bronzeville elite. As Edward Brunner contends, like her showgirl character Torchy, "Ormes herself is an entertainer in a mass culture medium."[6] In *Torchy Brown in "Dixie to Harlem"* the cartoonist blurs the lines between the real and the fantastic to show and promote African Americans' social achievements and cultural contributions. Torchy encounters real stars like Bill "Bojangles" Robinson, Cab Calloway, and Duke Ellington in the Cotton Club, and as a celebrity in her own right Ormes was featured in the *Pittsburgh Courier*'s society pages as a revered fashionista. "Jackie can wear sweaters with swank, and all the form fitting little numbers that we hefties sigh for," Toki Schalk Johnson praises in her notable people-sighting digest. "She came to town in a black skirt, orange sweater, with a gold belt of metal . . . a leopard coat and black Cassock hat."[7] Ormes's protagonists were not just her alter egos; she and her characters exemplified pedestal figures of black womanhood. With limited opportunities for black cartoonists in mainstream newspapers, and few opportunities for women cartoonists anywhere, Ormes challenged the racial and gender boundaries constituting Jane Crow oppression.

In the context of mid-twentieth-century African American fiction, Ormes's illustrations are more daring with the discursive territory they broach than the majority of the period's novels. The established history of comics as a means of artful political commentary gave cartoonists more leeway in articulating social critiques. Although they were sometimes depreciated as juvenile amusements, comics participated in extant cultural debates. Their characteristic humor likely allowed artists to be more provocative in their visual texts. For example, William Gropper was a popular proletarian pictorial satirist, and illustrators for *The Crisis*, the official organ of the NAACP, counteracted racial stereotypes with their own images.[8] Ormes's contemporary Ollie Harrington created illustrations and editorial cartoons for the *Pittsburgh Courier* and *Chicago Defender* newspapers as well as Adam Clayton Powell Jr.'s *The People's Voice*, Paul Robeson's *Freedom*, and the Communist Party's *Daily World*.[9] By the mid-1940s critics and publishers were skeptical of overtly political writers in the vein of Richard Wright's classic social realism blueprint, but the humor in Harrington's popular single-panel comic *Dark Laughter* often conveyed its political orientation with the antics of its Harlem protagonist Bootsie, whose escapades touched on the war as well as postwar lynching. Ormes expanded this political milieu by embracing issues of female sexuality and middle-class black life that were neglected or censured in contemporaneous novels. Whereas social protest fiction spoke to emphatically interracial audiences, Ormes's comics were specifically created for the unmediated African American audiences of the *Pittsburgh Courier* and *Chicago Defender*. The investments of white cultural brokers and the desires of white readers had less influence on the content of her comics and their reception by the newspapers' black readers.

Social realist fiction largely ignored the black middle class due to its foregrounding of the working-class masses (except for Dorothy West's novel *The Living Is Easy*). In contrast Ormes's comic *Patty-Jo 'n' Ginger* spotlights the fabulous life of the black middle class and emphasizes its expectations for attaining education, engaging politics, following fashion fads, and accessing material goods. The weekly cartoon concomitantly envisioned blacks' economic and social progress and authenticated the readership's upward mobility as a reality.[10] Five-year-old Patty-Jo speaks her mind on controversial political topics such as elections, restrictive covenants, and H-bombs. Ormes also used the character to substantiate and stimulate black middle-class consumerism by briefly producing a doll for the Terri Lee Doll Company; Patty-Jo was a hand-painted plastic effigy complete with a mischievous sideways glance, full lips, and an extensive wardrobe.[11] Meanwhile teenage Ginger embodies the material desires of the black middle class, as she is dressed trendily and the family's home is decorated with chic furniture and urbane art.

By rendering black women's selfhood through fashionable means, Ormes's comics imagined their sexuality beyond the social and literary strictures placed upon black female bodies and black female-centered texts during the Jane Crow era. Ormes sanctioned black women's sexual agency by displaying the early and later versions of Torchy like a pin-up beauty in bikinis, lingerie, and skimpy clothing. This legitimization of black female sexuality is especially significant for Candy in light of her literary predecessor, Bessie Mears, who uses alcohol to assuage her economic exploitation as a maid and her sexually abusive relationship with Bigger Thomas in Wright's novel *Native Son*. Ormes's oeuvre created an expansive and fluid narrative of black womanhood across class divides that boldly defies the representations of black women in white media discourses, the mandates mainstream publishers imposed upon African American writing, and the black community's restrictive politics for racial uplift. Thus the racial and sexual discourse in Ormes's combination of scintillating words and desirable images are a departure from that articulated in Jane Crow novels, specifically in regard to the juxtaposition of black and white women in *Candy*, negotiation of African American girlhood and young adult womanhood in *Patty-Jo 'n' Ginger*, and reconciliation of black women's sexual vulnerability and desire in *Torchy in Heartbeats*.

In *Candy* Ormes inverts the traditional power dynamic between the domestic worker and her employer and elevates the economically vulnerable figure of black womanhood over the wealth and appurtenances of the aptly named Mrs. Goldrocks. For example, Candy buys factory-manufactured cigarettes, while the thrifty Mrs. Goldrocks has the maid roll hers. Candy also demythologizes the trope of the angel of the house when she passes up a party to babysit for her inept employer. She exclaims, "I just couldn't trust those poor kids with their mother!"[12] Another installment features Candy criticizing Mrs. Goldrocks's excessive eating while bringing attention to her own svelte figure in a conspicuously flirty pose. "Gee, I hope Mrs. Goldrocks doesn't gain any more weight," she says coyly, looking at herself in the mirror. "I can't possibly wear a size larger."[13] In Ann Petry's novel *The Street* Lutie Johnson admires her white employers' elite status despite their dysfunction and, more important, the institutional structures of racism and sexism that overdetermine her inability to attain the white family's domestic ideal. In contrast, with textual and graphic cues Candy invokes these white values as the butt of her joke, and her oppositional reading predates the domestic worker militancy Trudier Harris finds in Alice Childress's newspaper columns, collectively published as *Like One of the Family . . . Conversations from a Domestic's Life*. Black women's systematic relegation to domestic work exploits them economically and sexually, but Candy consistently asserts her agency in her one-sided conversations with her employer. In her debut panel, Candy clarifies, "Course, Mrs. Goldrocks, you realize these first few weeks you'll be on probation!"[14] The employer is always physically absent from the comic, but her exotic home decor and social privilege are repeatedly on display (Figure 8). Candy, however, is not another eroticized exploit; her pin-up pose, fitted uniform, and strappy shoes convey her self-constructed femininity, not her sexual exploitation. Her no-nonsense stance confirms her authority in this exchange, as her right foot steps outside the frame of customary interracial relations.

Candy's critique of the cult of true white womanhood is coded in contemporaneous fashion discourse. Despite cleaning Mrs. Goldrocks's

FIGURE 8. Caption: "'Course, Mrs.
Goldrocks, you realize these first few
weeks you'll be on probation!" *Candy,
Chicago Defender*, national edition, March
24, 1945, original artwork. (Tim Jackson
Collection; reprinted by permission)

house, washing her clothes, and cooking for her social gatherings,
Candy claims Mrs. Goldrocks's domestic space, costly costumes, and
social status as her own. Ormes explicitly reveals Candy's curvaceous
figure in one installment by dressing her in a slip and likening her to a
1940s sweater girl in the pattern of movie stars like Lana Turner. Holding up her employer's garment, now bearing the imprint of her own
bust, Candy muses, "Hmmm . . . Maybe I'd better tell Mrs. Goldrocks
I borrowed her sweater last night!"[15] The verbal gag licenses Candy with
ownership of Mrs. Goldrocks's clothes, and the image of the molded
sweater signals Candy as the new model of womanhood (Figure 9).
This affirmation of the black female body outweighs the objectification
Candy's undergarments might elicit. As Nancy Goldstein argues, "The

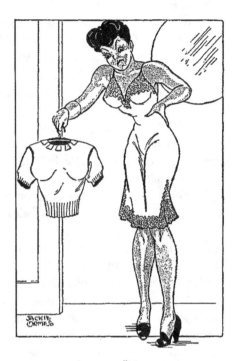

FIGURE 9. Caption: "Hmmm . . .
Maybe I'd better tell Mrs. Goldrocks
I borrowed her sweater last night!"
Candy, Chicago Defender, national
edition, May 19, 1945, original artwork.
(Tim Jackson Collection; reprinted by
permission)

family newspaper was a relatively safe place for [Ormes] to show a body
like her own, and it was safe as well for readers in their own homes to
gaze sometimes upon a barely dressed black woman."[16] Ormes could
liberally display Candy's figure because of the inviolable racial intimacy the *Defender*'s readership sought. As a result Ormes characterizes
her protagonist as unabashedly aware of her desirability and in control
of her sexuality. In a holiday episode Candy directly explains to readers, "I'm supposed to start the fireworks at the lawn party tonight, so
I decided to dress accordingly."[17] Her star-patterned, patriotic romper
replaces her typical uniform and symbolizes her refusal to play the role
of asexual maid as well as her ambition to be desired; she is hot enough
to set off sparks in her strapless short set.

Ormes's longest running comic, *Patty-Jo 'n' Ginger*, explores the characters' incipient emergence into African American womanhood from their respective stages of girlhood. Whereas Candy talks back to white women in her narrative, loquacious Patty-Jo delivers brazen one-liners while Ginger embodies material and sexual desire. Patty-Jo virtually echoes Candy when she brags, "And I just tol' 'em my big sister's got more by accident than Marilyn Monroe has on PURPOSE!"[18] Standing at her vanity in heels and a wrap that exposes her undies, garter, and stockings, Ginger reifies her little sister's boast. The narrative coherence created by the sisters' verbal and visual comedic routine is the basis of the series: Patty-Jo relays the clever joke, and Ginger furthers the humor either with her shocked responses to her sister's audaciousness or her suggestive posturing. Each episode in the single-panel comic essentially models a situational comedy. Sometimes Patty-Jo interrupts her sister while reading a book or newspaper, which demonstrates Ginger's shared intelligence. At other times Patty-Jo makes her quip in the midst of Ginger dressing, undressing, or sunbathing, which frames the latter as a pin-up beauty. Most of the time Ginger is a fashion plate draped in stylish clothes marking the girls' middle-class status. For example, in a couple of panels Patty-Jo references the "new look" of designer Christian Dior, whose Edwardian hemlines, voluminous skirts, and corseted dresses redefined the body and cultural identity of women who had become accustomed to the functional garments and sparing material of wartime fashion.[19] One panel shows Ginger shortening the length of Patty-Jo's dress as the latter acquiesces, "Ok—Ok—You're makin' it . . . But I just know this 'new look' is bound to catch up with me too, sooner or later!"[20] A follow-up image shows the benefits of Dior's longer hemlines, with Patty-Jo walking under Ginger's skirt in the rain. With Patty-Jo stating the advertising message and Ginger modeling the "new look," the girls represent the coming of age of the newly configured black middle class. Besides her adult-like intuitiveness, Patty-Jo's comedic bits communicate her childish innocence, savvy precociousness, and self-indulgent mischievousness.[21] She feigns wonder at her empty piggy bank, criticizes McCarthyism, and encourages the eye-catching Ginger to talk to Santa Claus on her behalf. In other words, Patty-Jo gets the laughs and demands readers' critical engagement; Ginger is the object of desire and the epitome of the "new" black woman.

Patty-Jo's commentary on black womanhood is ironic given that she is a child far from adolescence. Yet it is because of her age that Ormes portrays the five-year-old as the unfiltered voice of the sex exhorting traditional gender performance. When gifting Ginger an umbrella, Patty-Jo kindly explains, "For your birthday, sis—it's guaranteed not to open without the

FIGURE 10. Caption: "No WONDER your
luck's rotten, Sis . . . those men over there
said the BAIT's on the wrong end of the
pole!" *Patty-Jo 'n' Ginger, Pittsburgh Courier,*
city edition, July 2, 1949, original artwork. (Tim
Jackson Collection; reprinted by permission)

help of a MAN!"[22] Part of the joke is that Patty-Jo is boy crazy and obsessed
with finding Ginger a beau throughout the series. The joke also addresses
the inanity of women who feign demureness and dependence on men.[23]
Patty-Jo, however, frequently schools Ginger on how to negotiate her feminine wiles, and she revels in her newly acquired knowledge while Ginger
fishes: "No WONDER your luck's rotten, Sis . . . those men over there said
the BAIT's on the wrong end of the pole!" (Figure 10).[24] The cartoon's gags
unexpectedly deconstruct patriarchal conceptualizations of femininity by
articulating Patty-Jo's eagerness to be what she has been socialized to believe
a woman is. Consequently the comic also betrays a cultural anxiety about
traditional gender roles through humor. For example, in one episode Ginger
bends over to arrange her hair while dressed in only her bra and panties, and
Patty-Jo proclaims, "'Course I count on my fingers while I'm little, but later
on I'll more'n likely count on my LEGS!"[25] The punch line wittily points out

the way children learn math and how women rely on their beauty. Patty-Jo shows her fervor to enact the latter by directing her gaze at Ginger's bottom and legs, which signifies on male readers' objectification.

Ormes makes similar nods toward her readers' desiring of Ginger through multiple allusions to a lusting gaze. In heteronormative convention, men would likely want to be with Ginger and women would conceivably want to be her. Because Ormes caters to both audiences in the comic's metanarrative moments, she makes fun of the male readers' voyeurism and vivifies the female readers' fantasy. In one panel Ginger steps out of the bathroom in a towel hiked up on her thigh, and Patty-Jo, who is holding the phone, informs her sister, "It's Biff Banks . . . I still think this guy can see over the phone: Listen to 'im whistle!"[26] Apparently Biff does not need to see Ginger to sexualize her, but in his absence the comic's readers look at her eroticized image. In another episode Ginger takes a bath, and Patty-Jo, who is hiding behind the bathroom door, sends in a walking toy cowboy to peep in on her (Figure 11). Patty-Jo and her toy stand in for Ginger's admiring readers, while the text reminds those readers that intimate spaces are not always private. Interestingly in Brooks's novel, Maud Martha fears the loss of privacy in black newspapers' society pages, and yet being noticed is something she also secretly craves. Ormes regularly exposes Ginger in the *Pittsburgh Courier* by way of Patty-Jo's cheeky capers. However, *Patty-Jo 'n' Ginger* presents no lascivious threat to the girls; Ormes deploys their potential overexposure in order to deconstruct the patriarchal gaze.

A series of related panels published over the course of several years replicates and escalates this voyeuristic theme by explicitly casting Patty-Jo as the desirous reader. In a 1949 installment, budding photographer Patty-Jo snaps a wide-eyed Ginger sitting in her underwear with her leg propped up in the privacy of her bedroom (Figure 12). A shocked Ginger looks directly at the reader as Patty-Jo instructs, "Turn around, will ya, Sis? The fellas at the corner drugstore DEVELOP my pictures for FREE when I wind up each roll with a candid shot of you!"[27] Between the verbal gag and the visual joke there is no doubt that the little sister attempts to capitalize on the older sister's sexuality. Insofar as Ginger's positioning of her body is not simply a candid pose, Patty-Jo's capturing of this erotic moment is not for the guys at the drugstore alone. Ormes targets the male reader and implicitly criticizes the selling of sex as well as the commodification of the race in publications like *Ebony* and *Tan Confessions*. She employed virtually the same image and gag in 1953 (with Ginger wearing a slightly more demure bra). She used the same concept in 1954, when Patty-Jo spies on a fully clothed Ginger and her beau. In this

FIGURE 11. Caption: "Oooops! . . . Howdy,
Ma'am!" *Patty-Jo 'n' Ginger, Pittsburgh
Courier,* city edition, June 17, 1950, original artwork. (Tim Jackson Collection;
reprinted by permission)

variation Patty-Jo exclaims, "Hold still, will ya, Ginger? I'm sick of that
Phil down at the drug store not taking my photography seriously!"[28] This
time the voyeuristic gaze is intruding not on an erotic moment but on a
romantic one, as Ginger appears to be listening to her suitor's proposal or
declaration of love. Ormes recycles the line in yet another panel depicting Ginger posing in her bedroom for Patty-Jo's camera. In this installment, published just two weeks later, Ginger is not shocked by Patty-Jo's
fetishization. She coyly looks at the reader with a tilted head and a subtle
smile while Patty-Jo takes the photo kneeling on the bed.[29] Ginger's tacit
flirtation and Patty-Jo's sexual innuendo in this last iteration increase
the eroticism of these related panels. Still, the fact that a clothed Patty-
Jo and not Ginger sits on the bed and that Ormes ultimately teases the
libidinous male reader mitigates the girls' objectification.

    Finally, Ormes's comic strip *Torchy in Heartbeats* returns to her
original alter ego and delineates black female desire with the trials and

FIGURE 12. Caption: "Turn around, will ya, Sis? The fellas at the corner drugstore DEVELOP my pictures for FREE when I wind up each roll with a candid shot of you!" *Patty-Jo 'n' Ginger, Pittsburgh Courier*, city edition, January 29, 1949, original artwork. (Tim Jackson Collection; reprinted by permission)

tribulations of the heroine's romantic escapades. Torchy finds love, loses love, and eventually finds love again. Unlike Ormes's other comics, *Torchy in Heartbeats* was syndicated in the *Pittsburgh Courier*'s weekly color comics section. After several months the strip fostered readers' appreciation of the complexity of black female subjectivity with the addition of an adjacent *Torchy Togs* panel, which included a paper doll of the protagonist, several selections from her wardrobe, and a few fashion tips. Ormes was not the first woman cartoonist to use paper dolls to complement her comic strip. Dale Messick, for example, included cut-out figures of her glamorous and adventurous reporter Brenda Starr in the *Chicago Tribune*. However, *Torchy Togs* are significant in the context of the flat, stock representations of African Americans in hegemonic media (and sometimes black media discourses) because they moved beyond the romantic drama propelling the plot of *Torchy in Heartbeats* and realized erotic desire in the fashionable body. Goldstein infers that *Torchy Togs* "solved [Ormes's] sartorial conflict" by providing the cartoonist a vehicle to stage the black female body as well as her own tailored designs.[30] *Torchy in Heartbeats* focuses on the character's quixotic adventures, whereas the *Torchy Togs* served as a toy for little girls, a fashion mannequin for women, and a pin-up for men.

The ephemera had symbolic value because they concretized a model of black femininity similar to that affirmed and glamorized in black beauty contests and fashion shows. Such eventful displays expressed the black community's pride and belief that the black body should be looked upon as beautiful.[31] Accordingly in one *Torchy Togs* the paper doll speaks to her twofold function and gendered audience: "Here we go again, gals! Get your scissors and see how these dresses look on me. Or—if you're a guy, a pin is all you need!"[32] In another *Torchy Togs* the character urges readers to appreciate her body, warning, "Girls! . . . Cut carefully along the heavy black outlines so they'll fit me! And *please* . . . do right by my figure, too. Go slow around the curves."[33] The paper doll also assists her female fans in presenting their best body in public. "Let's start from scratch with pretty, fresh underthings, girls!" she advises. "Cut me out smoothly, making no bulges where you find none. . . . This week, I'm showing my favorite curve-controls, such are a must for perfect grooming."[34] The paper doll implies that undergarments not only determine one's respectability but also undergird one's desirability.

Together *Torchy in Heartbeats* and *Torchy Togs* represent the spectrum of black female subjectivity, but the pictorial narratives' relevance to each other varies from issue to issue. The comic strip's story arc and cut-out fashion show are not in sync for the most part. On the few occasions the two are in concert, the illustrations rewrite the familiar script of black female sexual exploitation. For example, in one episode Torchy sunbathes on a freighter ship's deck while traveling to South America for a new job. She lies on a checkered blanket as pulley ropes traverse her figure in one sequential frame. These illustrated cues alert readers to the impending danger the ship's leering first mate poses, but the accompanying *Torchy Togs* is disconnected from this menace and showcases the designs of Ormes's aspiring readers. In a subsequent installment the ship's first mate attempts to rape Torchy while the *Torchy Togs* discusses the perfect socializing frock (Figure 13). "Want to whirl in his arms as gay as an autumn leaf?" the caption asks. "Then try this gay date dress with the large leaf motif on screen print silk."[35] The sailor maintains his pursuit after Torchy verbally and physically rejects his advances, while the paper doll curtly questions,

FIGURE 13. *Torchy in Heartbeats* (*Pittsburgh Courier*, Chicago edition, February 23, 1952; image courtesy of Nancy Goldstein)

"OK?" Presumably she refers to her clothing selections in the *Torchy Togs*, not Torchy's consent in the drama. In *The Street* Lutie's sexual assault ends with her murdering her attacker, which has dire consequences for her and her child; she leaves her son in reform school with the misguided hope that he will be better off. Comparably in *Third Ward Newark* Wonnie's constant sexual exploitation

FIGURE 14. *Torchy in Heartbeats* (*Pittsburgh Courier*, Chicago edition,
October 25, 1952; image courtesy of Nancy Goldstein)

jeopardizes her psyche and concludes with her death. Even though Torchy is
similarly sexually vulnerable, she is a damsel, not a victim. A storm rages long
enough to sweep her assailant out to sea and then suddenly calms, and the
dashing Dr. Paul Hammond thwarts another attack by an exploitative banana
plantation owner.

Equally important is the fact that these sexual dangers never threaten Torchy's fashion sense. When *Torchy Togs* tacitly responds to the action in the comic strip, the clothes endorse Torchy's sexual agency—especially when she needs to use her sexuality to keep or get her man. Early in the strip Torchy fears that her love interest, Earl Lester, is too consumed by his desire to become a famous jazz pianist. Hence the *Torchy Togs* inspires women to use clothing to make people notice: "Who says there's no glamour in wearing rags and tatters? This'll make them *stop, look and listen!*"[36] Later, when insects in the Brazilian jungle bite Torchy, her new love interest, Paul, advises her to take advantage of a nearby pool to relieve her smarting skin and to use strategically placed leaves to dry herself (Figure 14). This building sexual moment is mirrored in the *Torchy Togs* with the paper doll's leafy undergarments.[37] Whether or not the panels are synchronized, the intertextual dialogue between *Torchy in Heartbeats* and *Torchy Togs* establishes black women's double jeopardy without compromising their sexual identities or social power. In her final adventure Torchy helps her doctor beau save a southern community from a health epidemic caused by the local chemical plant owned by a racist. At the comic strip's end, Torchy attains environmental justice and a marriage proposal. She fulfills her collective and personal desires with these achievements as well as with her gorgeous costumes. *Torchy Togs* is a collaborative text that manifests the erotics of fashion and recruits readers as participants in the construction of black femininity.

Ormes stakes a self-assured claim to black female sexuality in *Candy, Patty-Jo 'n' Ginger,* and *Torchy in Heartbeats.* By serially illustrating black women's efforts to give value to their labor, transition into womanhood, and express their sexuality, the cartoonist problematized racist stereotypes of black women. She also disregarded prevailing patriarchal conventions by imbuing the desirable black female body with agency. Her cultural work challenged the limitations of the Jane Crow text, as she empowered the erotic reductively defined or denied in mid-twentieth-century African American fiction. Yet Ormes's comics too are Jane Crow texts. As is the case for mid-twentieth-century black women writers and those who worked in popular culture mediums, Ormes's illustrations remained relatively obscure because comics were dismissed generally as an inferior literature due to their discursive accessibility, and they were forgotten typically due to their material temporality. Ormes's Jane Crow texts bypass circumspection and celebrate personal triumphs, but they do not envisage social change outside of the traditional gender frameworks maintained with marriage proposals and beauty rites. Her texts' innovation is in visualizing black women's lives, activism, and art in spite of their Jane Crow oppression.

Notes

Introduction

1. *Ethnic Notions.*
2. Baldwin, "Going to Meet the Man," 232.
3. Woodward, *Strange Career of Jim Crow*, 8.
4. Murray, "Why Negro Girls Stay Single," 4. Murray points out the pervasiveness of Jane Crow by noting black women's glaring absence from an issue of *Ebony* magazine dedicated to black lawyers. She asks, "What quirk of the editor's attitude had permitted him or her to ignore the contributions of women"? The editor's negligence slights Murray the woman and Murray the lawyer. Ironically black entrepreneur John H. Johnson published both *Ebony* and *Negro Digest.*
5. Wade-Gayles, *No Crystal Stair*, 9.
6. Murray, "Liberation of Black Women," 186.
7. Holloway, *Private Bodies, Public Texts*, 9.
8. Robert Reid-Pharr challenges the belief in the "inevitability" of racial identity that constructs black subjects, particularly the writer, as products of history and not as agents. He suggests that race is "lived as desire" and the assumption that African Americans have no choice in their subject formation "is, in fact, an affirmation of the racial status quo" (*Once You Go Black*, 7, 4, 8).
9. Wright, review of *Their Eyes Were Watching God*, 16, 17.
10. Hurston, review of *Uncle Tom's Children*, 3.
11. Hurston and Wright's art-versus-politics debate is the discursive contest in mid-twentieth-century African American literary history. William J. Maxwell argues that the writers' conflict "underwrites genealogies of audacious black women's writing burdened by Wright's male line" while it "dramatizes less intensely gendered oppositions undergirding the black modern within contemporary African-American criticism, oppositions such as race versus class, modernism versus naturalism, Harlem Renaissance versus Chicago Renaissance, black nationalism versus Marxism, and so on" (*New Negro, Old Left*, 155–56).

12. Johnson, "What My Job Means to Me," 74.

13. Shockley, *"We, Too, Are Americans,"* 2.

14. The details of Recy Taylor's rape case come from Danielle L. McGuire's study *At the Dark End of the Street*. The historian argues that from 1940 until 1975 interracial sexual violence and rape was "one crucial battleground upon which African Americans sought to destroy white supremacy and gain personal and political autonomy." She identifies Betty Jean Owens's trial in Tallahassee, Florida, as a watershed case that led to convictions in Alabama, North Carolina, and South Carolina, including the sentencing of a white marine to the electric chair (*At the Dark End of the Street*, xx).

15. Hine, "Rape and the Inner Lives of Black Women," 41.

16. Robinson, *Montgomery Bus Boycott and the Women Who Started It*, viii.

17. Burks, "Trailblazers," 71.

18. Edwards, *Charisma and the Fictions of Black Leadership*.

19. Mitchell and Davis, "Dorothy West and Her Circle," 40.

20. In the interview West also intimates that white literary agent Carl Van Vechten made sexually inappropriate comments toward her (McDowell, "Conversations with Dorothy West," 291).

21. Similar to the Harlem Renaissance of the 1920s, many black writers, musicians, and painters converged in Chicago during the 1940s and 1950s. For example, Archibald Motley, Louis Armstrong, Arna Bontemps, Margaret Walker, Mahalia Jackson, Willard Motley, and Katherine Dunham utilized the city's publishing outlets, leftist organizations, philanthropic endowments, and black enclaves to redefine their relationship to African American literature and culture as well as society at large. For more on this creative milieu, see Hine and McCluskey, *Black Chicago Renaissance*; Bone and Courage, *Muse in Bronzeville*.

22. Shockley, *Renegade Poetics*, 2, 8. Shockley notes that the "qualities of 'blackness'" outlined in the Black Arts Movement as well as Houston Baker's and Henry Louis Gates's canonizing theories of the African American literary tradition "seem to weigh more heavily upon women writers" (8).

23. Hill and Holman, "Preface," 296.

24. Gloster, "Race and the Negro Writer," 369. For a discussion of the evolution of *Phylon* as a journal of literary criticism after World War II, see Johnson and Johnson, *Propaganda and Aesthetics*.

25. Glicksberg, "The Alienation of Negro Literature," 50.

26. Young, *Black Writers, White Publishers*.

27. Stephanie Brown argues that African American literature had to "bear witness to an experiential blackness positioned as the repository of all that technological advances and material gain have stripped from white American men in the name of progress and the Cold War" (*Postwar African American Novel*, 25).

28. Locke, "Self-Criticism," 394. Gender themes are not included on Locke's list of censured black subjects. Candice M. Jenkins explains that the oversight is not on the grounds of "straightforward sexism" but male critics' inability to recognize the significance of such issues "within depictions of the racial intimate—the domestic sphere and the sexual and familial relationships constituting that sphere" (*Private Lives, Proper Relations*, 41–42).

29. Wright, "Blueprint for Negro Writing," 82.

30. Baldwin, "Everybody's Protest Novel," 23.

31. Maxwell, *New Negro, Old Left*, 3.

32. In "Love Jones," David Ikard points out that Bob's critique of racial oppression is significantly gendered. Ikard focuses his analysis on the secondary character Ella Mae and her critique of Bob's desire to be white (via his relationship with light-skinned, middle-class Alice) and his desire for white women (the hated white woman, Madge, with whom he works).

33. Himes, *If He Hollers Let Him Go*, 88.

34. Petry, "Novel as Social Criticism," 94. The writer argues that social criticism does not originate with Marx's proletariat but is as old as the biblical story of Abel and Cain. Alex Lubin's edited collection *Revising the Blueprint* develops new frameworks for reading Petry's oeuvre even as it nods at Wright's proscriptions for black writing in his 1937 essay. Contributors Farah Jasmine Griffin, Bill V. Mullen, Paula Rabinowitz, Rachel Rubin, James Smethurst, and John Charles situate Petry in relation to various progressive communities and highlight the naturalist and pulp fiction aesthetics in her work.

35. Gene A. Jarrett acknowledges, "Gender politics is crucial to our understanding of the historical dialectic between deans and truants, racial realism and anomalies." However, his survey of the dean and truant paradigm includes only one dissenting black female writer: Toni Morrison (*Deans and Truants*, 25).

36. Awkward, *Inspiriting Influences*, 4.

37. Although I refer to Murray's autobiography by its original title, *Song in a Weary Throat*, all quotes are from a 1989 edition of her memoir titled *Pauli Murray*. This later edition includes a brief note acknowledging the editorial contributions made to Murray's final manuscript of *Song in a Weary Throat*.

38. Gilmore, *Defying Dixie*, 288.

39. Anastasia Curwood reports that Murray "clearly transgressed feminine decorum" and redefined black women's sexual autonomy by "adopt[ing] a masculine persona" during her independent travels in the 1930s (*Stormy Weather*, 100).

40. Murray, *Pauli Murray*, 189.

41. Ibid., 191.

42. Murray, "Mr. Roosevelt Regrets," in *Dark Testament and Other Poems*, 34. The poem's title may be a riff on Cole Porter's song "Miss Otis Regrets," which was widely known in Popular Front circles. The song's lyrics satirically repeat that the lynched "Miss Otis regrets she's unable to lunch today."

43. Murray, *Pauli Murray*, 388.

44. Additionally, on behalf of the American Civil Liberties Union, Murray contributed to a brief for a landmark federal court case that argued racial and sexual discrimination on juries violated the Fourteenth Amendment. Among her many influential publications, Murray wrote with Mary O. Eastwood the law review article "Jane Crow and the Law: Sex Discrimination and Title VII" (1965) to expose both antifeminism and racism as human rights issues. See Edenfield, "American Heartbreak." Finally, although a founder of NOW, Murray parted with the organization due to its neglect of race issues. For more on Murray's decision to leave NOW and direct her feminist efforts in her civil rights and religious affiliations, see Hartmann, "Pauli Murray and the 'Juncture of Women's Liberation and Black Liberation.'"

45. Murray, *Pauli Murray*, 204.

46. Wolcott, *Remaking Respectability*.

47. Murray, *Pauli Murray*, 182, 162, 88, 183–84. Although Harvard Law School traditionally accepted Howard Law School's valedictorian for graduate work, Murray's application was rejected because of her sex (Gilmore, *Defying Dixie*, 399).

48. Ibid., 147, 99. Prior to Rosa Parks's activism in the Montgomery bus boycott, Claudette Colvin and Mary Louise Smith had similar bus desegregation cases. Yet neither woman fit the respectable image the movement wanted to project: Colvin was a pregnant teenager, and it was rumored that Smith's father struggled with alcoholism. Comparably Bayard Rustin's homosexuality also challenged notions of respectability. Even though he was a pioneer in the movement, Rustin was often asked to retire from the public at pivotal moments. See Robnett, *How Long? How Long?*; Anderson, *Bayard Rustin*.

49. Murray, *Pauli Murray*, 203, 205.

50. Honey, *Bitter Fruit*, 17.

51. Standley, "Role of Black Women in the Civil Rights Movement," 183, 184. The essay compares the memoirs of Daisy Bates, Jo Ann Gibson Robinson, Ella Baker, and Septima Clark.

52. Braxton, *Black Women Writing Autobiography*, 207.

53. Murray, *Pauli Murray*, 96.

54. Murray dressed in traditional feminine and masculine attire in a series of photographs under titles like "The Poet," "The 'Crusader,'" "The Vagabond," "The Imp!," "Peter Pan," and "The Dude." In pictures with Holmes, Murray identifies herself as "Pete." For more discussion of Murray and Holmes's relationship, see Drury, "'Experimentation on the Male Side.'"

55. Murray, *Pauli Murray*, 8, 10.

56. Expanding the term *queer*, Johnson employs the concept "quare" to also address "the material effects of race in a white supremacist society" ("'Quare' Studies," 135).

57. Murray, *Pauli Murray*, 57.

58. Ibid., 58.

59. Jenkins, *Private Lives, Proper Relations*.

60. Drury, "'Experimentation on the Male Side.'"

61. Scott, *Pauli Murray and Caroline Ware*, 38.

62. Rosenberg, "Conjunction of Race and Gender," 69–70.

63. Rupp and Taylor, "Pauli Murray," 84.

64. Murray, *Pauli Murray*, 22.

65. Smith, "Toward a Black Feminist Criticism," 164.

66. Olney, "Autobiography and the Cultural Moment," 22.

67. Murray, "Dark Testament," in *Dark Testament and Other Poems*, 22. For a discussion of Murray's protest poetry, see Bucher, "Pauli Murray."

68. Murray, *Pauli Murray*, 436.

69. Murray, "Without Name," in *Dark Testament and Other Poems*, 74.

70. Warren, *What Was African American Literature?*, 9.

71. Mary Helen Washington claims *Freedom* as a "founding text of black left feminism" because Paul Robeson's wife, Eslanda Robeson, Shirley Graham Du Bois, and Lorraine Hansberry were all involved in the newspaper's production. Washington also reveals that Childress wrote *Florence* in response to the sexism of the Harlem Left ("Alice Childress, Lorraine Hansberry, and Claudia Jones," 193).

72. After World War II civil rights reform became critical to U.S. foreign relations.

The country tried to change its image abroad to one that modeled the democracy it professed by promoting racial progress (Dudziak, *Cold War Civil Rights*).

1 / At the Point of No Return

1. Wright, "How Bigger Was Born," 434.

2. Ibid., 461.

3. My discussion of "Black Hope," based on my careful examination of the manuscript archived in the Richard Wright Papers in the Yale Collection of American Literature at the Beinecke Rare Book and Manuscript Library, includes few direct quotes from the work because permission to do so from the Wright Estate was not granted at this time.

4. Wright, *Native Son*, 103.

5. "Negro Hailed as New Writer," 28.

6. Wilder, "Wright, Negro Ex-Field Hand, Looks Ahead to New Triumphs," 37.

7. Binggeli, "Burbanking Bigger and Bette the Bitch," 476n3.

8. Gilroy, *Black Atlantic*, 174.

9. Rowley, *Richard Wright*, 188.

10. Fabre, *Unfinished Quest of Richard Wright*, 189–90.

11. Rowley, *Richard Wright*, 188.

12. Brody, *Punctuation*, 108.

13. Nancy F. Cott traces the evolving meaning of feminism in the early twentieth century, when the word comes into regular use. She explains that feminism was "broader in intent, proclaiming revolution in all the relations of the sexes, and narrower in the range of its willing adherents. As an *ism* (an ideology) it presupposed a set of principles not necessarily belonging to every woman—nor limited to women" (*Grounding of Modern Feminism*, 3).

14. William Z. Foster contends that feminism blames men instead of the social system that oppresses them. "The bourgeois feminist would counterpose to the male superiority 'theory' the equally unscientific notion of female superiority," he writes, "which leads only into the blind alley of the 'battle of the sexes'" ("On Improving the Party's Work among Women," 276).

15. Walker, *Richard Wright, Daemonic Genius*, 108. Italics mine. "Medusa is also the woman in *him*," Walker writes, "the capricious feminine self that was part of his acute sensitivity. She turned up as a whimsical, unpredictable, and often perverse or perfidious woman in every relationship." Walker's reference to the classic allusion insinuates that Wright was a homosexual, but no other biographers have suggested such a claim. In his work Robert Reid-Pharr distinguishes queer black intellectuals from "funny" post–World War II black intellectuals like Wright, who negotiated their marginality and representativeness through public performances of masking and passing (*Once You Go Black*, 39).

16. Jarrett, *Deans and Truants*, 21.

17. Baldwin, "Everybody's Protest Novel," 22–23. Michael Davitt Bell argues that Wright became increasingly wary of naturalism's restrictions as he wrote his first novel. Bell suggests that "*Native Son* is thus less the monument of naturalist narrative it has been supposed to be than it is a product of Wright's struggle with naturalism's generic imperatives" ("African-American Writing, 'Protest,' and the Burden of Naturalism," 191).

18. Claudia Tate theorizes that celebrated black writers' anomalous works reflect "the tensions between the discourses of personal desire and political demand in black

texts that cohere around what might respectively be called their latent and manifest narratives." In her psychoanalytic reading of Wright's understudied novel *Savage Holiday*, Tate observes a conscious and unconscious textual desire for matricide, which she contends is an "ur-text" masked in his more canonical works (*Psychoanalysis and Black Novels*, 5).

19. Fabre, *Unfinished Quest of Richard Wright*, xxv.

20. For example, Robert Butler examines the pivotal and positive images of women in Wright's novella *Rite of Passage*, completed in 1945 and published in 1994. The black foster mother and the white female teacher of Wright's protagonist Johnny Gibbs make home and school nurturing spaces for him, in contrast to the violence in the male-dominated street. Butler observes, "Wright consistently associates Johnny's best self with feminine values and influence while he links his worst self with masculine values and influence" ("Invisible Woman in Wright's *Rite of Passage*," 188).

21. Wright, "Ethics of Living Jim Crow," 7.

22. Ibid., 8.

23. Ibid., 12, 13.

24. Wright, "Long Black Song," 147.

25. Joyce, "Richard Wright's 'Long Black Song,'" 379.

26. Wright, "Long Black Song," 149, 152.

27. Williams, "Papa Dick and Sister-Woman," 396.

28. Wright, "Bright and Morning Star," 225.

29. Ibid., 235.

30. Baker, *Workings of the Spirit*, 116.

31. Wright, *12 Million Black Voices*, 37.

32. Ibid., 131.

33. Griffin, *"Who Set You Flowin'?,"* 75.

34. Brooks, "kitchenette building," 3.

35. Petry, *Street*, 28.

36. Wright, *12 Million Black Voices*, 131.

37. Wright, "How Bigger Was Born," 434.

38. Wright, "Man of All Work," 115, 116.

39. Harris, *From Mammies to Militants*, 86.

40. Wright, "Man of All Work," 154.

41. Johnson, "'Quare' Studies," 126.

42. Wright, "Man of All Work," 138.

43. Ibid., 153, 154.

44. Mootry, "Bitches, Whores, and Women Haters," 123, 124, 126.

45. Wright, *Native Son*, 229.

46. Gilroy, *Black Atlantic*, 176.

47. Rowley, *Richard Wright*, 198.

48. In Wright's screenplay, Bigger murders Bessie only because he realizes too late that she does not betray his whereabouts to the police. Wright also redeems Bessie with the workingwoman's blues. "If Bessie had ever been blind," Baker argues, "her blues reveal clearly that now she sees all" in the film (*Workings of the Spirit*, 130).

49. Wright's personal life also demanded his attention. For example, in 1943 the Harper & Brothers editor Edward C. Aswell expressed his hope that the uncertainty about the writer's draft status would not prevent him from making revisions to the

manuscript. "I am very keen about publishing that book," he writes. Edward C. Aswell, letter to Richard Wright, March 30, 1943, qtd. in Rowley, *Richard Wright*, 277. Although not drafted, Wright temporarily secured a special commission to the army's propaganda services through his literary agent, Paul R. Reynolds. According to Reynolds, "Wright thought he could be used to improve the moral [*sic*] of Black soldiers. He also had the somewhat fanciful notion that he could help strengthen the morale of Black men in Africa." Wright promised to write a statement expressing his commitment to the war effort and not racial politics. However, Wright's recommender lost his reputation when boxer Joe Louis became the subject of a tax scandal; both Louis and Wright lost their special commission (Reynolds, *Middle Man*, 118).

50. Paul R. Reynolds, letter to Richard Wright, April 13, 1942, qtd. in Rowley, *Richard Wright*, 265, 264.

51. Richard Wright, letter to Paul R. Reynolds, February 6, 1940, qtd. in Rowley, *Richard Wright*, 187.

52. Fabre, *Unfinished Quest of Richard Wright*, 190.

53. Fabre contends that a 1939 article published in the *New York Daily Mirror* may have inspired "Black Hope." Reportedly a black couple posed as servants to white employers in order to hide the fact that they owned the house in an exclusive white neighborhood.

54. Wright may have gotten the idea of arsenic poisoning from Horace Cayton, who sent Wright a reference for a *New York Times* article about using it as a skin lightener.

55. Spencer's shady deals in Mexico are added in the undated manuscript designated as the late draft in the Richard Wright Papers.

56. Rowley, *Richard Wright*, 188, 189.

57. Wright, *Black Boy*, 41.

58. Paul R. Reynolds, letter to Richard Wright, February 15, 1940, qtd. in Rowley, *Richard Wright*, 188.

59. Gilbert and Gubar, *Madwoman in the Attic*, 77.

60. *The Madwoman in the Attic* was written in the 1970s during the second wave of feminism; hence it is not surprising that subsequent developments in the field criticize the text, such as Spivak's "Three Women's Texts and a Critique of Imperialism." Feminist scholars working on women of color and transnationalism argue that Gilbert and Gubar privilege white womanhood, while poststructural feminist scholars criticize Gilbert and Gubar's transhistorical and essentialist framing.

61. Mitchell, "Slave Markets Typify Exploitation of Domestics," 230. Mitchell notes that two million women were in domestic work, as it was the largest occupational group for women. Half of these domestic workers were black.

62. Rowley, *Richard Wright*, 228.

63. In *Native Son*, Vera exclaims, "I ain't no dog," when Bigger stares at her. Later in the novel a neglected Bessie admits that she would settle for a "Hello, dog!" from Bigger. Comparably the prosecutor refers to Bigger as a "black mad dog" in court (Wright, *Native Son*, 103, 132, 409).

64. Hurston, *Their Eyes Were Watching God*, 6.

65. Wright, review of *Their Eyes Were Watching God*, 16.

66. Dora Jones founded the Domestic Workers' Union in Harlem in 1934, but most unions established during this time were short-lived and only locally effective. Domestic workers were difficult to unionize. Not only was domestic work a large industry,

but women also worked long hours and shared the widespread negative perception of unions. Despite these difficulties, Jones's union organized 350 members after five years, 75 percent of whom were black women. See Cooke, "Modern Slaves."

67. Smith, *Visions of Belonging*, 169.

68. White, "Regrets He Has No Words," 7.

2 / Gender Conscriptions, Class Conciliations

1. Wadelington and Knapp, *Charlotte Hawkins Brown and Palmer Memorial Institute*, 11.

2. Brown, *Correct Thing to Do—to Say—to Wear*, 49.

3. Denard, introduction to *Mammy*, xxxii. Denard posits that Brown's fiction and etiquette book are the products of her dual-strategy race work: first, appeal to sympathetic whites and, second, supplement African Americans' formal education with rules for appropriate social behavior.

4. Brown, *Correct Thing to Do—to Say—to Wear*, 49.

5. Murray, *Pauli Murray*, 204.

6. Wolcott, *Remaking Respectability*, 7.

7. Brown, "Negro and the Social Graces."

8. Ida Cox, "Wild Women Don't Have the Blues," in Davis, *Blues Legacies and Black Feminism*, 38.

9. Park and Wald, "Native Daughters in the Promised Land," 617. See also Christian, "Images of Black Women in Afro-American Literature"; Carby, *Reconstructing Womanhood*.

10. Petry, *Street*, 229.

11. West, *Living Is Easy*, 39–40.

12. Davis, *Blues Legacies and Black Feminism*, xv.

13. Carby, "It Jus Be's Dat Way Sometime," 749.

14. In "Punks, Bulldaggers, and Welfare Queens," Cohen argues that queer theory can build coalitions between diverse oppressed subjects, as marginal members of society still exist outside of dominant cultural norms despite their heterosexuality.

15. Ramsey, *Race Music*, 46. Ramsey identifies the blues muse or "blues-ing" in various vernacular forms such as the emergence of independent blues record labels, jazz singer Dinah Washington's double entendres, Theodore Frye's gospel strut, and Mahalia Jackson's riffing and riding.

16. Ibid., 45.

17. duCille, *Coupling Convention*, 84.

18. Jones, *Rereading the Harlem Renaissance*, 137.

19. Griffin, *"Who Set You Flowin'?,"* 52.

20. Quoted in ibid., 53–54.

21. Muñoz, *Disidentifications*, 11.

22. Ibid., 15.

23. Codman, review of *The Living Is Easy*, 265.

24. Cromwell, afterword to *The Living Is Easy*, 361.

25. Johnson, *Appropriating Blackness*, 144.

26. Hurston, "What White Publishers Won't Print," 170.

27. McDowell, "Conversations with Dorothy West," 296.

28. Davis, *Blues Legacies and Black Feminism*, 314.

29. West, *Living Is Easy*, 39, 43.

30. Ibid., 24.

31. Sanders, "Feminism of Dorothy West's *The Living Is Easy*," 439.

32. Hine, "Rape and the Inner Lives of Black Women in the Middle West," 912.

33. West, *Living Is Easy*, 25.

34. Ibid., 106, 42, 21.

35. duCille, *Coupling Convention*, 113.

36. West, *Living Is Easy*, 91.

37. Baker, *Blues, Ideology, and Afro-American Literature*, 13.

38. Johnson argues, "What frames a performance as performance, then, has as much to do with context as it does with the aesthetics of the event itself." In doing so, he extends the boundaries of performance beyond the traditional understanding of stage and audience (*Appropriating Blackness*, 11).

39. West, *Living Is Easy*, 17, 30, 29, 22, 35, 150.

40. Ibid., 146.

41. Boehm, *Making a Way Out of No Way*, 100–101.

42. West, *Living Is Easy*, 5, 44, 200–201.

43. Tate, *Psychoanalysis and Black Novels*, 13.

44. Griffin, *"Who Set You Flowin'?,"* 85.

45. West, *Living Is Easy*, 22.

46. Ibid., 235.

47. For a psychological portrait of Cleo's identity formation as a sister, see Rueschmann, "Sister Bonds."

48. West, *Living Is Easy*, 141.

49. Ibid., 235, 308.

50. Petry, *Street*, 323.

51. Wright, *12 Million Black Voices*, 93.

52. Ivey, "Ann Petry Talks about First Novel," 49.

53. Petry, *Street*, 206.

54. Petry, "Novel as Social Criticism," 94.

55. Petry, *Street*, 19.

56. Ivey, "Mrs. Petry's Harlem," 154.

57. McKay, "Ann Petry's *The Street* and *The Narrows*," 135.

58. Jenkins, *Private Lives, Proper Relations*, 43.

59. Davis, *Blues Legacies and Black Feminism*, 16.

60. Petry, *Street*, 28, 29, 199.

61. Ibid., 76, 30.

62. Ervin, "Hidden Hand of Feminist Revolt in Ann Petry's *The Street*," 183.

63. Pryse, "'Pattern against the Sky,'" 127.

64. Petry, *Street*, 67, 432.

65. Ibid., 10.

66. Given Lutie's celibacy and Lil's sensuality, Jenkins questions whether Lutie resents Lil because she has "easy access to carnal pleasures, unconstrained by the legal strictures of marriage" (*Private Lives, Proper Relations*, 55).

67. Petry, *Street*, 3.

68. Drake and Cayton, *Black Metropolis*, 595.

69. Petry, *Street*, 243, 307–8, 57. See Drake, "Women on the Go," 77–80.

70. Petry, *Street*, 368, 15–16.

71. Ibid., 64, 312–13.

72. Ibid., 147, 148.

73. Barrett, *Blackness and Value*, 113.

74. Early, "Her Picture in the Papers," 93.

75. Holiday and Dufty, *Lady Sings the Blues*, 50, 86.

76. Tucker, *Swing Shift*, 214.

77. Holiday and Dufty, *Lady Sings the Blues*, 32.

78. Tucker, *Swing Shift*, 213.

79. Petry, *Street*, 222.

80. Ibid., 156.

81. Ibid., 161.

82. In *Love for Sale*, Clement demonstrates that the sexual politics of treating and prostitution were intricate, and the boundaries between treating and dating murky. Workingwomen believed that their employment was proof that they were not prostitutes. Meanwhile many women were engaged in treating in private, but that did not change the public discourse on premarital chastity.

83. Petry, *Street*, 249.

84. Mullen, "Object Lessons," 46.

85. Davis, *Blues Legacies and Black Feminism*, 16.

86. Petry, *Street*, 422.

87. Baraka traces "the changing same" throughout *Blues People*, but he defines the term in "Changing Same (R&B and New Black Music)."

88. Petry, *Street*, 188.

89. Davis, *Blues Legacies and Black Feminism*, 54.

90. Holiday, "Lady Sings the Blues."

91. Mootry, "Bitches, Whores, and Women Haters," 126.

92. Wright, *Black Boy*, 214.

93. Ellison also employs the vernacular in his novel *Invisible Man*. In *Punctuation*, Brody argues that Ellison's use of topography, specifically ellipses, creates an aural and visual figuration that invites improvisation and provides a means for understanding black performance.

3 / "Nobody Could Tell Who This Be"

1. Amy Lee argues that the intervention of Louella's white female employer "suggests a new level of feminine consciousness during her time among some individuals, for her decision to treat her laundress as her equal challenges the issues of value and propriety in the public and political realms" ("Narrator as Feminist Ally in Ann Petry's 'The Bones of Louella Brown,'" 123).

2. Petry, "Bones of Louella Brown," 168, 167. First published in *Opportunity* 25.4 (October–December 1947): 189–92, 226–30, the short story is based on the account of Sister Rose Jackson, a black woman whose grave stood in the rear of a cemetery in Petry's hometown, Old Saybrook, Connecticut. Whereas whites' gravestones faced the front of the cemetery, Jackson's looked at the rear. Petry explains in an autobiographical essay that this organization was "the nineteenth-century equivalent of the back of the bus" ("Ann Petry," 256).

3. Petry, "Bones of Louella Brown," 177.

4. Ibid., 180.

5. O'Grady, "Olympia's Maid," 14.

6. Fikes, "Escaping the Literary Ghetto," 105.

7. For another reading of Petry's use of the white-plot novel genre, see Bernard, "'Raceless' Writing and Difference."

8. Tate, *Psychoanalysis and Black Novels*, 148. Regarding Hurston's film ambitions, see Carby, foreword to *Seraph on the Suwanee*, x.

9. O'Grady, "Olympia's Maid," 14.

10. Schultz, "Out of the Woods and into the World," 69.

11. Gates, "Zora Neale Hurston," 294.

12. Johnson, "Thresholds of Difference," 279.

13. Hurston, *Mules and Men*, 19.

14. Langston Hughes also explores the dynamic between a black female artist and a white female patron in his short story "The Blues I'm Playing" (1933). His protagonist secures a white patron for her art, but she realizes that her financed trips to Europe and classical musical training isolate her from her true loves: her future husband and black folk culture.

15. Story, "Patronage and the Harlem Renaissance," 285.

16. Hurston, "Drenched in Light," 17, 22, 25.

17. Ibid., 25.

18. Eric Lott contends that whites' blackface minstrelsy is a dialectic between "moments of domination and moments of liberation." In "minstrelsy's mixed erotic economy of celebration and exploitation," whites show sincere appreciation for black folk culture even though they also misappropriate it (*Love and Theft*, 18, 6).

19. Hurston, "How It Feels to Be Colored Me," 152, 153.

20. Hurston, *Dust Tracks on a Road*, 34.

21. Critics note the self-conscious, myth-making nature of Hurston's autobiography. Mary Helen Washington labels it "a strangely disoriented book," and Alice Walker contends that the text is "filled with evasion, posturing, all kinds of self-concealment, though it is ostensibly an autobiography" (Washington, "Zora Neale Hurston," 19–20; Walker, *I Love Myself When I am Laughing*, 27).

22. Johnson, *Appropriating Blackness*, 3.

23. Davies, *Black Women, Writing and Identity*, 46.

24. Hurston, *Dust Tracks on a Road*, 34.

25. Ross, *Manning the Race*, 225.

26. Hurston, *Dust Tracks on a Road*, 145.

27. Huggins, *Harlem Renaissance*, 133. Huggins also discusses Langston Hughes's and Louise Thompson's conflicts with Mason. Hughes rejected the primitivism Mason required of her artists, whereas Huggins reports that Thompson ended her collaboration "not for artistic integrity . . . but for her womanness" (130).

28. Carby notes in her foreword to *Seraph* that the novel earned measurable initial success, but it was quickly overshadowed when Hurston was accused of child molestation in 1948. When the *Baltimore Afro-American* broke the story on the sodomy allegation against the writer, it suggested the novel "advocated sexual aggressiveness in women and then used selected sentences from the novel as if they provided evidence of the author's immorality" (Carby, foreword to *Seraph on the Suwanee*, xiii). Though the charges against Hurston were dropped, she did little to promote *Seraph*. Hurston

writes to Carl Van Vechten that the scandal was "the blow that knocked me loose from all that I have ever looked to and cherished" (Zora Neale Hurston, letter to Carl Van Vechten and Fania Marinoff, October 30, 1948, in Kaplan, *Zora Neale Hurston*, 571).

29. In his introduction, titled "Not Necessarily Race Matter," Gene A. Jarrett contends that white-plot novels are anomalies of African American literature because critics "[allow] race to *over*determine" their understanding of the tradition, which prevents more comprehensive interpretations of racial representation (Jarrett, introduction to *African American Literature Beyond Race*, 2).

30. Washington, "Zora Neale Hurston," 21. The literary critic labels the novel a failure because Hurston's white characters use the same dialect as the black folks of Eatonville in *Their Eyes Were Watching God*. For Hurston's discussion on the similarities between black and poor southern white dialect, see her December 22, 1948, Christmas card to Marjorie Kinnan Rawlings in Kaplan, *Zora Neale Hurston*, 577. Some critics see the novel as a failure because of Arvay's less than feminist conclusion in comparison to some of Hurston's other women-centered work; other critics trace thematic connections between *Seraph* and Hurston's earlier work. See Jackson, "Waste and Whiteness"; Rieger, "Working-Class Pastoral of Zora Neale Hurston's *Seraph on the Suwanee*."

31. Meisenhelder, *Hitting a Straight Lick with a Crooked Stick*, 92.

32. duCille, *Coupling Convention*, 127.

33. In "'Some Other Way to Try,'" Shawn E. Miller argues that Tea Cake's domestic violence is one of the novel's flaws that goes unproblematized in feminists' recovery of the text.

34. duCille, *Coupling Convention*, 127.

35. Hurston, *Seraph on the Suwanee*, 126.

36. Zora Neale Hurston, letter to Burroughs Mitchell, September 3, 1947, in Kaplan, *Zora Neale Hurston*, 555.

37. Jacobson, *Whiteness of a Different Color*, 129.

38. Jackson, "Waste and Whiteness," 642.

39. Zora Neale Hurston, letter to Burroughs Mitchell, October 2, 1947, in Kaplan, *Zora Neale Hurston*, 557–58.

40. Hurston, *Seraph on the Suwanee*, 7. For more on the history of Irish racial assimilation, see Ignatiev's *How the Irish Became White* and Omi and Winant's *Racial Formation in the United States*.

41. Hurston, *Seraph on the Suwanee*, 61, 46, 126, 113.

42. Ibid., 106, 68, 57, 129, 144, 68, 131.

43. Ibid., 202. Kenny develops his talent for playing the pic box under Joe Kelsey's instruction, and later he becomes a successful jazz musician. As compensation, Kenny pays for "Uncle Joe" to accompany him north, and Arvay outfits Joe with "changing-clothes" as thanks for training and nurturing her son. The gifts are a kind of "reparation" that Kenny, the white minstrel, provides Joe, his black muse (251; Lott, *Love and Theft*, 59). For a lengthier discussion of the cultural exchanges between black and white in Hurston's oeuvre, see Hardison, "Crossing the Threshold."

44. Hurston, *Seraph on the Suwanee*, 110, 112.

45. Ibid., 113, 114, 115.

46. Ibid., 242, 207, 212, 202. Italics mine.

47. Meisenhelder, *Hitting a Straight Lick with a Crooked Stick*, 109.

48. Hurston, *Seraph on the Suwanee*, 161.

49. Laura Dubek concludes her reading of the novel with the assertion, "As long as white women are socially constructed to have relationships with their husbands only . . . they will remain both victimized by and complicit in social forces intent on maintaining white male supremacy" ("Social Geography of Race in Hurston's *Seraph on the Suwanee*," 351).

50. Hurston, "What White Publishers Won't Print," 173.

51. Bell, "Ann Petry's Demythologizing of American Culture and Afro-American Character."

52. Japtok, "'Gospel of Whiteness.'"

53. Petry, *Street*, 28, 50–51, 51.

54. Petry, *Country Place*, 66, 263.

55. Bernard, "'Raceless' Writing and Difference," 107.

56. Petry, *Country Place*, 58, 211.

57. Dubek, "White Family Values in Ann Petry's *Country Place*," 73.

58. Petry, *Narrows*, 260.

59. Ibid., 171, 7, 308, 35, 8.

60. Ibid., 138, 145.

61. Wilson and Petry, "MELUS Interview," 81, 82.

62. Weir, "*Narrows*."

63. Melina Vizcaíno-Alemán argues more broadly that in Petry's writing "double consciousness divides the black middle-class home and generates the contradictory fissures that enable and simultaneously disable interracial and feminist coalitions" ("Counter-Modernity, Black Masculinity, and Female Silence," 121).

64. Petry, *Narrows*, 136, 91.

65. Ibid., 162, 58. Interestingly Link also confuses seemingly rigid gender and sexual boundaries. After Major's death, Abbie's friend Frances Jackson aids Abbie in her mourning. "She was here so often," Link tells Abbie, "that I used to think she was my father and you were my mother." In acknowledging that Frances becomes a substitute for Major, Link suggests that the performance of gender—like race and class—can be ambiguous and mutable (14).

66. Ibid., 68, 72, 68.

67. Ibid., 249.

68. Vizcaíno-Alemán, "Counter-Modernity, Black Masculinity, and Female Silence," 126.

69. Petry, *Narrows*, 253.

70. Ibid., 21, 23, 25.

71. Ibid., 60, 56, 58, 275, 126.

72. Ibid., 320, 303–4, 300.

73. Ibid., 414, 414–15, 419.

74. In his reading of the novel, Michael Barry contends that "respecting our brothers does not fully explain why so many prejudices in society are rewarded by its structural features: [Petry's] call to respect urges an individual to transcend history, but it does not envision historical improvement or change" ("'Same Train Be Back Tomorrow,'" 154).

75. Petry, *Narrows*, 329.

76. Griffin, "Hunting Communists and Negroes in Ann Petry's *The Narrows*," 137.

234 / NOTES TO CHAPTERS 3 AND 4

I would also add that before Ann Allen Shockley's black lesbian in *Loving Her* (1974), there was Frances, the gender-bending, sexually ambiguous figure in *The Narrows*.

77. "Like a Winding Sheet" was first published in *The Crisis* 52.11 (November 1945): 317–18, 331–32. It is also included in Petry's collection *Miss Muriel and Other Stories*. Although a disenfranchised black man is the main actor, Jennifer DeVere Brody argues that the dilemma about "what it is to be a woman" is critical to the short story because the text "vividly illustrates the danger of relying on a binary opposition between race and gender" ("Effaced into Flesh," 187, 185).

78. Hurston, "What White Publishers Won't Print," 171.

79. Schultz, "Out of the Woods and into the World," 82.

80. Childress, *Florence*, 121.

81. Childress, "In the Laundry Room," in *Like One of the Family*, 108.

82. Zora Neale Hurston, letter to William Bradford Huie, September 6, 1954, in Kaplan, *Zora Neale Hurston*, 719.

83. Hurston, *Dust Tracks on a Road*, 197.

84. duCille, *Coupling Convention*, 82.

85. Ann Petry, journal, January 11, 1992, qtd. in Petry, *At Home Inside*, 67.

86. Ann Petry, letter to Elisabeth Petry, July 16, 1977, qtd. in Petry, *At Home Inside*, 61.

4 / "I'll See How Crazy *They* Think I Am"

1. Bates, *Long Shadow of Little Rock*, 24, 15, 16, 29, 21. In response to white men's verbal abuse, attempted sexual assault, and aggressive molestation, black women also pursued legal prosecution. See Shockley, *"We, Too, Are Americans."*

2. Wright, *Native Son*, 227-228, 331.

3. Sielke, *Reading Rape*, 117.

4. Petry, *Street*, 429.

5. Lucas, *Third Ward Newark*, 50. Italics are mine. Whereas Lucas transparently employs psychological language to describe Wonnie's melancholia and borderline hysteria, social psychiatrists use Wright's characterization of Bigger Thomas to diagnose disenfranchised black men with what they termed "black rage" (Scott, *Contempt and Pity*, 86–89, 98–103). For contemporaneous psychological evaluations of black men, see McLean, "Psychodynamic Factors in Racial Relations"; Charles, "Optimism and Frustration in the American Negro."

6. Lucas, *Third Ward Newark*, 60.

7. Cheng, "Melancholy of Race," 58.

8. Eng and Han, "Dialogue on Racial Melancholia," 365.

9. Lucas, *Third Ward Newark*, 197.

10. Ibid., 38, 83.

11. Dietzel, "African American Novel and Popular Culture."

12. Yerby, "How and Why I Write the Costume Novel," 150.

13. Brantley, "Racial Conflict."

14. Conroy, "Off The Book Shelf."

15. "Novel about Third Ward."

16. A few scholars reference Lucas's novels in larger critical studies. Lawrence R. Rodgers references *Flour Is Dusty* in his work *Canaan Bound*. Carl Milton Hughes includes a summary of *Third Ward Newark* in his overview *The Negro Novelist*. Noel

Schraufnagel argues, "Wonnie has the temperament of a Bigger Thomas, rather than a Lutie Johnson, but she lacks the opportunity to take advantage of her tendencies toward violence" (*From Apology to Protest*, 44).

17. James, *American Civilization*, 119.

18. Rabinowitz, *Black and White and Noir*, 18.

19. Spillers, "'All the Things You Could Be by Now, If Sigmund Freud's Wife Was Your Mother,'" 138.

20. Cohen, "Deviance as Resistance," 30.

21. Davis, *Women, Race and Class*, 182.

22. Lucas, *Third Ward Newark*, 6, 7.

23. Ibid., 10.

24. Clement, *Love for Sale*, 3.

25. Lucas, *Third Ward Newark*, 12.

26. Ibid., 21.

27. Lauren Berlant acknowledges that "Diva Citizenship" does not radically change society, but she contends that it "occurs when a person stages a dramatic coup in a public sphere in which she does not have privilege" (*Queen of America Goes to Washington City*, 223).

28. Lucas, *Third Ward Newark*, 22.

29. Catharine A. MacKinnon observes that rape laws ignore social hierarchies between white and black, legal versus various kinds of illegal status, and differing economic classes. She also argues for a redefinition of rape that would replace the idea that exchanging money provides consent with the idea that money is a means of sexual force (*Women's Lives, Men's Laws*, 245–48).

30. Lucas, *Third Ward Newark*, 22.

31. Ibid., 23.

32. Ibid., 24, 31, 32.

33. Unofficially the legal system problematically distinguishes between "technical" and "real" rape. Women may "technically" experience a rape, but cultural opinion reductively considers cases in which the rapist is a stranger, the perpetrator uses a weapon, or there is visible evidence of force as "real" rapes. See Estrich, *Real Rape*.

34. Lucas, *Third Ward Newark*, 25.

35. Ibid., 28, 38.

36. Ibid., 35.

37. Holloway, *Private Bodies, Public Texts*, 7, 9.

38. Lucas, *Third Ward Newark*, 38, 40.

39. Quoted in Stetler, "Writers, Famous and Obscure, Captured the Mood of Newark before the Riots." The Newark riots began in July 1967 when community members witnessed the police abuse a black cab driver following a routine traffic stop. After five days, Newark sustained twenty-six deaths (including one white police officer and a white firemen), over a hundred injuries, 1,400 arrests, and millions of dollars in property damage. For more on the riots, see Price, *Freedom Not Far Distant*.

40. The Detroit riots in June 1943 resulted in thirty-four deaths, 675 injuries, roughly 1,900 arrests, and $2 million in property damage and only ended with the arrival of federal troops. The New York riots in August of that same year ended in five deaths (all black), five hundred injuries, hundreds of arrests, and $5 million in

property damage. See Trotter, "From a Raw Deal to a New Deal?"; Brandt, *Harlem at War*; White, *What Caused the Detroit Riot?*

41. Lucas, *Third Ward Newark*, 44.

42. Wright, *Native Son*, 343.

43. Lucas, *Third Ward Newark*, 48–50, 51, 58, 61.

44. Ibid., 54.

45. Cheng, *Melancholy of Race*, 11.

46. Lucas, *Third Ward Newark*, 61.

47. Ibid., 123–24, 115, 116.

48. Price, *Freedom Not Far Distant*, 194.

49. Lucas, *Third Ward Newark*, 75, 140.

50. Feldstein, *Motherhood in Black and White*, 41. Tracking the popularity of psychological jargon during World War II, Feldstein examines how ideals of motherhood and codes of masculinity framed gendered and racial conceptions of citizenship.

51. During the war, black women finished training school for various industrial jobs only to be denied positions by employers and disenfranchised by the lack of federal enforcement of nondiscrimination policies. For example, several black women sued the Warner and Swasey Company and Thompson Products in Cleveland, Ohio, under Roosevelt's Executive Order 8802, but the judge upheld the companies' discriminatory practices (Parker, "Women Sue Cleveland Plants," 226–27).

52. Lucas, *Third Ward Newark*, 161.

53. Anderson, "Last Hired, First Fired," 86–87.

54. Anderson explains that white women used "hate strikes" or walkouts at their jobs to protest sharing bathroom facilities because they feared black women were infected with venereal disease, which demonstrates that "an important persisting dimension of racism that was particularly divisive among women was the virgin/whore dichotomization of feminine personality expressed in racial terms" (*Wartime Women*, 37).

55. Lucas, *Third Ward Newark*, 194.

56. Ibid., 172.

57. Samuel, *Pledging Allegiance*, xiv.

58. Lucas, *Third Ward Newark*, 156, 159.

59. Cohen, *Consumers' Republic*, 8.

60. Lucas, *Third Ward Newark*, 192.

61. Ibid., 184.

62. Johnson, "Phenomenology of the Black Body," 126.

63. Lucas, *Third Ward Newark*, 202.

64. Ibid., 213.

65. Mumford, *Newark*, 149.

66. Lucas, *Third Ward Newark*, 228, 235.

67. For more on spatial theory and monuments, see Lefebvre, *Production of Space*; Young, *Texture of Memory*.

68. Cheng explains that the mourner kills the lost one while the melancholic internalizes him or her. As a result, "the good mourner turns out to be none other than an ultrasophisticated, and more lethal, melancholic" ("Melancholy of Race," 53).

69. Lucas, *Third Ward Newark*, 237.

70. Jenkins, *Private Lives, Proper Relations*, 13–14.

71. "Pleads Well."

72. Outlining the topography of the female psyche in contemporary postfeminist culture, Laura Kipnis argues that "upping women's awareness and anger about rape has also had the unintended—and probably not so beneficial—by-product effect of reinforcing conventional feminine fear and vulnerability, which also impedes women's lives" (*Female Thing*, 130–31).

73. See Lovisi, "Lion Books," 223–26; Tuttle, "An Interview with Arnold Hano," 227–30.

74. Queer pulp cover art employed markers such as hair color and the positioning of same-sex characters, while their titles used signifiers like "strange" and "shadows," as code for the novels' exploration of lesbian and gay sexuality. For more on decoding homosexuality in pulp novels, see Stryker, *Queer Pulp*; Zimet, *Strange Sisters*; the website Women in the Shadows: Lesbian Pulp Fiction Collection.

75. Relatively little is known about the pulp illustrators, as publishers kept few of the original paintings. Pulp paperback covers are collectible items now, but they were created originally as ephemera. For more on this fiction, see O'Brien, *Hardboiled America*.

76. Pulp cover art reached its peak after World War II, but O'Brien contends that by 1955 it became more restrained and had entered "the realm of good taste" due to the House Select Committee on Current Pornographic Materials' investigation in 1952 (*Hardboiled America*, 45).

77. Lucas interview with the *Newark Evening News*, qtd. in Stetler, "Writers, Famous and Obscure, Captured the Mood of Newark before the Riots."

5 / Rereading the Construction of Womanhood

1. Dirthrower, "Negro Press," 98. Dirthrower writes from Panama, which indicates the global implications of having the African American press "shepherd" black readers.

2. Brooks, *Maud Martha*, 39.

3. Ibid., 2, 82, 52.

4. Ibid., 39.

5. Jablon, *Black Metafiction*, 27.

6. Dworkin, "'Evading Eye,'" 34.

7. Brooks, *Report from Part One*, 191.

8. Hughes, "Outstanding Autumn Headliners in 1953 Are Books, the Theatre and the Blues," 11.

9. Brooks, *Maud Martha*, 71.

10. Lattin and Lattin, "Dual Vision in Gwendolyn Brooks's *Maud Martha*," 184.

11. In "Speaking in Tongues," Mae Gwendolyn Henderson theorizes the limitations of both hegemonic and nonhegemonic discourses. Henderson differentiates between the titular fugitive slave's self-definition and the hegemonic historical inscriptions of her in Sherley Ann Williams's novel *Dessa Rose* (1986). The critic also stresses the black community's inability to ascribe meaning to the eponymous black female protagonist's birthmark in Toni Morrison's novel *Sula* (1973).

12. Petry, *Street*, 50, 412.

13. Dworkin, "'Evading Eye,'" 50; Washington, "'Taming All That Anger Down,'" 457.

14. Washington, "Plain, Black, and Decently Wild," 272.

15. Brooks, *Maud Martha*, 24, 133.

16. Elizabeth Lawrence, letter to Gwendolyn Brooks, October 17, 1952, Selected Records of Harper & Brothers. The literary club scene was a carryover from an earlier draft in which Helen and not Maud Martha (previously named Evelina) was the focus of Brooks's manuscript, which she began in the 1940s and titled "American Family Brown." In her letter Lawrence writes, "It is so difficult, so almost impossible to make lit'ry people or groups ring true. Try to fix them to paper and people who feed upon books become static at best and pretentious bores at worst."

17. Brooks, *Maud Martha*, 163.

18. Cohen, *Consumers' Republic*, 7.

19. Walker, "Introduction," 7.

20. Brooks, *Maud Martha*, 48, 49. Italics mine.

21. Ibid., 53.

22. Hughes, "Harlem Sweeties," 245.

23. Brooks, *Maud Martha*, 51.

24. Hughes, "Harlem," 426.

25. Walker, "Promised Land," 24.

26. Brooks, *Maud Martha*, 21, 22.

27. Ibid., 56–57.

28. Willis, *Posing Beauty*, xxvi.

29. Sontag, *On Photography*, 3.

30. Gwendolyn Brooks, letter to Elizabeth Lawrence, January 21, 1952, Selected Records of Harper & Brothers. Brooks specifically suggested the work of Bronzeville photographer Gerald Cogbill; Lawrence felt the pictures would be inappropriate.

31. Clarke, *Photograph*, 114.

32. "Mrs. Bill Robinson Stars in Important Role—'A Wife.'"

33. "Other Robinson—'Mrs. Bill.'"

34. "Camera Record of Married Life of Joe and Marva."

35. Monroe, "Marva Tells Why She Split with Joe."

36. Brooks, *Maud Martha*, 62, 61.

37. Sontag, *On Photography*, 23.

38. Brooks, *Report from Part One*, 59.

39. Brooks, *Maud Martha*, 58.

40. Streeter-Dixon, "Words of Wisdom from a Housewife."

41. Brooks, *Maud Martha*, 59.

42. Ibid., 69–70, 71, 151.

43. Muriel Donnelly, "Letter and Pictures to the Editor," *Ebony*, December 1945, 51.

44. "Goodbye Mammy, Hello Mom," 36.

45. Green, *Selling the Race*, 170.

46. Thea Thauner, "Letters and Pictures to the Editor," *Ebony*, February 1947, 49.

47. Jackie Ormes, *Patty-Jo 'n' Ginger, Pittsburgh Courier*, city edition, May 10, 1952.

48. DeKnight, "Quick Coffee Breads for Sunday Morning," 38.

49. Green, *Selling the Race*, 139.

50. DeKnight, "How to Glorify the Apple," 26.

51. DeKnight, "Tamale Pie for New Year's Eve," 42.

52. DeKnight, "Fruit Pies," 45.

53. DeKnight, "Budget Meals for Vet Wives," 27.

54. DeKnight, "Cakes for Halloween," 30.

55. Brooks, *Maud Martha*, 151, 152.

56. Frazier, "Domestic Epic Warfare in *Maud Martha*," 133.

57. Brooks, *Maud Martha*, 152.

58. DeKnight, "Dinner of Leftovers," 26.

59. Brooks, *Maud Martha*, 152–53.

60. DeKnight, "Date with a Cook Book," 44.

61. Brooks, "Why Negro Women Leave Home," 27.

62. Ibid., 28.

63. Brooks, *Maud Martha*, 73, 101, 120, 121.

64. Radway, "Readers and Their Romances," 580.

65. Brooks, *Maud Martha*, 66, 67.

66. Frazier, "Domestic Epic Warfare in *Maud Martha*," 137.

67. Jessamyn Neuhaus observes that the authors and editors of cookbooks often sexualized cooking as the way to catch or keep a man; they also gendered different types of food such as barbecue as masculine and decorative food as feminine ("Way to a Man's Heart," 538–39).

68. *Tan Confessions*, April 1950, 51.

69. *Tan Confessions*, February 1951, 4.

70. *Tan Confessions*, November 1950, 4.

71. *Tan Confessions*, June 1951, 4.

72. Rooks, *Ladies' Pages*, 115.

73. *Tan Confessions*, November 1950, 1.

74. Bernice Jackson, "Letters to the Editor," *Tan Confessions*, January 1951, 3.

75. In regard to a feminist reading methodology, Patrocinio P. Schweickart draws on Stanley E. Fish and explains that "the production of the meaning of a text is mediated by the interpretive community in which the activity of reading is situated: the meaning of the text depends on the interpretive strategy one applies to it, and the choice of strategy is regulated (explicitly or implicitly) by the canons of acceptability that govern the interpretive community" ("Reading Ourselves," 34).

76. Greer, "'Some of Their Stories Are Like My Life, I Guess,'" 147.

77. Betty Martin, "Letters to the Editor," *Tan Confessions*, February 1951, 3.

78. Georgia Elliott, "Letters to the Editor," *Tan Confessions*, December 1950, 6.

79. Myrtle Hartgrove, "Letters to the Editor," *Tan Confessions*, December 1950, 6.

80. Charles E. Walker, "Letters to the Editor," *Tan Confessions*, January 1951, 3. In "'Strange Love,'" Leisa D. Meyer contends the magazine provided a discursive space for readers to engage and deliberate diverse sexual subjectivities.

81. C. N. Daniel, "Letters to the Editor," *Tan Confessions*, January 1952, 6.

82. Rooks, *Ladies' Pages*, 139.

83. C. M. Ward, "Letters to the Editor," *Tan Confessions*, February 1951, 3.

84. Ruth Manor, "Letters to the Editor," *Tan Confessions*, April 1951, 3.

85. In her study, Radway argues that in "a mass-production system [the act of purchase] can just as easily testify to the existence of an ongoing, still only partially met, need" ("Readers and Their Romances," 577).

86. Jane White, "Letters to the Editor," *Tan Confessions*, December 1950, 6.

87. Hughes, "Sex in Front," 97.

88. "The Press."

89. Brooks, "Luther," 74. It reasons that "Luther" is a revised chapter from "American Family Brown" not included in *Maud Martha*. In her comments on a draft of *Maud Martha*, Brooks's editor expressed doubt that Paul would not know what a communist was.

90. *Tan Confessions*, January 1953, 4.

91. Hughes, "Sex in Front," 100.

92. Brooks, *Maud Martha*, 100.

93. Gwendolyn Brooks, letter to Elizabeth Lawrence, March 26, 1958, Selected Records of Harper & Brothers. Brooks enclosed two chapters of the sequel in her correspondence with Lawrence, but the editor disliked the idea of the new novel depending on readers' familiarity with the prequel.

94. Quoted in Hull and Gallagher, "Update on *Part One*," 26.

95. Hutcheon, *Narcissistic Narrative*, 6. Italics in original.

96. Brooks, *Maud Martha*, 135, 134.

97. Washington, "Plain, Black, and Decently Wild," 282.

98. Brooks, *Maud Martha*, 140.

99. Brooks, *Report from Part Two*, 15.

100. Brooks, *Report from Part One*, 176.

101. Brooks, *Maud Martha*, 17.

102. Brooks, "To Those of My Sisters Who Kept Their Naturals," 121.

103. Childress, "If You Want to Get Along with Me," in *Like One of the Family*, 21.

104. Brooks, *Maud Martha*, 179.

105. Reading the significance of the "feminine" in Brooks's novel, Hortense J. Spillers argues that "the central artistic purpose of *Maud Martha* is to express the essentially heroic character of the unheroic by altering our opinion of 'heroism' in the first place" ("'An Order of Constancy,'" 233).

106. Review of *Maud Martha*, 15.

6 / The Audacity of Hope

1. Thompson, "Negro Publications and the Writer," 304.

2. Era Bell Thompson, "Bell's Lettres," *Negro Digest*, April 1950, 72. In a draft of this column archived in the Era Bell Thompson Papers, the essay's title is "I Speak No More."

3. Thompson, *American Daughter* (1986), 117.

4. Ibid., 152.

5. Era Bell Thompson, "Full Circle," speech, Bismarck Junior College, Bismarck, ND, April 27, 1977, 6, Era Bell Thompson Papers; Thompson, *American Daughter*, 82.

6. I signify on President Barack Obama's political biography *The Audacity of Hope*. The phrase was the title of his 2004 Democratic National Convention speech, and hope was a running theme in his 2008 presidential campaign.

7. Era Bell Thompson, "An Editor Looks Back: Adjustment," *Together* (Chicago Urban League), 7, Era Bell Thompson Papers.

8. "Resident Comes Full Circle," *Bismarck Tribune*, July 28, 1977, 24, qtd. in Anderson, "Era Bell Thompson," 314. The bracketed date is Anderson's addition.

9. Anderson, "Era Bell Thompson," 310.

10. Coincidentally Wright's ethnography *Black Power* and Thompson's travelogue *Africa, Land of My Fathers* were published the very same week in 1954. The two writers did not have an obvious direct conflict, as did Hurston and Wright, who wrote critical reviews

of each other's fiction, or West and Wright, who fought over the political direction of the literary magazine *New Challenge*. However, Thompson and Wright seemed to "meet" at various career high points. In his study of their work on Africa, James Campbell describes such happenstances as evidence of the "strange magnetism between them, some force that repeatedly drew them together and then prised them apart" (*Middle Passages*, 268). A letter from Ben Burns, who was then the executive editor of *Ebony*, documents that Thompson had knowledge of Wright's research for *Black Power*. Burns informs her, "[Wright's] book incidentally—I know you're interested since it might be competition—is about his stay only *in the Gold Coast*." In *Black Power* Wright criticizes the tribalism he found in Ghana perpetuating the ignorance as well as the political and psychological damages of colonialism. Thompson's *Africa, Land of My Fathers*, in contrast, discusses but does not stress the continent's colonial history. In a letter to an acquaintance who worked in the Foreign Service in the State Department, she conceptualizes her text as "a sort of 'return of this native' to the 'Motherland,' complete with mother's reactions. Needless to say, it will be light, and I hope, humorous" (Ben Burns, letter to Era Bell Thompson, November 1, 1953, and Era Bell Thompson, letter to Roene Brooks, February 9, 1953, Era Bell Thompson Papers).

11. Ellison, "Richard Wright's Blues," 128.

12. See Fishburn's *Richard Wright's Hero*; Smith's *Self-Discovery and Authority in Afro-American Narrative*. Critics analyze *Native Son* as social realism, but they also point out the fictionalization of Wright's autobiography by arguing that his "black boy" is as much a writing persona as a real representation of the writer's childhood. For instance, Robert B. Stepto in "I Thought I Knew These People" and Jerry W. Ward Jr. in his introduction to *Black Boy* identify similar themes in *Black Boy* and slave narratives: hunger, the quest for literacy, the questioning of Christianity, and the desire to follow the North Star. Additionally Timothy Dow Adams posits that Wright's narrative is a "truthful account" that "often does not ring true; and that this inability to tell the truth is Wright's major metaphor of self" ("'I Do Believe Him Though I Know He Lies,'" 302).

13. Thompson, *Africa, Land of My Fathers*, 162; "How Richard Wright Looks at *Black Boy*," 65.

14. Era Bell Thompson, speech, University of Chicago tea, May 5, 1946, Era Bell Thompson Papers. Although the speech for her book's release emphasized her inclusion, Thompson did not turn a blind eye to the discrimination she suffered during a banquet for contributors to the *Chicago Tribune*. In her grievance letter, she explains, "I am a respectable citizen, a member of the N.A.A.C.P., the Board of Directors of the Chicago Y.W.C.A. and am on a fellowship writing a book—trying to write a story without malice and without bitterness. Sometimes the writing is very hard" (Era Bell Thompson, letter to Hilda Butler Farr, May 12, 1945, Era Bell Thompson Papers).

15. Thompson, *American Daughter* (1986), 296.

16. Braxton, *Black Women Writing Autobiography*, 146.

17. Though Hurston and Wright published their memoirs during the apex of their literary careers, both writers published autobiographical sketches before *Their Eyes Were Watching God* (1937) and *Native Son* (1940): "How It Feels to Be Colored Me" (1928) and the "The Ethics of Living Jim Crow" (1937), respectively.

18. Gates, "Introduction," 7.

19. Braxton, *Black Women Writing Autobiography*, 159.

20. Davies, *Black Women, Writing and Identity*.

21. Era Bell Thompson, "Rockerfeller [sic] Foundation," July 11, 1944, Era Bell Thompson Papers.

22. John K. Young draws upon editorial theory to distinguish the "'individual' zone of composition," or the writer's creative process, from the "the hybrid sphere of publication," or a creative web of publishers, editors, and other writers (*Black Writers, White Publishers*, 19).

23. These edits, Arnold Rampersad argues, "worked to de-intellectualize Wright, to return him to his childhood and adolescence." Similarly Rampersad contends that Wright's acquiescence to his editors' criticisms of *Native Son* "almost emasculated Bigger Thomas." Wright deleted a scene in which Mary Dalton appears in a newsreel and Bigger and his friend masturbate in the movie theater as well as language that suggests Mary desires Bigger. Such revisions illustrate the creative limitations imposed on black writers by the economic power of white cultural brokers. The edits were restored later in the Library of America edition of the novel (Rampersad, "Too Honest for His Own Time," 165).

24. Raynaud, "'Rubbing a Paragraph with a Soft Cloth'?," 35.

25. Thompson, "Full Circle," 7.

26. Algren, "Mulatto Family Struggles with Soil of North Dakota," 19.

27. Caliri, review of *American Daughter*, 55.

28. Olney, "Autobiography and the Cultural Moment," 25.

29. Era Bell Thompson, letter to Johnny Erp, July 30, 1950, Era Bell Thompson Papers.

30. Thompson, "Full Circle," 1, 2.

31. Era Bell Thompson, "At Library-Parg," November 3, 1945, Era Bell Thompson Papers.

32. Era Bell Thompson, letter to Stanley Pargellis, May 24, 1944, Era Bell Thompson Papers.

33. Stanley Pargellis, letter to Era Bell Thompson, July 11, 1944, Era Bell Thompson Papers.

34. Stanley Pargellis, letter to Era Bell Thompson, June 11, 1945, Era Bell Thompson Papers. Pargellis references Thompson as Tovey, her nickname in her autobiography.

35. Era Bell Thompson, "Newberry Library to Sponsor Writing about Midwest," May 1944, Era Bell Thompson Papers.

36. Era Bell Thompson, "Flowers," October 10, 1945, Era Bell Thompson Papers.

37. Couch, "Publisher's Introduction," xxii–xxiii.

38. Jackson, *Indignant Generation*, 185.

39. Era Bell Thompson, "Couch," October 20, 1945, Era Bell Thompson Papers.

40. Era Bell Thompson, "Max Siegel," April 3, 1945, Era Bell Thompson Papers.

41. Era Bell Thompson, "Bobbs Merrill Report," March 5, 1945, Era Bell Thompson Papers.

42. Era Bell Thompson, letter to Stanley Pargellis, March 11, 1945, Era Bell Thompson Papers.

43. Era Bell Thompson, "Committee Report," January 20, 1945, Era Bell Thompson Papers.

44. Raynaud, "'Rubbing a Paragraph with a Soft Cloth'?," 56.

45. Thompson, speech, University of Chicago tea. Phrases in parentheses are handwritten additions to Thompson's typed speech.

46. Thompson, *American Daughter*, University of Chicago Press dust jacket, second printing, Era Bell Thompson Papers.

47. Era Bell Thompson, "Called Flowers," February 2, 1946, Era Bell Thompson Papers. For the 1986 Minnesota Historical Society Press edition, *American Daughter*'s cover is a black-and-white high school graduation photograph of Thompson. The portrait exhibits her racial subjectivity rather than the western premise of the original dust jacket.

48. Ellison, "Stepchild Fantasy," 26.

49. Era Bell Thompson, personal letter, July 12, 1982, qtd. in Anderson, "Era Bell Thompson," 315.

50. Eleanor D. Wallace, review of *American Daughter*, by Era Bell Thompson, *The First Church Review* 24.6 (October 19, 1946), Era Bell Thompson Papers.

51. Rushmore, "Story of a Negro Girl."

52. Bernice Langert, "Testament to the Ability of an Individual," *Chicago Daily Law Bulletin*, May 15, 1946, 2, Era Bell Thompson Papers.

53. Hayakawa, "Second Thoughts," April 27, 1946.

54. Elder, "Minority Saga," 307.

55. Culley, "What a Piece of Work Is 'Woman'!," 8.

56. Era Bell Thompson, letter to Stanley Pargellis, July 11, 1944.

57. Thompson, *American Daughter* (1986), 193.

58. Ibid., 13. Thompson changes the names of her brothers (William Hobart, Stewart, and Carl), aunt and uncle (James and Ada Garrison), and white foster family (Mabel and Robert O'Brian) for legal purposes.

59. Thompson, *American Daughter* (1986), 15.

60. Johnson, "'This Strange White World,'" 103.

61. Thompson, *American Daughter* (1986), 16, 22. Italics mine.

62. Braxton, *Black Women Writing Autobiography*, 3.

63. Thompson, *American Daughter* (1986), 20.

64. Braxton, *Black Women Writing Autobiography*, 144.

65. Thompson, *American Daughter* (1986), 47.

66. Brooks, *Maud Martha*, 59.

67. Era Bell Thompson, "The Teen Age Book Parade," review of *My Ántonia*, by Willa Cather, Broadcast Music, Inc. (BMI), 1951, 4, Era Bell Thompson Papers.

68. Jean C. Griffith contends that in Cather's work "northern European, Nordic immigrants become independent, professionally minded New Women who transcend traditional gender roles and succeed in widening the scope of acceptable spheres for women" ("How the West Was Whitened," 398).

69. Thompson, *American Daughter* (1986), 147, 48.

70. Ibid., 37, 24, 97, 98.

71. Ibid., 108, 109.

72. Ibid., 55, 23.

73. Griffin, *"Who Set You Flowin'?,"* 28.

74. Thompson, *American Daughter* (1986), 113.

75. In their analysis of Thompson's memoir, "Religion, Idealism, and African American Autobiography in the Northern Plains," Cole and Weins connect the presence of God in the text, which links Thompson to a tradition of black women's spiritual autobiographies, to Thompson's utopian descriptions of nature.

76. Thompson, *American Daughter* (1986), 49, 33.

77. Thompson and Greenlee, *Interview with Era Bell Thompson*, 33.

78. Thompson, *American Daughter* (1986), 83, 141, 128.

79. David Laird also sees "the reenactment of those various constraints and limitations that characterize the social landscape of more settled, more traditional societies" in the frontier depicted in Willa Cather's fiction ("Willa Cather's Women," 246).

80. Thompson, *American Daughter* (1986), 142, 127.

81. Ibid., 219, 268.

82. Thompson and Greenlee, *Interview with Era Bell Thompson*, 15.

83. Anderson, "Era Bell Thompson," 313.

84. Thompson, *American Daughter* (1986), 208, 209.

85. Thompson and Greenlee, *Interview with Era Bell Thompson*, 35.

86. Thompson, *American Daughter* (1986), 240, 241. In his autobiography, Ben Burns recalls Thompson criticizing his efforts to increase *Ebony*'s circulation by including representations of interracial couples. "As the only female executive at *Ebony*, her opinion regarding any story on mixed marriage carried much weight," he writes. "She was a formidable antagonist in any wrangling over articles concerning sex or interracial romance, and we crossed words frequently" (*Nitty Gritty*, 139).

87. Braxton, *Black Women Writing Autobiography*, 170. Thompson was also critical of notions of "white" guardianship when she wrote a customer complaint to Neiman Marcus. She had ordered a rubber profile of a man advertised in the *Chicago Daily News* as a safeguard for lone women drivers. "As I am a Negro," she wrote, "send colored man only." Finding only a profile of a white man in the store's catalogue, Thompson followed up with a second letter to Neiman Marcus: "Unfortunately, I cannot use your inflatable man, as there are areas in which it would invite aggression rather than provide protection" (Era Bell Thompson, letter to Neiman Marcus, December 2, 1967, and letter to Edward Marcus, December 7, 1967, Era Bell Thompson Papers).

88. Era Bell Thompson, letter to Stanley Pargellis, May 24, 1944, Era Bell Thompson Papers.

89. Thompson, *American Daughter* (1986), 158–59, 113, 164, 195.

90. Thompson does not name this Chicago magazine in her autobiography, but she shares in an interview that her first writing job was at the St. Paul–Minneapolis *Spokesman* (McNeese, "Era Bell Thompson, Writer and Journalist").

91. Thompson, *American Daughter* (1986), 197, 201.

92. Ibid., 248, 267–68, 267, 268.

93. Ibid., 250.

94. Thompson, "Full Circle," 6.

95. Thompson, *American Daughter* (1986), 253, 255, 281.

96. Ibid., 258.

97. Johnson, "'This Strange White World,'" 107.

98. Thompson, *American Daughter* (1986), 268, 255.

99. Wright, *Black Boy*, 253.

100. Thompson, *American Daughter* (1986), 296, 294, 279. Many writers of the Black Chicago Renaissance (including Richard Wright, Willard Motley, Arna Bontemps, Margaret Walker, and Fenton Johnson) were professionalized through their work with the Federal Writers Project and Federal Theatre Project, which were part of the WPA. See Tracy, *Writers of the Black Chicago Renaissance*.

101. Thompson, *American Daughter* (1986), 279, 296.

102. Thompson, *American Daughter* (1967), 7.

103. Era Bell Thompson, "Bell's Lettres," *Negro Digest*, March 1950, 63.

104. Era Bell Thompson, "Bell's Lettres," *Negro Digest*, June 1950, 91. In the Era Bell Thompson Papers, the essay's title is "My Clowning Glory."

105. Thompson also coedited *White on Black* with Herbert Nipson. In the essay collection, writer Lillian Smith discusses her image of Harlem, actor Bobby Darin explains his portrayal of a bigot in the film *Pressure Point* (1962), and boxer Jack Dempsey examines black men's domination of the sport. The collection also includes essays by writers Pearl S. Buck on interracial adoption and William Faulkner on gradual integration.

106. Petry, "What's Wrong with Negro Men?," 4, 5.

107. Thompson, "What's Wonderful about Negro Men?," 9, 10. Italics mine.

108. Thimmesch, "John H. Johnson," 94. In a letter to the editors of *Fortune*, Burns denies responsibility for *Ebony*'s sensationalism. Instead he blames publisher John H. Johnson's desire for quick circulation gains; he also argues that Johnson supervised everything that went into the magazine (Burns, "Credit Denied," 82).

109. Georgia Douglas Johnson, letter to Era Bell Thompson, January 13, 1950, Era Bell Thompson Papers. Mary McLeod Bethune similarly praised Thompson's leadership at *Negro Digest* for "filling a vacancy in our Field of Literature that we all needed so much, but did not know just exactly what it took to bring to us the stimulus, inspiration and information that we needed in certain areas of thinking" (Mary McLeod Bethune, letter to Era Bell Thompson, December 6, 1950, Era Bell Thompson Papers).

110. Era Bell Thompson, letter to John H. Johnson, February 18, 1952, Era Bell Thompson Papers.

111. McNeese, "Era Bell Thompson, Writer and Journalist," 70. Thompson wrote the editorials for ten or twelve years, which most readers believed were written by a man.

112. For example, Michel Fabre and Addison Gayle hold Ben Burns responsible for *Ebony*'s refusal to publish Richard Wright's controversial essay "I Choose Exile" because it criticized American discrimination and thus would offend the magazine's advertisers. Burns maintained that although he was the executive editor, *Ebony* was under editor-in-chief Johnson's "rigid and unyielding direction" (Ben Burns, letter to Addison Gayle, August 29, 1989, Era Bell Thompson Papers).

113. Thompson and Greenlee, *Interview with Era Bell Thompson*, 39.

114. Ibid., 29.

Epilogue

1. Ormes was the only black women to achieve this accomplishment with her comic strip *Torchy Brown in "Dixie to Harlem*," which appeared in all editions of the *Pittsburgh Courier*, until Barbara Brandon-Croft's comic strip *Where I'm Coming From*, which was published first in the *Detroit Free Press* in 1989 and nationally syndicated in 1991. For more on the history of women in comics, see Robbins, *Great Women Cartoonists*.

2. Hayakawa, "Second Thoughts," April 21, 1945. In 1947 Florence Murray analyzed the results of a survey about representations of African Americans in popular culture. She reported that the stage and then the novel were the most liberal in portraying

complex black characters, whereas film was the worst in perpetuating stereotypes. Murray noted that comics had made "a commendably progressive stand" in their depiction of black soldiers since World War II, but she did not mention the reconfiguring of black womanhood in Ormes's comics (Murray, *Negro Handbook*, 259).

3. Jackie Ormes, *Candy*, *Chicago Defender*, national edition, April 21, 1945.

4. Jackie Ormes, *Patty-Jo 'n' Ginger*, *Pittsburgh Courier*, city edition, November 24, 1945.

5. Bongco, *Reading Comics*.

6. Brunner, "'Shuh! Ain't Nothin' to It,'" 33. Brunner argues that the Cotton Club in *Torchy Brown* is a metonym for the North, where blacks could attain success and recognition.

7. Johnson, "Toki Types."

8. For more on William Gropper's influence on political cartoonists, see Lozowick, *William Gropper*, and for more on the illustrators working for *The Crisis*, see Kirschke, *Art in Crisis*.

9. Harrington, "How Bootsie Was Born"; Dolinar, *Black Cultural Front*.

10. Brunner, review of *Jackie Ormes*, 103.

11. For more on Ormes's production and marketing of the doll, see Goldstein, "Patty-Jo."

12. Jackie Ormes, *Candy*, *Chicago Defender*, national edition, May 5, 1945.

13. Jackie Ormes, *Candy*, *Chicago Defender*, national edition, March 31, 1945.

14. Jackie Ormes, *Candy*, *Chicago Defender*, national edition, March 24, 1945.

15. Jackie Ormes, *Candy*, *Chicago Defender*, national edition, May 19, 1945.

16. Goldstein, *Jackie Ormes*, 83.

17. Jackie Ormes, *Candy*, *Chicago Defender*, national edition, July 7, 1945.

18. Jackie Ormes, *Patty-Jo 'n' Ginger*, *Pittsburgh Courier*, city edition, April 18, 1953.

19. For more on the cultural phenomenon Dior initiated with his "new look" for the post–World War II American woman, see Pochna, *Christian Dior*; Spindler, "Dior's Look, 50 Years Ago and Now."

20. Jackie Ormes, *Patty-Jo 'n' Ginger*, *Pittsburgh Courier*, city edition, October 11, 1947.

21. In his review of *Jackie Ormes*, Brunner differentiates the cartoonist's work in the *Pittsburgh Courier* from Ollie Harrington's comic *Dark Laughter*, which features the misadventures of the hapless, overweight, working-class, and silent Bootsie. Someone is always talking to Bootsie in Harrington's gag line.

22. Jackie Ormes, *Patty-Jo 'n' Ginger*, *Pittsburgh Courier*, city edition, July 9, 1949.

23. As Elsa Barkley Brown points out, even *Patty-Jo 'n' Ginger*'s less overtly political strips "carried a political, if more subtle, message, by suggesting the absurdity of women who exist for others merely as helpless sex objects" ("Ormes," 903).

24. Jackie Ormes, *Patty-Jo 'n' Ginger*, *Pittsburgh Courier*, city edition, July 2, 1949.

25. Jackie Ormes, *Patty-Jo 'n' Ginger*, *Pittsburgh Courier*, city edition, December 7, 1946.

26. Jackie Ormes, *Patty-Jo 'n' Ginger*, *Pittsburgh Courier*, city edition, November 12, 1949.

27. Jackie Ormes, *Patty-Jo 'n' Ginger*, *Pittsburgh Courier*, city edition, January 29, 1949.

28. Jackie Ormes, *Patty-Jo 'n' Ginger*, *Pittsburgh Courier*, city edition, October 23,

1954. In the April 29, 1950 *Patty-Jo 'n' Ginger*, Ormes uses this very same image but Patty-Jo's joke is different: "Just a reminder, sis . . . if you keep on dragging this thing out a few years more, you'll have me to contend with!" In this version the child remarks upon the fact that Ginger has not settled down to marriage. Goldstein believes Ormes struggled to draw later in her career due to pains in her joints and that this might account for the repetition of images in later years. However, there is still an unintentional rhetorical effect of these reworked gags and images.

29. Jackie Ormes, *Patty-Jo 'n' Ginger*, *Pittsburgh Courier*, city edition, November 13, 1954.

30. Goldstein, "*Torchy Togs* Paper Doll Cutouts," 30.

31. In their discussion of how black beauty contests define the black middle class, Shane White and Graham J. White argue, "Against an unvarying background of demeaning visual portrayals of African American bodies in cartoons, magazine illustrations, advertisements, and film, black beauty contests and fashion shows were not merely vivid repudiations of black physical and aesthetic inferiority but salutary expressions of African American pride" (*Stylin'*, 218).

32. Jackie Ormes, *Torchy in Heartbeats*, *Pittsburgh Courier*, Chicago edition, March 31, 1951.

33. Jackie Ormes, *Torchy in Heartbeats*, *Pittsburgh Courier*, Chicago edition, January 27, 1951.

34. Jackie Ormes, *Torchy in Heartbeats*, *Pittsburgh Courier*, Chicago edition, March 17, 1951.

35. Jackie Ormes, *Torchy in Heartbeats*, *Pittsburgh Courier*, Chicago edition, February 23, 1952.

36. Jackie Ormes, *Torchy in Heartbeats*, *Pittsburgh Courier*, Chicago edition, September 9, 1951.

37. Jackie Ormes, *Torchy in Heartbeats*, *Pittsburgh Courier*, Chicago edition, October 25, 1952.

Works Cited

Adams, Timothy Dow. "'I Do Believe Him Though I Know He Lies': Lying as Genre and Metaphor in *Black Boy.*" In *Richard Wright: Critical Perspectives Past and Present,* edited by Henry Louis Gates Jr. and K. A. Appiah, 302–15. New York: Amistad, 1993.

Algren, Nelson. "Mulatto Family Struggles with Soil of North Dakota." Review of *American Daughter,* by Era Bell Thompson. *Chicago Daily News,* April 24, 1946.

Anderson, Jervis. *Bayard Rustin: Troubles I've Seen: A Biography.* New York: HarperCollins, 1997.

Anderson, Karen Tucker. "Last Hired, First Fired: Black Women Workers During World War II." *Journal of American History* 69, no. 1 (1992): 82–97.

———. *Wartime Women: Sex Roles, Family Relations, and the Status of Women During World War II.* Westport, CT: Greenwood Press, 1981.

Anderson, Kathie R. "Era Bell Thompson: A North Dakota Daughter." In *The Centennial Anthology of North Dakota History, Journal of the Northern Plains,* edited by Janet Daley Lysengen and Ann M. Rathke, 307–19. Bismarck: State Historical Society of North Dakota, 1996.

Awkward, Michael. *Inspiriting Influences: Tradition, Revision, and Afro-American Women's Novels.* New York: Columbia Press, 1989.

Baker, Houston A., Jr. *Blues, Ideology, and Afro-American Literature: A Vernacular Theory.* Chicago: University of Chicago Press, 1984.

———. *Workings of the Spirit: The Poetics of Afro-American Women's Writing.* Chicago: University of Chicago Press, 1991.

Baldwin, James. "Everybody's Protest Novel." In *Notes of a Native Son,* 13–23. Boston: Beacon Press, 1955.

———. *Giovanni's Room*. 1956. Reprint, New York: Delta Trade Paperbacks, 2000.

———. "Going to Meet the Man." In *Going to Meet the Man*, 229–249. New York: Dial Press, 1965.

———. *Go Tell It on the Mountain*. 1953. Reprint, New York: Delta Trade Paperbacks, 2000.

Baraka, Amiri. *Blues People: Negro Music in White America*. 1963. Reprint, New York: HarperPerennial, 1999.

———. "The Changing Same (R&B and New Black Music)." In *Black Music*, 180–212. New York: William Morrow, 1968.

Barrett, Lindon. *Blackness and Value: Seeing Double*. Cambridge, UK: Cambridge University Press, 1999.

Barry, Michael. "'Same Train Be Back Tomorrow': Ann Petry's *The Narrows* and the Repetition of History." *MELUS* 24, no. 1 (1999): 141–59.

Bates, Daisy. *The Long Shadow of Little Rock: A Memoir*. Fayetteville: University of Arkansas Press, 1987.

Bell, Bernard W. "Ann Petry's Demythologizing of American Culture and Afro-American Character." In *Conjuring: Black Women, Fiction, and Literary Tradition*, edited by Marjorie Pryse and Hortense J. Spillers, 105–15. Bloomington: Indiana University Press, 1985.

Bell, Michael Davitt. "African-American Writing, 'Protest,' and the Burden of Naturalism: The Case of *Native Son*." In *Culture, Genre, and Literary Vocation: Selected Essays on American Literature*, 189–216. Chicago: University of Chicago Press, 2001.

Berlant, Lauren. *The Queen of America Goes to Washington City: Essays on Sex and Citizenship*. Durham, NC: Duke University Press, 1997.

Bernard, Emily. "'Raceless' Writing and Difference: Ann Petry's *Country Place* and the African-American Literary Canon." *Studies in American Fiction* 33, no. 1 (2005): 87–177.

Binggeli, Elizabeth. "Burbanking Bigger and Bette the Bitch." *African American Review* 40, no. 3 (2006): 475–92.

Boehm, Lisa Krissoff. *Making a Way Out of No Way: African American Women and the Second Great Migration*. Jackson: University Press of Mississippi, 2009.

Bogar, Jeff. *My Gun, Her Body*. New York: Lion Books, 1952.

Bone, Robert, and Richard Courage. *The Muse in Bronzeville: African American Creative Expression in Chicago, 1932–1950*. New Brunswick, NJ: Rutgers University Press, 2011.

Bongco, Mila. *Reading Comics: Language, Culture, and the Concept of the Superhero in Comic Books*. New York: Garland, 2000.

Brandt, Nat. *Harlem at War: The Black Experience in WWII*. Syracuse, NY: Syracuse University Press, 1996.

Brantley, Frederick. "Racial Conflict." Review of *Third Ward Newark*, by Curtis Lucas. *New York Times*, December 15, 1946.

Braxton, Joanne M. *Black Women Writing Autobiography: A Tradition within a Tradition*. Philadelphia: Temple University Press, 1989.

Brody, Jennifer DeVere. "Effaced into Flesh: Black Women's Subjectivity." In *On Your Left: The New Historical Materialism*, edited by Ann Kibbey et al., 184–205. New York: New York University Press, 1996.

———. *Punctuation: Art, Politics, and Play*. Durham, NC: Duke University Press, 2008.

Brontë, Charlotte. *Jane Eyre*. 1847. Reprint, New York: Norton, 2000.

Brooks, Gwendolyn. "kitchenette building." In *Selected Poems*, 3. New York: Harper & Row, 1963.

———. "Luther." *Tan Confessions*, October 1952, 36, 73–74.

———. *Maud Martha*. 1953. Reprint, Chicago: Third World Press, 1993.

———. *Report from Part One*. Detroit: Broadside Press, 1972.

———. *Report from Part Two*. Chicago: Third World Press, 1996.

———. "To Those of My Sisters Who Kept Their Naturals." In *The Essential Gwendolyn Brooks*, edited by Elizabeth Alexander, 120–21. New York: Library of America, 2005.

———. "Why Negro Women Leave Home." *Negro Digest*, March 1951, 26–28.

Brown, Charlotte Hawkins. *The Correct Thing to Do—to Say—to Wear*. Sedalia, NC: Charlotte Hawkins Brown, 1940.

———. "The Negro and the Social Graces." *Wings over Jordan*. CBS Radio. Cleveland, OH: WGAR, March 10, 1940. "Charlotte Hawkins Brown Museum." *North Carolina Historic Sites*. Accessed January 29, 2011. http://www.nchistoricsites.org/chb/chb-radio.htm.

Brown, Elsa Barkley. "Ormes, Zelda Jackson 'Jackie' (1917–1986)." In *Black Women in America: An Historical Encyclopedia*, edited by Darlene Clark Hine, 2: 903. New York: Carlson, 1993.

Brown, Stephanie. *The Postwar African American Novel: Protest and Discontent, 1945–1950*. Jackson: University Press of Mississippi, 2011.

Brown, William Wells. *Clotel; or the President's Daughter*. 1953. Reprint, New York: Modern Library, 2001.

Brunner, Edward. Review of *Jackie Ormes: The First African American Woman Cartoonist*, by Nancy Goldstein. *American Periodicals* 19, no. 1 (2009): 102–4.

———. "'Shuh! Ain't Nothin' to It': The Dynamics of Success in Jackie Ormes's *Torchy Brown*." *MELUS* 32, no. 3 (2007): 23–49.

Bucher, Christina G. "Pauli Murray: A Case for the Poetry." *North Carolina Literary Review* 13 (2004): 59–73.

Burks, Mary Fair. "Trailblazers: Women in the Montgomery Bus Boycott." In *Women in the Civil Rights Movement: Trailblazers and Torchbearers, 1941–1965*, edited by Vicki L. Crawford, Jacqueline Anne Rouse, and Barbara Woods, 71–83. Bloomington: Indiana University Press, 1993.

Burns, Ben. "Credit Denied." *Fortune*, February 2, 1968, 82.

———. *Nitty Gritty: A White Editor in Black Journalism.* Jackson: University Press of Mississippi, 1996.

Butler, Gerald. *The Lurking Man.* New York: Lion Books, 1952.

Butler, Robert J., ed. *The Critical Response to Richard Wright.* Westport, CT: Greenwood Press, 1995.

———. "The Invisible Woman in Wright's *Rite of Passage.*" In *The Critical Response to Richard Wright,* 185–89. Westport, CT: Greenwood Press, 1995.

Caliri, Fortunata. Review of *American Daughter,* by Era Bell Thompson. *The Sign,* June 1946, 55.

"Camera Record of Married Life of Joe and Marva." *Chicago Defender,* July 12, 1941.

Campbell, E. Simms. "Are Black Women Beautiful?" *Negro Digest,* June 1951, 16–20.

Campbell, James. *Middle Passages: African American Journeys to Africa, 1787–2005.* New York: Penguin, 2006.

Carby, Hazel V. Foreword to *Seraph on the Suwanee,* by Zora Neale Hurston, vii–xviii. New York: HarperPerennial, 1991.

———. "It Jus Be's Dat Way Sometime: The Sexual Politics of Women's Blues." In *Feminisms: An Anthology of Literary Theory and Criticism,* edited by Robyn R. Warhol and Diane Price Herndl, 746–58. New Brunswick, NJ: Rutgers University Press, 1991.

———. *Reconstructing Womanhood: The Emergence of the Afro-American Woman Novelist.* New York: Oxford University Press, 1987.

Cather, Willa. *My Ántonia.* 1918. Reprint, New York: Oxford University Press, 2006.

Charles, Charles V. "Optimism and Frustration in the American Negro." *Psychoanalytic Review* 29 (1942): 270–99.

Cheng, Anne Anlin. "The Melancholy of Race." *Kenyon Review* 19, no. 1 (1997): 49–61.

———. *The Melancholy of Race: Psychoanalysis, Assimilation, and Hidden Grief.* New York: Oxford University Press, 2001.

Chesnutt, Charles W. *The Colonel's Dream.* 1905. Reprint, New Milford, CT: Toby Press, 2004.

Childress, Alice. *Florence.* 1949. Reprinted in *Wines in the Wilderness: Plays by African American Women from the Harlem Renaissance to the Present,* edited by Elizabeth Brown-Guillory, 110–21. Westport, CT: Greenwood Press, 1990.

———. *Like One of the Family: Conversations from a Domestic's Life.* 1956. Reprint, Boston: Beacon Press, 1986.

Christian, Barbara. *Black Women Novelists: The Development of a Tradition, 1892–1976.* Westport, CT: Greenwood Press, 1980.

———. "Images of Black Women in Afro-American Literature: From Stereotype to Character." 1975. In *Black Feminist Criticism: Perspectives on Black Women Writers,* 1-30. New York: Pergamon Press, 1985.

Clarke, Graham. *The Photograph*. New York: Oxford University Press, 1997.

Clement, Elizabeth Alice. *Love for Sale: Courting, Treating, and Prostitution in New York City, 1900–1945*. Chapel Hill: University of North Carolina Press, 2006.

Codman, Florence. Review of *The Living Is Easy*, by Dorothy West. *Commonweal* 48, no. 11 (1948): 264–65.

Cohen, Cathy. "Deviance as Resistance: A New Research Agenda for the Study of Black Politics." *DuBois Review* 1, no. 1 (2004): 27–45.

———. "Punks, Bulldaggers, and Welfare Queens: The Radical Potential of Queer Politics?" *GLQ* 3, no. 4 (1997): 437–65.

Cohen, Lizabeth. *A Consumers' Republic: The Politics of Mass Consumption in Postwar America*. New York: Vintage Books, 2003.

Cole, Kevin L., and Leah Weins. "Religion, Idealism, and African American Autobiography in the Northern Plains: Era Bell Thompson's *American Daughter*." *Great Plains Quarterly* 23, no. 4 (2003): 219–29.

Conroy, Jack. "Off the Book Shelf." Review of *Third Ward Newark*, by Curtis Lucas. *Chicago Defender*, December 7, 1946.

Cooke, Marvel. "Modern Slaves." *Amsterdam News*, October 16, 1937. Reprinted in *Black Women in White America: A Documentary History*, edited by Gerda Lerner, 231–34. New York: Vintage Books, 1973.

Cott, Nancy F. *The Grounding of Modern Feminism*. New Haven, CT: Yale University Press, 1987.

Couch, W. T. "Publisher's Introduction." In *What The Negro Wants*, edited by Rayford W. Logan, ix–xxiii. Chapel Hill: University of North Carolina Press, 1944.

Cox, Ida. "Wild Women Don't Have the Blues." In *Blues Legacies and Black Feminism: Gertrude "Ma" Rainey, Bessie Smith, and Billie Holiday*, by Angela Y. Davis, 38. New York: Vintage Books, 1999.

Crawford, Vicki L., Jacqueline Anne Rouse, and Barbara Woods, eds. *Women in the Civil Rights Movement: Trailblazers and Torchbearers, 1941–1965*. Bloomington: Indiana University Press, 1993.

Cromwell, Adelaide M. Afterword to *The Living Is Easy*, by Dorothy West, 349–64. New York: Feminist Press at CUNY, 1982.

Culley, Margo. "What a Piece of Work Is 'Woman'! An Introduction." In *American Women's Autobiography: Fea(s)ts of Memory*, 3–31. Madison: University of Wisconsin Press, 1992.

Curwood, Anastasia. *Stormy Weather: Middle-Class African American Marriages between the Two World Wars*. Chapel Hill: University of North Carolina Press, 2010.

Davies, Carole Boyce. *Black Women, Writing and Identity: Migrations of the Subject*. New York: Routledge, 2005.

Davis, Angela Y. *Blues Legacies and Black Feminism: Gertrude "Ma" Rainey, Bessie Smith, and Billie Holiday*. New York: Vintage Books, 1999.

————. *Women, Race and Class.* New York: Random House, 1981.

DeKnight, Freda. "Budget Meals for Vet Wives." *Ebony*, September 1947, 27–28.

————. "Buffet Bridge Luncheon." *Ebony*, May 1948, 60–61.

————. "Cakes for Halloween." *Ebony*, October 1947, 30.

————. "Date with a Cook Book." *Ebony*, June 1948, 44–45.

————. "Dinner of Leftovers." *Ebony*, May 1947, 26.

————. "Fruit Pies." *Ebony*, March 1948, 45.

————. "Hot Roll Mix." *Ebony*, October 1948, 58.

————. "How to Glorify the Apple." *Ebony*, October 1946, 26.

————. "Lena Horne's Valentine Party." *Ebony*, February 1947, 17–18.

————. "Quick Coffee Breads for Sunday Morning." *Ebony*, March 1947, 38–39.

————. "Tamale Pie for New Year's Eve." *Ebony*, January 1947, 42–43.

————. "Vacation Cookies." *Ebony*, September 1949, 39.

Denard, Carol C. Introduction to *Mammy: An Appeal to the Heart of the South / The Correct Thing to Do—to Say—to Wear*, by Charlotte Hawkins Brown, xv–xxxv. New York: G. K. Hall, 1995.

Dietzel, Susanne B. "The African American Novel and Popular Culture." In *The Cambridge Companion to the African American Novel*, edited by Maryemma Graham, 156–70. Cambridge, UK: Cambridge University Press, 2004.

Dirthrower, Johnny. "Negro Press." *Negro Digest*, February 1950, 98.

Dolinar, Brian. *The Black Cultural Front: Black Writers and Artists of the Depression Generation.* Jackson: University Press of Mississippi, 2012.

Drake, Kimberly. "Women On the Go: Blues, Conjure, and Other Alternatives to Domesticity in Ann Petry's *The Street* and *The Narrows*." *Arizona Quarterly* 54, no. 1 (1998): 65–95.

Drake, St. Clair, and Horace R. Cayton. *Black Metropolis: A Study of Negro Life in a Northern City*, Vol. 2. 1945. Reprint, New York: Harper Torchbooks, 1962.

Drury, Doreen Marie. "'Experimentation on the Male Side': Race, Class, Gender, and Sexuality in Pauli Murray's Quest for Love and Identity, 1910–1960." Ph.D. diss., Boston College, 2000.

Dubek, Laura. "The Social Geography of Race in Hurston's *Seraph on the Suwanee*." *African American Review* 30, no. 3 (1996): 341–51.

————. "White Family Values in Ann Petry's *Country Place*." *MELUS* 29, no. 2 (2004): 55–76.

DuBois, W. E. B. *Dark Princess.* 1928. Reprint, Jackson: University Press of Mississippi, 1995.

duCille, Ann. *The Coupling Convention: Sex, Text, and Tradition in Black Women's Fiction.* New York: Oxford University Press, 1993.

Dudziak, Mary L. *Cold War Civil Rights: Race and the Image of American Democracy.* Princeton, NJ: Princeton University Press, 2000.

Dworkin, Ira. "'The Evading Eye': The Transgeneric Prose of Gwendolyn Brooks." *CLA* 47, no. 1 (2003): 32–54.

Early, Gerald. "Her Picture in the Papers: Remembering Some Black Women." In *Tuxedo Junction: Essays on American Culture*, 83–112. New York: Ecco Press, 1989.

Edenfield, Paul L. "American Heartbreak: The Life of Pauli Murray." *Legal Studies Forum* 27 (2003): 733–78.

Edwards, Erica R. *Charisma and the Fictions of Black Leadership*. Minneapolis: University of Minnesota Press, 2012.

Elder, Louise H. "Minority Saga." Review of *American Daughter*, by Era Bell Thompson. *Phylon* 7, no. 3 (1946): 307.

Ellison, Ralph. *Invisible Man*. 1952. Reprint, New York: Vintage, 1990.

———. "Richard Wright's Blues." 1945. Reprinted in *The Collected Essays of Ralph Ellison*, edited by John F. Callahan, 128–44. New York: Modern Library, 2003.

———. "Stepchild Fantasy." Review of *American Daughter*, by Era Bell Thompson. *Saturday Review*, June 8, 1946, 25–26.

Eng, David L., and Shinhee Han. "A Dialogue on Racial Melancholia." In *Loss: The Politics of Mourning*, edited by David L. Eng and David Kazanjian, 343–71. Berkeley: University of California Press, 2003.

Ervin, Hazel Arnett, ed. *African American Literary Criticism, 1773 to 2000*. New York: Twayne, 1999.

———. "The Hidden Hand of Feminist Revolt in Ann Petry's *The Street*." In *The Critical Response to Ann Petry*, edited by Hazel Arnett Ervin, 179–94. Westport, CT: Praeger, 2005.

Estrich, Susan. *Real Rape*. Cambridge, MA: Harvard University Press, 1987.

Ethnic Notions. Directed by Marlon T. Riggs. San Francisco: California Newsreel, 1986.

Fabre, Michel. *The Unfinished Quest of Richard Wright*. 2nd ed. Urbana: University of Illinois Press, 1993.

Farrar, Helen. *Murder Goes to School*. New York: Ziff-Davis, 1948.

Feldstein, Ruth. *Motherhood in Black and White: Race and Sex in American Liberalism, 1930–1965*. Ithaca, NY: Cornell University Press, 2000.

Fikes, Robert, Jr. "Escaping the Literary Ghetto: African American Authors of White Life Novels, 1946–1994." *Western Journal of Black Studies* 19, no. 2 (1995): 105–12.

Fishburn, Katherine. *Richard Wright's Hero: The Faces of a Rebel-Victim*. Metuchen, NJ: Scarecrow Press, 1977.

Forbes, Murray. *Hollow Triumph*. New York: Ziff-Davis, 1946.

Foster, William Z. "On Improving the Party's Work among Women." 1948. Reprinted in *Against the Tide: Pro-Feminist Men in the United States, 1776–1990: A Documentary History*, edited by Michael S. Kimmel and Thomas E. Mosmiller, 274–77. Boston: Beacon Press, 1992.

Frazier, Valerie. "Domestic Epic Warfare in *Maud Martha*." *African American Review* 39, nos. 1–2 (2005): 133–41.

Freud, Sigmund. "Mourning and Melancholia." 1917. In *The Standard Edition of the Complete Psychological Works of Sigmund Freud*, translated by James Strachey, 14: 243–58. London: Hogarth Press, 1966.

Gates, Henry Louis, Jr. "Introduction: On Bearing Witness." In *Bearing Witness: Selections from African-American Autobiography in the Twentieth Century*, 3–9. New York: Pantheon Books, 1991.

———. "Zora Neale Hurston: 'A Negro Way of Saying.'" Afterword to *Dust Tracks on a Road*, by Zora Neale Hurston, 287–97. New York: HarperPerennial, 1996.

Gates, Henry Louis, Jr., and K. A. Appiah, eds. *Richard Wright: Critical Perspectives Past and Present*. New York: Amistad, 1993.

Gilbert, Sandra M., and Susan Gubar. *The Madwoman in the Attic: The Woman Writer and the Nineteenth-Century Literary Imagination*. New Haven, CT: Yale University Press, 2000.

Gilmore, Glenda Elizabeth. *Defying Dixie: The Radical Roots of Civil Rights, 1919–1950*. New York: Norton, 2008.

Gilroy, Paul. *The Black Atlantic: Modernity and Double Consciousness*. Cambridge, MA: Harvard University Press, 1993.

Glicksberg, Charles I. "The Alienation of Negro Literature." *Phylon* 11, no. 1 (1950): 49–58.

Gloster, Hugh M. "Race and the Negro Writer." *Phylon* 11, no. 4 (1950): 369–71.

Goldstein, Nancy. *Jackie Ormes: The First African American Woman Cartoonist*. Ann Arbor: University of Michigan Press, 2008.

———. "Patty-Jo: A Terri Lee Doll." *Doll News* 56, no. 4 (2007): 42–49.

———. "*Torchy Togs* Paper Doll Cutouts, Created by Jackie Ormes, the First Black American Woman Cartoonist." *Doll News* 57, no. 2 (2008): 28–33.

"Goodbye Mammy, Hello Mom." *Ebony*, March 1947, 36–37.

Gordon, James. *The Lust of Private Cooper*. New York: Lion Books, 1952.

Green, Adam. *Selling the Race: Culture, Community, and Black Chicago, 1940–1955*. Chicago: University of Chicago Press, 2007.

Greer, Jane. "'Some of Their Stories Are Like My Life, I Guess': Working-Class Women Readers and Confessional Magazines." In *Reading Sites: Social Difference and Reader Response*, edited by Patrocinio P. Schweickart and Elizabeth A. Flynn, 135–65. New York: Modern Language Association of America, 2004.

Griffin, Farah Jasmine. "Hunting Communists and Negroes in Ann Petry's *The Narrows*." In *Revising the Blueprint: Ann Petry and the Literary Left*, edited by Alex Lubin, 137–49. Jackson: University Press of Mississippi, 2007.

———. "*Who Set You Flowin'?*": The African-American Migration Narrative. New York: Oxford University Press, 1995.

Griffith, Jean C. "How the West Was Whitened: 'Racial' Difference on Cather's Prairie." *Western American Literature* 41, no. 4 (2007): 393–417.

Guttman, Sondra. "What Bigger Killed For: Rereading Violence against

Women in *Native Son*." *Texas Studies in Literature and Language* 43, no. 2 (2001): 169–93.

Hardison, Ayesha K. "Crossing the Threshold: Zora Neale Hurston, Racial Performance, and *Seraph on the Suwanee*." *African American Review*, forthcoming.

Harrington, Oliver W. *Dark Laughter: The Satiric Art of Oliver W. Harrington*. Edited by M. Thomas Inge. Jackson: University Press of Mississippi, 1993.

———. "How Bootsie Was Born." In *Why I Left America and Other Essays*, edited by M. Thomas Inge, 26–34. Jackson: University Press of Mississippi, 1993.

Harris, Trudier. *From Mammies to Militants: Domestics in Black American Literature*. Philadelphia: Temple University Press, 1982.

Hartmann, Susan M. "Pauli Murray and the 'Juncture of Women's Liberation and Black Liberation.'" *Journal of Women's History*, 14, no. 2 (2002): 74–77.

Hayakawa, S. I. "Second Thoughts." *Chicago Defender*, April 21, 1945.

———. "Second Thoughts." Review of *American Daughter*, by Era Bell Thompson. *Chicago Defender*, April 27, 1946.

Henderson, Mae Gwendolyn. "Speaking in Tongues: Dialogics, Dialectics, and the Black Woman Writer's Literary Tradition." In *African American Literary Theory: A Reader*, edited by Winston Napier, 348–68. New York: New York University Press, 2000.

Hill, Mozell C., and M. Carl Holman. "Preface." *Phylon* 11, no. 4 (1950): 296.

Himes, Chester. *If He Hollers Let Him Go*. 1945. Reprint, New York: Thunder's Mouth Press, 2002.

Hine, Darlene Clark. "Rape and the Inner Lives of Black Women in the Middle West." *Signs* 14, no. 4 (1989): 912–20.

———. "Rape and the Inner Lives of Black Women: Thoughts on the Culture of Dissemblance." In *Hine Sight: Black Women and the Re-construction of American History*, 37–47. Brooklyn: Carlson, 1994.

Hine, Darlene Clark, and John McCluskey Jr., eds. *The Black Chicago Renaissance*. Urbana: University of Illinois Press, 2012.

Holiday, Billie. *The Best of Billie Holliday: 20th Century Masters*. Universal City, CA: Hip-O Records, 2002.

Holiday, Billie, and William Dufty. *Lady Sings the Blues*. 1956. Reprint, New York: Penguin Books, 1984.

Holloway, Karla F. C. *Private Bodies, Public Texts: Race, Gender, and a Cultural Bioethics*. Durham, NC: Duke University Press, 2011.

Honey, Maureen, ed. *Bitter Fruit: African American Women in World War II*. Columbia: University of Missouri Press, 1999.

———. *Creating Rosie the Riveter: Class, Gender, and Propaganda During World War II*. Amherst: University of Massachusetts Press, 1984.

"How Richard Wright Looks at *Black Boy*." *PM* 15, April 1945, 3–4. Reprinted in *Conversations with Richard Wright*, edited by Keneth Kinnamon and Michel Fabre, 63–66. Jackson: University Press of Mississippi, 1993.

Huggins, Nathan Irvin. *Harlem Renaissance*. New York: Oxford University Press, 1971.

Hughes, Carl Milton. *The Negro Novelist: A Discussion of the Writings of American Negro Novelists, 1940–1950*. New York: Citadel Press, 1953.

Hughes, Langston. "The Blues I'm Playing." In *The Portable Harlem Renaissance Reader*, edited by David Levering Lewis, 619–27. New York: Penguin Books, 1994.

———. "Harlem." In *The Collected Poems of Langston Hughes*, edited by Arnold Rampersad, 426. New York: Knopf, 1994.

———. "Harlem Sweeties." In *The Collected Poems of Langston Hughes*, edited by Arnold Rampersad, 245–46. New York: Knopf, 1994.

———. "Outstanding Autumn Headliners in 1953 Are Books, the Theatre and the Blues." Review of *Maud Martha*, by Gwendolyn Brooks. *Chicago Defender*, October 10, 1953.

———. "Sex in Front." In *Simple Stakes a Claim*, 96–101. New York: Rinehart, 1957.

Hull, Gloria T., and Posey Gallagher. "Update on *Part One*: An Interview with Gwendolyn Brooks." *CLA* 21 (1977): 19–40.

Hurst, Fannie. *Imitation of Life*. 1933. Reprint, Durham, NC: Duke University Press, 2004.

Hurston, Zora Neale. "Drenched in Light." 1924. Reprinted in *The Complete Stories*, edited by Henry Louis Gates Jr., 17–25. New York: HarperCollins, 1995.

———. *Dust Tracks on a Road*. 1942. Reprint, New York: HarperPerennial, 1995.

———. "How It Feels to Be Colored Me." 1928. Reprinted in *I Love Myself When I Am Laughing . . . and Then Again When I Am Looking Mean and Impressive*, edited by Alice Walker, 152–55. New York: Feminist Press at CUNY, 1993.

———. *Mules and Men*. 1935. Reprint, New York: Harper & Row, 1970.

———. Review of *Uncle Tom's Children*, by Richard Wright. *Saturday Review of Literature*, April 2, 1938. Reprinted in *Richard Wright: Critical Perspectives Past and Present*, edited by Henry Louis Gates Jr., and K. A. Appiah, 3–4. New York: Amistad, 1993.

———. *Seraph on the Suwanee*. 1948. Reprint, New York: HarperPerennial, 1991.

———. *Their Eyes Were Watching God*. 1937. Reprint, New York: Perennial Classics, 1998.

———. "What White Publishers Won't Print." 1950. Reprinted in *I Love Myself When I Am Laughing . . . and Then Again When I Am Looking Mean and Impressive*, edited by Alice Walker, 169–73. New York: Feminist Press at CUNY, 1993.

Hutcheon, Linda. *Narcissistic Narrative: The Metafictional Paradox*. New York: Methuen, 1980.

Ignatiev, Noel. *How the Irish Became White*. New York: Routledge, 1995.

Ikard, David. "Love Jones: A Black *Male* Feminist Critique of Chester Himes's *If He Hollers Let Him Go.*" *African American Review* 36, no. 2 (2002): 299–310.

Ivey, James W. "Ann Petry Talks about First Novel." *The Crisis*, February 1946, 48–49.

———. "Mrs. Petry's Harlem." Review of *The Street*, by Ann Petry. *The Crisis*, May 1946, 154–55.

Jablon, Madelyn. *Black Metafiction: Self-Consciousness in African American Literature.* Iowa City: University of Iowa Press, 1997.

Jackson, Chuck. "Waste and Whiteness: Zora Neale Hurston and the Politics of Eugenics." *African American Review* 34, no. 4 (2000): 639–60.

Jackson, Lawrence P. *The Indignant Generation: A Narrative History of African American Writers and Critics, 1934–1960.* Princeton, NJ: Princeton University Press, 2010.

Jacobson, Matthew Frye. *Whiteness of a Different Color: European Immigrants and the Alchemy of Race.* Cambridge, MA: Harvard University Press, 1998.

James, C. L. R. *American Civilization*, edited by Anna Grimshaw and Keith Hart. Cambridge, MA: Blackwell, 1993.

JanMohamed, Abdul R. *The Death-Bound-Subject: Richard Wright's Archaeology of Death.* Durham, NC: Duke University Press, 2005.

Japtok, Martin. "'The Gospel of Whiteness': Whiteness in African American Literature." *Amerikastudien/American Studies* 49, no. 4 (2004): 483–98.

Jarrett, Gene A. *Deans and Truants: Race and Realism in African American Literature.* Philadelphia: University of Pennsylvania Press, 2007.

———. "Not Necessarily Race Matter." Introduction to *African American Literature Beyond Race: An Alternative Reader*, 1–24. New York: New York University Press, 2006.

Jenkins, Candice M. *Private Lives, Proper Relations: Regulating Black Intimacy.* Minneapolis: University of Minnesota Press, 2007.

Johnson, Abby Arthur, and Ronald Maberry Johnson. *Propaganda and Aesthetics: The Literary Politics of Afro-American Magazines in the Twentieth Century.* Amherst: University of Massachusetts Press, 1979.

Johnson, Barbara. "Thresholds of Difference: Structures of Address in Zora Neale Hurston." *Critical Inquiry* 12, no. 1 (1985): 278–89.

Johnson, Charles. "A Phenomenology of the Black Body." In *The Male Body: Features, Destinies, Exposures*, edited by Laurence Goldstein, 121–36. Ann Arbor: University of Michigan Press, 1994.

Johnson, E. Patrick. *Appropriating Blackness: Performance and the Politics of Authenticity.* Durham, NC: Duke University Press, 2003.

———. "'Quare' Studies, or (Almost) Everything I Know about Queer Studies I Learned from My Grandmother." In *Black Queer Studies: A Critical Anthology*, edited by E. Patrick Johnson and Mae G. Henderson, 124–57. Durham, NC: Duke University Press, 2005.

Johnson, Hortense. "What My Job Means to Me." *Opportunity*, April 1943.

Reprinted in *Bitter Fruit: African American Women in World War II*, edited by Maureen Honey, 71–75. Columbia: University of Missouri Press, 1999.

Johnson, Michael K. "'This Strange White World': Race and Place in Era Bell Thompson's *American Daughter*." *Great Plains Quarterly* 24 (2004): 101–11.

Johnson, Toki Schalk. "Toki Types: About People Here and There." *Pittsburgh Courier*, December 28, 1946.

Jones, Gayl. *Corregidora*. 1975. Reprint, Boston: Beacon Press, 1986.

Jones, Sharon L. *Rereading the Harlem Renaissance: Race, Class, and Gender in the Fiction of Jessie Fauset, Zora Neale Hurston, and Dorothy West*. Westport, CT: Greenwood Press, 2002.

Joyce, Joyce Ann. "Richard Wright's 'Long Black Song': A Moral Dilemma." *Mississippi Quarterly* 42 (1989): 379–85.

Kane, April L. *Newark's Literary Lights*. Newark, NJ: Newark Public Library, 2002.

Kaplan, Carla, ed. *Zora Neale Hurston: A Life in Letters*. New York: Doubleday, 2002.

Kellum, David W. "Marva Draws Up 5-Point Plan for Reconciliation: Still in Love with Joe She Admits to *Defender*." *Chicago Defender*, July 12, 1941.

Kinnamon, Keneth, and Michel Fabre, eds. *Conversations with Richard Wright*. Jackson: University Press of Mississippi, 1993.

Kipnis, Laura. *The Female Thing: Dirt, Sex, Envy, Vulnerability*. New York: Pantheon Books, 2006.

Kirschke, Amy Helene. *Art in Crisis: W. E. B. DuBois and the Struggle for African American Identity and Memory*. Bloomington: Indiana University Press, 2007.

Laird, David. "Willa Cather's Women: Gender, Place, and Narrativity in *O Pioneers!* and *My Ántonia*." *Great Plains Quarterly* 12, no. 4 (1992): 242–53.

Lattin, Patricia H., and Vernon E. Lattin. "Dual Vision in Gwendolyn Brooks's *Maud Martha*." *Critique* 25, no. 4 (1984): 180–88.

Lee, Amy. "The Narrator as Feminist Ally in Ann Petry's 'The Bones of Louella Brown.'" In *Ann Petry's Short Fiction: Critical Essays*, edited by Hazel Arnett Ervin and Hilary Holladay, 119–24. Westport, CT: Praeger, 2004.

Lefebvre, Henri. *The Production of Space*. Translated by Donald Nicholson-Smith. Cambridge, MA: Blackwell, 1991.

Lerner, Gerda, ed. *Black Women in White America: A Documentary History*. New York: Vintage Books, 1973.

Lewis, Julian. "What Color Will Your Baby Be?" *Negro Digest*, November 1946, 4–7.

The Life and Times of Rosie the Riveter. Directed by Connie Field. 1980; Franklin Lakes, NJ: Clarity Educational Productions, 2007.

Locke, Alain. "Self-Criticism: The Third Dimension in Culture." *Phylon* 11, no. 4 (1950): 391–94.

Lott, Eric. *Love and Theft: Blackface Minstrelsy and the American Working Class*. New York: Oxford University Press, 1993.

Lovisi, Gary. "Lion Books: Noir Paperback Icons." In *The Big Book of Noir*, edited by Lee Server, Ed Gorman, and Martin H. Greenberg, 223–26. New York: Carroll & Graf, 1998.

Lozowick, Louis. *William Gropper*. Philadelphia: Art Alliance Press, 1983.

Lubin, Alex, ed. *Revising the Blueprint: Ann Petry and the Literary Left*. Jackson: University Press of Mississippi, 2007.

Lucas, Curtis. *Angel*. New York: Lion Books, 1953.

———. *Flour Is Dusty*. Philadelphia: Dorrance, 1943.

———. *Forbidden Fruit*. New York: Beacon Press, 1953.

———. *Lila*. New York: Lion Books, 1955.

———. *So Low, So Lonely*. New York: Lion Books, 1952.

———. *Third Ward Newark*. New York: Ziff-Davis, 1946.

MacKinnon, Catharine A. *Women's Lives, Men's Laws*. Cambridge, MA: Belknap Press of Harvard University Press, 2005.

Maxwell, William J. *New Negro, Old Left: African-American Writing and Communism between the Wars*. New York: Columbia University Press, 1999.

McDowell, Deborah E. "Conversations with Dorothy West." In *The Harlem Renaissance Re-examined*, edited by Victor A. Kramer and Robert A. Russ, 285–303. Troy, NY: Whitson, 1997.

McGuire, Danielle L. *At the Dark End of the Street: Black Women, Rape, and Resistance—A New History of the Civil Rights Movement from Rosa Parks to the Rise of Black Power*. New York: Knopf, 2011.

McKay, Nellie Y. "Ann Petry's *The Street* and *The Narrows*: A Study of the Influence of Class, Race, and Gender on Afro-American Women's Lives." In *Women and War: The Changing Status of American Women from the 1930s to the 1950s*, edited by Maria Diedrich and Dorothea Fischer-Hornung, 127–40. New York: Berg, 1990.

McLean, Helen V. "Psychodynamic Factors in Racial Relations." *Annals of the American Academy of Political and Social Science* 244 (1946): 159–66.

McNeese, LaVern Arnetta. "Era Bell Thompson, Writer and Journalist." Ph.D. diss., Southern Illinois University, 1983.

Meisenhelder, Susan Edwards. *Hitting a Straight Lick with a Crooked Stick: Race and Gender in the Work of Zora Neale Hurston*. Tuscaloosa: University of Alabama Press, 1999.

Meyer, Leisa D. "'Strange Love': Searching for Sexual Subjectivities in Black Print Popular Culture during the 1950s." *Feminist Studies* 38, no. 3 (2012): 625–57.

Miller, Monica L. *Slaves to Fashion: Black Dandyism and the Styling of Black Diasporic Identity*. Durham, NC: Duke University Press, 2009.

Miller, Shawn E. "'Some Other Way to Try': From Defiance to Creative

Submission in *Their Eyes Were Watching God.*" *Southern Literary Journal* 37, no. 1 (2004): 74–95.

Mitchell, Louise. "Slave Markets Typify Exploitation of Domestics." *Daily Worker,* May 5, 1940. Reprinted in *Black Women in White America: A Documentary History,* edited by Gerda Lerner, 229–31. New York: Vintage Books, 1973.

Mitchell, Verner D., and Cynthia J. Davis. "Dorothy West and Her Circle." Introduction to *Where the Wild Grape Grows: Selected Writings, 1930–1950,* 3–48. Amherst: University of Massachusetts Press, 2005.

Monroe, Al. "Marva Tells Why She Split with Joe: 'Too Much Glamour Killed Our Marriage.'" *Chicago Defender,* October 2, 1943.

Mootry, Maria K. "Bitches, Whores, and Women Haters: Archetypes and Typologies in the Art of Richard Wright." In *Richard Wright: A Collection of Critical Essays,* edited by Richard Macksey and Frank E. Moorer, 117–27. Englewood Cliffs, NJ: Prentice-Hall, 1984.

Morgan, Stacy I. *Rethinking Social Realism: African American Art and Literature, 1930–1953.* Athens: University of Georgia Press, 2004.

Morrison, Toni. *Playing in the Dark: Whiteness and the Literary Imagination.* Cambridge, MA: Harvard University Press, 1992.

———. *Sula.* 1973. Reprint, New York: Vintage, 2004.

Motley, Willard. *Knock on Any Door.* 1947. Reprint, Chicago: Northern Illinois University Press, 1989.

"Mrs. Bill Robinson Stars in Important Role—'A Wife.'" *Chicago Defender,* January 20, 1940.

Mullen, Bill V. "Object Lessons: Fetishization and Class Consciousness in Ann Petry's *The Street.*" In *Revising the Blueprint: Ann Petry and the Literary Left,* edited by Alex Lubin, 35–48. Jackson: University Press of Mississippi, 2007.

Mumford, Kevin J. *Newark: A History of Race, Rights, and Riots in America.* New York: New York University Press, 2007.

Muñoz, José Esteban. *Disidentifications: Queers of Color and the Performance of Politics.* Minneapolis: University of Minnesota Press, 1999.

Murray, Florence, ed. *The Negro Handbook 1946–1947.* New York: Current Books, 1947.

Murray, Pauli. *Dark Testament and Other Poems.* Norwalk, CT: Silvermine, 1970.

———. "The Liberation of Black Women." 1970. Reprinted in *Words of Fire: An Anthology of African-American Feminist Thought,* edited by Beverly Guy-Sheftall, 186–97. New York: New Press, 1995.

———. *Pauli Murray: The Autobiography of a Black Activist, Feminist, Lawyer, Priest, and Poet.* Knoxville: University of Tennessee Press, 1989.

———. "Why Negro Girls Stay Single." *Negro Digest,* July 1947, 4–8.

Murray, Pauli, and Mary O. Eastwood. "Jane Crow and the Law: Sex Discrimination and Title VII." *George Washington Law Review* 43, no. 2 (1965): 232–56.

"Negro Hailed as New Writer." *New York Sun*, March 4, 1940. Reprinted in *Conversations with Richard Wright*, edited by Keneth Kinnamon and Michel Fabre, 28–30. Jackson: University Press of Mississippi, 1993.

Neuhaus, Jessamyn. "The Way to a Man's Heart: Gender Roles, Domestic Ideology, and Cookbooks in the 1950s." *Journal of Social History* 32, no. 3 (1999): 529–55.

"A Novel about Third Ward: Negro Author's Portrayal of Newark Section to Be Published Tomorrow." *Newark (NJ) Evening News*, December 1, 1946.

Obama, Barack. *The Audacity of Hope: Thoughts on Reclaiming the American Dream*. New York: Three Rivers Press, 2006.

O'Brien, Geoffrey. *Hardboiled America: The Lurid Years of Paperbacks*. New York: Van Nostrand Reinhold, 1981.

O'Grady, Lorraine. "Olympia's Maid: Reclaiming Black Female Subjectivity." *Afterimage* 20, no. 1 (1992): 14–15, 23.

Olney, James. "Autobiography and the Cultural Moment: A Thematic, Historical, and Bibliographical Introduction." In *Autobiography: Essays Theoretical and Critical*, 3–27. Princeton, NJ: Princeton University Press, 1980.

Omi, Michael, and Howard Winant. *Racial Formation in the United States: From the 1960s to the 1990s*. New York: Routledge, 1994.

"The Other Robinson—'Mrs. Bill.'" *Chicago Defender*, January 20, 1940.

Ottley, Roi. "What's Wrong with Negro Women." *Negro Digest*, December 1950, 71–74.

Park, You-me, and Gayle Wald. "Native Daughters in the Promised Land: Gender, Race, and the Question of Separate Spheres." *American Literature* 70, no. 3 (1998): 607–33.

Parker, Albert. "Women Sue Cleveland Plants." *Militant*, January 2, 1943. Reprinted in *Fighting Racism in World War II: C. L. R. James, George Breitman, Edgar Keemer, and Others*, edited by Fred Stanton, 226–27. New York: Monad Press, 1980.

Petry, Ann. "Ann Petry." In *Contemporary Authors Autobiography Series*, edited by Adele Sarkissian, 6: 253–69. Detroit: Galenet Research, 1988.

———. "The Bones of Louella Brown." In *Miss Muriel and Other Stories*, 163–80. New York: Dafina Books, 2008.

———. *Country Place*. Boston: Houghton Mifflin, 1947.

———. *The Narrows*. 1953. Reprint, New York: Beacon Press, 1988.

———. "The Novel as Social Criticism." In *African American Literary Criticism, 1773 to 2000*, edited by Hazel Arnett Ervin, 94–88. New York: Twayne, 1999.

———. *The Street*. 1946. Reprint, New York: Mariner Books, 1974.

———. "What's Wrong with Negro Men?" *Negro Digest*, March 1947, 4–7.

Petry, Elisabeth. *At Home Inside: A Daughter's Tribute to Ann Petry*. Jackson: University Press of Mississippi, 2009.

Pinky. Directed by Elia Kazan. Los Angeles: 20th Century Fox, 1949.

"Pleads Well." Review of *Third Ward Newark*, by Curtis Lucas. *Winnipeg Free Press*, May 24, 1947.

Pochna, Marie-France. *Christian Dior: The Biography*. Translated by Joanna Savill. New York: Overlook Duckworth, 2008.

"The Press: Purpose without Passion." *Time*, September 22, 1952. Accessed February 21, 2011. http://www.time.com/time/magazine/article/0,9171,822525,00.html.

Price, Clement Alexander. *Freedom Not Far Distant: A Documentary History of Afro-Americans in New Jersey*. Newark: New Jersey Historical Society, 1980.

Pryse, Marjorie. "'Pattern against the Sky': Deism and Motherhood in Ann Petry's *The Street*." In *Conjuring: Black Women, Fiction, and Literary Tradition*, edited by Marjorie Pryse and Hortense J. Spillers, 116–31. Bloomington: Indiana University Press, 1985.

Pryse, Marjorie, and Hortense J. Spillers, eds. *Conjuring: Black Women, Fiction, and Literary Tradition*. Bloomington: Indiana University Press, 1985.

Rabinowitz, Paula. *Black and White and Noir: America's Pulp Modernism*. New York: Columbia University Press, 2002.

Radway, Janice. "The Readers and Their Romances." In *Feminisms: An Anthology of Literary Theory and Criticism*, edited by Robyn R. Warhol and Diane Prince Herndl, 574–608. New Brunswick, NJ: Rutgers University Press, 1997.

Rampersad, Arnold. "Too Honest for His Own Time." *New York Times*, December 29, 1991. Reprinted in *The Critical Response to Richard Wright*, edited by Robert J. Butler, 163–65. Westport, CT: Greenwood Press, 1995.

———, ed. *The Collected Poems of Langston Hughes*. New York: Knopf, 1994.

Ramsey, Guthrie P., Jr. *Race Music: Black Cultures from Bebop to Hip-Hop*. Berkeley: University of California Press, 2003.

Raynaud, Claudine. "'Rubbing a Paragraph with a Soft Cloth'? Muted Voices and Editorial Constraints in *Dust Tracks on a Road*." In *De/colonizing the Subject: The Politics of Gender in Women's Autobiography*, edited by Sidonie Smith and Julia Watson, 34–64. Minneapolis: University of Minnesota Press, 1992.

Reid-Pharr, Robert. *Once You Go Black: Choice, Desire, and the Black American Intellectual*. New York: New York University Press, 2007.

Review of *Maud Martha*, by Gwendolyn Brooks. *New Yorker*, October 10, 1953, 153. Reprinted in *On Gwendolyn Brooks: Reliant Contemplation*, edited by Stephen Caldwell Wright, 15. Ann Arbor: University of Michigan Press, 1996.

Reynolds, Paul R. *The Middle Man: The Adventures of a Literary Agent*. New York: William Morrow, 1972.

Rieger, Christopher. "The Working-Class Pastoral of Zora Neale Hurston's *Seraph on the Suwanee*." *Mississippi Quarterly* 56, no. 1 (2002–3): 105–24.

Robbins, Trina. *The Great Women Cartoonists*. New York: Watson-Guptill, 2001.

Robinson, Jo Ann Gibson. *The Montgomery Bus Boycott and the Women Who Started It: The Memoir of Jo Ann Gibson Robinson*, edited by David J. Garrow. Knoxville: University of Tennessee Press, 1987.

Robnett, Belinda. *How Long? How Long? African-American Women in the Struggle for Civil Rights.* New York: Oxford University Press, 1997.

Rodgers, Lawrence R. *Canaan Bound: The African-American Great Migration Novel.* Urbana: University of Illinois Press, 1997.

Rooks, Noliwe M. *Ladies' Pages: African American Women's Magazines and the Culture That Made Them.* New Brunswick, NJ: Rutgers University Press, 2004.

Rosenberg, Rosalind. "The Conjunction of Race and Gender." *Journal of Women's History,* 14, no. 2 (2002): 68–73.

Ross, Marlon B. *Manning the Race: Reforming Black Men in the Jim Crow Era.* New York: New York University Press, 2004.

Rowley, Hazel. *Richard Wright: The Life and Times.* Chicago: University of Chicago Press, 2008.

Rueschmann, Eva. "Sister Bonds: Intersections of Family and Race in Jessie Redmon Fauset's *Plum Bun* and Dorothy West's *The Living Is Easy.*" In *The Significance of Sibling Relationships in Literature*, edited by JoAnna Stephens Mink and Janet Doubler Ward, 120–32. Bowling Green, OH: Bowling Green State University Popular Press, 1993.

Rupp, Leila J., and Verta Taylor. "Pauli Murray: The Unasked Question." *Journal of Women's History* 14, no. 2 (2002): 83–87.

Rushmore, Howard. "Story of a Negro Girl." Review of *American Daughter*, by Era Bell Thompson. *New Leader*, May 25, 1946.

Samuel, Lawrence R. *Pledging Allegiance: American Identity and the Bond Drive of World War II.* Washington: Smithsonian Institution Press, 1997.

Sanders, Pamela Peden. "The Feminism of Dorothy West's *The Living Is Easy*: A Critique of the Limitations of the Female Sphere through Performative Gender Roles." *African American Review* 36, no. 3 (2002): 435–46.

Schraufnagel, Noel. *From Apology to Protest: The Black American Novel.* Deland, FL: Everett/Edwards, 1973.

Schultz, Elizabeth. "Out of the Woods and into the World: A Study of Interracial Friendships between Women in American Novels." In *Conjuring: Black Women, Fiction, and Literary Tradition*, edited by Marjorie Pryse and Hortense J. Spillers, 67–85. Bloomington: Indiana University Press, 1985.

Schweickart, Patrocinio P. "Reading Ourselves: Toward a Feminist Theory of Reading." In *Speaking of Gender*, edited by Elaine Showalter, 17–44. New York: Routledge, 1989.

Schweickart, Patrocinio P., and Elizabeth A. Flynn, eds. *Reading Sites: Social Difference and Reader Response.* New York: Modern Language Association of America, 2004.

Scott, Anne Firor. *Pauli Murray and Caroline Ware: Forty Years of Letters in Black and White*. Chapel Hill: University of North Carolina Press, 2006.

Scott, Daryl Michael. *Contempt and Pity: Social Policy and the Image of the Damaged Black Psyche, 1880–1996*. Chapel Hill: University of North Carolina Press, 1997.

Server, Lee, Ed Gorman, and Martin H. Greenberg, eds. *The Big Book of Noir*. New York: Carroll & Graf, 1998.

Shockley, Ann Allen. *Loving Her*. 1974. Reprint, Boston: Northeastern University Press, 1997.

Shockley, Evie. *Renegade Poetics: Black Aesthetics and Formal Innovation in African American Poetry*. Iowa City: University of Iowa Press, 2011.

Shockley, Megan Taylor. *"We, Too, Are Americans": African American Women in Detroit and Richmond, 1940–54*. Urbana: University of Illinois Press, 2004.

Sielke, Sabine. *Reading Rape: The Rhetoric of Sexual Violence in American Literature and Culture, 1790–1990*. Princeton, NJ: Princeton University Press, 2002.

Smith, Barbara. "Toward a Black Feminist Criticism." In *All the Women Are White, All the Blacks Are Men, but Some of Us Are Brave*, edited by Gloria T. Hull, Patricia Bell Scott, and Barbara Smith, 157–75. New York: Feminist Press at CUNY, 1982.

Smith, Judith E. *Visions of Belonging: Family Stories, Popular Culture, and Postwar Democracy, 1940–1960*. New York: Columbia University Press, 2004.

Smith, Valerie. *Self-Discovery and Authority in Afro-American Narrative*. Cambridge, MA: Harvard University Press, 1987.

Sontag, Susan. *On Photography*. New York: Farrar, Straus and Giroux, 1977.

Spillers, Hortense J. "'All the Things You Could Be by Now, If Sigmund Freud's Wife Was Your Mother': Psychoanalysis and Race." In *Female Subjects in Black and White: Race, Psychoanalysis, Feminism*, edited by Elizabeth Abel, Barbara Christian, and Helene Molgen, 135–58. Berkeley: University of California Press, 1997.

———. "'An Order of Constancy': Notes on Brooks and the Feminine." *Centennial Review* 29, no. 2 (1985): 223–48.

Spindler, Amy M. "Dior's Look, 50 Years Ago and Now." *New York Times*, December 13, 1996. Accessed July 2, 2011. http://www.nytimes.com/1996/12/13/arts/dior-s-look-50-years-ago-and-now.html?pagewanted=all&src=pm.

Spivak, Gayatri. "Three Women's Texts and a Critique of Imperialism." *Critical Inquiry* 12, no. 1 (1985): 243–61.

Standley, Anne. "The Role of Black Women in the Civil Rights Movement." In *Women in the Civil Rights Movement: Trailblazers and Torchbearers, 1941–1965*, edited by Vicki L. Crawford, Jacqueline Anne Rouse, and Barbara Woods, 183–202. Bloomington: Indiana University Press, 1993.

Stepto, Robert B. "I Thought I Knew These People: Richard Wright and the Afro-American Literary Tradition." In *Chant of Saints: A Gathering of*

Afro-American Literature, Art, and Scholarship, edited by Michael S. Harper and Robert B. Stepto, 195–211. Urbana: University of Illinois Press, 1979.

Stetler, Carrie. "Writers, Famous and Obscure, Captured the Mood of Newark before the Riots." *Star-Ledger (Newark, NJ)*. Accessed December 10, 2007. http://blog.nj.com/ledgernewark/2007/07/writers_famous_and_obscure_cap.html.

Story, Ralph D. "Patronage and the Harlem Renaissance: You Get What You Pay For." *CLA* 32, no. 3 (1989): 284–95.

Streeter-Dixon, Edwina. "Words of Wisdom from a Housewife." *Chicago Defender*, January 21, 1933.

Stryker, Susan. *Queer Pulp: Perverted Passions from the Golden Age of the Paperback*. San Francisco: Chronicle Books, 2001.

Tate, Claudia. *Psychoanalysis and Black Novels: Desire and the Protocols of Race*. New York: Oxford University Press, 1998.

Thimmesch, Nick. "John H. Johnson: The Man behind *Ebony*." *Saturday Evening Post*, October 1975, 36–37, 94–96.

Thompson, Era Bell. *Africa, Land of My Fathers*. Garden City, NY: Doubleday, 1954.

———. *American Daughter*. 1946. Reprint, Chicago: Follett, 1967.

———. *American Daughter*. 1946. Reprint, St. Paul: Minnesota Historical Society Press, 1986.

———. "Negro Publications and the Writer." *Phylon* 11, no. 4 (1950): 304–6.

———. "What's Wonderful about Negro Men?" *Negro Digest*, August 1947, 9–10.

Thompson, Era Bell, and Marcia M. Greenlee. *Interview with Era Bell Thompson, March 6 and 10, 1978*. Schlesinger Library, Radcliffe College, 1980.

Thompson, Era Bell, and Herbert Nipson, eds. *White on Black: The Views of Twenty-two White Americans on the Negro*. Chicago: Johnson, 1963.

Tracy, Steven C., ed. *Writers of the Black Chicago Renaissance*. Urbana: University of Illinois Press, 2011.

Trotter, Joe William, Jr. "From a Raw Deal to a New Deal? 1929–1945." In *To Make Our World Anew: A History of African Americans*, edited by Robin D. G. Kelley and Earl Lewis, 409–44. New York: Oxford University Press, 2000.

Tucker, Sherrie. *Swing Shift: "All-Girl" Bands of the 1940s*. Durham, NC: Duke University Press, 2000.

Tuttle, George. "An Interview with Arnold Hano." In *The Big Book of Noir*, edited by Lee Server, Ed Gorman, and Martin H. Greenberg, 227–30. New York: Carroll & Graf, 1998.

Vizcaíno-Alemán, Melina. "Counter-Modernity, Black Masculinity, and Female Silence in Ann Petry's Fiction." In *Revising the Blueprint: Ann Petry and the Literary Left*, edited by Alex Lubin, 120–36. Jackson: University Press of Mississippi, 2007.

Wade-Gayles, Gloria. *No Crystal Stair: Visions of Race and Gender in Black Women's Fiction*. Revised and updated edition. Cleveland, OH: Pilgrim Press, 1997.

Wadelington, Charles W., and Richard F. Knapp. *Charlotte Hawkins Brown and Palmer Memorial Institute: What One Young African American Woman Could Do.* Chapel Hill: University of North Carolina Press, 1999.

Walker, Alice. *I Love Myself When I Am Laughing . . . and Then Again When I Am Looking Mean and Impressive.* New York: Feminist Press at CUNY, 1993.

———. "Looking for Zora." 1975. Reprinted in *In Search of Our Mothers' Gardens: Womanist Prose*, 93–116. San Diego: Harcourt Brace Jovanovich, 1983.

Walker, Juliet E. K. "The Promised Land: The Chicago *Defender* and the Black Press in Illinois, 1862–1970." In *The Black Press in the Middle West, 1865–1985*, edited by Henry Lewis Suggs, 9–50. Westport, CT: Greenwood Press, 1996.

Walker, Margaret. *Richard Wright, Daemonic Genius: A Portrait of the Man, a Critical Look at His Work.* New York: Amistad, 1993.

Walker, Nancy A. "Introduction: Women's Magazines and Women's Roles." In *Women's Magazines 1940–1960: Gender Roles and the Popular Press*, 1–20. Boston: Bedford/St. Martin's, 1998.

Ward, Jerry W., Jr. Introduction to *Black Boy (American Hunger): A Record of Childhood and Youth*, by Richard Wright, xi–xix. New York: HarperPerennial, 1993.

Warren, Kenneth W. *What Was African American Literature?* Cambridge, MA: Harvard University Press, 2011.

Washington, Mary Helen. "Alice Childress, Lorraine Hansberry, and Claudia Jones: Black Women Write the Popular Front." In *Left of the Color Line: Race, Radicalism, and Twentieth-Century Literature of the United States*, edited by Bill V. Mullen and James Smethurst, 183–204. Chapel Hill: University of North Carolina, 2003.

———. "Plain, Black, and Decently Wild: The Heroic Possibilities of *Maud Martha*." In *The Voyage In: Fictions of Female Development*, edited by Elizabeth Abel, Marianne Hirsch, and Elizabeth Langland, 270–86. Hanover, NH: University Press of New England, 1983.

———. "'Taming All That Anger Down': Rage and Silence in Gwendolyn Brooks' *Maud Martha*." *Massachusetts Review* 24, no. 2 (1983): 453–66.

———. "Zora Neale Hurston: A Woman Half in Shadow." Introduction to *I Love Myself When I Am Laughing . . . and Then Again When I Am Looking Mean and Impressive*, edited by Alice Walker, 7–25. New York: Feminist Press at CUNY, 1993.

Weir, Sybil. "*The Narrows*: A Black New England Novel." *Studies in American Fiction* 15, no. 1 (1987): 81–93.

West, Dorothy. *The Living Is Easy.* 1948. Reprint, New York: Feminist Press at CUNY, 1982.

White, Shane, and Graham J. White. *Stylin': African American Expressive Culture from Its Beginnings to the Zoot Suit.* Ithaca, NY: Cornell University Press, 1999.

White, Walter. "Regrets He Has No Words of Praise For 'Pinky.'" *Chicago Defender*, October 29, 1949.

———. *What Caused the Detroit Riot? An Analysis*. New York: NAACP, 1943.

Wilder, Roy. "Wright, Negro Ex-Field Hand, Looks Ahead to New Triumphs." *New York Herald Tribune*, August 17, 1941. Reprinted in *Conversations with Richard Wright*, edited by Keneth Kinnamon and Michel Fabre, 36–39. Jackson: University Press of Mississippi, 1993.

Williams, Sherley Anne. "Papa Dick and Sister-Woman: Reflections on Women in the Fiction of Richard Wright." In *American Novelists Revisited: Essays in Feminist Criticism*, edited by Fritz Fleischmann, 394–414. Boston: G. K. Hall, 1982.

Willis, Deborah. *Posing Beauty: African American Images from the 1890s to the Present*. New York: Norton, 2009.

Wilson, Mark K., and Ann Petry. "A MELUS Interview: Ann Petry. The New England Connection." *MELUS* 15, no. 2 (1988): 71–84.

Wolcott, Victoria W. *Remaking Respectability: African American Women in Interwar Detroit*. Chapel Hill: University of North Carolina Press, 2000.

"Women in the Shadows: Lesbian Pulp Fiction Collection." *Sallie Bingham Center for Women's History and Culture*. Accessed July 20, 2006. http://library.duke.edu/specialcollections/bingham/guides/lesbianpulp/.

Woodward, C. Vann. *The Strange Career of Jim Crow*. New York: Oxford University Press, 1966.

Wright, Richard. *Black Boy (American Hunger): A Record of Childhood and Youth*. Introduction by Jerry W. Ward Jr. New York: HarperPerennial, 1993.

———. "Blueprint for Negro Writing." 1937. Reprinted in *African American Literary Criticism, 1773 to 2000*, edited by Hazel Arnett Ervin, 82–90. New York: Twayne, 1999.

———. "Bright and Morning Star." 1938. In *Uncle Tom's Children*, 221–63. Reprint, New York: HarperPerennial, 2004.

———. "The Ethics of Living Jim Crow." 1937. Reprinted in *Uncle Tom's Children*, 1–15. New York: HarperPerennial, 2004.

———. "How Bigger Was Born." 1940. Reprinted in *Native Son*, 433–62. New York: HarperPerennial, 1993.

———. "Long Black Song." 1938. In *Uncle Tom's Children*, 125–56. Reprint, New York: HarperPerennial, 2004.

———. "Man of All Work." 1961. In *Eight Men*, 109–54. New York: HarperPerennial, 1996.

———. *Native Son*. 1940. Reprint, New York: HarperPerennial, 1993.

———. *The Outsider*. 1953. Reprint, New York: HarperPerennial, 2008.

———. Review of *Their Eyes Were Watching God*, by Zora Neale Hurston. *New Masses*, October 5, 1937. Reprinted in *Zora Neale Hurston: Critical Perspectives Past and Present*, edited by Henry Louis Gates Jr., and K. A. Appiah, 16–17. New York: Amistad, 1993.

———. *Savage Holiday.* 1954. Reprint, Jackson: University Press of Mississippi, 1994.

———. *12 Million Black Voices: A Folk History of the Negro in the United States.* New York: Viking Press, 1941.

———. *Uncle Tom's Children.* 1938. Reprint, New York: HarperPerennial, 1993.

Yerby, Frank. *The Foxes of Harrow.* New York: Dial Press, 1946.

———. "How and Why I Write the Costume Novel." *Harper's,* October 1959, 145–50.

Young, James E. *The Texture of Memory: Holocaust Memorials and Meaning.* New Haven, CT: Yale University Press, 1993.

Young, John K. *Black Writers, White Publishers: Marketplace Politics in Twentieth-Century African American Literature.* Jackson: University Press of Mississippi, 2006.

Zimet, Jaye. *Strange Sisters: The Art of Lesbian Pulp Fiction 1949–1969.* New York: Viking Studio, 1999.

Archives

Era Bell Thompson Papers. Vivian G. Harsh Research Collection of Afro-American History and Literature, Chicago Public Library.

Richard Wright Papers. Yale Collection of American Literature, Beinecke Rare Book and Manuscript Library.

Selected Records of Harper & Brothers. Manuscripts Division, Department of Rare Books and Special Collections, Princeton University Library.

Index